PROLOGUE TO ANNIHILATION

STUDIES IN ANTISEMITISM
Alvin H. Rosenfeld, editor

PROLOGUE TO ANNIHILATION

Ordinary American and British Jews Challenge the Third Reich

—⚊—

STEPHEN H. NORWOOD

INDIANA UNIVERSITY PRESS

This book is a publication of

Indiana University Press
Office of Scholarly Publishing
Herman B Wells Library 350
1320 East 10th Street
Bloomington, Indiana 47405 USA

iupress.org
© 2021 by Stephen H. Norwood

Manufactured in the United States of America
First printing 2021

Library of Congress Cataloging-in-Publication Data

Names: Norwood, Stephen H. (Stephen Harlan), 1951- author.
Title: Prologue to annihilation : ordinary American and British Jews challenge the Third Reich / [Stephen H. Norwoord].
Description: Bloomington, Indiana : Indiana University Press, [2021] | Series: Studies in antisemitism | Includes bibliographical references and index.
Identifiers: LCCN 2020047239 (print) | LCCN 2020047240 (ebook) | ISBN 9780253053619 (hardback) | ISBN 9780253053626 (paperback) | ISBN 9780253053633 (ebook)
Subjects: LCSH: Jews—Persecutions—Germany—History—20th century. | Jews—Persecutions—Press coverage—United States. | Jews—Persecutions—Press coverage—Great Britain. | Nazis—Press coverage—United States. | Nazis—Press coverage—Great Britain. | Jews—United States—Attitudes. | Jews—Great Britain—Attitudes. | Holocaust, Jewish (1939-1945)—Causes. | Germany—Foreign public opinion, American | Germany—Foreign public opinion, British
Classification: LCC DS134.255 .N67 2021 (print) | LCC DS134.255 (ebook) | DDC 940.53/1830941—dc23
LC record available at https://lccn.loc.gov/2020047239
LC ebook record available at https://lccn.loc.gov/2020047240

To Eunice G. Pollack

CONTENTS

PROLOGUE TO ANNIHILATION

INTRODUCTION

Foundations of the Final Solution

IN EXPLAINING HOW AND WHEN the Hitler regime decided to annihilate the Jews, Holocaust scholars have concentrated on the period from the Kristallnacht pogroms in November 1938 through the early years of World War II. The few scholars who have addressed Western responses to the plight of European Jewry also dwell mainly on the years after Kristallnacht.[1] This examination of American and British responses focuses instead on the critical early years of the Third Reich, illuminating how much was known in the West about Nazi ambitions at the time. This was the period in which Western actions could still have precluded the ensuing catastrophe to Jewry and Europe.

Widening the lens of scholarship on Nazism and the Holocaust, *Prologue to Annihilation* demonstrates how the Nazis' early policies and atrocities formed the foundation of the Final Solution. It argues that developments in the early years of Hitler's rule, and in the years immediately preceding it, foreshadowed what was to come. I show that from the establishment of the Nazi Party, its explicitly racial antisemitism was the central focus of its ideology. Of the twenty-five points in the party platform, endorsed in 1920, "ten were aimed directly at the Jews." In one point, the Nazis made it clear that they intended to strip Jews of their citizenship on racial grounds: "Only one who is of German blood irrespective of religion, can be a member of the nation. No Jew, therefore can be a member of the nation." The Jew could "live in Germany only as a guest, and must be subject to alien legislation." The Hitler regime made this official in 1935 by introducing the Nuremberg race laws. The party platform's very first point telegraphed the Nazis' expansionist designs, calling for "the union of all Germans in a greater Germany."[2] The antisemitic terror that the Nazis openly directed at the Jews in the Saar, which Germany annexed after its victory in

1

the January 13, 1935, plebiscite, clearly signaled the fate awaiting all Jews in the steadily expanding "greater Germany." As the journalist William L. Shirer observed, "The most important [of the twenty-five points] . . . were carried out by the Third Reich, with consequences disastrous to millions of people."[3]

Some newspapers were quick to recognize the menace Nazis presented to Jews and sounded the alarm. A little more than a month after Adolf Hitler became chancellor, the London *Daily Telegraph* pointed out that the Nazi Party's practice of unleashing violent attacks on Jews was long-standing and warned that this would not change after the party assumed the "responsibilities" of government. The editors asked rhetorically, "Can a party that has been fed for years upon little but hysterical hatred and counsels of violence settle down [and direct] a government that does not destroy and persecute?"[4]

Although not addressed in the newspapers, the Nazis promoted their lethal program by drawing heavily on Christianity's teachings about the Jews. The Nazis routinely presented Jews not only as the root of all of Germany's miseries but also as bent on taking over the world, subjugating the "Aryan race," and destroying Christian civilization—goals that only a people evil and powerful enough to have murdered a god would pursue and could effect. Conflating theological and racial antisemitism, Nazi leaders roused their followers by invoking the image of the Jews as Christ killers and Satan's allies, while also characterizing them as subhuman. In a 1932 speech in Nuremberg, Julius Streicher urged his audience to "listen to Christ who said to the Jews: 'You are children of the devil.'" He confirmed that "all Jews have one common aim: 'World dominion.'" As the leader of the Nazis' April 1, 1933 national boycott of Jewish stores and offices, Streicher proclaimed to an audience of one hundred thousand in Munich, "Golgotha has not yet been avenged." He pledged that *this* time it would be the Jews themselves, the crucifiers of Jesus and arch-enemy of the German people, who would meet their punishment there. Drawing on the medieval libel that Jews murdered Christian children to extract their blood to mix with matzo at Passover, he denounced the Jews as "a nation of bloodsuckers."[5]

As early as April 1, 1933, the *Manchester Guardian* warned that Hitler appeared to telegraph the Nazis' annihilationist intentions even in 1925, when he graphically described Jews in *Mein Kampf* as "a spiritual pestilence"—"the worm of destruction gnawing at the tree of civilization." The survival of civilization demanded the wiping out of the "pestilence," the killing of the "worm."[6] In a German press interview on May 21, 1933, Hitler combined a hoary Christian antisemitic accusation dating from the fourteenth century with annihilationist imagery similar to that highlighted in the *Guardian*. Jews were "well-poisoners of the German and Christian world-soul," and "this lousy pest, this infection, degenerate in soul and spirit," was something one must exterminate if Germans and Christians were to thrive.[7]

From the beginning, the Nazis made their rationale for ridding the world of this pestilence explicit. In what can be called annihilation inversion, the Nazis attributed their own genocidal intentions to the Jews. On April 1, 1933, the Nazi Women's Federation justified that day's national boycott of Jewish stores and offices by explaining that the Jews' objective was "the destruction of the German people." The federation claimed that it was the Jews who were responsible for Germany's defeat in the world war and for the "2,000,000 war dead" and the starvation "of old men, women, and children"—steps toward their ultimate goal. With the Nazis in power, the Jews were now determined "to deprive awakened Germany of all possibility to live."[8] The pro-Nazi German newspaper *Kölnischer Zeitung* denounced the March 27, 1933 mass rally in New York's Madison Square Garden to protest Nazi antisemitism as a "great auto da fé," alluding to the Spanish Inquisition's public burning at the stake of conversos (whom the Nazis, as racial antisemites, considered Jews).[9] Now it was the Jews who had become the new inquisitors—who would burn Germans.

The Berlin pogroms of 1930 and 1931, even before Hitler came to power—in which organized bands of Nazis shouting, "Perish Judaea!" savagely beat Jews in the streets, smashed the large plate-glass windows of Jewish-owned department stores with paving stones, and wrecked Jewish-owned cafés—foreshadowed the infamous Kristallnacht of 1938.[10] Similarly, the Nazis' "declaration of war against Germany's 600,000 Jews . . . broadcast . . . from every wireless station in the country," which preceded their April 1, 1933 national boycott of Jewish stores and offices, loudly foretold the impending disaster. The London *Daily Herald*, the British Labour Party newspaper, commented that "there was hardly any need for this official announcement," because "crowds up and down the country" were "already taking the law into their own hands." They attacked Jewish stores "at Eberswalde, Schwedt, Goettingen, Emden, Kiel, Wernigerode, Ereinwalde and Dortmund—that is to say from north to south and east to west of Germany."[11] In yet another prelude to the Night of Broken Glass, at Passover in 1934, Christian residents of the Bavarian town of Ellwangen inflicted pogromist violence on their Jewish neighbors, shattering the windows of their homes while shouting "in chorus," "In this Pesach there flows no Christian but Jewish blood"—an inversion of the entrenched medieval blood libel, as Germans (Lutherans and Catholics) finally exacted revenge for the crucifixion and the centuries of Jews' alleged murder of Christian children.[12]

Indeed, from the beginning of Hitler's rule, the Nazis used the blood libel to incite violent assaults on Jewish communities in Germany—and this too was openly reported at the time. On March 17, 1933, the Paris correspondent of the London *Daily Herald* wrote that anti-Nazi refugees who had fled to the French capital from Germany told him "how the Nazi speakers were . . . spreading false reports of preparation by Jews for the 'ritual murder' of Christian infants during the coming Passover festival."[13]

Jewish journalists wrote early of looming disaster. Jacob Fishman, managing editor of the New York *Jewish Morning Journal*, warned in March 1933 that the Nazi *Sturmabteilung* (storm troops), whom he had encountered on a trip to Germany in July 1932, comprised a "pogrom- army" threatening the existence of German Jewry. He estimated their number at six hundred thousand and described them as young, armed, housed in barracks, and "permitted to wreak their will" on the Jews without police interference. These storm troops, Fishman cautioned, surpassed in both size and power czarist Russia's Black Hundreds and Romania's Iron Guard. He presciently concluded that "the situation of the Jews in Germany today has no counterpart in all the history of pogroms."[14]

On March 3, 1933, the London *Daily Herald* drew readers' attention to the lines in the Nazi Party anthem, the "Horst Wessel Lied," sung by storm troopers at their marches and rallies, which expressed joy about Jewish blood gushing from the knife. The paper stressed that every Jew had become a target for severe bodily harm or death: "Vengeance threatens every man, woman, and child of the Jewish community." German Jewry's situation had become desperate: "Only the mass pressure of world opinion, the vigorous expression of outraged humanity, can avert catastrophe."[15]

In May 1934, Frederick Birchall, Berlin correspondent for the *New York Times*, told the publisher, Arthur Hays Sulzberger, of a chilling luncheon encounter with a leader of the elite SS division of the storm troops that unmistakably telegraphed the Nazis' genocidal intentions. Birchall described the SS leader as about thirty years old, polished, well educated, and well traveled, speaking perfect English. After listening to him extol the storm troops as a "band of brothers" committed to eliminating class distinctions in Germany, Birchall asked how he could defend Nazi treatment of the Jews. The SS man responded by first criticizing the Hitler regime for moving too quickly to destroy German Jewry. He told Birchall that it had thrown Jewish physicians and technicians out of the hospitals too fast, noting that the Jews "have given us the Koch tuberculosis serum, the Wasserman test, the Salvarsan remedy—he went on to reel off a whole lot of things." Then the SS man confided, "If we had given them another three years . . . I am certain they would have produced a cancer cure." At that point, he leaned over the table and declared excitedly to Birchall, "And *then* we could have done it to them!"

Birchall reported to Sulzberger that as the SS man enthused about the annihilation of the Jews, "I just stared at him open-mouthed." He "was so animated, so deadly in earnest, so utterly unconscious of the vile treachery, the thorough rottenness of his own mentality." When Birchall indicated his disapproval, the Nazi leader was "amazed," contending that the United States was also suffering from the machinations of Jews, a criminal race. To him, none of the Jews' contributions to civilization and human betterment could offset their evil essence and designs. Birchall "ended the lunch as soon as possible" and would not return the SS man's subsequent telephone calls or accept his invitations.[16]

In the spring of 1933, the American and British press detailed Nazis' and German mobs' degradation and literal animalization of the Jews. They told of Nazis exhibiting Jews in slaughterers' carts and cattle trucks—forebodings of the cattle cars that would be used to transport Jews to the annihilation camps during the Holocaust. They reported events that were rehearsals for the Kristallnacht to come. In April, after an antisemitic mob staged demonstrations against Jewish stores and wrecked the synagogue in Goettingen, three Jewish businessmen were thrown into an animal cart. The next morning, "the principal business streets presented a scene of devastation. The pavements were full of glass; the shop fronts were boarded up, dumb but eloquent witnesses to what had gone on during the night."[17] Notably, the same month, as antisemitic terror in the Reich continued to escalate, the *Brooklyn Jewish Examiner* reported that the German minister of agriculture had just attempted to prohibit bringing dancing bears to perform in Germany, on the grounds that their keepers treated them cruelly. The *Examiner* commented sarcastically that this offended German sensibilities.[18]

Prologue to Annihilation analyzes the extensive transnational efforts of Jews, from the first weeks of Nazi rule, both to alert the world to the unprecedented horrors in Germany and to call on the American and British governments to officially condemn the persecution of Jews and take punitive measures against the Hitler regime. While American and British scholarship on responses to antisemitism has focused largely on the organizational leadership and prominent figures in the movement, my study gives considerable attention to the central role of the Jewish grassroots. Indeed, working- and lower-middle-class Jews in the United States and Britain were often the movers and shakers in the struggle, forcing the Jewish leadership, or significant parts of it, to follow their path. It was the fierce agitation of ordinary Jews that drove the American Jewish Congress leadership to sponsor an enormous mass rally against Nazi antisemitism at New York's Madison Square Garden on March 27, 1933, less than two months after the Nazis assumed power in Germany. On that day, an estimated one million Jews participated in street protests and gatherings in cities across the United States. Inspired by the example of American Jews, from March 27 to March 30 Jews in Egypt, Tunisia, Mexico, Argentina, Brazil, and Poland staged mass rallies to protest Nazi persecution of Jews. Jews fasted throughout Palestine and in Beirut. The boycott of German goods and services (the most effective means of resistance available to Jews, given their governments' unwillingness to take action against the Nazi regime) also developed spontaneously among the rank-and-file Jews of New York and the East End of London—notably, over the objections of the established British Jewish leadership and months before most of the major American Jewish leaders endorsed it.

As the Nazis steadily escalated their persecution of German Jewry, Jews at the grassroots level in the United States and Britain not only drew on older tactics long deployed in the fight against antisemitism but also developed new approaches to meet the current challenge. In addition to demonstrations and rallies, often involving tens and even hundreds of thousands of Jews in major cities, and well-coordinated boycotts, the Jewish activists systematically accumulated, organized, and widely disseminated massive amounts of information about Nazism and the history of antisemitism, mounting arguments to blunt the impact of Germany's extensive propaganda campaigns in the West. American Jews also produced pageants to express pride in Jewishness and to highlight the long tradition of Jews' resistance to persecution. The most notable was the spectacular *The Romance of a People*, opening in Chicago in July 1933 before an audience of more than 120,000 and performed before enormous crowds in America's largest cities. Jewish organizations also publicized cutting-edge anthropological research in their resolve to counter Nazi "racial science." They staged mock trials of Hitler and printed and widely distributed pamphlets in the United States and Britain that presented harrowing accounts of Nazi antisemitic atrocities, many provided by victims and eyewitnesses.

Prologue to Annihilation delineates the persistent refusal of the American and British governments in these years to denounce Nazi terrorist violence against Jews, despite the attention the Western media drew to it. On March 26, 1933, even as Americans all over the country deluged the White House and State Department with demands for forceful condemnation of and action against the Nazis' antisemitic atrocities, Secretary of State Cordell Hull remained dismissive, commenting that anti-Jewish violence in Germany had largely come to an end—insistent that "responsible" leaders of the German government like Chancellor Hitler were committed to maintaining "law and order." The US embassy in Berlin had assured Hull that the situation would soon be "normal." The *New York Herald Tribune* concluded that the secretary's statement "obviates any present possibility" that the US government would make "official representations to the German government in behalf of the Jews there." President Roosevelt and Secretary Hull were inclined to rely instead on the "sense of responsibility among the Nazi leadership."[19]

The British ambassador to Germany, Sir Horace Rumbold, although acknowledging that Germany's Jews faced "a much more serious danger than mere bodily maltreatment," because many were being "ruthlessly dismissed" from their jobs and would soon be reduced to penury, held the Jews partly responsible for their predicament. Swallowing German propaganda and ignoring all the evidence against it, Sir Horace claimed that under the Weimar Republic, Jews had "practically monopolized some professions and ha[d] obtained the plums of a great many others." They were positioned to completely take over "the teaching professions, medicine, law, the press, imaginative literature, architecture, and the like." Sir Horace found it "only natural" that German youth "should bitterly resent" this, especially "when the learned professions in Germany" were "hopelessly overcrowded." In addition, the British ambassador pointed to what he insisted was the "supremacy of the Jews in the domain of finance."[20]

Prologue to Annihilation examines the considerable sympathy in the American and British governments and among mainstream non-Jewish Americans for appeasing Nazi Germany and allowing German rearmament, a critical Nazi goal. It delves into how Nazi Germany spread propaganda in the United States in these early years in a determined effort to preclude American intervention in the next European war, a central issue to which scholars have devoted little attention. Indeed, *Prologue to Annihilation* shows the success of the Hitler regime in the period 1933–1936 in forging friendly ties with the US and British military leaders, especially naval leaders, as well as in securing the support of non-Jewish veterans' groups in both nations and of prominent American academics. In the mid-1930s, the Nazi government sent swastika-bedecked navy cruisers on extended visits to US and British ports, where they were received enthusiastically and where the US Navy assisted them in training exercises. Numerous civic and business groups invited the officers of the Nazi cruisers to enlighten them about the achievements of the Third Reich and the "injustices" the West had inflicted on Germany. In 1935, the principal British veterans' group, the British Legion, sent its leaders to fraternize with pro-Nazi veterans' groups in the Third Reich. These visits were reciprocated and provided the opportunity for British Legion officers to promote a highly positive view of the Reich, including of its concentration camps. Similarly, leading American universities sent representatives to academic conferences in the "New Germany" that served as platforms for the dissemination and promotion of Nazi racial ideology and that legitimized the Nazified institutions of higher learning that had already staged massive burnings of Jewish and other "un-German" books. Nazi Germany benefited considerably from the fraternal bonds established through these contacts, which convinced many American and British people to consider it a respectable, wronged member of the community of nations.

These efforts to whitewash the Third Reich were conducted, as the following chapters make clear, at the same time as some of the journalists most knowledgeable about the situation in Germany in 1933 and early 1934 had become so alarmed about the predicament of the Jews and the danger of Nazi rearmament that they were calling on the Western democracies to threaten, or even to initiate, a preventive war against Germany. These journalists were especially distressed by the indifference of the British government to what they already understood to be a cataclysm that could envelop Europe. On October 3, 1933, Robert Dell of the *Manchester Guardian* wrote to his editor from Berlin that it was "best to strike now when Germany cannot offer serious resistance." The only chance to avoid a catastrophic war, he urged, was to make Hitler "understand that the other Powers mean business and will walk into Germany if necessary." Dell castigated the British government for floundering and called for "the dismemberment of Germany into small countries." Similarly, Dell's colleague, Frederick Voigt, the *Guardian's* Paris correspondent, warned on February 9, 1934, that "the shadow of Germany rearming is all over Europe." Assessing the current menace, he charged unforgettably that "the great difference between the German and British governments [is] that the German government has a ... conviction of dynamic force, like Islam (unless this is understood there can be no understanding of Germany) but the British government has no conviction at all."[21]

NOTES

1. Among the most important scholarly works on American responses to the Holocaust focusing on the World War II period are David S. Wyman, *The Abandonment of the Jews: America and the Holocaust, 1941–1945* (New York: New Press, 2007 [1984]); Laurel Leff, *Buried by the Times: The Holocaust and America's Most Important Newspaper* (New York: Cambridge University Press, 2005); Rafael Medoff, *FDR and the Holocaust: A Breach of Faith* (Washington, DC: David S. Wyman Institute for Holocaust Studies, 2013); and Monty Penkower, *The Jews Were Expendable: Free World Diplomacy and the Holocaust* (Urbana: University of Illinois Press, 1981). Bat-Ami Zucker, *In Search of Refuge: Jews and*

US Consuls in Nazi Germany, 1933–1941 (London: Vallentine Mitchell, 2001)
focuses on the role of US consuls in obstructing Jewish immigration from
Germany and German-occupied areas to the United States through July 1941.
Except for Leff's book, these studies concentrate on government policy and
the refugee issue, as well as reactions within the American Jewish leadership.
Deborah Lipstadt's study of American journalists' response to Nazism and the
Holocaust, *Beyond Belief: The American Press and the Coming of the Holocaust,
1933–1945* (New York: Free Press, 1986), contains several chapters on the prewar
period. Michaela Hoenicke Moore's analysis of the American public's and
government's perceptions of Nazi Germany, *Know Your Enemy: The American
Debate on Nazism, 1933–1945* (New York: Cambridge University Press, 2010),
devotes two chapters to the interwar period, one of which discusses the
commentary of several major journalists. Wyman's first book, *Paper Walls:
America and the Refugee Crisis, 1938–1941* (Amherst: University of Massachusetts
Press, 1968), covers the years immediately preceding US intervention in World
War II. Journalist Arthur D. Morse's *While Six Million Died: A Chronicle of
American Apathy* (Woodstock, NY: Overlook Press, 1998 [1967]), emphasizes the
US government's refugee policy during the war but contains several chapters on
the late 1930s. In the preface to the 2007 edition of *The Abandonment of the Jews*,
Wyman stated, "Much additional research needs to be done on many aspects of
the U.S. response to the plight of German Jewry in the 1930s" (xv).

Scholarship on British responses to Nazism has focused largely on
appeasement, beginning with Martin Gilbert's pioneering *The Roots of
Appeasement* (London: Weidenfeld and Nicholson, 1966) and Martin Gilbert
and Richard Gott, *The Appeasers* (Boston: Houghton Mifflin, 1963). Richard
Griffiths's *Fellow Travellers of the Right: British Enthusiasts for Nazi Germany,
1933–39* (London: Constable, 1980) also provides a useful account. The British
were, of course, far more engaged with issues of German expansionism than was
the United States.

Like Gilbert, I consider the failure of Britain's leadership to respond
effectively to Germany's rapid rearmament during the early years of Hitler's rule
critically important. Gilbert emphasized that Winston Churchill referred to
this period as "the locust years," a wasted time: "when Britain, if differently led,
could have easily rearmed, and kept well ahead of the German military and air
expansion, which Hitler had begun in 1933 from a base of virtual disarmament."
Hitler had concluded that Britain "would not stand up to aggression beyond its
borders, and . . . would not be in a position to act effectively even to defend its
own cities." Gilbert, *In Search of Churchill: A Historian's Journey* (New York: John
Wiley and Sons, 1994), 106. I devote a chapter to the consequences of British and
American failure to react to the antisemitic terror in the Saar from 1933 through
1935, a subject scholars have largely neglected, which signaled the appeasement

and capitulation that followed on a larger scale. I dedicate another chapter to US and British complicity in German naval rearmament.

Little effort has been accorded to comparing American and British responses to Nazism. One of the few such works, Naomi Cohen's article "The Transatlantic Connection: The American Jewish Committee and the Joint Foreign Committee in Defense of German Jews, 1933–1937," *American Jewish History* 90 (December 2002): 353–84, relies on a limited institutional approach. Cohen claims that "until the Nuremberg Laws of 1935, Western Jews preferred to close their eyes to the long-term danger of Nazism to their fellow-Jews in Europe" (354). By contrast, my social-historical study shows that masses of working- and lower-middle-class Jews in both the United States and Britain spontaneously mobilized against the Nazi threat and displayed considerable militancy as soon as Hitler assumed power. The Jewish masses forced the hand of the major Jewish organizations and pushed them to take stronger action. Throughout this study, I give considerable attention to American and British Jews' anti-Nazi activism from the bottom up.

2. M. J. April, "The Role of Antisemitism in the National Socialist Movement Prior to 1933," D21F7, American Jewish Committee (hereafter, AJC) Archives, New York, NY; Israel Cohen, *The Jews in Germany* (London: John Murray, 1933), 2; William L. Shirer, *The Rise and Fall of the Third Reich* (New York: Simon and Schuster, 1960), 41.

3. Shirer, *Rise and Fall of the Third Reich* 1, 40–41.

4. *New York Times*, March 8, 1933, 10.

5. Streicher's speech in Nurnberg, April 21, 1932 (extract from *Kampf dem Welfeind*, 134), and "100,000 Demonstrate in Koenigsplatz against the Jewish Incitement to Cruelty" (extract from the *Muenschener Beobachter*, daily supplement to the *Voelkischer Beobachter*, no. 91/92, April 1–2, 1933), International Military Tribunal, British Document Book: Julius Streicher, D22F11, AJC Archives; *Daily Herald* (London), April 1, 1933, 1, 11.

6. *Manchester Guardian*, April 1, 1933, 13.

7. Shaplen, translation of interview with Hitler in the *Staats-Zeitung und Herold*, May 21, 1933, box 175, Arthur Hays Sulzberger Collection (hereafter, Sulzberger Papers), Archives and Manuscript Division, New York Public Library (hereafter, NYPL), New York, NY.

8. *New York Times*, April 2, 1933, 29.

9. "Black Monday in America. Germany Is Burned Up," *Kölnische Zeitung*, April 13, 1933, box 175, Sulzberger Papers, NYPL.

10. Lucy S. Dawidowicz noted that "department stores by Nazi definition 'Jewish' were a particular target" of the party. The 1920 program had demanded that they "be immediately communalized and rented cheaply to small ["Aryan"]

tradespeople." Dawidowicz, *The War Against the Jews, 1933–1945* (New York: Bantam Books, 1986 [1975]), 52.

11. "Nazis Launch Onslaught on Jews," *Daily Herald* (London), March 30, 1933, 3.

12. "Report from Nurenberg. Easter 1934 (March-April)," folder H2, James G. McDonald Papers, Rare Book and Manuscript Library, Butler Library, Columbia University, New York, NY.

13. *Daily Herald* (London), March 17, 1933.

14. Jacob Fishman, letter to the editor, *New York Herald Tribune*, March 24, 1933, 10.

15. *Daily Herald* (London), March 3, 1933, 1.

16. [Frederick] Birchall to [Arthur Hays] Sulzberger, May 13, 1934, box 175, Sulzberger Papers, NYPL.

17. "The Tragedy of German Jewry—Vigorous Economic Persecution Continues—Starvation for 600,000 Jews," *Jewish Chronicle* (London), April 14, 1933, 16.

18. *Brooklyn Jewish Examiner*, April 7, 1933, 1.

19. Cordell Hull, Secretary of State, to Rabbi Stephen S. Wise, March 26, 1933, box 6782, Central Decimal Files 1930–39, Department of State General Records, Record Group 59, National Archives, College Park, MD; *New York Herald Tribune*, March 27, 1933, 1, 4.

20. Horace Rumbold, "Recent Persecutions in Germany of Jews and Other Persons. Despatch from His Majesty's Ambassador in Berlin to the Secretary of State for Foreign Affairs," April 13, 1933, Records of the Cabinet Office, National Archives, Kew Gardens, London, UK.

21. Robert Dell to Crozier, October 3, 1933, 210/1–86, and Frederic Voigt to Crozier, February 9, 1934, 211/86–136, GDN Foreign Correspondence, *Manchester Guardian* Archives, John Rylands Library, Manchester, UK.

ONE

—〰—

PORTENTS

September 1930 to January 1933

IN AN ADDRESS TO THE American Jewish Congress (AJCongress) National
Executive Committee on March 8, 1931, its chair, Dr. Joseph Tenenbaum, declared that a "hurricane" of anti-Jewish hatred raged across Europe, from the
Ural Mountains to the Rhine River and from the Baltic Sea to the Black Sea,
"sweeping disaster upon the heads" of the Jewish people. He noted that in the
years immediately following World War I, as "peacemakers" haggled in Paris,
a "wave of well-organized and... premeditated pogroms" ravaged Jewish communities in Eastern Europe, making it the "bloodiest and saddest" period in
Jewish history. But now in Germany, the Nazi movement promoted a form
of antisemitism that was "far more venomous and destructive than murder
and pillage." It combined aggressive economic boycotts of Jewish stores and
offices, destruction of Jewish property, desecration of synagogues and Jewish
cemeteries, dissemination of vicious anti-Jewish propaganda, and relentless
harassment, punctuated by outbursts of violence. This onslaught had already
reduced many flourishing Jewish businesses to "a desolate condition" and de-
moralized sizeable numbers of Jews. Over the long term, it threatened Jewish
existence in Germany.[1]

A year later, on March 6, 1932, Tenenbaum reported that German Jewry's
plight had worsened: it was "on the brink of disaster." The Nazis' antisemitic
campaign had paralyzed "Jewish commerce and industry," and "poverty and
ruin" were "spreading rapidly." Hundreds of Jewish families had already been
forced to flee their country, a land their ancestors had inhabited for centuries.
Tenenbaum predicted that should the Nazis assume control in Germany, its
Jewish citizens would face "mass expulsion, confiscation of property [and] exclusion from schools and employment." He warned that even highly educated

Nazis harbored annihilationist intentions, pointing out that the recent Nazi Congress of Physicians and Pharmacists in Leipzig had seriously considered a proposal "to sterilize all Jews." On December 8, 1931, the *New York Times* reported that speakers at the congress had identified the "'racial' purification of Germany" to be a "prime objective" of a Nazi regime "once the party assumed the reins of government." The "Nordics" would be "nurtured preeminently, tolerance being extended to the group next below as a sort of suffered helots, while the lowest group [Jews] would be eliminated through compulsory sterilization." Special "race bureaus" maintaining information on the "racial" background of all Germans were to be established to prevent "miscegenation," which the Nazis would prohibit by law.[2]

Addressing the AJCongress's annual sessions in Washington, DC, in June 1932, Tenenbaum stated that "poisonous" propaganda maligning Jews, disseminated throughout Germany in a hundred newspapers, twenty-five magazines, news agencies, and feature syndicates that the Nazis controlled, had precipitated physical "assaults and attacks" against Jews that were "repeated almost daily." Stiffening boycotts against Jewish enterprises had impoverished Jews in many parts of Germany. Tenenbaum stressed that legislation Nazi leaders had introduced in the Prussian chamber and elsewhere portended disaster for German Jewry. This legislation required the dismissal of all Jewish state and municipal employees and the termination of Jews' right to vote or hold office. Tenenbaum also underlined Nazi deputies' proposals in the Bavarian and Thuringian Landtags that any unsolved case of a murder committed since 1840 be classified as a Jewish ritual murder.[3]

As early as the summer of 1926, bills were introduced in Thuringia's Landtag that barred Jews from teaching in state and communal schools or in the provincial university; excluded Jewish students from state and communal schools because of the "innate ... outlook and moral ideas and other peculiarities of the Jewish race" and the "moral and physical danger" of mixing the sexes when Jews were among Christians; prohibited Jews from serving as physicians because they lacked the "moral purity which is natural to a born-German but foreign to a Jew"; and expelled Jews of Eastern European origin from Thuringia and confiscated their property.[4]

Highlighting Nazism's extreme brutality and expansionist designs, Tenenbaum called it a movement with "no parallel since Genghis Khan," who had "set out to destroy western civilization." The Nazis, who already administered many municipalities, were "a controlling power" in Prussia, Germany's largest and most populous state, where nearly three-quarters of the Jewish population resided. The Nazis were poised to take over Germany's government.[5]

On a speaking tour in the United States in January 1932, Pierre van Paassen, an internationally renowned non-Jewish European journalist whose column was syndicated in numerous American newspapers, provided an analysis of German Jewry's condition and prospects that was similar to Tenenbaum's. Van Paassen wrote that Hitler's plan for German Jewry "surpasses . . . in cruelty and evil intent" both the czarist pogrom and "wholesale expulsion." It imposed "a ruthless system of taxation and economic and social pressure," designed to "force the mass of German Jewry into the ranks of the poorest strata of the population within a decade," enabling Hitler "to administer the coup de grace." A Hitler aide explained to van Paassen that this was how the Nazis planned "ruthlessly and without mercy . . . [to] rid these Germanic countries of the Semitic vermin that has sucked away our strength and our blood for centuries."[6] In referring to Jews as "vermin," the aide not only drew on annihilationist imagery but also ominously invoked the medieval blood libel, which held that Jews murdered innocent Christian children to extract their blood for use in Jewish religious rituals.

In a December 2, 1932 column entitled "In Darkest Germany," the London *Jewish Chronicle* emphasized that the Nazis used medieval images of bloodsucking Jews as a principal weapon in their relentless drive to foment anti-Jewish violence. The Nazis published articles filled with antisemitic invective and distributed large quantities of postcards featuring "diabolical caricatures" of Jews, the fount of all evil. Their songs were "designed to rouse the thirst for Jewish blood." Introduced in 1930, the party anthem, the "Horst Wessel Lied," promised, "When Jewish blood spurts from the knife, then will the German people prosper." Other Nazi songs associated German liberation with inflicting pain on Jews and killing them. The "Song of the Storm Columns," "chanted by marching brownshirts on the streets of Berlin from 1928 onwards," announced, "So stand the Storm Columns, for racial fight prepared / Only when Jews bleed, are we liberated." This appeared in the Sturmabteilung's (SA) *Kampflied der SA (SA Songs of Struggle)*, published in the *Kleines Naziliederbuch: Deutsche Erwache! (Little Nazi Songbook: Germany Awake!)*[7]

As an example of the Nazis' "diabolical accusation" against German Jewry, the *Jewish Chronicle* cited a lecture by Reichstag deputy Dr. Robert Ley, who became head of the German Labor Front when Hitler was Germany's chancellor. Entitled "Judaism, Race, and Revolution," it was printed in the Nazi newspaper *Westdeutscher Beobachter* on July 25, 1931. Here, Ley compared Jews to vampires, explaining that there were Jewish men whose "race instinct" drove them to consume the blood of non-Jewish "races."[8]

The Nazis' intention to reduce German Jewry to a lower caste was evident to many Jewish and non-Jewish observers in the West who monitored the situation in Germany during the three years before Hitler's assuming the chancellorship. In October 1930, the British ambassador to Germany, Sir Horace Rumbold, a non-Jew, sent the British Foreign Office a lengthy summary of "the basic tenets of the Nazi creed." It was drawn from his analysis of the Nazi Party program, formulated in 1920, and a commentary that Alfred Rosenberg, a leading Nazi racial theorist, had written on it in 1922. Rumbold emphasized the Nazis' determination to deprive German Jews of the rights of citizenship once they gained power. They accomplished this in September 1935 by enacting the Nuremberg race laws. Rumbold also directed attention to the platform's call to prohibit Jews from serving as editors or correspondents for a German newspaper. In an address entitled "Hitlerism and the Status of the Jews in Germany" delivered before a Jewish audience in New York City in December 1932, Morris Waldman, secretary of the American Jewish Committee (AJC), one of the two largest American Jewish defense organizations, also highlighted the platform's demand that German Jews be denied rights of citizenship. Waldman pointed out that this demand derived from the Nazis' contention that Jews were racially different from Germans, and he stressed that the platform stipulated that "he who is not a citizen may live in Germany only as a guest . . . governed by the laws regulating foreigners."⁹

TOWARD THE HOUR OF RECKONING

The London *Times*, reporting in August 1932 on "outrages" in Königsberg, where rampaging Nazis had smashed Jewish store windows and sent threatening letters to Jewish storekeepers, noted that Nazi leaders had long spoken of "the hour of reckoning" with the Jews and the "fearful vengeance" they would inflict on them. Three months before, the London *Jewish Chronicle*'s special correspondent in Berlin had drawn attention to a pervasive atmosphere of menace toward Jews across Germany. He described towns, villages, and hamlets "drowned in anti-Semitic banners." A high state of tension prevailed in Berlin, where during the eight days of Passover the city "was virtually deluged with swastikas." The correspondent observed that "over roofs, over balconies [and] from windows, the [swastika] flags were streaming, as if to issue the warning: 'Look out! We are coming!'" Jews emerging from nearly every shul in Berlin were confronted with a swastika banner placed opposite the building, warning that "inevitable sorrow and grief were in store" for the Jews "and would come soon, very soon."¹⁰

During the 1920s, the Nazis linked their charge that Jews had deprived Germany of certain victory in World War I by stabbing it in the back with the

Protocols of the Elders of Zion, a turn-of-the-century forgery by the Russian czarist secret police, which became arguably the twentieth century's most perni-
cious piece of antisemitic propaganda. Antisemites claimed that the document
revealed a Jewish conspiracy to dominate the world, originating at the First
World Zionist Congress in Basel, Switzerland, in 1897. The *Protocols* circulated
widely in Germany, brought there and to other Western and Central European
countries by White Russian émigrés fleeing from the Bolshevik Revolution.
Antisemites deduced that Jews had started the world war and caused Germany's defeat as part of their goal to undermine Christian civilization and
establish "a Jewish world empire." The Nazis quickly embraced the *Protocols.*
Alfred Rosenberg published a text of the *Protocols,* including a commentary on
it that sold fifty thousand copies.[11]

Influenced by the *Protocols,* a favorite Nazi song depicted Jews as wealthy,
cowardly, and unpatriotic and accused them of starting World War I for financial profit: "Jewish money kindled / the great world-conflagration and in every
office [in safe, unmanly jobs] / the Jew-boys sit / Everywhere their faces grin /
except in the trenches!" An antisemitic cartoon in the January 17, 1931 issue
of *Der Stürmer,* a major Nazi weekly newspaper published in Nuremberg, is
indicative of the *Protocols'* influence on the Nazi outlook. The cartoon featured
an "enormous bloated Jew" whose face and shirt were stained with blood. The
Jew stood "nearly up to the waist in a sea of blood." In his skeletal hands he held
a placard marked "World War." *Der Stürmer's* caption was "Pan-Juda Wades
through a Sea of Blood on His Way to World Domination."[12]

The Nazis' involvement in the assassination of Germany's foreign minister,
Walther Rathenau, a Jew, on June 24, 1922, and their desecration of memorials to him reflected their virulent antisemitism and violent, often murderous,
impulses toward Jews, as well as the strong impact of the *Protocols.* A German
patriot, Rathenau had held one of the government's most important positions
during the world war, directing the War Materials Office. In this capacity he
was charged with overseeing the raw materials used in production for Germany's war effort, as well as the nation's food supply. He was the man who
had "kept the people shooting and the army eating."[13] As Germany's minister
of reconstruction after the war, Rathenau had signed the reparations agreement with France, but afterward he had steadily pressed for a revision of the
indemnity. Still, Rathenau's young Nazi assassins, members of the viciously
antisemitic paramilitary Ehrhardt Brigade, claimed that Rathenau was "one
of the 300 Elders of Zion who was seeking to bring the world under the rule of
the Jews."[14] In his 1934 autobiography, *I Was a German,* Ernst Toller, a leading
German Jewish dramatist and refugee from Nazism who settled in the United

States soon after Hitler assumed power, recalled that before Rathenau's assassination, the Nazi students compared Rathenau to a pig that deserved to be slaughtered, another common antisemitic image dating to the Middle Ages. They would sing: "The rifles ring out—tack, tack, tack / On all the swine both red and black / And Mr. Walther Rathenau / Will find his days are precious few: / Let fly at Walther Rathenau / The God-damned dirty Jew."[15]

The assassins timed Rathenau's murder close to the summer solstice, the brightest time of the year, stamping out the darkness and evil of the Jew.[16] They murdered Rathenau in "a hail of bullets" and hand grenades while he was leaving home in his open automobile on the way to his office. On June 29, 1931, Nazis desecrated the memorial that marked the spot where Rathenau was killed, smearing it with paint and destroying a wreath placed there by supporters of the Weimar Republic.[17]

THE BERLIN POGROMS

Severe antisemitic riots in Berlin's major commercial district marked the opening of the fifth Reichstag of the German Republic on October 13, 1930, which became an arena for Nazi verbal attacks on Jews and disorderly, sometimes violent, behavior designed to undermine parliamentary government. The Nazis had won a smashing victory in the September 14, 1930, general election, on a scale that surprised even the party leaders, polling 6.5 million votes—an 800 percent increase—and winning 107 seats in the Reichstag. Their numbers were second only to the Social Democrats. This was an immense gain for the Nazis, who in 1928 had been the ninth-largest party, receiving only 810,000 votes and holding only 12 seats. In the 1930 election, the Nazis had demonstrated strength with almost every social group.[18] The Nazis' showing in the election gave them tremendous momentum.

Guido Enderis, head of the *New York Times* Berlin bureau, wrote that the election "virtually makes [the Nazis] the largest single group definitely sworn to anti-Semitic politics in European parliamentary history for the past fifty years." He reported that foreign correspondents who telephoned the Nazi Party's Berlin headquarters for information or interviews during the election campaign were immediately asked if they represented a Jewish newspaper. Ambassador Horace Rumbold informed the queen of Spain that when news of the Nazi electoral success came over the wireless, the faces of Jews in the German capital's cafés and restaurants turned white with horror.[19]

Toni Sender, a Social Democratic deputy in the Reichstag from 1920 to 1933, called the September 14, 1930, elections "a turning point in German history" for having brought "the new barbarians" into the Reichstag as a sizeable bloc for the first time. The husband of Walther Rathenau's niece informed AJC president Cyrus Adler, who had left Germany three or four days before the election, that "nothing but a miracle can avert a grave danger to the Jews in Germany." Arthur Koestler, who resided in Berlin from the day of the election until July 1932, predicted that "the final showdown was approaching."[20]

German elections from 1930 to 1933 heightened the danger to Jews, because they provided the opportunity for the Nazis (and antisemitic candidates in other parties) to slander them before enormous crowds. Hitler spoke to gatherings of as many as twenty thousand during the 1930 campaign.[21]

The first session of the new Reichstag on October 13, 1930 proved the most "spectacular and [the] loudest" in German parliamentary history, as swaggering Nazi deputies appeared ready to pounce on Communist deputies and expressed contempt for the body's Jewish members. The Nazis waited until the other deputies were seated and then, led by Dr. Wilhelm Frick, Thuringia's minister of the interior, marched single file into the chamber, wearing brown-shirt uniforms (forbidden in Prussia), Sam Browne belts, and swastika armbands. They slapped their hips and cried, "Germany, awake!" To prevent arrest, some Nazi deputies wore coats over their uniforms on the way to the Reichstag; others changed into them upon arrival. Parliamentary immunity prevented their arrest once inside the building. According to the London *Times*, as Carl Herold, presiding as the oldest Reichstag member, called the roll of the 577 deputies, the Nazis "made mocking noises" whenever he came to a Jewish name. When Herold called the name of the first Nazi, he responded by shouting, "Heil Hitler!" As Josef Goebbels entered the chamber, all the Nazi deputies rose in unison and gave the Nazi salute. Sigrid Schultz, Berlin correspondent of the *Chicago Tribune*, noted that as the Nazi and Communist deputies hurled invectives at each other, moderate deputies huddled together terrified.[22]

Sender recalled that when she entered the Reichstag hall that day, she immediately noticed the tightly knit gaggle of brown-shirted Nazis: "a noisy, shouting" gang, many of whom had "the faces of criminals and degenerates." So "this was the elite of the Aryan race!" she thought. Sender felt degraded to have to sit in the room with them. She commented, "Whoever glanced once at them had to be prepared for all the crimes, all the cruelties and perverse acts that were to take place little more than two years later [when Hitler assumed power]."[23]

Among the Nazi deputies was Edmund Heines, an SA leader, who in 1928 had been sentenced to prison for committing a political murder in 1920. He was convicted of manslaughter and sentenced to fifteen years (reduced to five on appeal) but was released after about eighteen months. On his campaign posters for the Reichstag, the Nazis had boasted, "*Feme*-murderer Heines will speak!" Heines had belonged to the Freikorps, an illegal, antisemitic, antirepublican paramilitary group, during the years immediately following World War I. The Freikorps established the Feme as a unit to murder "traitors" without trial. Alan Bullock, author of a major biography of Adolf Hitler, wrote that "the *Freikorps* were the training schools for the political murder and terrorism [carried out by the Nazis] which disfigured German life up to 1924, and again after 1929." Germany's postwar republican government had, under Allied pressure, ordered the Freikorps dissolved. The Nazis had established the SA as a successor to the Freikorps.[24] In December 1930, when a Social Democratic deputy referred to the killing that Heines had committed as "particularly abominable" on the Reichstag floor, the Nazis in the chamber shouted back, "Just the same thing is going to happen to you!"[25]

Shortly after the first Reichstag session ended, Nazi mobs celebrated their party's emergence as a powerful presence by rampaging through the nearby fashionable shopping districts, hurling rocks through the plate-glass windows of numerous Jewish-owned department stores and other Jewish enterprises, and shouting insults at—and beating—anyone they believed to be a Jew. Having severely damaged Jewish cafés, a Jewish silk firm, and several other Jewish-owned stores, the mob proceeded to Jewish-owned Wertheim's, one of Berlin's largest department stores. At a given signal, they flung huge cobblestones that shattered thirty-six plate-glass windows, nearly all the windows on the ground level. The *New York Herald Tribune*'s Berlin bureau reported that "the Nazis hailed the crash of the falling glass with jubilant shouts of 'All out, Jews!' and 'Perish Judea!'" Celebrating the demolition, the mob marched down Leipziger Strasse, Berlin's major shopping street, singing Nazi "war songs" and battle cries: "Germany, awake!" and "Down with the Jews!" They left a trail of broken shopwindows half a mile long on Berlin's busiest thoroughfares. On several occasions, the police fired "alarm shots" over the heads of the mob in order to summon reinforcements. Members of the mobs and onlookers fired shots as well, and by evening any remaining fragments of windows were pocked with bullet holes.[26]

Leading American newspapers gave prominent coverage to the Berlin pogroms, with the *New York Herald Tribune* and the *New York Times* on October 14 highlighting the antisemitic attacks on their front pages. The *Herald Tribune* banner headline announced, "Fascist Mobs Strike at Jews in Berlin as Reichstag Opens." The article was illustrated with three photographs. The *Times* page 1 headline read, "Hitlerites in Riots, Stone Jewish Shops as Reichstag Opens." In Britain, the *Manchester Guardian* ran stories about the pogrom on inside pages on both October 14 and 15. It made very clear that the violence was directed solely at Jews: "[It] had nothing to do with Communism or with the unemployed. They were not bread riots. . . . They were exclusively anti-Semitic."[27]

The *New York Times* reported that all over Berlin, one heard the warning: "This is just the beginning." The *New York Herald Tribune* noted the next day that Hitler had "promised to expel the Jews and to abolish department stores," which he believed to be largely Jewish owned, and editorialized that the Berlin rioters had "translated [the Nazi Party's] proposals into action."[28]

The Berlin police were convinced that the Nazis had carefully organized the rioting, commenting that otherwise it would have been impossible to smash thirty-six of Wertheim's windows simultaneously and escape undetected. The police identified 45 of the 108 they arrested as members of the Nazi Party and most of the others as Nazi sympathizers. They detained only 31 of those arrested.[29]

On October 17, 1930, four days after the street violence, Gregor Strasser, a Nazi Party leader, read in the Reichstag "from a carefully prepared manuscript" and in a "bellowing voice" issued a series of demands, which included "the elimination of Jews from German life." When Strasser finished, Nazi deputies introduced a motion that called for the expropriation without compensation of property of East European Jews who had immigrated to Germany after August 1, 1914, and that of their relatives. Later in the session, Strasser proclaimed that the Jews had failed to follow Moses and his laws, and "they were just the same then as they are now."[30]

In December 1930, the Nazis disrupted the Berlin premiere of the antiwar film *All Quiet on the Western Front*, based on Erich Maria Remarque's novel. Organized by Josef Goebbels, the disruption sparked violent antisemitic riots inside and outside the theater. As the film began, Nazis shouting, "Germany, awake!" and "Death to the Jews!" released mice and hurled stench bombs. Cries of "Death to the Jews!" rang from all corners of the theater, which was forced to shut down the film. The London *Jewish Chronicle* reported that in the streets outside, a huge crowd assaulted "persons of Jewish appearance," inflicting "a large number of casualties."[31] In Vienna, the film opening the next month triggered hours-long antisemitic riots in three districts, with pro-Nazi demonstrators marching from one deserted Jewish-owned café to another, smashing plate-glass windows. After two days, Austria's minister of the interior prohibited further showings of *All Quiet on the Western Front* because of "the imminent danger to persons and property."[32]

On the first day of Rosh Hashanah, 1931, eleven months after the Berlin street riots that marked the Reichstag's opening, the Nazis staged another pogrom against Jews on Berlin's Kurfürstendamm, the center of the city's nightlife, and along adjoining streets. An estimated fifteen hundred Nazis marched down the Kurfürstendamm, and in a "carefully planned" operation, they assaulted "every Jewish-looking person they could lay their hands on," including many who had emerged from synagogue services. A London *Times* journalist who witnessed the pogrom stated that groups of Nazi storm troopers appeared to have been assigned certain stretches of the Kurfürstendamm, and at a given signal they would launch an attack against Jews. He observed that Nazi leaders wearing black armbands were stationed on street corners directing and inciting their followers. The Jewish Telegraphic Agency (JTA) reported that the Nazis, having set up a megaphone near the famous Romanische Café, "kept up a constant shout of 'Death to the Jews' and 'Perish Judea! Germany Awake!'" (*"Juda verrecke! Deutschland erwache!"*). The Nazis knocked down Jews and clubbed them with heavy cudgels, then stomped on them with heavy boots. The JTA reporter witnessed an elderly Jewish couple knocked down in Knesebeck Strasse, where the Jewish Joint Distribution Committee's European offices were located; the man was then "beaten senseless." In many of the streets, "blood was running." The JTA stated that the Uhlandstrasse, the Rankestrasse, the Tauentzienstrasse, and other streets through which Jews walked home from the Nollendorf Platz synagogue resembled a battlefield, the "Jews, with battered and bleeding heads, pursued by triumphant Hitlerites shouting their war cries." Dr. Leo Lowenstein, one of those the Nazis wounded in the pogrom, was a former German army captain and president of the Federation of Jewish Front-Fighters, the organization of German Jewish World War I combat veterans.[33]

The Nazis also invaded cafés and restaurants owned or frequented by Jews, in search of Jews to pummel. The *Manchester Guardian* reported that "the attacks in the cafés appeared to have been disciplined and organized" hunts for Jews, adding that "all fair-haired people had been unmolested." Fifty Nazis broke into the Reimann Café and fired shots at the Jewish customers, driving them out in a panic. Then they broke a window, smashed crockery, and overturned and destroyed marble tables.[34]

The *Manchester Guardian* commented that these Nazi beatings and destruction made it "difficult to give any assurance that Germany is a country safe for Jews." The London *Times* observed that many "solid" German citizens watching the anti-Jewish violence on the streets or from restaurants appeared to approve of it.[35]

In a caustic letter to *New York Times* soon-to-be publisher Arthur Hays Sulzberger on October 1, 1931, AJC secretary Morris Waldman conveyed his displeasure with the paper's very brief and inaccurate coverage of the pogrom. He informed Sulzberger that "Jewish newspapers express profound disappointment over the fact that so influential a journal as the *New York Times* should be so poorly represented in so important a center as Berlin." Waldman assessed the *New York Times*'s coverage as vastly inferior to that of the London *Times* and *Manchester Guardian,* and he enclosed their articles. The *New York Times* had not published an article about the event until September 16, two days after the British newspapers (and the *Chicago Tribune*). Consisting of two very short paragraphs and titled "Berlin Riot a Mild Affair," it erroneously stated that no one was seriously injured. The article also claimed that the "demonstration . . . did not constitute an organized movement of any sort." The London *Times*'s September 14 article, headlined "Attack on Jews in Berlin," had designated the Nazis' violence "organized hooliganism." Waldman emphasized to Sulzberger that the London *Times* correspondent, an eyewitness to the disturbances, described them as "having borne all the earmarks of a planned attack." On September 14, the *Guardian* had called the attacks "the worst anti-Semitic excesses there have yet been in Germany." It reported that "many people were struck on the head . . . or knocked down. Some were badly hurt. Elderly men could be seen with bleeding heads staggering beneath the blows."[36]

Count Wolf von Helldorf (head of the Berlin SA), some of his SA commanders, and about thirty others were tried for offenses committed during the pogrom. The Berlin High Court was relatively lenient, although the Boston *Jewish Advocate* noted that the sentences were "unprecedented [in Germany] for offenses of this nature." They ranged from nine months to twenty months in prison for disturbing the public peace and conspiring against religion. Nobody was convicted of assault and battery, despite the many seriously injured Jews. The Philadelphia *Jewish Exponent* reported that after the court announced the sentences, the Central Verein of German Jews, the nation's leading Jewish organization, received letters threatening to set synagogues ablaze, to drench Jewish passersby in oil and set them on fire, and warning that Jewish families would be "seized, beaten, and imprisoned in cellars" until they died of hunger.[37] Josef Goebbels's *Der Angriff* justified the attacks, claiming they had been carried out by starving, unemployed men incited by Jews walking about dressed in holiday finery.[38]

Von Helldorf asserted that the Nazis had not targeted individual Jews but were merely expressing opposition to "the Jewish capitalistic system." The public prosecutor interrupted to ask how he could then explain why the Nazis had attacked the Reimann Café, known as a gathering spot for poor Jewish artists and the Jewish intelligentsia. Fourteen Berlin police officers and sergeants testified that the anti-Jewish attacks had been "systematically planned and organized."[39]

After hearing further testimony, on November 7, 1931, a new court sentenced von Helldorf to six months' imprisonment for disturbing the peace. It ruled,

however, that the riots were not "planned by the Nazi command," and it acquitted von Helldorf of leading them. The court thus accepted the SA chieftain's
"main contention," despite the testimony of numerous witnesses. Two brothers stated they had been driving just behind von Helldorf's car and heard him
give orders to beat Jews. Police officers made the same claim. Dr. Alfred Apfel,
a Jewish lawyer who lived in the Kurfürstendamm near the Fasanenstrasse
synagogue, told the court that he had seen fifteen hundred storm troopers pass
by his house, all "acting clearly under the orders of recognized leaders." Five
or six of the leaders sent a group of the SA men to a corner, where a man with a
loudspeaker issued commands. He also repeatedly barked out, "Juda!" to which
the storm troopers shrieked, "Perish!" Dr. Apfel testified that he had seen about
fifteen storm troopers knock down and stomp on "a Jewish-looking man." A
non-Jew, Dr. Möhring, whom the pogromists mistook for a Jew, stated that a
troop of Nazis had pushed him into the gutter. When an SA man blew a whistle,
storm troopers converged from all sides and began clubbing him, shouting,
"Shoot the Jew down!" He ran into the Reimann Café, but the storm troopers
pursued him inside, pounding him with cudgels until he fell unconscious. Herr
Reimann, the proprietor, also testified that he had heard the storm troopers
responding to their leaders' commands.[40]

Upon appeal, Count Helldorf was acquitted even of disturbing the peace and
was only required to pay a trifling fine of one hundred marks for "using offensive language against the police." The appeals court also reduced the sentences
of nineteen of the other previously convicted Nazis.[41]

In February 1932, Israel Cohen reported in the London *Jewish Chronicle*
that since the Rosh Hashanah pogrom in Berlin, "hardly a week has passed
without some additional evidence of the ferocious enmity of the Nazis against
their Jewish fellow citizens." He cited the Munich Nazi newspaper *Illustrierter
Beobachter*'s characterization of Jews as "the abortion of world history," creatures who were worse than cannibals, and its call to abolish Jews' civil rights.
Cohen found that Nazi lawyers were demanding that Jews be prevented from
serving as magistrates or judges. He learned that a commission of Nazi physicians had visited all of Berlin's hospitals to prepare for dismissing Jewish doctors once Hitler came to power.[42]

ANTI-JEWISH TERROR IN THE PROVINCES

Writing in the London *Jewish Chronicle* in June 1932, Israel Cohen drew attention to the persecution of Jews in Germany's provincial towns, where they were
"more conspicuous" and easier to isolate and target. He reported that the Jewish

shopkeepers, physicians, and lawyers were boycotted, and Jewish schoolchildren "molested or ostracized." Similarly, in September 1932 the Brooklyn *Jewish Examiner* stressed that although Jews' situation was increasingly precarious throughout Germany, it was especially perilous in the provinces, where Nazi boycotts and threats had caused many to liquidate their businesses and flee to the cities. In the smaller towns, the Nazis even picketed Jewish stores to prevent customers from entering. In some towns, the Nazis threatened to publish blacklists of "traitors"—persons who purchased from Jews. Not a day went by without the Nazi press publishing "some poisonous libel against the Jews." Fearing physical assault, Jewish families in the provinces "barred their doors and tremble[d] through the night."[43] The London *Jewish Chronicle*'s Berlin correspondent had observed that Nazis campaigning in rural villages during the September 14, 1930, general election had promised German gentiles that a Nazi victory would result in the expulsion of Jews and the confiscation of their houses, which would be distributed among the gentiles.[44]

In his book *Germany Puts the Clock Back*, published in early 1933, Edgar Ansel Mowrer, Berlin correspondent for the *Chicago Daily News*, described the anti-Jewish terror that prevailed in the spring of 1932 in the Nazi-administered Protestant town of Neustadt-on-the-Aisch, population five thousand, in Central Franconia. The municipal government conducted business only with gentile firms. Mowrer noted that Nazi sentinels stood in front of Jewish-owned stores writing down the name of anyone shopping there, who would then be shunned. Peasants coming to town were "directed to stores kept by Germans." Christians who had Jewish friends dared not acknowledge them on the streets.[45]

In 1931 and 1932, the Nazis also launched boycotts of Jewish stores in German and Austrian cities. In the 1931 Christmas shopping season, they distributed hundreds of thousands of leaflets warning "No Jewish goods on your Christmas tree." In a 1932 boycott, Nazis invoked the almost two-millennium-old deicide accusation, using the slogan "not a single penny for the crucifiers of Christ."[46]

As reported in the London *Jewish Chronicle* and the *Manchester Guardian*, by the end of 1932 the Nazis were escalating their effort to shut down Jewish-owned department stores by tossing tear gas bombs into them, forcing customers to flee in panic. On December 23, 1932, the *Jewish Chronicle* described how Nazis had thrown tear gas bombs into three Jewish department stores in Giessen, a town in Hessen, and into three in Mayence (Mainz) in the Rhineland, creating terror in the crowds of shoppers. It pointed to similar attacks in Worms, Darmstadt, and other German towns, "suggesting that there is a systematic campaign." Two days earlier, the *Guardian* described similar Nazi tear gas attacks on crowded Jewish department stores, which had just occurred in Vienna.[47]

Jewish shopkeepers in provincial towns had become targets of terrorist violence as well as boycotts. On August 9, 1932, the *Manchester Guardian* reported that antisemites had thrown a bomb at a store owned by a Jew in Allenstein in East Prussia. The bomb smashed the door and caused considerable damage to the inventory. The *Guardian* added that bombs had also been thrown at three Jewish-owned stores in Neidenburg, another East Prussian town. It stated that "attacks in the local Nazi press, insults and menaces . . . boycotts [and] now— open violence have plunged innumerable Jews who have harmed no one and are almost defenseless into ruin and despair."[48]

Jews in major cities were the targets of violent attacks as well, foreshadowing the reign of terror that followed the formation of the Hitler government in early 1933. On June 27, 1932, the JTA reported that the Social Democratic newspaper *Vorwärts* had just warned that the Nazis were preparing to launch systematic raids in the Berlin subway, aimed at throwing Jews and socialists out of moving trains. The JTA noted that on the previous night, Nazi storm troopers had attempted to do this to Jews at or near the Kurfürstendamm station in Berlin.[49]

Jewish children and adolescents in both towns and cities were also subjected to unceasing torments and threats of physical harm. Mowrer noted that German police had convinced the Association of Jewish Boy Scouts (*Jüdischer Pfadfinderbund Deutschlands*) not to hold its open-air summer camp in 1932 because they could not (or would not) protect them from violent "attacks of racial rowdies." The JTA reported on July 19, 1932, that antisemites had assaulted Jewish boy scouts on their way to Bavaria. Mowrer emphasized that many Jewish pupils in the schools were also "enduring hell at the hands of their merciless Christian companions."[50]

The Nazis' huge gains in the general election of July 31, 1932, following the dissolution of the Reichstag that had been elected on September 14, 1930, led to increased and intensified antisemitic violence throughout Germany. The Nazis more than doubled their number of seats, from 107 to 230, making them the largest party in the Reichstag. Their vote doubled from 6.4 to 13.1 million, nearly 40 percent of ballots cast. A few days before the election, *New York Times* Berlin correspondent Frederick Birchall emphasized that the Nazis' "racial creed" held that the only people "worth preserving" were "of the Nordic breed." Their program called for confining Jews in ghettos, prohibiting them from serving as judges or educators, barring them from the military, and ending Jewish immigration into Germany. He added that the Nazis had recently paraded before major Jewish-owned publishing houses in Berlin "shouting in unison, 'Judea verrecke!'" ("Perish Judaea!")[51]

The trial of nine storm troopers for murdering an unemployed laborer of Communist sympathies, Konrad Pietzuch, in his home at 1:30 a.m. on August 10, 1932, in the Upper Silesian town of Potempa and the sentencing of five of them to death sparked fierce anti-Jewish demonstrations, which resulted in damage to Jewish stores and other businesses. The brownshirts had broken into Pietzuch's cottage while he slept and had brutally beaten, stabbed, and shot him in his mother's presence. They had also torn his throat. The trial was conducted in the nearby Silesian town of Beuthen. Walter Lütgebrune, a leading Nazi Party attorney and close colleague of SA chief Ernst Röhm, represented the accused storm troopers. Recently passed antiterrorism decrees, which Chancellor von Papen's government assumed would primarily be used against Communists, required the death penalty for political murders. Edmund Heines, *Gruppenführer* of the Silesian SA, attended every session of the trial. The trial received international publicity.[52]

In what the *Manchester Guardian* called "an open declaration of war on the German government," Hitler denounced the court's verdict as "monstrous" and called von Papen "the executioner of patriotic fighters for freedom." The London *Times* reported that the editor of the official Nazi Party newspaper *Völkischer Beobachter*, Alfred Rosenberg, claimed that equality before the law was not in the national interest. Judging a person accused of a crime must take into consideration his or her race or political outlook. Rosenberg justified this view by referring to the lynching of African Americans in the United States and the short sentences that German courts had given reactionaries convicted of political murder during the previous decade. "For the Nazis," he emphasized, "one soul is not equal to another."[53]

To the Nazis, the convicted men were prisoners of war, not criminals. *Der Angriff* endorsed the murder of Pietzuch, whom they labeled a "Communist bandit," as an act of "just defense against the Marxist terror," which they considered Jewish directed and inspired.[54]

As soon as the verdict was announced on August 22, Heines incited the crowd outside the courthouse, which included many uniformed storm troopers, to go on a rampage through the streets of Beuthen, smashing the windows of Jewish-owned stores. Jewish shopkeepers "hurriedly closed their premises and put up shutters." The next day Josef Goebbels published a "violent" article in *Der Angriff* entitled "The Jews are to Blame," which attributed the death sentences to Jewish influence on the German government. Goebbels implied that when the Nazis came to power they would unleash pogroms against the

Jews, promising they "will never escape the judgment they deserve." He railed that the Jews had ruled Germany for fourteen years, during which they had starved German workers, "poisoned the nation's morals," and "encouraged the police ... to persecute patriotic Germans with clubs."[55] In Breslau, crowds assaulted and robbed Jewish pedestrians and broke the windows of Jewish-owned stores. They shrieked, "Down with the Bloody Jewish Judges!" and "Death to the Jews!"[56]

ANTISEMITIC TERROR AND VIOLENCE
IN GERMAN UNIVERSITIES

From 1930 until the advent of the Hitler regime in early 1933, Germany's universities served as important bases for Nazi agitation and were dangerous environments for Jews. The historian Richard Evans noted that well before 1930 German universities had become "political hotbeds of the extreme right." They provided significant support for the Freikorps after the world war.[57] In March 1931, the *New York Times* published an article headlined "German Students Are Mostly Nazis." Not only students but also many professors were fiercely antisemitic and hostile to the Weimar Republic. In November 1930, a few weeks after returning to the United States from Germany, AJC president Cyrus Adler stressed the urgency of defending German Jewry against "the high-brow scientific agitation which is being carried on against them." Virulently antisemitic doctrines were being spread by German "professors of theology [and] anthropologists and biologists, who claim to have discovered by microscopic investigation a totally different blood as between Jews and Teutons."[58] In March 1931, German Jewish refugee Dr. Saloman Flink, a City College of New York professor, stated that the University of Berlin's faculty had excluded Albert Einstein from social affairs because he was a Jew. Flink reported that the University of Vienna faculty had ignored the seventieth birthday of Sigmund Freud.[59]

Many associated with Germany's prestigious medical faculties embraced Nazi racial doctrines. In *Germany Puts the Clock Back*, Mowrer cited a July 1932 report in the German left-wing intellectual journal *Die Weltbühne* that the University of Berlin medical faculty had barred Jews from the front seats at clinical demonstrations. He noted that women students in the anatomical laboratories of the University of Berlin "carved their beloved swastika into the flesh of the cadavers," providing "a foretaste of the Third Reich." The historian Fritz Stern recalled that his father, a prominent physician in Weimar Germany, "witnessed a bizarre prelude to what was to come" while in the medical auditorium in Breslau, attending a demonstration of a psychosis. When the psychotic patient suddenly launched into "violent outbursts against Jews and other criminals," the students and some of the doctors applauded.[60]

In the years immediately preceding Hitler's assuming the chancellorship, German university students launched numerous assaults on Jews, often using dangerous weapons to inflict serious injuries. The Nazis' goal was the expulsion of Jewish students or a rigid numerus clausus (quota) to restrict their admission to a very low percentage.[61] Sometimes they demanded that Jews be segregated on the campus. The Associated Press reported in December 1931 that "Germany's halls of learning" had taken on "the turbulent atmosphere of the ringside." Fists flew in university corridors. Nazi students regularly disrupted the lectures of Jewish professors, often demanding their termination. The JTA reported that antisemitic riots in late June 1931 had forced the University of Berlin to close for the first time in a decade. After classes were suspended, the Nazis continued to savagely beat Jewish students in the streets surrounding the university.[62] Students at the University of Jena successfully pressed for the establishment of a chair in *Rassenkunde* (racial science) for Nazi professor Hans Günther, to validate Nazi racial doctrines.[63]

The London *Jewish Chronicle* stated in July 1931 that the wave of antisemitic disturbances that had recently shaken all German universities "represent, without a doubt, a concentrated action, managed from Munich by Hitler." It noted that early in the year the Nazi Party headquarters in Munich had signaled Nazi students to start antisemitic riots at the University of Vienna, which were followed by similar outrages at the University of Munich and then, "simultaneously, [at the universities of] Berlin, Hamburg, Kiel, Cologne, Leipzig, Brunswick [and] Greifswald." At the University of Vienna on February 3, 1931, Nazi students attacked socialist and Jewish students with cattle whips and clubs. By using cattle whips on the Jews, the Nazis communicated once again that Jews were animals. Vienna's liberal press condemned "the inaction of the authorities." A month later, Vienna's Nazi students "rushed into lecture rooms, throwing out and beating Jewish students." They set on fire a kiosk exhibiting an anti-Nazi poster. The university's rector, whom the *New York Times* called "strongly antisemitic," agreed with the student incendiaries that the poster was "insulting" and promised the Nazis that he would prohibit it from being displayed. In Vienna in January 1932, Nazi assaults on Jewish and socialist students caused all faculties at the university to close down.[64]

Nazi students continued their violent antisemitic rampages through the time Hitler assumed power. At the University of Vienna in June 1931, shouting "Germans, awake! Jews, retreat!" they beat Jewish students with cudgels, leaving them "battered and bleeding." The attacks, which lasted five days, followed a decision by Austria's Constitutional Court that the "Students' Racial Regulation" was unconstitutional. This regulation, shaped by Nazi racial antisemitism, had been introduced by the previous rector and placed students into racial associations. All students with the smallest fraction of "Jewish blood," including converts to Christianity, were considered Jews and forced into a Jewish racial association. Austrians of "pure Teutonic blood" were considered Germans and part of the German racial organization. After the attacks, Vienna's Nazi students declared a "Jewless week" at the university, forcing every Jew they encountered off campus. The *New York Times* reported that "at the end of the week they intend to serenade the rector because of his sympathies with them."

Noah Fabricant, an American physician engaged in postgraduate work at the University of Vienna who witnessed the antisemitic rioting, emphasized the complicity of the rector and the police, who would not stop the beatings that left more than twenty, mostly Jewish, students badly injured. Fabricant concluded, "By his passivity during the violence in the buildings under his charge, Professor Übersberger, the present rector of the university, may be said to have condoned the attacks." Fabricant reported that police officers posted around the university "but carefully refraining from entering it offered practically no aid to the victims" of the beatings.[65]

The American minister to Austria reacted angrily to a letter of protest signed by six American physicians attending courses at the University of Vienna, including Fabricant, that denounced the "inhumanity" of "mobs of fifty to a hundred" attacking a single person. The protest stated that for failing to protect the targeted students the rector was not fit to remain in office. The protestors declared that they were notifying B'nai B'rith, a prominent Jewish organization, of their outrage. They demanded better protection for Jewish students from the American diplomatic representatives stationed in Vienna. When Dr. Samuel Marcus, the American Jewish physician who led the protest, visited the US minister to Austria, G. B. Stockton, to discuss the matter, Stockton "flew into a rage," shaking his fist in the physician's face. The US minister threatened to terminate Dr. Marcus's stay in Vienna and warned, "If the authorities or the rioters get after you, I will not protect or defend you." The AJC Executive Committee, meeting on October 25, 1931, decided to ask Dr. Marcus for a signed statement describing his conversation with US Minister Stockton, to be submitted to the US State Department in the hope that it would investigate Stockton's response to the antisemitic riot.[66]

In the 1930s, the US State Department and diplomatic corps were pervaded with antisemitism and essentially off-limits to Jews. A sizeable proportion of men in their upper ranks were products of elite preparatory schools and colleges where Jews were unwelcome. Minister Stockton's angry response to the six physicians set the stage for the State Department's and diplomats' indifference to European Jewry's plight over the next decade and a half.[67] More than a year later, the continuing attacks on Jewish students at the University of Vienna caused a delegation of twenty-five Americans studying there, the majority apparently Jewish, to ask the American minister to Austria if it was advisable for them to return to the United States.[68]

The student violence against Jews at the University of Vienna ignited similar outrages at the Universities of Berlin and Munich in June and July 1931. In Berlin, the Nazis beat left-wing and Jewish students so brutally they were covered in blood. "Uttering anti-Semitic war cries," the Nazis tried to force their way into the main building. The disorders forced the university to close on July 2. At Munich, Nazi students disrupted the lectures of professor of constitutional law Hans Nawiasky, a Jew who had characterized the Versailles treaty as no harsher than the treaties of Bucharest and Brest-Litovsk, which Germany had imposed on its defeated enemies, Romania and Russia. The London *Observer* stated that the students' attacks on Nawiasky "took on a violent antisemitic color." Nazis crowded into his classroom, and one called for his removal. A student who protested this was beaten unconscious. The Nazis followed Nawiasky into the hallway and physically attacked him. When he returned for his class later that week, students interrupted his lecture with shouts of "Death to the Jews!" The students forced the university to close "until further notice." At the University of Hamburg, antisemitic students seized buildings and hoisted the swastika flag over them.[69]

At Frankfurt, where the atmosphere had been more liberal than at other German universities, three hundred "well-drilled" Nazi students protesting the rector's ban on the wearing of uniforms on campus stormed the school, savagely beating Jews and liberal and Social Democratic students. All the Nazi students wore the brownshirt uniform, with sword belts, troop emblems, black high boots, breeches, caps, and swastika armbands. Some of the students the Nazis attacked were knocked unconscious and had to be hospitalized. An English woman attending the university told the *Manchester Guardian* that a student whom the Nazis had beaten and had to be taken to the hospital recalled that he had come onto the scene unaware of what was happening. One of the Nazis spotted him and called out to his comrades, "Here! On to the black-haired Jew!" Twenty Nazis then "detached themselves from the rest, encircled him, and knocked him down." They "us[ed] their boots and their sword-belts freely." The English woman noted that the victim's wounds, "as those of the others, show traces of the 'fighting rings'—the favorite Nazi weapon." It consisted of "steel rings with five sharp points, carried round the fist." She emphasized that it was "capable of splitting a head open." No arrests were made. The *Chicago Tribune* stated that the Nazis had injured thirteen students using brass knuckles, belt buckles, and batons.[70]

Two days later, on July 1, the *Guardian* reported that Nazi students had engaged in "anti-Semitic rowdyism" at the University of Berlin that day, similar to that in Frankfurt. The Nazi students' leader informed the rector that it was "dishonorable for a German to be in the same room as a Jew." The Nazi students demanded the expulsion of all Jews from the university. The *Guardian* found the Nazis' beating and kicking of female students "particularly repulsive."[71]

Violent antisemitic Nazi student rampages also occurred outside the universities. The tear gas bombs used in the attack on the Gerngross family department store in Vienna were manufactured by a Nazi cell known as the "Technical Storm," composed of chemistry students at the University of Vienna. The bombs were thrown when the store was filled with hundreds of shoppers, causing many to be knocked down and trampled in the rush to escape.[72]

In January 1933, two weeks before Hitler became chancellor, antisemitic rioting broke out again at the University of Berlin in opposition to the inclusion of Jews in the student body and to Ernst Cohn's recent reinstatement as professor of commercial law at the University of Breslau. In November 1932, Nazi students at Breslau had disrupted the newly appointed Cohn's class because they refused to "tolerate the delivery of lectures by a Jew." Seated in the front benches of his classroom, they "began to heap abuse on him . . . singing anti-Jewish songs" as soon as he began his lecture. Nazi students physically attacked him as he left the campus. Followed "by a shouting mob of Nazi students," the police had to call for reinforcements to escort Cohn home. When he resumed lecturing on January 23, Nazi students disrupted university proceedings by releasing evil-smelling and lachrymatory chemicals (similar to tear gas) and exploding fireworks filled with gunpowder, which caused the police to clear the campus. Crowds then gathered outside the university and chanted antisemitic slogans.[73]

At the University of Berlin on January 17, 1933, shortly after Prussian minister of education Kaehler had intervened to restore Cohn to his position at Breslau, two hundred Nazi students hurled chairs, tables, and glassware at the Jewish students in the campus restaurant, injuring five of them, including three women. They then proceeded to throw the Jewish students out of the campus buildings, shouting, "Perish Judaea!" and "Down with Kaehler!" The rector made no effort to intervene.[74]

*   *   *

In the three years preceding the establishment of the Hitler regime, many well-informed commentators in the United States and Britain, both Jewish and non-Jewish, publicly voiced fear that the Nazis' steady advance portended disaster for German Jewry. They pointed to the explicitly antisemitic goals in the Nazi Party program, formulated in 1920, including stripping Jews of citizenship rights. Reports in the American and British press and by on-the-scene observers described aggressive Nazi boycotts of Jewish stores in many German localities, sometimes accompanied by blacklists of all seen shopping in them. Major metropolitan newspapers in the United States and England, as well as the Jewish press, freely described the frequent eruptions of anti-Jewish violence between 1930 and the time the Nazis assumed power in early 1933. News of the antisemitic pogroms in Berlin in October 1930 and on Rosh Hashanah in 1931 circulated widely in Britain and the United States, as did reports of violent Nazi assaults on Jewish students and the severe harassment of Jewish professors at German universities. American and English readers learned of the Nazi tear gas attacks designed to drive shoppers away from Jewish-owned department stores.

Nazi anti-Jewish boycotts had a devastating impact on Jews employed in the theatrical professions in Germany as well as on those engaged in mercantile activity. The Nazis sometimes used violence to enforce their theatrical boycotts. On January 13, 1933, about two weeks before Hitler became chancellor, the *Brooklyn Jewish Examiner* reported that "a furious boycott campaign against Jews has resulted in an alarming decrease in employment among Jewish artists and musicians," including many of international renown. Their plight was so desperate that serious consideration was given to establishing a Jewish traveling theater to make a world tour, "the proceeds of which would be used to alleviate distress among Jewish artists."[75]

Outside the major cities, the Jews' situation was especially perilous. Nazi boycotts against Jewish shopkeepers and tradespeople, isolated in towns and villages and lacking a Jewish support network, drove many out of business and into penury. Threats of violence or actual beatings led to a noticeable Jewish migration to the larger cities. Berlin rabbi Joachim Prinz recalled officiating at a funeral in a small German town in mid-1931, where the tiny Jewish community had no rabbi. He noted that although when a funeral passed in the street German gentiles customarily removed their hats in a gesture of respect, no one did so at this funeral. Instead, the hundreds of onlookers reacted with "jeers and laughter," some throwing stones at Rabbi Prinz. He understood that he was "in enemy territory."[76]

The Nazis insisted that Jews' racial inferiority and innate evil rendered them unworthy of even minimal respect and security. In October 1930, the

Manchester Guardian reported that when an American Jewish woman, representing "an important organization," called on Josef Goebbels in Berlin, she "was not only informed that [he] refused 'as a matter of principle' to talk to Jews, but was greatly insulted by a noisy menacing throng of Nazi stalwarts (male and female)." The *Guardian* commented that "she had no alternative except to leave the building at once."[77]

Nazi speeches and publications drew on the most venomous medieval antisemitic images, depicting Jews as ritual murderers, a pestilence, "plant lice." The American Berlin correspondent Edgar Ansel Mowrer in his *Germany Puts the Clock Back*, written in 1932, cited the Nazi periodical *Der Stürmer*'s claim that the Jew was "forced by his blood to ruin and to decompose all other races." Mowrer described the portrayal of the Jew in *Der Stürmer*'s recent series of posters as a demonic lecher and parasite: "wading through seas of Christian blood . . . releasing snakes from a box marked 'The Talmud' upon a naked Christian woman," kicking a pregnant Christian woman in the abdomen, and "picking the pocket of a pilloried German workman."[78]

When Rabbi Joachim Prinz visited Ulm in 1931, Albert Einstein's birthplace and a town in which Jews had lived for centuries, he warned the Jewish community that it was doomed. Upon meeting Rabbi Prinz, Ulm's Jewish leaders told him that they were about to build a Jewish community center. Prinz responded that Hitler would soon come to power, and he predicted, "As soon as you have finished building the new community center, it will be destroyed and you will be killed."[79]

NOTES

1. Joseph Tenenbaum, "Economic Anti-Semitism: A Review of Political and Economic Conditions of the Jews" (address, Meeting of the Executive Committee of the American Jewish Congress, New York, NY, March 8, 1931), RG 21.001.02*09, Joseph and Sheila Tenenbaum Collection (hereafter Tenenbaum Collection), US Holocaust Memorial Museum Archives (hereafter USHMMA), Washington, DC.

2. Joseph Tenenbaum, "The Growing Menace to the Jews," Sunday English edition of *The Day* [*Der Tog*], March 6, 1932, RG 21.001.03*01, Scrapbook 1, 1927–34, Tenenbaum Collection, USHMMA; *New York Times*, December 8, 1931, 1.

3. Joseph Tenenbaum, "European Jewry Facing Gravest Emergency" (address, Annual Sessions of the American Jewish Congress, Washington, DC, June 25–27, 1932), reel 73, ACC/3121/E03/141–42, Board of Deputies of British Jews Papers, USHMMA.

4. M. J. April, "The Role of Anti-Semitism in the National Socialist Movement Prior to 1933," D21 F7, American Jewish Committee (hereafter AJC) Archives, American Jewish Committee, New York, NY.

5. Tenenbaum, "European Jewry Facing Gravest Emergency."

6. *American Israelite*, January 21, 1932, 1.

7. "In Darkest Germany," *Jewish Chronicle* (London), December 2, 1932, 22; Richard J. Evans, *The Coming of the Third Reich* (New York: Penguin, 2003), 269; *Manchester Guardian*, April 9, 1932, 11.

8. "In Darkest Germany," 22.

9. Martin Gilbert, *Sir Horace Rumbold* (London: Heinemann, 1973), 338; *Jewish Exponent* (Philadelphia), December 30, 1932, 1.

10. *Times* (London), August 3, 1932, 9; "The Shadow of the Swastika: A Letter from Berlin," *Jewish Chronicle* (London), May 6, 1932, 19.

11. April, "Role of Anti-Semitism."

12. *Manchester Guardian*, April 9, 1932, 11.

13. *New York Times*, June 25, 1922, 2.

14. April, "Role of Anti-Semitism." Techow, who drove the assassins' car, testified at the trial that Kern, one of the two who fired at Rathenau, had told him this. April stated that "the origin of the accusation is a statement Rathenau made in 1909 when he warned: 'In the impersonal democratic field of economics . . . three hundred men, all of whom know one another, direct the economic destiny of Europe and choose their successor from among themselves.' The German anti-Semites, their heads filled with the *Protocols of the Elders of Zion*, dug up Rathenau's warning and changed the words to read 'three hundred Jewish bankers' and 'three hundred Elders of Zion.'"

15. Ernst Toller, *I Was a German* (New York: William Morrow, 1934), 274.

16. Modris Eksteins, *Rites of Spring: The Great War and the Birth of the Modern Age* (New York: Doubleday, 1989), 319.

17. *New York Times*, June 25, 1922, 1; Fritz Stern, *Five Germanys I Have Known* (New York: Farrar, Straus and Giroux, 2006), 64; Jewish Telegraphic Agency, July 1, 1931. Stern notes that "never before (or after) was a Jew to have such a preeminent post in German political life."

18. Karl Dietrich Bracher, *The German Dictatorship* (New York: Praeger, 1970), 182; Evans, *Coming of the Third Reich*, 209, 259, 261; Gilbert, *Sir Horace Rumbold*, 329, 334; William L. Shirer, *The Rise and Fall of the Third Reich* (New York: Simon and Schuster, 1960), 138.

19. *New York Times*, September 21, 1930, E3; Sir Horace Rumbold to the queen of Spain, October 31, 1930, MS 38, Sir Horace Rumbold Papers, Bodleian Library, University of Oxford, Oxford, UK.

20. Toni Sender, *The Autobiography of a German Rebel* (New York: Vanguard, 1939), 274–75; Cyrus Adler to Mortimer L. Schiff, November 3, 1930, box 14, AJC

Papers, AJC Archives; Arthur Koestler, *Arrow in the Blue: An Autobiography* (New York: Macmillan, 1952), 249–51. Nazi Party membership soared from 293,000 to 389,000 from September 1930 to December 31, 1930. Bracher, *The German Dictatorship*, 184.

21. *Brooklyn Jewish Examiner*, September 30, 1932, M8; Evans, *Coming of the Third Reich*, 255.

22. *New York Herald Tribune*, October 14, 1, 12, and October 15, 1930, 20; *Chicago Tribune*, October 14, 1930, 1, 12; *Times* (London), October 14, 1930, 14; *Jewish Exponent* (Philadelphia), October 17, 1930, 1; Rumbold to queen of Spain, October 31, 1930. The *Manchester Guardian* reported that "once or twice it did seem as though the Nazis and Communists would come to blows." October 14, 1930, 11.

23. Sender, *Autobiography of a German Rebel*, 276–77.

24. Alan Bullock, *Hitler: A Study in Tyranny* (New York: Harper and Row, 1962), 63, 73; Sender, *Autobiography of a German Rebel*, 277. The name *Fehme* was drawn from the "old knightly court, in which leaders sat in secret and passed sentence of death upon real or supposed informers." Edgar Ansel Mowrer, *Germany Puts the Clock Back* (New York: William Morrow, 1933), 92. On Heines's trial for the murder, see *Observer* (London), May 6, 1928, 17; *Times* (London), November 6, 1930, 13. The *Times* reported that Heines had murdered his victim by shooting him twice in the back of the head.

25. *Times* (London), December 8, 1930, 11.

26. *New York Herald Tribune*, October 14, 1930, 1, 12; *New York Times*, October 14, 1930, 1, 16; *Chicago Tribune*, October 14, 1930, 1.

27. *New York Herald Tribune*, October 14, 1930, 1; *New York Times*, October 14, 1930, 1; *Manchester Guardian*, October 14, 1930, 11, and October 15, 1930, 11.

28. *New York Times*, October 14, 1930, 1; *New York Herald Tribune*, October 15, 1930, 20.

29. *Times* (London), October 15, 1930, 12.

30. *New York Times*, October 18, 1930, 1, 8; *Los Angeles Times*, October 18, 1930, 4. Sigrid Schultz called Strasser's speech "blood curdling." *Chicago Tribune*, October 18, 1930, 8. American press reports of the Reichstag session prominently featured the Nazis' antisemitic demands. The *New York Times* placed its article, obtained from the Associated Press, on its front page and referred to the Nazis' proposed "ban on Jews" in the headline.

31. *Times* (London), December 9, 1930, 13; *New York Times*, December 6, 1930, 10; *Los Angeles Times*, December 6, 1930, 4; "German Anti-Semitic Theatre Riots," *Jewish Chronicle* (London), December 12, 1930, 23.

32. *Times* (London), January 8, 1931, 10, and January 10, 1931, 8.

33. *Manchester Guardian*, September 14, 1931, 12; *Times* (London), September 14, 1931, 12; *Jewish Telegraphic Agency*, September 15, 1931; Brigitte Granzow,

A Mirror of Nazism: British Opinion and the Emergence of Hitler, 1929–1933 (London: Victor Gollancz, 1964), 154. Granzow points out that the usual English translation of *"Juda verrecke!"*—"Perish Judaea!"—fails to adequately convey the expression's viciousness toward, and biting contempt for, Jews. She notes that *verrecke* is a "coarse vulgar word for dying as vermin die when crushed by a boot."

34. *Manchester Guardian*, November 9, 1931, 4; Jewish Telegraphic Agency, September 15, 1931; *Times* (London), September 14, 1931, 12; "Rosh Hashanah in Berlin: Anti-Jewish Rioting," *Jewish Chronicle* (London), September 18, 1931, 16.

35. *Manchester Guardian*, September 14, 1931, 12; *Times* (London), September 14, 1931, 12.

36. Morris D. Waldman to Arthur Hays Sulzberger, October 1, 1931, box 176, Arthur Hays Sulzberger Papers, Archives and Manuscripts Division, New York Public Library, New York, NY. Waldman surmised that Sulzberger's correspondent's "handling of the incident gives very strong ground for the suspicion that he was caught napping, and, to escape from the consequences of his negligence, sought to convey the impression that the affair was a matter not deserving of his notice." *New York Times*, September 16, 1931, 10; *Manchester Guardian*, September 14, 1931, 12; *Times* (London), September 14, 1931, 12.

37. *Times* (London), September 24, 1931, 11; *Jewish Advocate* (Boston), September 29, 1931, 1; *Jewish Exponent* (Philadelphia), October 2, 1931, 7.

38. Jewish Telegraphic Agency, September 19, 1931.

39. Jewish Telegraphic Agency, September 24 and October 28, 1931.

40. *New York Times*, November 8, 1931, 14; *Manchester Guardian*, November 9, 1931, 4; Jewish Telegraphic Agency, October 28 and 31, 1931; *Times* (London), November 9, 1931, 11.

41. "Count Helldorf Acquitted," *Jewish Chronicle* (London), February 19, 1932, 19.

42. Israel Cohen, "The Situation in Germany," *Jewish Chronicle* (London), February 19, 1932, 18.

43. Israel Cohen, "A Letter from Berlin: The Menacing Situation," *Jewish Chronicle* (London), June 24, 1932, 20; *Brooklyn Jewish Examiner*, September 30, 1932, M5, M8.

44. "The Black Forest Well Named/German Jewry's Ordeal/The Situation in the Provinces," *Jewish Chronicle* (London), January 23, 1931, 16.

45. Mowrer, *Germany Puts the Clock Back*, 226–27.

46. Jewish Telegraphic Agency, December 21, 1931, and December 14, 1932.

47. "A Letter from Berlin: Tear Bomb Outrages," *Jewish Chronicle* (London), December 23, 1932, 20; *Manchester Guardian*, December 21, 1932, 13; "Austria: The Nazi Boycott Campaign," *Jewish Chronicle* (London), December 23, 1932, 20.

48. *Manchester Guardian*, August 9, 1932, 13.

49. Jewish Telegraphic Agency, June 27, 1932.

50. Mowrer, *Germany Puts the Clock Back*, 236–37; Jewish Telegraphic Agency, July 19, 1932.

51. Evans, *Coming of the Third Reich*, 293; Sender, *Autobiography of a German Rebel*, 293; *New York Times*, July 27, 1932, 7. In the November 6, 1932 election the Nazis' vote declined from 37.3 to 33.1 percent, but "they still remained by far the largest party" in the Reichstag. Bullock, *Hitler*, 230.

52. Richard Bessel, "The Potempa Murder," *Central European History* 10 (September 1977): 243–45, 248–49; Sender, *Autobiography of a German Rebel*, 293. The postmortem showed that it was the stabbing and beating that caused Pietzuch's death. *Manchester Guardian*, August 23, 1932, 9. The trial and its aftermath received coverage in major American newspapers including the *New York Times*, *Chicago Tribune*, *Washington Post*, and *Los Angeles Times*, as well as from the Associated Press and United Press, to which numerous US newspapers subscribed. In Britain there was extended coverage in such newspapers as the London *Times* and the *Manchester Guardian*.

53. *Manchester Guardian*, August 24, 1932, 4; *Times* (London), August 26, 1932, 10.

54. Bessel, "Potempa Murder," 251; *Manchester Guardian*, August 23, 1932, 9. *Der Angriff*'s reference to Pietzuch as a bandit made the victim the criminal, instead of the murderers.

55. *Manchester Guardian*, August 23, 1932, 9; and August 25, 1932, 4.

56. Jewish Telegraphic Agency, August 25, 1932.

57. Evans, *Coming of the Third Reich*, 132; Bracher, *German Dictatorship*, 164.

58. *New York Times*, March 22, 1931, E4; Adler to Schiff, November 3, 1930, box 14, Cyrus Adler Papers, AJC Archives. The *Times* article stated that even the German Social Democrats acknowledged that more than half of German university and technical school students were supporters of the extreme right.

59. *New York Herald Tribune*, March 9, 1931, 17.

60. Mowrer, *Germany Puts the Clock Back*, 177, 233; Stern, *Five Germanys*, 76. A little more than a week before Hitler became chancellor, Godehard Ebers, rector of the University of Cologne, stated, "The influx of Jewish medical students from North America is absolutely undesirable." *Chicago Tribune*, January 22, 1933, 15. The *Chicago Tribune* reported that of the University of Cologne's 5,400 students, only 129 were foreigners, and of those only 33 (0.006 percent) came from North America. Jews were probably a minority of those 33.

61. There was no basis for the Nazi claim that Jews were crowding "Germans" out of student bodies and in this manner were "capturing the professions," used to justify restricting Jewish admissions. According to the 1925 German census, Jews made up 0.9 percent of the German population. In 1930 they comprised 3.7 percent of the university student enrollment (4,972 out of 132,090). Of the 4,972 Jewish students, 1,269 were foreigners, likely to return to their home countries and take jobs there upon graduation. Jews in Germany were also

"practically excluded [from employment] in all state and municipal services."
The only opportunities for Jews outside of commerce were in the professions.
The proportion of women students among Jews was considerably higher than
among non-Jewish Germans, and women were less able to secure jobs in the
professions than men, particularly after marriage. "Jewish Students in Germany,"
Jewish Chronicle (London), December 5, 1930, 18. The proportion of Jews in the
fields of law and medicine in Prussia had declined sharply since 1913, from 12.8
percent to 6.9 percent in medicine and from 10.3 percent to 5.2 percent in law.
"The Numerus Clausus," *Jewish Chronicle* (London), February 6, 1931, 18. Jews
also resided disproportionately in cities, where most universities were located.
Travel and housing costs placed universities out of reach for many rural families.
Mária M. Kovács makes this point about post–World War I Hungary; it also
applied to Germany. Kovács, "The Numerus Clausus in Hungary, 1920–1945,"
in *Alma Mater Antisemitica: Akademisches Milieu, Juden und Antisemitismus an
den Universitäten Europas zwischen 1918 und 1939*, ed. Regina Fritz, Grzegorz
Rossoliński-Liebe, and Jana Starek (Vienna: New Academic, 2016), 95–98.

62. The Associated Press story appeared in the *Washington Post*, December 27,
1931, M7; Jewish Telegraphic Agency, July 1, 1931.

63. Mowrer, *Germany Puts the Clock Back*, 169; Leonidas E. Hill, "The Nazi
Attack on 'Un-German' Literature, 1933–1945," in *The Holocaust and the Book:
Destruction and Preservation*, ed. Jonathan Rose (Amherst: University of
Massachusetts Press, 2001), 11.

64. "Hitler's Part in University Riots," *Jewish Chronicle* (London), July 10, 1931,
22; *New York Times*, February 4, 1931, 9; *Manchester Guardian*, January 29, 1932,
13.

65. *New York Times*, June 24, 1931, 26; Noah Fabricant, "Intolerance in
Vienna," *Nation*, October 21, 1931, 442. Fabricant stated that in addition to
the Jews, some Hungarian students and one Egyptian were badly injured. He
reported that "one youth, when set upon by thirty or forty rioters, jumped out of
a second-story window to escape their assault and suffered a broken leg."

66. Fabricant, "Intolerance in Vienna," 442–43; Minutes of American Jewish
Committee Executive Committee, October 25, 1931, ajcarchives.org.

67. Martin Weil, *A Pretty Good Club: The Founding Fathers of the U.S. Foreign
Service* (New York: W. W. Norton, 1978); Bat-Ami Zucker, *In Search of Refuge:
Jews and US Consuls in Nazi Germany, 1933–1941* (London: Vallentine Mitchell,
2001), 173–78.

68. *Washington Post*, October 30, 1932, 13.

69. *New York Times*, July 1, 1931, 8; *Observer* (London), July 5, 1931; Mowrer,
Germany Puts the Clock Back, 176; "Anti-Semitic Rioting at Universities," *Jewish
Chronicle* (London), July 3, 1931, 24.

70. "Letter to the Editor from an English Girl Student," *Manchester Guardian*, June 29, 1932, 16; *Chicago Tribune*, June 23, 1932, 10.

71. *Manchester Guardian*, July 1, 1932, 14.

72. "Austria: The Nazi Boycott Campaign," 20; *Manchester Guardian*, December 21, 1933, 13.

73. Jewish Telegraphic Agency, November 11, 1932; *Chicago Tribune*, November 11, 1932, 17; *Manchester Guardian*, January 18, 1933, 4; *Times* (London), January 26, 1933, 11. Breslau's university senate used Cohn's response to a question posed by a journalist as to whether he favored granting Leon Trotsky asylum in Germany as their excuse for depriving him of his post. Cohn, who was not engaged in politics, had replied that such a question required careful consideration and that the government should examine other countries' experiences with Trotsky. He stated that "an intellectual worker will always appear worthy of protection." The Nazis stridently denounced this answer, claiming that Cohn had "emphasized the intellectual eminence of Trotsky." Identifying all Jews with Communism, they called Trotsky Cohn's "Jewish-Bolshevist racial associate." *Times* (London), December 27, 1932, 9.

74. Jewish Telegraphic Agency, January 18, 1933.

75. *Brooklyn Jewish Examiner*, January 13, 1933, 1. The *Jewish Examiner* stated that "unofficial statistics reveal that 94 percent of Jewish artists in Germany are affected by the anti-Semitic boycott in German theatres." The Nazis often used violence to enforce theater boycotts. For example, in November 1930, in the Bavarian town of Würzberg, several hundred Nazis blocked the entrance to the municipal theater to prevent a performance by the Habimah, a well-known Hebrew dramatic troupe. The Nazis "pushed around and threatened" persons who attempted to enter the theater. While some Nazis "held the would-be patrons at bay, others distributed Hitlerite leaflets." The performance was delayed for nearly two hours, until police arrived to disperse the Nazis. Jewish Telegraphic Agency, November 23, 1930.

76. Joachim Prinz, *Joachim Prinz, Rebellious Rabbi: An Autobiography—the German and Early American Years*, ed. Michael Meyer (Bloomington: Indiana University Press, 2008), 84–85.

77. *Manchester Guardian*, October 7, 1930, 6.

78. Mowrer, *Germany Puts the Clock Back*, 232, 236. Mowrer quoted Nazi deputy Bauer of the Prussian Diet announcing that the Nazis' Third Reich "will treat the Jews like plant lice."

79. Prinz, *Joachim Prinz, Rebellious Rabbi*, 83.

TWO

—⚬—

BARBARISM AND ENTRAPMENT

The Cold Pogrom, 1933–1934

IN APRIL 1933, NEWSPAPERS ACROSS the United States published a photograph smuggled out of Germany that featured grinning Nazi storm troopers parading a Jewish man around the town of Chemnitz, Saxony, in a garbage wagon. The caption related that the storm troopers had rounded up Chemnitz's Jews and forced them to scrub walls "before jeering crowds." When the Jewish man refused to comply with the storm troopers' order, they placed him on exhibit in the garbage wagon. A Jewish woman in the hamlet of Roundup, Montana, seeing the photograph and accompanying report in the *Billings Gazette* (Montana), immediately wrote to Montana's US senators, John Erickson and Burton Wheeler, appealing to them to ask the American government to pressure Germany "to stop these unspeakable humiliations" of Jews.[1] The same month, the *Manchester Guardian* and London *Jewish Chronicle*, which were available on newsstands in New York and other American cities, reported that in Worms, Germany, the Nazis had imprisoned Jews in a pigsty.[2]

In 1933, the press in both the United States and Britain frequently published accounts of Nazis publicly displaying Jews in a manner that associated them with garbage and human excrement. Readers could readily discern that the Nazis considered Jews not merely subhuman but "waste" that German society must discard.

After escaping from Germany in 1934, Rabbi Max Abraham, who had been imprisoned in the Oranienburg concentration camp in 1933, published an account in both the United States and Britain in which he described how the SS guards impressed on Jewish inmates that they were lower than animals. On the first Jewish holiday after his arrival at the camp, the guards drove Rabbi Abraham and the other Jews into a manure pit and ordered him to conduct his religious service there. When he refused, the guards beat him unconscious. The Oranienburg SS assigned Jewish inmates the task of cleaning the camp latrines and referred to them as the "sanitary company." This work was reserved for the Jewish Sabbath. The SS forced Rabbi Abraham, whom they addressed as "you Jewish pig," to dig into the feces with his bare hands, as they denied him even a cloth. The camp's storm troop leader nicknamed Rabbi Abraham "Director of Latrines."[3]

SS guards in the concentration camps subjected Jews to especially degrading treatment. Wolfgang Langhoff, a non-Jew imprisoned in the Börgermoor concentration camp near Papenburg in 1933 and 1934, stated in an account of his experience published in 1935 that the guards had marched Ernst Heilmann, a Jew and former head of the Social Democrats in the Prussian Landtag, to the latrine with an imprisoned Jewish lawyer, handed them shovels, and ordered them to use them to hurl feces at each other. The SS also made Heilmann crawl into a kennel, sniff the dog's hindquarters, and bark. That Heilmann had been severely wounded as a soldier in the German army during the world war meant nothing to the SS.[4] A prisoner who had escaped from the Sonnenburg concentration camp told the *Manchester Guardian* and the *New Statesman* in January 1934 that the guards had ordered two young Jewish prisoners to run and jump with pails of feces. They had to put back by hand what fell out.[5] In another concentration camp, the SS made Jews smear feces on their faces when cleaning the latrine. At the Brandenburg concentration camp, the Jewish prisoners received no regular rations but had to eat the leavings from the meals of non-Jewish inmates from one bowl, without implements. Jews there were also forced to lick saliva off the ground.[6]

In July 1933, leading American and British newspapers reported that Nazi storm troopers in Nuremberg had seized about 260 Jewish men ranging in age from seventeen to seventy-six, including many physicians, lawyers, and businessmen, and forced them to act as if they were cattle. The storm troopers ordered the Jews to leave their homes, offices, stores, and an early morning synagogue service and herded them through Nuremberg's main streets to a field outside the city. Elderly men unable to keep pace were driven on by the storm troopers' kicks. At the field, the storm troopers gave the Jews picks and shovels and demanded that they remove all the weeds. Many were forced to crawl on their hands and knees pulling the weeds out with their teeth, like cattle. Some of the Jews "committed suicide" or were "shot while trying to escape."[7]

Jacob Billikopf, executive director of the Federation of Jewish Charities of Philadelphia, who interviewed several non-Jewish German witnesses to these brutalities shortly after they had occurred, informed New York's governor, Herbert Lehman, that the Nuremberg storm troopers had also inflicted "other cruelties of an unmentionable nature" on the Jews in the field. They warned the Jews, "Today you have just gotten a taste of what is in store for you!"[8]

From the beginning, the Nazis singled out Jews for especially violent treatment. In March 1933, American newspapers, including the *Los Angeles Times* and the Boston *Jewish Advocate*, drawing on accounts of refugees who had fled from Germany to Austria after Hitler assumed power, reported that the Nazis asked all new arrivals at Spandau prison in Berlin whether they were Jewish. If the answer was affirmative, the Jew was stomped and kicked into unconsciousness.[9] British Labour Party MP Ellen Wilkinson, who traveled to Germany in 1933 to investigate Nazi persecution of Jews and political dissidents, reported that "the Nazis' first attention to their Jewish prisoners is to smash the nose as a symbolic act," because antisemites always caricatured Jews as having big noses. She stated that the Nazis had revived Jews they had beaten unconscious and made them lick each other's wounds. Wilkinson noted that the Nazis blamed the Jews for luring the Communists away from their national allegiance.[10]

Within two months of the time Hitler became chancellor, American and British newspapers were publishing articles detailing Nazi atrocities against Jews, often giving them prominence of place. Refugees escaping from Germany—to France, Austria, Czechoslovakia, the Saar, and even Poland—were a prime source of information for Western journalists. On March 17, 1933, the London *Daily Herald*'s Paris correspondent presented reports from German Jewish refugees who "form the vanguard of the destitute thousands who are secretly moving across Germany towards the [French] frontier." The article ran under a two-column top-of-the-page headline reading, "Children Shot in Streets by Nazis. Jewish Refugees Tell of Their Ordeal." Jewish workers who had fled Chemnitz and Leipzig informed the correspondent that "the Nazis systematically pillaged Jewish shops under the tolerant eye of the police." A young Jewish Leipzig furrier who had escaped to Paris told of Nazis murdering Jewish children in the streets when they hurled words of defiance at them. Another German Jewish refugee had seen Nazis shooting into a Jewish eating house in Cologne without provocation, killing three and wounding sixteen.[11]

On March 22, 1933, the *Cleveland Plain Dealer* carried a front-page article headlined, "U.S. Probes Nazi Cruelty against Jews." It reported that indignation against Nazi antisemitic atrocities had spread to the United States Congress and noted the grassroots pressure "to open the doors of the country to Jewish refugees from Germany."[12]

German Jewish novelist Lion Feuchtwanger, who fled to Paris after Hitler's agents invaded his home, destroyed his manuscripts, and confiscated his wife's automobile, informed the *New York Times* in March 1933 that the Nazis had been carrying out "pogroms such as Germany has not seen since the . . . fourteenth century." He stated that the atrocities of the world war paled in comparison with the accounts of German Jewish refugees with whom he had spoken in Paris. The refugees had told Feuchtwanger that "every Jew in Germany . . . must expect to be assaulted in the street or to be dragged out of bed and arrested, to have his goods and property destroyed."[13]

There were frequent reports in 1933 in the American and British press of another form of torture reserved for Jews: storm troopers and other Germans seized Jewish men and tore off, plucked out, or set fire to their beards. In March, Pierre van Paassen, a distinguished European journalist whose column was widely syndicated in American newspapers, wrote, for example, that he had seen storm troopers carting a half-naked Jewish man through the streets of Munich, his hands tied and half his beard torn out. This foreshadowed German soldiers' "game" of "beards" during the Holocaust in which they sliced off the beards of Jewish men with their bayonets.[14]

FEAR OF EXTERMINATION

From the earliest months of Nazi rule, many American and British Jewish and non-Jewish observers expressed fear that German Jewry would be exterminated. The *Brooklyn Jewish Examiner*, in its summary of the year 5692 issued on September 30, 1932, had concluded that "if Hitler seeks the defeat of his political opponents, he doubly seeks the destruction of Jewry." By March 10, 1933, it considered the situation so desperate that "only a miracle can save the German Jews from complete annihilation." In May 1933, British industrialist Lord Melchett stated that Germany had become "an absolute death trap" for its six hundred thousand Jews.[15] The same month, American journalist Dorothy Thompson, wife of novelist Sinclair Lewis, who had made several trips to Germany immediately before and after Hitler assumed power, warned that the Nazis were carrying out a "cold pogrom" of economic strangulation designed to exterminate German Jewry within a generation. A pogrom—a Russian word—is defined as an organized violent attack on Jews, often involving killings, beatings, rape, torture, and mutilation. By "cold pogrom," journalists in the 1930s meant eliminating German Jews' ability to earn a livelihood and curtailing their educational opportunities so that those unable to emigrate had no chance to survive beyond a generation or two.

Thompson reported that the Hitler regime was forcing Jews out of the professions, severely restricting Jews' admission to universities, and, in many sections of the country, boycotting and destroying Jewish businesses. Thompson emphasized that "every Jew in Germany, [all] 600,000 of them, is daily humiliated . . . and threatened with the withdrawal of his entire means of existence." She concluded that the cold pogrom "aims at nothing short of German Jewry's destruction." Thompson presciently declared that German Jewry would likely never recover.[16]

In May 1933, Dr. Jacob Sonderling, one of Germany's most eminent reform rabbis before his emigration to the United States in 1923 and a Jewish chaplain for the German army on the Russian front during the world war, spoke in Boston on the degradation of Germany's Jews under Hitler. Leading Jewish groups, including the American Jewish Congress (AJCongress) and the American Palestine Campaign, sponsored his lecture. Sonderling had been one of Theodor Herzl's first coworkers in the Zionist movement. He informed his audience that the purpose of the Nazi "cold pogrom tactics," which included "the economic strangling of the German Jews, discriminatory laws, [and] the closing of educational opportunities to Jewish youth," was "nothing short of German Jewry's complete destruction."[17]

Similarly, Professor Richard Gottheil of Columbia University, one of the world's leading scholars of Semitic languages, stressed in an interview with the London *Jewish Chronicle* the same month that "he felt perfectly certain that Hitler and his band wished to exterminate the Jews of Germany." Like Sonderling, Gottheil had been a close friend of Herzl. He predicted that unlike Spain, which expelled Europe's largest Jewish population in 1492, Germany would "kill off the Jews" by "slow degrees . . . by suppression of all means of livelihood, so that instead of a sudden death they shall come to their end in a lingering torture."[18]

The *Manchester Guardian*, which provided the most thorough documentation of Nazi atrocities against Jews of any metropolitan daily newspaper, noted in January 1934 that Germany's antisemitic laws were unparalleled in Europe. Its Berlin correspondent, Alexander Werth, declared a week after Hitler became chancellor that the antisemitism of Nazi leaders like Josef Goebbels surpassed that of the rulers or population of czarist Russia. The *Guardian's* Paris correspondent, Frederick Voigt, who was based in Germany from 1920 to early 1933 and who interviewed many anti-Hitler refugees in France, declared on March 15, 1933, that the Nazis' "Brown Terror" against Jews and political opponents was the "most horrible" atrocity he had ever seen in a "long experience [covering] war, famine, armed upheaval and oppression." It was a "frightfully dangerous inrush of barbarism into the civilized world." Voigt emphasized that the Brown Terror was systematic and should be considered "a war, and a particularly ferocious one, against . . . a people now unarmed and helpless." He warned that Hitler and the Nazi leaders "demand it and more of it."[19]

While savagely persecuting Germany's Jews, the Hitler government made Jewish emigration exceedingly difficult, prohibiting Jews from taking more than a small amount of funds or property out of Germany. This would ensure the "liquidation" of the Jewish question in Germany "for all time." The Nazis were aware that nearly all foreign countries severely restricted Jewish immigration and employment opportunities, so even those who managed to flee would have difficulty reestablishing themselves abroad. As Alexander Brin, publisher and editor of Boston's *Jewish Advocate*, commented, Germany's Jews were "trapped like wild beasts."[20]

In the autumn of 1933, Dr. Alice Hamilton of the Harvard medical faculty, recently returned from three months in Germany studying "the Nazi reign of terror," informed the National Executive Committee of the AJCongress that German Jews told her it was futile to send money to relieve their poverty and distress. The Hitler government confiscated all funds sent to German Jewish organizations.[21] When Americans desiring to mail money to German Jewish friends asked the US embassy in Berlin to receive it, fearing German banks would confiscate what they sent, they were told to use "the regular [German] banking channels."[22] In March 1933, a German Jewish leader informed the Board of Deputies of British Jews (BoD) that Jews in the Third Reich had begun "to liquidate Jewish assets and place them, so far as we can get hold of them, in non-German banks." He stressed, "We can only take out very little and we do not know how long we will be able to take out any money."[23]

Hamilton told the Boston *Jewish Advocate* that Jews with whom she spoke in Germany were emphatic that the Nazis' cold pogrom was "more cruel" than any Russian pogrom. They explained that it was "far better to have a savage massacre for a few days than a deliberate cold-blooded determination to make life impossible for some three million men, women, and children of Jewish blood."[24] (The Nazis defined as Jews not just the six hundred thousand who considered themselves Jewish but also persons who had one-quarter or one-half Jewish ancestry.)

Professor Sheldon Blank of Hebrew Union College in Cincinnati, who had traveled around Nazi Germany about the same time as Hamilton, reached the same conclusion. Blank's September 16, 1933, report to Rabbi Jonah Wise, national chairman of the American Jewish Joint Distribution Committee's German Relief Fund, was definitive: "Germany is no longer possible as a home for the Jews."[25]

A *New York Times* news article on April 18, 1933 stated that were Jews ever able to leave Germany, the "new exodus" could assume proportions "greater than the one led by Moses from Egypt." It reported that Jewish welfare organizations were "swamped by frantic people seeking aid and advice" about emigrating from Germany. Everywhere in Germany, Jews asked visitors from Western Europe and the United States about the possibilities of resettling in their countries. Berlin rabbi Joachim Prinz, who fled to the United States in 1938, recalled that soon after the Nazis came to power German Jews were joking to each other, "Are you an Aryan or are you learning English?"[26] American Jewish leaders and activists noted with horror in 1933 that conditions had become so abysmal for Jews in Germany that some were even attempting to escape into Poland, for centuries considered one of the world's most antisemitic countries.

Otto Tolischus, a senior New York Times correspondent in Berlin, wrote in September 1933 that the vast majority of Germany's Jews would leave the country immediately if they could, but they faced a very bleak future because most had no hope of gaining admission to any Western country. Tolischus reported that German Jews believed that the older generation was fated to "live a short while on charity and then die out."[27] Michael Williams, editor of the American Catholic magazine Commonweal, who traveled in Nazi Germany for several weeks during the summer of 1933, similarly concluded that most German Jews were doomed. He pleaded to Americans, "Will you not help to deliver at least the youthful members of the [German] Jewish people?"[28]

Jews fleeing into countries contiguous to Germany confronted severe antisemitic persecution. Pierre van Paassen commented in June 1933 that Jews were physically assaulted every day in Dutch cities. The New York Times reported in April 1933 that Switzerland would admit Jews only as temporary refugees and would not permit them to engage in business or acquire land. It threatened "criminal action" against any refugee engaging in anti-Nazi agitation.[29] The Jewish Telegraphic Agency (JTA), whose dispatches were regularly published in American Jewish newspapers and in some major American metropolitan dailies, reported on August 20, 1933, that Jews in France, the European country least inhospitable to the refugees, were in "despair." Resources available to support the refugees, never close to sufficient, were rapidly diminishing. The JTA emphasized that among the Jewish refugees in France "the misery is indescribable." Since 1930 there had been numerous anti-Jewish riots and demonstrations in Paris and other French cities and at the universities. Action Française, a leading voice of France's rapidly growing antisemitic movement, warned in the spring of 1933 that "the Semitic vultures, hav[ing] ruined Germany," were now "swooping down in France to ruin our land." [30]

Alexander Brin concluded in November 1933 in the Boston Jewish Advocate, drawing on his observations during several weeks spent that fall in the Third Reich, that German Jewry was "doomed." He reported that Germany's Jews were the victims of a cruelty unprecedented in the history of antisemitism. Nazi persecution of the Jews made the Spanish Inquisition "look like a mere brawl." Reduced to a class of lepers or untouchables, Germany's Jews faced the future "without a ray of hope." Although the Nazis were not yet capable of slaughtering or expelling all six hundred thousand of them in one day, Brin emphasized that the Hitler regime had implemented policies whose objective was to starve German Jewry into extinction within a generation. He wrote that the Nazis' goal was "to starve out more than half a million men, women, and children. . . . Their intent is murder, cold-blooded murder."[31]

The most informed American and European commentators in 1933 expressed no surprise that Germany had lurched back into the Dark Ages almost immediately after the Nazis assumed power. In a speech in Atlantic City, New Jersey, in June, Dorothy Thompson declared that the Nazis had carried out "a program which has been on the books of the Nazi Party for the last thirteen years."[32] The Brown Book of the Hitler Terror and the Burning of the Reichstag, the first book-length documentation of Nazi atrocities, published in the United States in 1933 by Alfred A. Knopf, similarly noted that "for fifteen years, in tens of thousands of meetings and tens of thousands of articles in the press," the Nazis had denounced the Jews as "a world plague [and] the most brutish of sub-men." For fifteen years, the Nazis had promised a "day of reckoning" when they would "extirpate the Jews." The Nazi movement's "main battle cry—'Perish Judah!'"—was annihilationist.[33]

Similarly, the Manchester Guardian emphasized that the Nazis had made these intentions explicit from the beginning. Frederick Voigt declared on March 15, 1933, that "Hitler, Goering, and the others [in the Nazi leadership] ha[d] for years" made clear their plan to unleash a violent antisemitic terror when they came to power. He had attended many Nazi gatherings "which were nothing but one incitement to lynch-law." On April 1, 1933, the Guardian reminded readers that in Mein Kampf Hitler called Jewry a "pestilence worse than the Black Death" of the Middle Ages, which threatened civilization's survival.[34]

On April 9, 1932, almost a year before Hitler came to power, the Manchester Guardian had drawn its readers' attention to his speeches and writings and those of other Nazi leaders that cast Jews as demonic, bent on world conquest and on Germany's destruction. The Guardian cited quotations and pointed to caricatures that could explain the Nazis' systematic campaign of antisemitic violence. Hitler condemned the "materialistic contamination" of Germany by "the Jewish pest," whose God was gold. The paper pointed to Der Stürmer's 1931 antisemitic cartoon captioned "Pan-Juda Wades Through a Sea of Blood on his Way to World Domination" as a graphic illustration of the Nazis' dangerous, deeply ingrained image of Jewry. The *Guardian* emphasized that such quotations and cartoons were "a commonplace" of Nazi propaganda and "could easily be multiplied a hundredfold."[35]

The Nazis' fierce antisemitism and determination to show German Jewry that it had no future found support among teachers and schoolchildren, who routinely tormented and humiliated Jewish pupils, making their experience so miserable that many refused to attend school. The Hitler regime introduced "ghetto benches" (the *Judenbank*) in many schoolrooms: segregated seating for Jews, usually in the rear. Jews were barred from participating in gymnastic exercises and sports and games with the gentile pupils. When teachers called on Jews to recite, they addressed them as "Jude" (Jew) and then their last name. By an order of Reich Minister of the Interior Frick on December 20, 1933, German pupils were required to stand and in unison return the teacher's "Heil Hitler!" and Nazi salute at the beginning and end of each lesson. By June 1933, the Nazis had made the teaching profession in Germany entirely *Judenrein*—devoid of Jews. Jews were only permitted to teach the Jewish religion to Jewish children.[36]

Nazi Germany's school curriculum was centered on inculcating a belief in "Aryan" superiority and the Jewish threat to "race purity." In 1933 a lesson in "race theory" was made compulsory in every school. The newspaper *Neue Deutsche Schule* (*New German School*) enjoined teachers, when lecturing schoolgirls about the "Jewish question," to "bring out the fact that Jews are of Asiatic descent and cannot mix with Aryans and that inter-marriage with Jews is out of the question." The *New York Times* reported in December 1933 that the textbook *German History as Racial Fate*, assigned in many schools in the Third Reich, characterized Judaism as "foreign" and dwelled on its "disintegrating and destructive might." The *Times* stated that "all biological instruction, which now takes the most prominent place on every curriculum, is along the same line." A teachers' magazine advised how to use popular fairy tales to promote antisemitism.[37]

The British anti-Nazi activist Lady Violet Bonham-Carter, daughter of former prime minister Herbert Asquith, reported that the school lessons offered "insult after insult" to Jews. She examined the notes of a fourteen-year-old girl taken in a "Staatsbürgerkunde" (civic knowledge) class, which included statements like "The Jews are not an inferior race, they are less than that" and "The Jews are guests in Germany, and you know what one does with guests one dislikes—one tells them to go."

It was not unusual for a teacher to call a Jewish pupil to the front of the classroom to demonstrate "race theory." The teacher would ask the gentiles to identify the classmate's "characteristically Jewish traits." Pierre van Paassen reported in February 1934 that German schools had introduced a book that listed sixteen distinguishing marks. In one case, a Jew's classmates pointed out her "nose, curly black hair, and sallow skin ... while the wretched girl stood trembling in front of the class." The teacher "expressed surprise that the children could point to nothing else," asking them, "Can't you see her deceitful look?"[38]

American Jewish travelers to Nazi Germany in 1933 and 1934 emphasized the severity of the abuse inflicted on Jewish pupils and their extreme mental anguish. Richard Neuberger, an American law student who spent seven weeks visiting smaller German towns in the summer of 1933, reported that German Jewish children lived "in constant terror and bewilderment." Teachers and gentile students "ridiculed and shunned" them; every day Judaism was "condemned to them." A Jewish girl showed him the welt on her forehead sustained when a gentile pupil struck her with an inkwell. The teacher, who wore the brown uniform of the Sturmabteilung (SA) in the classroom, "approved the deed."[39] The prominent Boston Jewish merchant Edward Filene, who traveled to Germany in the spring of 1933 to investigate antisemitic persecution, told the US State Department about the confinement of Jewish pupils to segregated back benches, their teachers forcing them to stand until all the "Aryan" pupils had been seated.[40] Rabbi Ferdinand Isserman of St. Louis learned from a German Jewish refugee whom he met in Paris in the summer of 1934 that the gentile pupils in his daughter's school wiped the bench after she sat on it.[41]

In November 1933, Alexander Brin stated that on his fall 1933 trip to Germany he had learned that Jewish pupils were "treated like dirt" in school, with some driven to suicide. They were "segregated on Jewish benches, denied crackers and milk [and] books," and taught that they were inferior to "Aryans" and the source of "all kinds of evils." Many schools assigned a textbook showing a "Jewish traitor stabbing the victorious German soldier in the back." The wife of a Jewish physician told Brin that the headmistress of her daughter's school required that she and the only other Jew among forty children alternate every other day in singing the Nazi "hymn of the national revolution" (the "Horst Wessel Lied") before the class: "How beautiful it is to see Jewish blood gushing under the Hitlerian knife." Another headmistress marched her pupils to a playground every day, lining them up to receive milk and a bun. The Jewish children were required to stand in file, but when they came to the head of the line, the headmistress spurned them: "Go away, Jews, next one please." The school considered it important that "Christian children ... witness this scene daily, so that they may learn how to treat a Jewish child who is hungry and asks for food."[42]

Lady Bonham-Carter cited an October 1933 *Manchester Guardian* article about how German kindergartens traumatized Jewish children by having them assume the role of pigs in games. The article reported that "after having been made a pig for several days in succession, a little Jewish girl of six refused to go to the school anymore." Classmates often cut swastikas into the Jewish children's clothes. In an art class, the teacher made a student whose father was Jewish draw "nothing but swastikas."[43]

In a February 1934 lecture in London, Lt. Colonel J. Sandeman Allen, a British MP just returned from Germany, reported on "Hitler propaganda in the nursery." He told the audience that in the house in which he was lodged, "I found children playing a game we know as snakes and ladders, but on their board the snakes were Jews, the ladders were swastikas, and the goal was Hitler."[44]

The endless harassment of Jewish students and the expulsion of Jewish teachers led German Jews to try to establish special Jewish schools, which most had previously strongly opposed. The London *Jewish Chronicle* reported that not only the Zionists but "even the most rabid Assimilationists" were now advocating separate Jewish schools "as the only relief for their mentally tortured children." On May 6, 1933, the Central British Fund for World Jewish Relief declared that maintaining a Jewish school system was "of the highest importance to Jews of all shades of opinion, as the attendance of state or municipal schools by Jewish children has been made practically impossible." It expressed alarm that since Hitler assumed power German Jewish schools' funding had declined drastically, as a result of the departure from the country of some of the wealthier Jewish families, the ruin of the Jewish professional class, and the Nazi threat to Jewish businesses and charities. The fund feared there would not be sufficient money to pay Jewish teachers' salaries in the coming months.[45]

On July 21, 1933, the *Brooklyn Jewish Examiner* reported that Jewish philanthropist Leo Simon had called for the United States to relax the immigration quota to admit twenty thousand German Jewish children, to be placed with American Jewish families, as a step toward saving "a whole generation of Jews." Simon underscored that Jewish children could no longer attend German schools because of the degradation to which they were subjected as a result of their teachers' antisemitic instruction and harassment and the "mockery and laughter with which their classmates greet these barbarities." The Jewish pupils told their parents that nothing could make them return to these "torture chambers."[46]

ECONOMIC STRANGULATION AND TERROR

The Nazis considered the boycott of Jewish stores and offices a major weapon in bringing about German Jewry's demise through economic strangulation and terror. It provided opportunities to mobilize Germans in violent attacks on Jews and their property. A Nazi mob had celebrated the party's dramatic gains in the September 1930 election, when it increased its representation in the Reichstag by 800 percent, by smashing the windows of Berlin's Jewish-owned department stores.[47] On February 13, 1933, Alexander Werth informed *Manchester Guardian* editor-in-chief William P. Crozier that the Nazis' anti-Jewish boycott had been underway for about three years, a product of their intense antisemitism. Werth observed that "there is an unwritten law against Jews which . . . is much more serious than any laws that Hitler may invent."[48]

Boycotts of Jewish businesses had been carried out in the 1920s by militant German rightist groups like the Queen Louise League, a national women's organization, and the Stahlhelm, the nation's largest veterans' association. The antisemitic boycotts became more frequent as the Nazi Party's membership and electoral strength grew dramatically between 1930 and its assumption of power in 1933. The damage the boycotts inflicted on Jewish shopkeepers pre-cipitated a significant Jewish migration to the larger cities from small towns and villages, where Jews were more easily identified and lacked the support of an organized Jewish community.[49]

On March 28, 1933, the *New York Evening Post* reported testimony by German Jewish refugees in Paris that anti-Jewish boycotts began "immediately after Chancellor Hitler assumed power." They "took the form of beating Jewish store proprietors, picketing their establishments with signs reading 'Buy only from Germans,' and threatening Gentiles who refused to obey." In early March 1933, the *Brooklyn Jewish Examiner* reported that the Nazis had launched "a terrific wave of guerilla warfare" against Jewish businesses in Germany's large cities and small towns. Brown-shirted SA men raided Jewish-owned businesses in Berlin, Hamburg, Frankfurt, Leipzig, Dresden, Breslau, and Königsberg, driving out the owners and raising the swastika flag over their stores.[50] On March 21, 1933, JTA correspondent Max Rhoade sent US Undersecretary of State William Phillips a summary of the Nazis' "concerted attack on Jewish stores and warehouses in many parts of Germany" that began in the first week of March. He reported that in Berlin the Nazis "shouted incessantly" to large crowds that assembled in front of Jewish-owned stores, "Germans, buy only from Germans!" In Berlin's Jewish quarter, this created a panic among shopkeepers, who hurriedly shut down their businesses. Seven gunshots were fired into the window of a Jewish-owned shop on March 10, and missiles were thrown at some of the stores.[51]

Similar anti-Jewish violence and intimidation occurred elsewhere in Germany at the same time. On March 10, outgoing US ambassador to Germany Frederic Sackett informed Secretary of State Cordell Hull that the Nazis had forced the closing of Jewish-owned department and chain stores in parts of Germany.[52] That same day, storm troopers positioned themselves in front of the Jewish-owned Tietz department stores in Kassel, photographing every customer and threatening to retaliate against them for shopping there. Storm troopers forced Jewish stores to close that day in Essen, Bottrop, and Mühlheim-on-Ruhr.[53]

The same day, Hermann Goering, Prussian minister of the interior and a top Nazi leader, made clear that the Hitler government did not consider Jewish business in Germany legitimate. He announced that policemen would not respond to Jews' pleas to stop mobs from harassing them and ruining their businesses, because their job was to protect only honest merchants, not "swindlers, tramps, usurers, and traitors."[54]

On April 1, 1933, the Nazis underscored German Jews' isolation and extreme vulnerability when they completely shut down Jewish commercial activity in a well-coordinated one-day national boycott of Jewish stores and offices. Julius Streicher, Nazi district leader in Franconia and one of the party's most rabid antisemites, had charge of the boycott. He made no effort to conceal that his ultimate objective was the destruction of German Jewry. At a rally in Munich the night before the boycott that drew one hundred thousand people, Streicher announced that "the Jews, who had crucified Christ, were now themselves on the way to Golgotha." He gloated that "the German people . . . would soon be free of the archenemy, the 'eternal wandering Jew,' whose crimes had been accumulating throughout the ages." Streicher would make "a clean job of the Jews."[55]

The *New York Times* reported that on the eve of the April 1 national boycott the Nazi Women's Federation appealed for an annihilationist "holy war" against the Jews. The Women's Federation declared that the boycott was part of an "inexorable" struggle that must continue until "Jewry has been destroyed." It emphasized that "the Jew must forever be eliminated from our people and our State."[56]

The Nazi leadership issued detailed instructions to party activists on how to conduct the boycott and established boycott committees even in the villages. The committees compiled lists of Jewish businesses, lawyers, and physicians. The Nazis plastered antisemitic posters across Jewish storefronts and on trucks, which they drove through commercial streets. Particularly chilling was the storm troopers' placement of a yellow circle above the boycotted places—the medieval symbol of Jewish humiliation. Storm trooper pickets were posted at the store and office doors, photographing, threatening, and sometimes assault- ing those who tried to enter.[57]

George Gordon, chargé d'affaires at the US embassy in Berlin, informed Secretary of State Hull that the Nazis had clearly been planning the boycott "for a long time" because it was "organized so systematically, on such a large scale, and carried out to the minutest detail." The Nazi claim that the boycott was a response to foreign Jews' "atrocity propaganda" had no validity. Gordon had concluded that the Hitler government's objective for Germany's Jews was their "complete ruination."[58]

Many American and British newspapers gave considerable attention to the atmosphere of antisemitic menace that pervaded the Nazis' April 1 boycott. Nearly all the articles pointed to the Nazis' resurrection of the dreaded medieval yellow circle to designate Jewish stores and offices. The *New York Herald Tri- bune* ran front-page articles about the boycott on both April 1 and April 2. In the April 1 issue, covering the final preparations for the boycott, the *Herald Tribune* reported that a Nazi "central committee of action" was posting "huge placards on all billboards and pillars throughout the Reich," displaying an antisemitic "manifesto" that explained the Hitler regime's purpose in organizing it. The manifesto presented the boycott as part of the Nazis' effort to thwart a nefari- ous Jewish conspiracy to take control of the world, which they claimed Theodor Herzl devised at the First Zionist Congress at Basel in 1897. According to the manifesto, Herzl had said, "As soon as a gentile state [in this case Germany] dares to offer resistance to the Jews, the Jews must be in a position to make the neighbors of this state declare war on it." Nazi resistance would frustrate the Jews' plan to transform Germany into a "Soviet Russian criminal colony."[59]

Herald Tribune Berlin correspondent John Elliott predicted that "matters will be made very unpleasant for citizens who defy the boycott." The Nazis had arranged to post motion-picture cameramen in front of Jewish stores, and "persons entering them may see themselves later shown on the screen in cin- ema houses or in the picture sections of the newspapers, held up to common obloquy." Elliott noted other forms of intimidation that the Nazis were al- ready using against anyone who defied the boycott. In Frankfurt-am-Main, the Nazis had broken up a meeting of Jews protesting the boycott and arrested forty Jewish merchants involved in it. In the Hamburg suburb of Altona, the Nazi police chief had ordered all Jewish storekeepers to place signs in their windows identifying the shop as Jewish owned, "on penalty of a heavy fine or prison sen- tence." The *Herald Tribune* also ran an Associated Press wire report stating that in the German town of Annaberg, where the boycott was already underway, Nazi pickets had stopped customers exiting Jewish stores and "pasted on their foreheads stamps reading: 'We traitors bought from the Jews.'"[60]

The next day, with the boycott officially begun, nearly all of the large Jewish-owned department stores remained closed all day, and with "husky Nazis" positioned in front of smaller Jewish stores, few persons dared enter them. Those "who did were greeted with cries of 'Shame!' and had to run a gauntlet of photographers and motion picture operators, with the risk of being exposed later on the screen and in the newspapers in the guise of unpatriotic Germans."

The *Herald Tribune* reported a "holiday spirit" in Berlin, with "gentile restaurants reap[ing] a harvest" as a result of the shutting down of Jewish eating establishments. Trucks filled with brownshirts drove about the streets, warning the public not to buy from Jewish merchants. The streetcars and buses were all bedecked with swastikas.[61]

The *New York Times*'s front-page story, written by its Berlin correspondent Frederick Birchall, highlighted the boycott's international focus: its purpose was to convey to "the whole world that the Jewish question was not a problem for Germany alone but for the whole of mankind." The Nazis were threatening Jews not just within Germany but beyond its borders as well. Birchall pointed out that Nazi storm troopers picketing Jewish stores carried signs warning shoppers in both German and English, "Germans, defend yourselves! Don't buy in Jewish shops!"

Birchall emphasized the boycott's wide range and impact. He described the yellow circles posted on Jewish lawyers' and physicians' offices, accompanied by signs reading, "Attention! A Jew! It is prohibited to visit him." Birchall reported that Jews were forbidden entry to the University of Berlin and to the reading room of Berlin's State Public Library.[62]

On April 1, 1933, Pulitzer Prize–winning correspondent H. R. Knickerbocker reported from Berlin on the *New York Evening Post*'s front page that storm troopers had forcibly prevented his *Evening Post* colleague Albion Ross from entering a Jewish-owned store in the Rosenthalerstrasse and had beaten him, shouting, "Damn dog!" A policeman looked on indifferently.[63]

The same day, a *Manchester Guardian* editorial warned that if the boycott were not called off, "it means the utter, irremediable ruin of all Jews within the Reich." The *Guardian* predicted that Jews would have to "sell their businesses at knock-down prices" and would find no opportunities to use their skills. With Jewish judges and physicians expelled from their posts, German Jews would have no hope of fair treatment. Germany might well be embarking on a path "which means expulsion or starvation for six hundred thousand Jews."[64]

Less than a week after the boycott, the *Boston Globe* carried a story about Munich Nazis' savage beating of correspondent Pierre van Paassen, at the time associated with the Foreign Bureau of the Toronto *Star*, during which a top Nazi leader expressed his desire to permanently shut down all Jewish stores. The Nazis observed van Paassen in a restaurant taking notes as he listened to Hermann Goering's antisemitic rant. Goering maintained that Jewish shopkeepers did not deserve protection. He called them "Asiatic scoundrels who ... suck[ed] the blood of the German people." Goering warned, "Let the Jewish bandits beware.... Our patience has its limits. We will crush them like snakes in the grass." When the Nazis demanded van Paassen's papers and learned he was a journalist who had visited the Soviet Union, they hit him in the jaw and arrested him. During his three hours in jail, van Paassen "was given a dose of the Nazi mailed fist."[65]

Dr. Leon Zeitlin, director of the Association of Large High Quality Shops in Berlin in 1933, who witnessed the April 1 boycott there, twenty years later called it "the prelude to the unparalleled crimes of Hitler's racial madness." He described Berlin's store windows on the major shopping boulevards as "grotesquely disfigured" that day with the Nazis' "coarse and sickening" antisemitic slogans. At noon he had begun receiving telephone calls from managers of Jewish-owned department stores informing him that the Nazis had presented them with an ultimatum to dismiss without notice all of their Jewish employees.[66]

Nobody made any effort to protect the Jews during the boycott. Robert Weltsch, another eyewitness, recalled that "the police stood by smiling," making no attempt to interfere with the storm troopers' and Nazi mobs' intimidation and violence. He noted that "in a cruel irony," it was their Jewish victims whom the police arrested, allegedly "to protect them from the ... fury of the people."[67] The prominent Berlin rabbi Dr. Leo Baeck, who was in the city during the boycott, stated that Germany's "churches, universities, courts, [and] chambers of commerce had all remained silent" about the Nazi boycotters' vicious antisemitic displays and violence.[68]

In many places Jews and gentiles who made purchases in Jewish stores were placed on public display in humiliating positions. In the town of Glogau, fifteen prominent Jewish residents, including two lawyers and a physician, were forced into a truck used to transport cattle, which was decorated with a swastika, and "slowly driven through the streets." In Kassel, a barbed-wire enclosure was erected in front of a Jewish shop, with a sign identifying it as a concentration camp for those who frequented Jewish-owned stores. A donkey was placed in the enclosure.[69] In Annaberg in Saxony, during or shortly after the April 1 boycott, Nazi pickets stamped "We are traitors; we have bought from the Jews" on the faces of persons leaving Jewish stores.[70]

After April 1, 1933, boycotts of Jewish stores, physicians, and attorneys persisted in many German localities. At the International Conference for the Relief of German Jewry, held in London from October 29 to November 1, 1933, and sponsored by the Central British Fund for World Jewish Relief, Professor David Cohen of the Jewish Central Information Office in Amsterdam reported that the anti-Jewish boycott was "still in full swing" in Germany's smaller towns. The boycott was enforced by the two-million-strong SA. Cohen explained that "in the country, small [Jewish-owned] stores are in a catastrophic state." Jewish peddlers throughout Germany were being "systematically ruined." Jewish traders were no longer admitted to public markets in most of Germany. Many German newspapers refused to accept any advertising from Jews. Cohen reported that in some German communities the Jews were "considering emigrating 'en bloc' as their condition becomes desperate."[71]

A *New York Times* correspondent reported on April 16, 1933, that all agencies of the German government were instructed not to make purchases from Jews. He explained that the German government, "through the many socialized industries, banks and insurance organizations that it controls . . . virtually dominates all business in the country." The government's embargo was "therefore almost a command to all other businesses" not to buy from Jews. The *Times* observed that many Jewish stores "in the small towns and villages whose customers are under neighborhood scrutiny and control" would "probably go to the wall."[72]

From Berlin, chargé d'affaires George Gordon notified Secretary of State Hull on April 10, 1933, that the Nazi removal of Jews from the professions, civil service, and private businesses was proceeding on a large scale. In Berlin, only 36 of what he estimated had been 1,750 Jewish lawyers were still allowed to try cases in court or perform notary work.[73] The Reich Press Law, passed on October 4, 1933, "stipulated that all editors must possess German citizenship, be of Aryan descent, and not married to a Jew."[74]

In November 1933, Leon Dominian, American consul general at Stuttgart, informed Secretary of State Hull that every day, for months, *Der Führer*, the leading magazine of Karlsruhe, capital of the state of Baden, had published a notice in the middle of its advertising section: "Kauft nicht bei Juden!" ("Do not buy from Jews!") Dominian found that such notices precipitated atrocities against Jews. He emphasized that *Der Führer* was the principal Nazi newspaper in Baden and thus expressed the view of the national government.[75]

The Nazis dramatized Jews' pariah status by suppressing Jewish stores' Christmas trade on theological grounds. On December 15, 1933, Raymond H. Geist, American consul in Berlin, informed Secretary of State Hull that the German press in many cities and towns was urging Germans not to purchase Christmas presents in stores owned by "Christ-Killers." Waldenburg's *Mittelschlesische Gebirgszeitung*, for example, reminded its readers that Jewish stores had no right to make money from "a German feast." It emphasized that Germans celebrated Christmas to honor the birth of "the same Christ whom the Jews in a shameful manner nailed on the Cross." In the city of Giessen in Hesse, the authorities ordered automobile owners to drive around with signs reading, "German Christians . . . do not buy your Christmas presents in Jewish stores." In Fulda in Hesse during the Christmas season, "Aryan" shopkeepers and their employees marched through the city demanding that Jewish one-price stores be shut down.[76]

A boycott of Jewish stores initiated in March 1934 in Franconia touched off a pogrom on Palm Sunday in Gunzenhausen, where two Jews were killed and a large number tortured and seriously injured. The *Manchester Guardian* reported that "these brutal attacks . . . resembled the prewar pogrom scenes in Russia." This in turn sparked similar outbreaks of anti-Jewish violence elsewhere in the region. A JTA correspondent in Prague who had toured the area reported that in the region around Nuremberg, Franconia's largest city, the Nazis had prohibited shops from selling bread to Jews, who were "starving as a result of the intense boycott." He stated that the Nazis required Jewish stores in the region to prominently display signs proclaiming, "The Jews are our misfortune." Many Franconian towns posted signs announcing, "Jews unwanted."[77]

The American consul general at Munich, Charles M. Hathaway Jr., trivialized Gunzenhausen's Palm Sunday pogrom in his report almost four months later to US ambassador to Germany William E. Dodd, denying the press accounts that Jews had been physically attacked. Hathaway conceded that SA, joined by a local mob, had "rounded up all the Jews in town that they could find, drove them in to the market place, lectured them on their position and place in life, [and] sang offensive songs at their expense and the like." But he accepted the Nazis' claim that the two dead Jews had committed suicide. Hathaway maintained that one of the Jews had "opened his own veins under the stress of his excited feelings," while the other "hanged himself." He did not foresee any similar trouble in the region in the future.[78]

EXTENDING THE WAR AGAINST THE JEWS: THE BOOK BURNINGS

The Nazi student association, backed by the Nazi Party, invoked the medieval association of Jews with poison when it organized coordinated nationwide mass burnings of "un-German" books at Germany's universities on the night of May 10, 1933, about six weeks after the nationwide boycott of Jewish stores and offices. The book burnings symbolized the Nazi determination to extend their war against the Jews from the economic to the cultural realm.[79] The Nazis defined as "un-German" any work authored by a Jew, as well as Marxist and pacifist writings. They announced that books written by Jews were an "insidious poison" that threatened "the very roots of Germandom" and must be destroyed. Students at the University of Berlin issued a manifesto entitled "Twelve Theses on the Non-German Spirit," including "Our most important enemy is the Jew and he who serves him" and "The Jew can only think Jewish." In the weeks before the book burnings, Nazi students gathered massive numbers of books from private households and public and university libraries.[80]

On the night of May 10, Nazi students in universities across Germany staged torchlight parades and then assembled to burn many of the world's greatest works of scholarship and literature. Large crowds of spectators loudly booed the names of the authors of the condemned works, such as Sigmund Freud and Albert Einstein. In Frankfurt, one of Germany's largest cities, the students hauled the "un-German" books to the bonfires in oxen-pulled manure wagons, again underscoring the Nazi identification of Jews with human and animal excrement. At the book burning in Berlin, the capital, Propaganda Minister Josef Goebbels, presiding at a swastika-draped podium, shouted, "Jewish intellectualism is dead!" The Berlin book burning was broadcast nationally on radio. The university's rector participated in the ceremony. The *New York Times* referred to the burning of books at "inquisitorial stakes," associating Nazism with the racially antisemitic Spanish Inquisition, which had also employed large-scale torture and execution by fire to suppress Judaism's influence. The AJCongress on May 6 compared the book burnings to the Inquisition's auto da fé, public spectacles in which conversos and Jews were burned at the stake, implying that they could portend the extermination of the Jews.[81]

In German academia and publishing, which were rapidly expelling Jews, the book burnings went virtually unchallenged. George Messersmith, American consul general in Berlin, informed Secretary of State Hull in June that German publishers "will no longer receive anything by a Jewish author."[82]

In enacting a law on April 7, 1933, barring Jews from the civil service, the Hitler government removed them from the professoriate, because German universities were state run. By the 1934–35 academic year, most Jewish faculty members, about eight hundred in all, including many of the world's most distinguished scholars, had been expelled from their positions. Martha Dodd, daughter of US ambassador to Germany William E. Dodd (1933–38), who lived with him in Berlin, stated that German universities under Hitler were just "elevated institutions of Nazi propaganda." A strict quota was imposed on Jewish enrollments, limiting them to no more than 1.5 percent of the student body. Initially, veterans and persons who held their posts before 1914 were exempted, as a result of pressure from President von Hindenburg.[83]

In June 1932, Joseph Tenenbaum, chairman of the AJCongress's National Executive Committee, estimated that of the 140,000 students enrolled in German universities, 100,000 "swear to the swastika."[84] Nazi students' physical assaults on and furious harassment of Jewish students and professors continued after Hitler assumed power, until in a very short time almost none remained in the universities. George Messersmith informed Secretary of State Hull on May 6, 1933, that "the Nazi student bodies in the various universities are in complete control of the universities and the constituted authorities in the universities must be their mouthpiece and servants, or they are immediately replaced." He added that German newspapers "carry every day announcements of further professors who are relieved from duty simply because they are not pleasing to the student body."[85]

Nazi students expressed solidarity with the April 1, 1933, national boycott of Jewish stores and offices and employed some of its tactics against Jewish professors at the universities. That day they picketed Jewish professors' classrooms, pressuring students not to enter. Later, they photographed students who attended Jewish professors' classes.[86]

MAKING JEWS PARIAHS

Throughout 1933 and 1934, the American, British, and world Jewish press reported rampant antisemitic terrorism in the German provinces, where towns and villages were denying Jews access to public facilities and driving them out. As early as March 1933, a Jewish industrialist who had escaped from Germany told the JTA that fear had led many Jews in the provinces to spend their nights in the forests or in cattle sheds. In January 1934, the American Jewish Committee explained that many German Jewish children were sleeping in the woods at night because there was no protection for them in the towns.[87]

Whole sections of Germany were made *Judenrein*, as in the Middle Ages, reinforcing Jews' pariah status. In December 1933, the *New York Times* stated that in many places Jews were prohibited from entering towns and villages or doing business in markets and fairs. It noted that many German high schools advertised themselves as "free of Jews." A year later, the *Palestine Post* (Jerusalem) reported that the Jews of Hesse were "outlawed": in the villages, placards warning Jews not to enter were posted "on almost every door." Residents of the

Franconian district of Hersbruck in May 1934 celebrated the departure of the last Jew by hoisting a swastika flag over his house.[88]

As soon as the Nazis became a significant bloc in the Reichstag in 1930, their virulent racial antisemitism led them to press aggressively for legislation to prohibit marriages and sexual relations between Jews and gentiles, anticipating the Nuremberg laws of September 1935, which banned both. On February 3, 1933, only days after Hitler became chancellor, the Philadelphia *Jewish Exponent* reported Hermann Goering's declaration that any German who married a Jew would automatically be stripped of his or her citizenship.[89]

On July 8, 1933, George Gordon predicted to the US acting secretary of state that the German government would soon make Jewish-Christian intermarriage illegal. Gordon emphasized that the purpose of such a law was to "reduce the German Jews to the position of ignominy to which they were subjected during the Middle Ages." He reminded the acting secretary that "Nazi leaders have repeatedly boasted . . . that one of the first acts of a Nazi regime would be to set up ghettos in Germany." Gordon reported that German schools and universities had elevated "racial hygiene" to "primary importance in the curriculum," with particular emphasis "on the evils of miscegenation." He added that the new civil service law prohibited any person "married to a non-Aryan" from retaining or securing a civil service position.[90]

Reports of German courts annulling or barring marriages between Jews and gentiles circulated in the United States and Britain in 1933 and 1934. In December 1933, the Philadelphia *Jewish Exponent* announced that a Berlin court had granted an annulment to a gentile husband who argued that marriage must be based on "consanguinity." In May 1934, a researcher reported to the BoD that a Hessian court had denied a nineteen-year-old Jewish man permission to marry a gentile pregnant with his child. The court ruled that the benefit to the state from legitimizing the child was less than that which accrued from preventing a "non-Aryan" from marrying an "Aryan." The community's interest superseded the child's. Moreover, the mother must be punished for "her levity and lack of responsibility" in having sexual relations with a Jew. The researcher also noted that the Reich commissioner for justice, Hans Frank, in a speech on April 24, 1934, at the Conference of Lawyers in Karlsruhe, had thanked a court there for granting a gentile a divorce from a Jew on the grounds that mixed marriages were "against nature." Frank declared that such unions were based on the mistaken notion that "the Jews were racial members of the German nation." About that time, the Hessen government placed an official notice in the newspapers stating that a Jewish man had been sent to a concentration camp for having sexual relations with an "Aryan" woman.[91]

In 1933 and 1934, the American and British press reported German crowds' noxious harassment and public humiliation of mixed couples. The *New York Times* and the *Manchester Guardian* reported in August 1933 that Nazi storm troopers in Nuremberg had seized a nineteen-year-old German gentile woman found in the company of a young Jewish man, shaved her head, and paraded her through the streets with a placard around her neck announcing "I have offered myself to a Jew." The storm troopers also took the woman, "who was in a state of collapse," to cabarets, placed her on stage and shouted threats and insults at her. Among those who witnessed the antisemitic spectacle were the son and daughter of recently arrived US Ambassador to Germany William Dodd and a party of British tourists, who expressed their disgust.[92]

In 1934, the almost two-millennia-old Christian antisemitic stereotyping of Jews as lascivious prompted one hundred Nazi youth in Munich to shut down a screening of *The Girl from Vienna*. They had erroneously assumed that the male lead, British actor Arthur Riscoe, was Jewish. Some of the Nazi youths rose "at a given signal and started booing." Others "howled out, 'Leave the cinema, Germans!'" and "It is scandalous that a Jew should flirt with a German girl!" Riscoe had several love scenes with the heroine, Magda Schneider. Nazi censors had banned a previous Riscoe film "because of his alleged Semitic appearance."[93]

From the beginning of Hitler's rule, the Nazis used film to defame and marginalize Jews. The state-run Universum-Film Aktiengesellschaft (UFA) in 1933 determined that the films it produced would cast Jews only in stereotypical roles like "swindlers, criminals, and pathological cases."[94] It required even foreign actors and actresses (and musicians) to prove that their grandparents were "Aryan" before they could appear in German films.[95] In March 1934, the German government made clear that the prohibition on Jews applied to foreign as well as German films when it banned *Catherine the Great*, produced in Britain, and the American-made *The Prizefighter and the Lady*, starring American Jewish heavyweight boxer Max Baer. *Catherine the Great*, featuring Galician-born Jewish actress Elisabeth Bergner, was withdrawn after an antisemitic demonstration at a major Berlin theater.[96]

The Hitler government signaled its intention to obliterate the Jewish presence in Germany and to legitimize antisemitic violence when it replaced all Jewish street and city square names, including those of converts to Christianity, with names of Nazi Party leaders and martyrs and German kings and built memorials to assassins of Jews. This also erased Jews' centuries-long contributions to German culture. One of the first changes, in February or March 1933, was that of Rathenauplatz, which had honored the Weimar Republic's Jewish foreign minister, Walther Rathenau, to Wilhelmplatz. Names like Horst Wessel or Julius Streicher were substituted for Heinrich Heine or Felix Mendelssohn. In July 1933, the *Chicago Tribune* reported that a memorial had been unveiled near Hammelburg honoring Rathenau's assassins, Erwin Kern and Hermann Fischer. Several Bavarian Nazi Party leaders attended the ceremony.[97]

SPREADING THE BLOOD LIBEL: DEMONIZING THE JEW

On May 1, 1934, a few weeks after Gunzenhausen's Palm Sunday pogrom, Julius Streicher published a special, widely distributed "ritual murder" issue of his weekly newspaper *Der Stürmer*, devoted to "documenting" how, over more than two millennia, Jews kidnapped, tortured, and murdered Christian children to reenact their crime of deicide and obtain blood to mix with their Passover matzo and Purim pastries. This libel first emerged in the Middle Ages and persists into the present century. German Jewish leaders had already reported to the BoD in March 1933 that Nazi organizations, especially women's groups, were circulating the ritual murder charge.[98]

Der Stürmer depicted Jews as driven by their racial traits and religious beliefs to murder Christians. The front-page headline trumpeted, "Jewish Murder Program against Non-Jewish Humanity Unveiled." An illustration depicted four rabbis sucking a Christian child's blood through straws. Another portrayed two hook-nosed Jews wearing yarmulkes: one held a blood-soaked knife; the other, a bowl filling with the blood pouring from the necks of Christian women and children. Leading newspapers, including the *New York Times*, the *Manchester Guardian*, and the London *Times*, made American and British readers aware of *Der Stürmer*'s antisemitic claims.[99]

Der Stürmer explicitly linked the "secret rites" with a Jewish compact with the devil against Christianity, suggesting that the only solution was indiscriminate murder. In a speech at a factory meeting a few weeks before the ritual murder issue appeared, Streicher instructed his listeners to "throw any Jew they happened to meet down the stairs until his blood spurted forth."[100]

The London *Times* identified Streicher as a member of Hitler's inner circle, which rendered his publication of the ritual murder charge and accompanying antisemitic illustrations especially alarming. William L. Shirer, one of the leading American correspondents reporting from Berlin during the 1930s, later recalled that when Streicher was in the dock at Nuremberg after World War II, charged with war crimes, it was the first time he had seen him "without a whip in his hand or in his belt." Streicher had been a follower of Hitler since the early 1920s and participated in the 1923 Beer Hall Putsch. He had directed the April 1, 1933, national anti-Jewish boycott and at the beginning of 1934 was appointed minister without portfolio in the Bavarian cabinet. As Nazi district leader of Franconia, he ruled the province "with unlimited powers."[101]

Streicher attracted strong grassroots support in Franconia and received the endorsement of local leaders in the Catholic Church. Several months after the pogrom, Gunzenhausen staged a large official reception for him. The town's pastor and sister superior welcomed him to the convent, where Streicher intoned, "Whoever links himself with the Jews, links himself with the devil."[102]

In speeches to German children and youth, Streicher emphasized Jews' demonic qualities. On March 19, 1934, he warned girls at a vocational training school in Nuremberg that after they graduated they would be in constant danger from predatory Jews. Like the devil, the Jews were lecherous and assumed many forms: "You, German girls, are in great danger when you leave school and enter life. The Jew for whom you are free game according to his laws will try to approach you in many shapes."[103]

The BoD reported that Streicher's power within the Nazi movement was increasing steadily. On February 11, 1935, Adolf Hitler traveled to Nuremberg to celebrate Streicher's fiftieth birthday with him. Over the next few months, Streicher delivered vitriolic antisemitic addresses to massive gatherings, including forty thousand in Hamburg and sixty thousand workers in Chemnitz and Zwickau. He spoke in Munich, Cologne, and many other cities. Streicher was accorded the honor of opening the annual Nazi Party Congress at Nuremberg that year.

Streicher set up *"Stürmer* cases" (*Stürmerkästen*), prominently displaying copies of the newspaper, in towns and villages throughout Germany, thereby greatly expanding the readership beyond its already large circulation. The government-controlled German Railway Company and the German Postal Service placed *"Stürmer* cases" on their premises.[104]

Der Stürmer made a significant contribution to a Nazi antisemitic campaign that "reached an astonishing pitch of obscenity" in 1934 and 1935. Streicher's newspaper introduced columns of fake Jewish want ads, which drew on the centuries-old Christian antisemitic images of carnal, bloodsucking Jews, the impetus for the expulsions that had made Western and much of Central Europe *Judenrein* by 1500 CE. Young Jewish men sought relationships with "blond Aryan girls." Unemployed rabbis offered to teach what the London *Daily Herald* described as "revolting vices." An advertisement listing "For sale, good Jewish wine mixed with human blood" appeared "mild compared with most of these so-called Jewish advertisements."[105]

On May 22, 1934, the president of the World Alliance for Combatting Anti-Semitism in London, Schachna Maurice Salomen, wrote to President Roosevelt requesting that he publicly denounce the ritual murder calumny that the Nazis were spreading throughout Germany. Salomen noted that every day the Nazis were circulating "millions of pamphlets confirming this terrible accusation ... among the Youth of Germany, poisoning their minds." On behalf of the World Alliance, Salomen "begged" Roosevelt to condemn this exceedingly dangerous propaganda and offer "a word of sympathy" for Germany's beleaguered Jews. Roosevelt's aide Louis Howe did not consider Salomen's plea worthy of the president's attention and referred it to the State Department, which refrained from issuing any public statement on the matter.[106]

GERMANY'S CONCENTRATION CAMPS: MEDIEVAL TORTURE AND JEWISH DEGRADATION

By the fall of 1933, the Jewish and labor press in the West, as well as several major metropolitan dailies, most notably the *Manchester Guardian* and London *Times*, had provided millions of readers with a considerable amount of information about the medieval horrors of Nazi concentration camps. The Hitler government was deeply concerned about the impact of this investigative journalism and testimony from refugees who had escaped from the camps, and it devoted much attention to attempting to refute the evidence. Concentration camps had been set up before as a war measure, notably by the Spanish in their conflict in Cuba during the 1890s and by the British in the Anglo-Boer war of 1899–1902, but the Nazis established them in peacetime to imprison political opponents and Jews without leveling charges.[107] This approach had been used, in a more limited manner, only in czarist Russia. The Soviets provided the closest parallel in terms of scale. The Nazis initially imprisoned political dissidents and Jews in torture cellars (called "butcher shops") in their Brown Houses and in rundown factories and barracks. Very soon, however, they transferred most to larger concentration camps. The first was Dachau, near Munich, initially just "empty huts and a gravel pit." In March 1933, it was enlarged to hold five thousand prisoners, and over the next months the Nazis built many more camps.[108]

On October 27, 1933, Frederick Birchall reported in the *New York Times* the German government's admission that it held twenty-two thousand prisoners in concentration camps. He pointed out, however, that the previous summer *Neues Vorwärts*, organ of the German Social Democratic refugees in Prague, claimed that forty to fifty thousand were imprisoned in the camps and an equal number in ordinary jails. The London *Times* stated that *Neues Vorwärts* had "compiled a nearly complete list of concentration camps in Germany with the approximate list of interned persons." It showed sixty-five operating concentration camps, the largest of which were Dachau (thirty-five hundred inmates), Siegburg (twenty-five hundred), Osnabrück (more than two thousand), and Oranienburg (two thousand).[109]

A London *Daily Herald* reporter who visited Dachau in late October 1933 wrote that the entire camp was "surrounded with war-like barbed wire entanglements." There were as many guards as prisoners, who still wore the clothes they had on when arrested. The camp lacked facilities for washing or drying clothes and for medical treatment. The reporter managed to speak briefly to a prisoner, who described the food as "garbage." All prisoners had to perform eight hours a day of manual labor, whatever their health or age. In November, Lord Dudley Marley and Ellen Wilkinson introduced to the British House of Commons a German refugee, Herr Tentz (not his real name), who had been imprisoned in the Sonnenberg concentration camp for seven months. The camp, which now housed one thousand prisoners, was "an old prison . . . condemned in 1930 as unhygienic." The water was "undrinkable." Tentz testified to the MPs that inmates were "kept in heavy chains; war cripples were beaten with carbines; [there were] special torture cells; . . . [and] men lying in the courtyard with the flesh torn from their arms and legs." Prisoners who were beaten to death "were hung up in their cells to create the impression they had committed suicide" and were then "carted away, no one knows where."[110]

After escaping in December 1933 from the Oranienburg concentration camp near Berlin, former Social Democratic Reichstag deputy Gerhart Seger told Americans in a 1934 lecture tour about the horrifying conditions there. Seger recalled that months before the Nazis assumed power they had already planned to establish concentration camps. During a debate in the Reichstag's foreign affairs committee in November 1932, Dr. Wilhelm Frick, a prominent Nazi deputy, had warned Seger that as soon as Hitler came to power, "persons like you will be sent to concentration camps right away." Seger noted that the word "concentration camp was unknown [to him] up until that time" and "indicated that the Nazis had already made their plans on how to do away with the political opposition once they assumed power." He stated that prisoners referred to the isolation cells, less than one yard square, where many inmates were confined, as "stone coffins." It was impossible to sit or lie down. Seger knew of a prisoner who was forced to stand in one for more than a week. Most prisoners were packed together in the old "ice cellars . . . body by body on straw on the floor." After his escape, Seger learned from a man who had been released from a concentration camp near Bremen that a former Social Democratic Reichstag deputy, Alfred Faust, who was over fifty and suffered from heart disease, had been tortured to death by Nazi camp guards. When he became tired or was unable to carry heavy coal sacks, the guards beat and kicked him, finally trampling him to death. Then "the Nazis actually played football with his body." Faust was "buried in a corner of the camp like a mad dog."[111]

The London *Times* on September 19, 1933, published an article sent from Switzerland by another former Oranienburg inmate, which described the public humiliation inflicted on him and a group of predominantly Jewish prisoners before their shipment to the camp. A non-Jew, he had been attending a Jewish-run agricultural school when he and the other students were arrested in June 1933 by SA men. About thirty of the forty-three students at the school were Jews. The heavily armed storm troopers forced them to leave their belongings behind, packed them tightly into trucks (beating some with cudgels), and drove them to the Adolf Hitler Haus in Berlin. The students remained in the trucks for three hours while the storm troopers told a crowd forming around them that the prisoners were Jews whose "fathers had robbed Germany of all its money since the War." At the camp, there were no beds, just straw, and only one hydrant for twenty-five hundred prisoners to wash. Every inmate suffered "his full share of beatings," many quite savage. The former inmate stated that in the camp, the 125 Jewish prisoners were forced to live in an enclosure about twenty-five yards square.[112]

Jews in the concentration camps were singled out for special degradation. The *Manchester Guardian* interviewed a recently discharged inmate of the Brandenburg concentration camp in December 1933, who reported that Jews "were treated with special cruelty" and "compelled to perform the hardest and most disagreeable tasks." In one section of the camp, Jews were denied food rations, forced to eat only what non-Jewish inmates left over, without knives or forks. The entire student body of a Jewish boys' school was imprisoned at Oranienburg for several weeks in "inhuman conditions." Each of the Jewish boys was subjected to homosexual rape.[113]

Nazi propagandists repeatedly denied that prisoners in concentration camps were treated harshly. The *New York Times* quoted Dr. Friedrich Schönemann, Hitler's leading authority on the United States, who lectured to Americans in late 1933 in the drive to promote support for Nazi policies, as telling a Drew University audience that when he visited a concentration camp, he found the inmates "living in cleanliness and order." The camp resembled a college dormitory. The Boston press reported that when he declared at that city's Ford Hall Forum that there was nothing "dirty, abnormal, or mean" in the concentration camps, the audience responded with "derisive laughter."[114] In March 1934, the London *Jewish Chronicle* reported that a book entitled *Concentration Camp Oranienburg* by the camp commandant, Storm Troop Leader Schaefer, had been published in Nazi Germany. The book provided "long descriptions of how the good-natured storm troopers and the willing prisoners worked hand in hand in brotherly love to build the camp." Schaefer expressed his disgust at the "'lying reports' in the foreign press about cruelty" in the camps. He specifically denounced the London *Times*'s article by the student from the Jewish agricultural school who had been imprisoned at Oranienburg.[115]

* * *

During the first year of Nazi rule, many of the journalists most informed about German affairs told the American and British public of their fears that German Jewry would be annihilated. These commentators included the non-Jews Dorothy Thompson and Pierre van Paassen, as well as leading Jewish authorities such as Dr. Jacob Sonderling, considered one of Germany's most eminent rabbis before his emigration to the United States a decade before, and world-renowned Semitics scholar Professor Richard Gottheil. They warned that the Nazis were carrying out a cold pogrom of economic strangulation designed to drive most of German Jewry to starvation within a generation. Almost as soon as Hitler became chancellor, his regime expelled Jews from the professions and civil service, barred them from many occupations, boycotted and shut down large numbers of Jewish businesses, and drastically reduced Jews' access to education.

From the beginning, the Nazis equated Jews with contaminants like garbage and excrement, which, if not quickly disposed of, would infect and destroy society. The Boston *Jewish Advocate* called Jews Germany's lepers. The American writer and journalist Mary Heaton Vorse emphasized in July 1933 that "in the minds of Hitler and his followers," the Jew was "not merely a stranger" but "a cancer" that must be eradicated. She noted that Germany's Jews had already been "degraded to untouchables." The Nazis saw the Jew as "the wrecker of nations."[116] The London *Jewish Chronicle* stated in April 1933 that the German government and the Nazi press had repeatedly denounced the Jews as "vermin" and satanic "monsters" who craved Christian blood, creatures "who forever plot" non-Jews' ruin. A British MP that month pointed out in the House of Commons that "night after night" the Nazis "proclaimed on the wireless that Jewry would be destroyed."[117]

NOTES

1. Mrs. Maurice J. Werner to Senator Erickson, April 17, 1933, box 6784, Central Decimal Files w1930–39 (hereafter, CDF), Department of State General Records, Record Group (hereafter, RG) 59, National Archives, College Park, MD (hereafter, NA-CP).

2. *Manchester Guardian*, April 8, 1933, 15; "The English Press–the *Manchester Guardian*'s Exposure," *Jewish Chronicle* (London), April 21, 1933, 26.

3. *The Yellow Spot: The Extermination of the Jews in Germany* (London: Victor Gollancz, 1936), 44–46.

4. Wolfgang Langhoff, *Rubber Truncheon: Being an Account of Thirteen Months Spent in a Concentration Camp* (New York: E. P. Dutton, 1935), 103, 201–2. Heilmann also served in the German Reichstag from 1928 until 1933, when the Nazis arrested him. Imprisoned in a series of concentration camps, he was "then murdered in Buchenwald at the age of 59 in 1940 in a particularly vicious manner." E. G. L., "News from Germany: Ernst Heilmann Remembered," *AJR Information*, March 1982, 9.

5. *New Leader* (UK), January 26, 1934, 3.

6. *Manchester Guardian*, January 22, 1934, 9; "Concentration Camps: Jews Still Imprisoned," *Jewish Chronicle* (London), November 23, 1934, 15A

7. Alfred M. Cohen, president of B'nai B'rith, to William Phillips, undersecretary of state, September 8, 1933, box 6786, CDF, Department of State General Records, RG 59, NA-CP. Newspapers reporting the roundup and public parading of the Jewish men included the *Manchester Guardian*, July 21, 1933, 9 and August 7, 1933, 12; *Times* (London), July 21, 1933, 15; *Washington Post*, July 21, 1933, 21; *Los Angeles Times*, July 21, 1933, 7; and *New York Times*, July 31, 1933, 1. Jacob Billikopf to Herbert Lehman, September 1, 1933, George S. Messersmith Papers, 0109 0288, Special Collections (hereafter, SC), University of Delaware Library, Newark, DE.

8. Billikopf to Lehman, September 1, 1933.

9. *Los Angeles Times*, March 16, 1933, 10; *Jewish Advocate* (Boston), March 14, 1933.

10. H. N. Brailsford, *The Nazi Terror: A Record* (London: Hereford Times, 1933), 12, citing Ellen Wilkinson, "Terror 1933," *Daily Herald* (London), March 27, 1933; Ellen Wilkinson, *The Terror in Germany* (London: British Committee for the Relief of the Victims of German Fascism, n.d.), 6.

11. *Daily Herald* (London), March 17, 1933.

12. Cleveland *Plain Dealer*, March 22, 1933, 1.

13. *New York Times*, March 21, 1933, 11.

14. *Chicago Tribune*, March 24, 1933, 3; *Philadelphia Inquirer*, May 12, 1933, 1, 4; "Being a Jew Means Being Less than an Animal," *Jewish Chronicle* (London), March 24, 1933, 27 and "An Eyewitness Account," 28; "The German Jewish Agony," *Jewish Chronicle* (London), May 5, 1933, 22; Pierre van Paassen, unidentified newspaper clipping, "Nazis' Reign of Blood Eclipses Massacres of Medieval Times," March 19 or 20, 1933, 4Zg42, Walter Winchell Papers, Dolph Briscoe Center for American History, University of Texas at Austin. On "beards," see Lucy Dawidowicz, *The War against the Jews, 1933–1945* (New York:

Bantam Books, 1986 [1975]), 201–2; Daniel Jonah Goldhagen, *Hitler's Willing Executioners: Ordinary Germans and the Holocaust* (New York: Alfred A. Knopf, 1996), 93, 189, 245–46. Goldhagen noted that tearing out, cutting off, or burning off Jews' beards, a "symbol of [their] manhood" and of their Jewish identity, was meant to communicate the Germans' "virtually limitless power" over Jews and "their denial that Jews possessed dignity." It transformed Jews into the Germans' "playthings." Goldhagen, *Hitler's Willing Executioners*, 245–46.

15. *Brooklyn Jewish Examiner*, September 30, 1932, M5, and March 10, 1933, 1; *Manchester Guardian*, May 17, 1933, 12. Lord Melchett (Henry Mond) was a former member of the House of Commons and close friend of Winston Churchill. Martin Gilbert, *Churchill and the Jews: A Lifelong Friendship* (New York: Henry Holt, 2007), 130.

16. *Cleveland Plain Dealer*, May 13, 1933; Jewish Telegraphic Agency, May 14, 1933.

17. *Jewish Advocate* (Boston), May 16, 1933, 1.

18. "Professor Richard Gottheil: American Savant Reviews the Situation," *Jewish Chronicle* (London), June 30, 1933, 16. Gottheil stated that the region that became Germany "has always been the home of anti-Semitism. Even in the early Middle Ages." He had witnessed antisemitic incitement while a student in Germany during the late nineteenth century. Gottheil had served as vice president and treasurer of the American Jewish Historical Society.

19. *Manchester Guardian*, January 22, 1934, 9; Werth to Crozier, February 7, 1933, and Voigt to Crozier, March 15, 1933, GDN Foreign Correspondence, *Manchester Guardian* Archives, John Rylands Library, University of Manchester, Deansgate, Manchester, UK.

20. *New York Times*, September 23, 1933, 9. Brin quoted in *Jewish Advocate* (Boston), November 10, 1933, 4.

21. *Jewish Advocate* (Boston), September 29, 1933, A6, October 6, 1933, 1, and June 15, 1934, 8. On October 1, 1933, Hamilton presented a public lecture at Boston's Ford Hall on the persecution of the Jews in Nazi Germany. *Jewish Advocate* (Boston), September 29, 1933, A6.

22. Mrs. Benjamin A. Kaiser, Boston, to State Department, April 6, 1933, and Herbert C. Hengstler, chief, Division of Foreign Service Administration, State Department, to Mrs. Benjamin A. Kaiser, April 20, 1933, box 6784, CDF, Department of State General Records, RG 59, NA-CP.

23. "Notes of Conversation with Dr. Kahn on Afternoon of Saturday, March 31st, 1933," ACC/3121/C11/012/021, Board of Deputies of British Jews (hereafter, BoD) Papers, London Metropolitan Archives (hereafter, LMA), London, UK.

24. *Jewish Advocate* (Boston), September 29, 1933, A6. Hamilton was not Jewish.

25. *New York Times*, September 17, 1933, 12.

26. Ibid., April 18, 1933, 10; Joachim Prinz, *Joachim Prinz, Rebellious Rabbi: An Autobiography—the German and Early American Years*, ed. Michael A. Meyer (Bloomington: Indiana University Press, 2008), 99.

27. *New York Times*, September 22, 1933, 13.

28. *Boston Globe*, August 6, 1933, 38.

29. *Brooklyn Jewish Examiner*, June 16, 1933, 1; *New York Times*, April 1, 1933, 10.

30. Jewish Telegraphic Agency, December 4, 1930 and August 20, 1933; "Riots in Paris," *Jewish Chronicle* (London), May 1, 1931, 24; *Brooklyn Jewish Examiner*, June 16, 1933, 1, 6; untitled report, n.d., reel 85, ACC/3121/E03/511, BoD Papers, US Holocaust Memorial Museum Archives (hereafter, USHMMA), Washington, DC.

31. *Jewish Advocate* (Boston), November 10, 1933, 1, 4, and November 24, 1933, 1, 4.

32. *Jewish Exponent* (Philadelphia), June 23, 1933, 8.

33. *The Brown Book of the Hitler Terror and the Burning of the Reichstag* (New York: Alfred A. Knopf, 1933), 227–29.

34. F. Voigt to Crozier, March 15, 1933, GDN Foreign Correspondence, 207/109–195, *Manchester Guardian* Archives, Rylands Library; *Manchester Guardian*, April 1, 1933, 13.

35. *Manchester Guardian*, April 9, 1932, 11.

36. "The German Barbarism: Branding the Children," *Jewish Chronicle* (London), March 16, 1933, 15; "Torturing Jewish Children in Schools," *Jewish Chronicle* (London), June 16, 1933, 18; unidentified newspaper clipping, probably *The Scotsman* (Edinburgh), 1933, 1658/7/1//9/18, Board of Deputies of British Jews Defence Committee Papers, Wiener Library for the Study of the Holocaust and Genocide, London, UK; Robert Dell, *Germany Unmasked* (London: Martin Hopkinson, 1934), 68; Lady Violet Bonham-Carter, *Child Victims of the New Germany: A Protest* (London: McCorquodale, 1934), 5. In an article entitled "Year of Hitler Nears End with Small Hope for Jews," the *New York Times* reported that the twelve-year-old daughter of an American diplomat in Germany, "full of pity" for the Jewish "pariahs" whom the teacher segregated from the "Aryan" pupils on a class excursion, tried to join the Jews but "was not permitted to do so." *New York Times*, December 24, 1933, E1.

37. Bonham-Carter, *Child Victims of the New Germany*, 5–6; *New York Times*, December 24, 1933, E1; *Palestine Post*, February 8, 1935, 4. The *Post* described a German school lesson in which the teacher pointed to the crucifix on the classroom wall and told the pupils how the Jews had murdered Jesus and "that ever since . . . they have been like a pestilence in every land in which they lived."

38. Bonham-Carter, *Child Victims of the New Germany*, 7–8; *Boston Globe*, February 9, 1934, 2.

39. *American Israelite* (Cincinnati), September 7, 1933, 1, 4. Neuberger's article "My Seven Weeks in Germany" was also published in the *Brooklyn Jewish Examiner*, September 8, 1933, 1, 6.

40. Hugh, London to J. Pierrepont Moffat, Chief Division of Western European Affairs, US State Department, July 24, 1933, with attached memorandum by Edward A. Filene, "A Report on Conditions in Germany," June 15, 1933, box 6786, CDF, Department of State General Records, RG 59, NA-CP.

41. *Jewish Exponent* (Philadelphia), September 21, 1934, 1. The article containing Rabbi Isserman's account was entitled "Desperate Plight of German Jewry. What Two Witnesses Beheld in the Reich Last Summer."

42. *Jewish Advocate* (Boston), November 24, 1933, 1, 4.

43. Bonham-Carter, *Child Victims of the New Germany*, 2–3, 6; *Manchester Guardian*, October 9, 1933, 9.

44. *Manchester Guardian*, February 22, 1934, 13.

45. "Memorandum Concerning Schools in Germany," May 6, 1933, 27/1/A, Central British Fund for World Jewish Relief Records, Wiener Library for the Study of the Holocaust and Genocide, London, UK.

46. *Brooklyn Jewish Examiner*, July 21, 1933, 1, 3. Simon's proposal foreshadowed the Wagner-Rogers bill, introduced in 1939, which would have allowed twenty thousand German Jewish children to settle in the United States unimpeded by the immigration quota. President Roosevelt would not support the bill, and it was not passed. Rafael Medoff, *FDR and the Holocaust: A Breach of Faith* (Washington, DC: David S. Wyman Institute for Holocaust Studies, 2013), 3.

47. *Manchester Guardian*, October 14, 1930, 11; *Jewish Exponent* (Philadelphia), October 17, 1930, 1.

48. Alexander Werth to Crozier, February 13, 1933, 207/45–108, *Manchester Guardian* Archives, Rylands Library, Manchester, UK.

49. "The Economic Boycott," Jewish Central Information Office (Amsterdam), November–December 1934, Central British Fund for World Jewish Relief (hereafter, CBFWJR) Papers, Wiener Library, London. This article cited as an example of a Stahlhelm and Queen Louise League antisemitic boycott their targeting of the Ascher Mayer dry goods firm in Prenzlau, a town of about twenty-five thousand in Brandenburg. This boycott forced Ascher Mayer, which had been selling to local peasants for three generations, into bankruptcy. The Queen Louise League was particularly effective because most shoppers were women. It was named for the Prussian queen who opposed Napoleon's invasion of her country. During the 1920s, many of its members were married to veterans in the Stahlhelm, facilitating cooperation between the two organizations in anti-Jewish boycotts.

50. *New York Evening Post*, March 28, 1933, 2; *Brooklyn Jewish Examiner*, March 10, 1933, 1; *Yellow Spot*, 38. The *Jewish Examiner* drew its report from a special cable from Copenhagen.

51. Max Rhoade to William Phillips, March 21, 1933, box 6782, CDF, Department of State General Records, RG 59, NA-CP. Rhoade's summary was based on dispatches from the New York Yiddish newspaper *Der Tog*.

52. Frederic Sackett to Secretary of State, March 10, 1933, box 6782, CDF, Department of State General Records, RG 59, NA-CP.

53. *Yellow Spot*, 37–38.

54. "The Economic Boycott," Jewish Central Information Office, November–December 1934, CBFWJR Papers, Wiener Library.

55. *Daily Herald* (London), April 1, 1933, 11; *Yellow Spot*, 39–40.

56. *New York Times*, April 2, 1933, 29.

57. Ibid.; *Yellow Spot*, 39–40.

58. George A. Gordon to Cordell Hull, April 10, 1933, CDF, box 6784, Department of State General Records, RG 59, NA-CP. The chargé d'affaires headed the embassy when the ambassador was away.

59. *New York Herald Tribune*, April 1, 1933, 1, 4.

60. Ibid., 1, 4.

61. *New York Herald Tribune*, April 2, 1933, 1.

62. *New York Times*, April 2, 1933, 1. *Chicago Tribune* Berlin correspondent Sigrid Schultz published three front-page articles on the boycott in early April 1933: *Chicago Tribune*, April 1, 1933, 1; April 2, 1933, 1; and April 4, 1933, 1.

63. *New York Evening Post*, April 1, 1933, 1.

64. *Manchester Guardian*, April 1, 1933, 13.

65. *Boston Globe*, April 7, 1933, 25.

66. Dr. Leon Zeitlin, "A Tragic April Fool's Day: April 1, 1933, *AJR Information*, April 1953, microfilm P.C. 3, reel 33, Wiener Library, London.

67. Robert Weltsch, "25 Years after Boycott Day," *AJR Information*, April 1958, microfilm P.C. 3, reel 33, Wiener Library, London. Weltsch was at the time the editor of the Berlin-based *Judische Rundschau*, journal of the Zionist Federation of Germany. Dimitry Shumsky, "Weltsch, Robert," in *Yivo Encyclopedia of Jews in Eastern Europe*, accessed August 5, 2019, https://yivoencyclopedia.org/article.aspx/Weltsch_Robert.

68. "The Nazi Boycott of German Jews," *Jewish Chronicle* (London), April 10, 1953, n.p.; C. C. Aronsfeld, "Memento of Emancipation: 25 Years after the Boycott," *Gates of Zion* (1958), 13, microfilm P.C. 3, reel 33, Wiener Library, London.

69. "The Martyrdom of German Jewry: Brutal Process of Economic Extinction," *Jewish Chronicle* (London), April 7, 1933, 24.

70. "The Tragedy of German Jewry—Vigorous Economic Persecution Continues—Starvation for 600,000 Jews," *Jewish Chronicle* (London), April 14, 1933, 16.

71. "International Conference for the Relief of German Jewry, October 29 to November 1, 1933," Central British Fund for World Jewish Relief Records, 27/6/35, Wiener Library, London.

72. *New York Times*, April 16, 1933, 21.

73. George A. Gordon to Secretary of State Cordell Hull, April 10, 1933, box 6784, CDF, Department of State General Records, RG 59, NA-CP.

74. William L. Shirer, *The Rise and Fall of the Third Reich* (New York: Simon and Schuster, 1960), 245.

75. Leon Dominian to Secretary of State, November 17, 1933, box 6786, CDF, Department of State General Records, RG 59, NA-CP.

76. Raymond H. Geist, American consul, Berlin, to Honorable Secretary of State, December 15, 1933, box 6786, CDF, Department of State General Records, RG 59, NA-CP. Geist noted that the "conservative" Reich minister of commerce, Kurt Schmitt, feared that the sudden closing of Jewish stores would adversely affect the German economy. Other members of the German cabinet opposed Schmitt, and his attempts to stop the closings were "totally ignored, especially in the provinces."

77. *Manchester Guardian* , March 31, 1934, 11; Jewish Telegraphic Agency, April 1, 1934.

78. Charles M. Hathaway Jr. to the Honorable William E. Dodd, July 24, 1934, "Subject: Anti-Semitism in Franconia," CDF, Department of State General Records, RG 59, NA-CP.

79. Saul Friedländer, *Nazi Germany and the Jews*, vol. 1, *The Years of Persecution, 1933–1939* (New York: HarperCollins, 1997), 57.

80. *New York Times*, May 6, 1933, 8, and May 10, 1933, 1, 11; George S. Messersmith to Secretary of State Cordell Hull, May 6, 1933, George S. Messersmith Papers, SC, University of Delaware Library, Newark, DE.

81. Leonidas E. Hill, "The Nazi Attack on 'Un-German' Literature, 1933–1945," in *The Holocaust and the Book: Destruction and Preservation*, ed. Jonathan Rose (Amherst: University of Massachusetts Press, 2001), 15–16; Michael Stephen Steinberg, *Sabers and Brownshirts: The German Students' Path to National Socialism, 1918–1935* (Chicago: University of Chicago Press, 1977), 140; *New York Times*, May 6, 1933, 8, and May 11, 1933, 1; *New York Evening Post* , May 11, 1933; *Chicago Tribune*, May 11, 1933, 4; "Bibliocaust," *Time*, May 22, 1933, 21; Lillie Shultz, director of publicity and research, American Jewish Congress, to Walter Winchell, May 6, 1933, 4Zg43, Walter Winchell Papers, Dolph Briscoe Center for American History, University of Texas at Austin.

82. Messersmith to Hull, June 17, 1933, George S. Messersmith Papers, SC, University of Delaware Library, Newark, DE.

83. Stephen H. Norwood, *The Third Reich in the Ivory Tower: Complicity and Conflict on American Campuses* (New York: Cambridge University Press, 2009), 4, 61.

84. Joseph Tenenbaum, "European Jewry Facing Gravest Emergency" (address, Annual Sessions of the American Jewish Congress, Washington, DC, June 25–27, 1932), BoD Papers, reel 73, ACC/3121/E03/141–142, USHMMA.

85. Messersmith to Hull, May 6, 1933.

86. Friedländer, *Nazi Germany and the Jews*, 1:56–57.

87. "Nazi Terror Described by German Fugitive," *Jewish Daily Bulletin*, March 27, 1933, 1; "Minutes of Meeting of Committee on Aid of German Children," January 3, 1934, American Jewish Committee Papers, ajcarchives.org.

88. *New York Times*, December 24, 1933, E1, and December 31, 1934, 4; *Palestine Post*, December 17, 1934, 5; *Times* (London), May 28, 1934, 14.

89. *Brown Book*, 278–79; *Jewish Exponent* (Philadelphia), February 3, 1933, 7.

90. George A. Gordon to Acting Secretary of State, July 8, 1933, in *Foreign Relations of the United States: Diplomatic Papers*, vol. 2, *1933* (Washington, DC: Government Printing Office, 1949), 356.

91. *Jewish Exponent* (Philadelphia), December 22, 1933; "Memorandum of the Information Department," May 14, 1934, ACC/3121/C/012/014, BoD Papers, LMA.

92. *New York Times*, August 19, 1933, 5; *Manchester Guardian*, August 23, 1933, 9.

93. *Daily Herald* (London), December 17, 1934.

94. *Brown Book*, 176.

95. "Memorandum for the Information Department," May 14, 1934, ACC/3121/C/012/014, BoD Papers, LMA.

96. *New York Times*, March 30, 1934, 26; *Jewish Advocate* (Boston), March 31, 1934; *Manchester Guardian*, March 31, 1934, 11.

97. Rhoade to Phillips, March 21, 1933, CDF, box 6782, Department of State General Records, RG 59, NA-CP; *Palestine Post*, March 18, 1935; *Chicago Tribune*, July 19, 1933, 14.

98. "Notes of Conversation with Dr. Kahn on afternoon of Saturday, March 31, 1933," ACC 3121/C11/012/021, BoD Papers, LMA.

99. *Der Stürmer* (*Ritualmord-Nummer*), May 1, 1934, in 882, Documents on Antisemitism and Ritual Murder, Wiener Library, London. See, for example, *New York Times*, May 4, 12, 17, and 20, 1934; *Manchester Guardian*, May 2, 3, 4, 5, and 18, 1934, and *Times* (London), May 2, 10, 11, 15, and 16, 1934.

100. "Memorandum of the Information Department," May 14, 1934, ACC/3121/C/012/014, BoD Papers, LMA.

101. "Ritual Murder Protest by Chief Rabbi," *Evening Standard* (London), May 11, 1934, 882/9, Documents on Antisemitism and Ritual Murder, Wiener Library, London; Shirer, *Rise and Fall of the Third Reich*, 50, 73; *Times* (London), May 16, 1934, 15; *Jewish Exponent* (Philadelphia), June 15, 1934; "Julius Streicher," November 28, 1935, ACC/3123/C11/12/21, BoD Papers, LMA.

102. "Streicher on Jesus," *Jewish Chronicle* (London), November 16, 1934, 16.

103. Louis W. Bondy, *Racketeers of Hatred: Julius Streicher and the Jew-Baiters' International* (London: Newman Wolsey, 1946), 43.

104. "Julius Streicher," November 28, 1935, ACC/3123/C11/12/21, BoD Papers, LMA; Bondy, *Racketeers of Hatred*, 45–46.

105. *Daily Herald* (London), February 1, 1935.

106. Schachna Maurice Salomen to President Franklin D. Roosevelt, May 22, 1934, box 6787, CDFR, Department of State General Records, RG 59, NA-CP. The following note was attached to Salomen's letter: "Louis McH. Howe—referred to State Dept."

107. Joseph Tenenbaum, *Race and Reich* (New York: Twayne, 1956), 162–63.

108. Ibid., 163; Martin Gilbert, *The Holocaust* (New York: Henry Holt, 1985), 32–33.

109. *New York Times*, October 27, 1933, 11; *Times* (London), August 26, 1933, 7.

110. *Daily Herald* (London), November 1 and December 1, 1933.

111. "The Reminiscences of Gerhart Henry Seger," December 1950, Oral History Research Office, Butler Library, Columbia University, New York, NY, 54–55, 66–67, 82; "Germany/New Acts of Terrorism," *Jewish Chronicle* (London), March 16, 1934, 18; *Daily Herald* (London), August 2, 1933.

112. *Times* (London), September 19, 1933, 13.

113. "Germany/Nazis' Revolution for 1934," *Jewish Chronicle* (London), January 5, 1934, 16; "Germany/New Acts of Terrorism," 18; *Manchester Guardian*, December 30, 1933, 13, and October 27, 1934, 8.

114. *New York Times*, October 25, 1933, 3; *Boston Herald*, November 27, 1933, 1, 3; *Boston Globe*, November 27, 1933, 1, 22; *Boston Post*, November 27, 1933, 1, 10; Norwood, *Third Reich in the Ivory Tower*, 28–29.

115. "The Concentration Camps," *Jewish Chronicle* (London), March 16, 1934, 18.

116. *Jewish Advocate* (Boston), October 10, 1933, 3; Mary Heaton Vorse, "Getting the Jews out of Germany," *New Republic*, July 19, 1933, 256–57.

117. "Germany: The Jewish Agony," *Jewish Chronicle* (London), April 21, 1933, 12; "The Debate in the House," *Jewish Chronicle* (London), April 21, 1933, 15; J. H. Hertz, "In Ancient Egypt and Present-Day Germany," *Jewish Chronicle* (London), April 21, 1933, 18.

THREE

—w—

A TIDAL WAVE OF PROTEST

March to May 1933

DURING THE EARLY MONTHS OF Hitler's rule, grassroots Jews in the United States and Britain staged massive protests against Nazi antisemitism, which much of the Jewish leadership in both countries discouraged and attempted to contain. These demonstrations and rallies, held in the streets, municipal auditoriums, synagogues, and schools, along with spontaneous boycotts of German goods and services, were influenced by the history of rank-and-file Jewish challenges to pogroms in Eastern Europe and the conviction of Captain Alfred Dreyfus in France, dating back to the late nineteenth century. The oldest and most well-established Jewish organizations, the American Jewish Committee (AJC) and the Board of Deputies of British Jews (BoD), representing the more affluent and acculturated Jews, were deeply alarmed about Nazi intentions but feared that aggressive public Jewish protest against Hitlerism, such as street marches, organized boycotts, and public rallies with predominantly Jewish speakers, would precipitate a dangerous antisemitic backlash in the United States and Britain and further endanger Germany's Jews. By contrast, the American Jewish Congress (AJCongress), whose constituency was largely working-class and lower-middle-class Jews of Eastern European background sympathetic to Zionism, supported most grassroots protest and helped coordinate it. The BoD did convene public rallies against Nazi persecution of Jews but with prominent non-Jews as the primary speakers. A year before Hitler became chancellor of Germany, the AJC, the BoD, and their French counterpart, the Alliance Israélite Universelle (AIU), began regular joint discussions about how to defend German Jewry in the event the Nazis assumed power.[1]

On January 21, 1932, Bernhard Kahn, secretary-general of the Jewish Joint Distribution Committee in Berlin, which provided social services to Jewish refugees, came to Paris and warned AIU officials that if the Nazis formed a government in Germany they would make German Jews' lives "impossible."[2] The Nazis' spectacular gains in the September 14, 1930 elections had made them a sizeable bloc. The AJC, the BoD, and the AIU recognized that a Nazi-controlled Germany was now a serious possibility.[3]

Kahn contended that the Nazis would not be able to achieve their objective—in his view, the removal of German Jews' citizenship rights—entirely by legal means. Anticipating the cold pogrom, he predicted that they would accomplish this by imposing arbitrary commercial taxes on Jews, boycotting their stores and offices, and evicting them from "administrative functions, university careers, [the] judiciary, etc."[4]

Traveling to New York and London, Kahn shared his assessment with leaders of the AJC and BoD. He called for a private meeting of Jewish leaders from London, New York, and Paris to discuss arranging shelter and support for German Jews in the event of the "massive exodus" that Nazi control of Germany would surely precipitate. In February 1932, the Joint Foreign Committee (JFC) of the BoD and Anglo-Jewish Association (AJA) met in London with another leader of German Jewry, Dr. Heinrich Stern, whose view of the situation was similar to Kahn's.[5]

In a February 2, 1932 letter to AJC president Cyrus Adler, the AIU wrote that the Nazis' "daily agitation through the press and rallies [and] storm troopers' violence" had convinced it that they might soon take control of Germany— legally or by force. Because the Nazis "openly proclaimed" their antisemitic program, the AIU proposed convening a private meeting of AJC, BoD, and AIU leaders to develop a strategy to protect German Jewry should the Nazis assume power. Responding to a similar inquiry from the BoD, Adler stated that the AJC had conferred with the AJCongress leadership, which favored Jewish organizations' initiating "agitation" on behalf of German Jewry. The AJC, he explained, preferred instead to persuade the mainstream press and "some outstanding non-Jewish personality" to take up German Jewry's cause.[6] Both organizations agreed in opposing a boycott. In August 1933, the AJCongress would break with the AJC and endorse the boycott movement that the Jewish masses in both the United States and Britain had established months before.

As early as the summer of 1932, American Jews at the grassroots had proposed an organized worldwide boycott of German goods and services should Hitler assume power. On August 19, 1932, the *Brooklyn Jewish Examiner* reported approvingly the Chicago *Jewish Courier*'s endorsement of such a boycott. The *Courier* saw the boycott as a powerful weapon against Nazism, because Jews "consume[d] more German products than all the Balkan countries together."

In muscular language, it proclaimed, "To vanquish Hitlerism, it is necessary to take the offensive." The next week, the *Examiner* reported that many of its readers had written, "demanding a universal boycott of German goods."[7]

In March 1933, Hitler established full dictatorial power and unleashed a "reign of terror" against Jews, political opponents, and trade unionists, intensifying the alarm not only of the Jewish communities and labor movements in the United States and Britain but also of many other supporters of democracy, civil liberties, and ethnic and religious tolerance. The Nazis savagely beat Jews in the streets, invaded homes, and arrested Jews, Social Democrats, and Communists. Many of the arrested were imprisoned in Nazi torture cellars; thousands were shipped off to concentration camps. The Reichstag had passed the Enabling Act that month, ceding its legislative power to Hitler's cabinet. Hitler's arrest of the Reichstag's Communist deputies, on whom he blamed the February 27 Reichstag fire, made possible the two-thirds majority required to enact the law. The mass dismissals of Jews from university faculties, which began shortly afterward, led to the flight from Germany of many of its leading scholars and intellectuals, including several Nobel Prize winners.

Aware that Jews at the grassroots were inundating the White House and the US State Department with letters and telegrams demanding a strong American diplomatic protest against Nazi antisemitism, the AJCongress's national executive committee met on March 12, 1933, to plan a coordinated national day of protest against the Nazis' antisemitic policies and atrocities. At the suggestion of Dr. Samuel Margoshes, editor of the New York Yiddish newspaper *Der Tog* (*The Day*), the national executive committee decided that a central feature of the protest would be a mass meeting at Madison Square Garden. Simultaneous street parades were scheduled for eleven major US cities, and many smaller communities around the country planned protest rallies.[8]

AJCongress president, Bernard S. Deutsch, informed the press that the national executive committee had deliberately scheduled its meeting on Purim in order to identify Adolf Hitler with Haman, the Persian official in the Hebrew Bible's book of Esther who had attempted to exterminate the Jews. The holiday celebrated Queen Esther's thwarting of Haman's genocidal plan. On Purim, 1933, rabbis across the United States devoted their sermons to denouncing Hitler as the modern Haman.[9]

On the evening of March 19, the AJCongress held a conference at the Astor Hotel in New York City, attended by fifteen hundred representatives of national, regional, and local Jewish organizations, to build public support for the day of mass anti-Nazi protest. Deutsch credited the Jewish masses for taking the initiative in calling for a day of protest. The AJCongress had issued the conference call "at the insistent and overwhelming demand of a practically unanimous Jewry impatient to express its horror and indignation" at Nazi antisemitism.[10]

Committed to quiet diplomacy and mistrustful of working-class Jews of East European origin, the AJC Executive Committee met earlier that day, hoping to persuade the AJCongress to delay action. Judge Irving Lehman doubted the AJC could succeed in this effort, because the "[AJ]Congress regards itself as a mouthpiece of the inarticulate Jewish masses of the United States, and is opposed on principle to holding them back from self-expression." James Rosenberg suggested that in any event, the AJC should issue a statement signed by members of its executive committee and other prominent persons "disavowing the intemperate expressions of the masses and expressing the sober hope . . . that the German Government would deal justly with all parts of the German population." Executive Board members Rosenberg and former New York Supreme Court justice Joseph Proskauer decided to attend the AJCongress conference in an effort to prevail upon it "to hold off demonstrations for the time being."[11]

Conference delegates were, however, nearly unanimous that evening in backing coordinated national street protests and rallies. Proskauer and Rosenberg, who claimed that "marches and meetings" would intensify Nazi persecution of Jews, provided the only dissent. Rabbi Stephen S. Wise, AJCongress honorary president, portrayed the AJC as marginal to the anti-Nazi struggle, declaring that its representatives "should not have waited all these years to attend a meeting under [the] auspices of the American Jewish Congress." J. George Fredman, national commander of the Jewish War Veterans of the United States (JWV), proposed an organized boycott of German goods and services, which the AJCongress leadership was not yet prepared to support.[12]

The AJCongress leadership mistrusted the JWV, which it considered "militant," and had not invited it to the conference. When a JWV delegation arrived at the Astor uninvited, conference organizers prevented them from entering the hotel elevator. After fierce protest, AJCongress executive director Abraham Cohen agreed to allow Fredman and a few other JWV members into the gathering.[13]

American Jews had demonstrated their ability to mobilize in huge numbers against antisemitic atrocities when, in the years immediately after World War I, they staged massive grassroots street demonstrations in America's largest cities to protest the waves of pogroms in Poland, Romania, and the Ukraine. Several hundred thousand Jews in New York City took part in "gigantic, spontaneous parades" on the Lower East Side on the afternoon of May 21, 1919. Most Jews employed in factories, both men and women, stopped work at noon to start the street demonstrations, and "tens of thousands of [Jewish] children left their classrooms. . . . Jewish men, women, and children, carrying banners in Yiddish and English paraded up and down the streets of the east side." "Hundreds of small shops" also shut down. The parades were often led by Jewish soldiers, veterans of the world war. The *New York Times* reported on its front page that this "big human protest . . . occurred without an advance plan or program, parades forming everywhere." Pushcart peddlers abandoned their stands to take part. That evening, a crowd that police estimated at between one hundred fifty thousand and two hundred thousand converged for a protest rally at Madison Square Garden, from seven to ten times its capacity. The main speaker, former US Supreme Court justice Charles Evans Hughes, denounced the pogroms as "ruthless barbarity" and called on all Americans to join the Jews in "a mighty protest."[14]

In May and June 1919, Jews in Chicago, Boston, Los Angeles, and Washington, DC, held similar parades and mass meetings protesting the pogroms. On the same day as the New York demonstrations, twenty-five thousand Jews in Chicago jammed sidewalks and blocked traffic in the Loop to express their outrage. A week later, fifteen thousand Jews paraded through the major downtown streets of Boston under the auspices of the Greater Boston Committee for the Protection of Jewish Rights in Poland and Eastern European Countries. In Los Angeles on June 11, ten thousand Jews marched behind a large contingent of Jewish soldiers and sailors. A line of Jewish children carried a banner that read, "Do Not Feed Baby Killers," urging a cessation of aid to Poland.[15]

On November 24, 1919, as many as half a million Jews in New York left work to stage a "Day of Sorrow" to mourn the massacres of one hundred thousand Jews in the Ukraine, participating in solemn processions, listening to addresses, and attending rallies. Rabbi Stephen Wise was one of the principal speakers at an evening protest meeting at Carnegie Hall, along with US Secretary of the Navy Josephus Daniels, Jewish leader Jacob Schiff, and New York mayor John Hylan. Marching in the major afternoon procession were numerous Jewish veterans of the US armed forces in the world war, the Spanish-American War, and the Civil War. Joining them were men who during the world war had served in the Jewish Legion of the British Army, the first Jewish armed force since the crushing of the Bar Kochba Rebellion in 135 CE.[16]

A few days after the March 19, 1933, AJCongress conference, the JWV, giving expression to growing grassroots Jewish militancy, demanded that President Roosevelt issue a formal protest to the Hitler government against its antisemitic policies and sever diplomatic and commercial relations with Germany. The JWV also announced that it would press President Roosevelt to appoint a Jew as US ambassador to Germany to indicate American disgust for Nazi antisemitism.[17]

On March 23, the JWV staged an anti-Nazi street parade in New York City to publicize these demands and its call for an organized boycott of German goods and services. About four thousand marched from St. Mark's Place on the Lower East Side to city hall, including seven hundred JWV members and an equal number from other veterans' organizations. They were joined by a large contingent from the heavily Jewish fur industry. Ten thousand New Yorkers watched from the sidewalks. The veterans marched in disciplined columns four abreast, carrying only the American and Zionist flags and veterans' organization banners. New York mayor John O'Brien and his staff reviewed the parade at city hall. O'Brien announced that he would speak at the March 27 Madison Square Garden anti-Nazi rally. After the parade ended, J. George Fredman and other JWV leaders proceeded to the British consulate and "presented an appeal to the British government . . . to temporarily set aside the quota and financial restrictions on Jewish immigration to Palestine."[18]

News of the JWV parade was transmitted "to the ends of the earth" by press, radio, and newsreels, informing a world audience of significant American opposition to Nazi antisemitism less than two months after Hitler came to power. The entire New York City press and many foreign newspapers carried reports of the parade. The *New York Herald Tribune* placed its story on page 1. The British Labour Party newspaper, the London *Daily Herald*, ran a banner headline about the JWV march that spanned six columns on the front page: "Jews World Boycott of Germany . . . Chant of Dead Sung in U.S." The headline referred both to Jewish grassroots militancy—at a time when the major Jewish organizations had yet to endorse the boycott—and to Jews' fear of Germany's annihilationist intentions. A London group called the Jewish United Defence Association circulated anti-Nazi leaflets including a photograph captioned, "American War Veterans in New York protest against Nazi terror."[19] In the military language favored by grassroots Jewish protestors, the JWV warned the Nazis that the march "was only the opening gun" in its struggle against them and emphasized that it had been "a mighty salvo."[20]

Energized by what it had billed as its "monster parade demonstration," the JWV became the first organization in the United States to initiate a systematic boycott of German goods and services. The day after the parade, the JWV sent one thousand form letters to businesses across the country asking them to boycott all German goods. The JWV offered seals to be affixed to letters that read "For Humanity's Sake—Don't Buy German Goods." It condemned as "apathetic" the "so-called leading Jewish organizations," which had failed to support an organized boycott. The JWV claimed that the AJC remained wedded to medieval Jewry's approach of "diplomacy, cringing, begging and praying." The AJCongress was too "old" and "conservative."[21]

The American Communist Party (CP) denounced the JWV's call for a boycott and its demand that the United States break diplomatic relations with Nazi Germany, although members of its veterans' group, the Workers Ex-Servicemen's League, participated in the march. The CP, following the Soviets' Third Period line, rejected any cooperation with groups to its right. During the Third Period, 1928 to 1935, the Communists argued that world capitalism was entering its death throes and that all advanced industrial nations, including Germany, were on the verge of proletarian revolution. All groups to the Communists' right were allies of a decaying bourgeoisie that would turn to fascism to suppress proletarian insurgency. Cooperating with mainstream Jewish organizations like the AJCongress or JWV (or with socialists or reformist trade unions) distracted workers from their "revolutionary tasks." The CP argued that the appeal to boycott German goods and services was only an American capitalist scheme to capture the German market. The day after the JWV parade, the CP newspaper *Daily Worker* condemned the JWV's call for a boycott and termination of US diplomatic relations with Nazi Germany as "reactionary chauvinistic demands that would . . . provok[e] a war situation" and harm "the German masses, who are being so savagely persecuted by the Nazi regime."[22]

The Communists, committed to a rigid class analysis, differed from mainstream Jewish organizations in deliberately downplaying Nazi antisemitism. For the CP, Nazism represented a desperate maneuver by an embattled bourgeoisie to maintain control of society and protect its profits in the last stage of capitalist decay. A *New York Evening Post* report on March 25 of a Communist demonstration at the German consulate in New York noted that nearly all the placards emphasized Nazi-Communist struggle "rather than the attacks on Jews."[23]

Many who enlisted in the JWV boycott campaign were aware that there was a precedent in the United States for a national boycott movement to protest antisemitism. In 1899 Jews in many major American cities had organized a boycott of French goods and of the Paris Exposition of 1900 to protest a French military tribunal's upholding of a guilty verdict in the case of Captain Alfred Dreyfus, a French Jewish artillery officer falsely accused of passing military secrets to Germany. Dreyfus's conviction had sparked pogroms in many French cities and towns and in Algeria. The boycott received especially strong support from working- and lower-middle-class Jews of Eastern European origin. Mass boycott rallies were staged in New York City, Chicago, and Washington, DC, and significant numbers of Jews in cities such as St. Louis and Kansas City committed themselves not to purchase French goods or visit the Paris Exposition. Editorials in prominent American metropolitan dailies like the *Chicago Tribune* endorsed the boycott. US Congressman Jefferson Levy, who represented a New York City district, had introduced a resolution in the House of Representatives to withdraw US government backing for the Paris Exposition because of the Dreyfus case.[24]

The JWV's boycott campaign alarmed the US State Department, which feared antagonizing the German government. A special agent of the department investigating the JWV reported in June 1933 that it had already written one hundred thousand letters to Jews throughout the United States urging them to join the boycott movement and had sent out five million boycott seals. This was impressive, because the JWV had only "a small desk-room" in New York for an office, with "but one girl on duty." The agent was alarmed by the JWV's plan to "forc[e] through other conventions of war veterans" pro-boycott resolutions similar to the one it was preparing to pass at its upcoming meeting in Atlantic City. He stated that although the JWV was "scrupulous in their efforts to dissociate themselves from the Communists," it "seem[ed] to approve" the Communists' "general views." This charge was highly inaccurate and reflected the influence of the Hitler government's propaganda, which claimed that the anti-Nazi movement outside Germany was Communist directed. In fact, American Communists had established their own veterans' organization, the Workers Ex-Servicemen's League, rather than join the anti-Communist JWV. JWV members barred a Communist from speaking from the audience at the March 27 anti-Nazi rally in Cleveland.[25]

From England, the *Manchester Guardian* reported that public outrage over the Nazi dictatorship's oppressive policies continued to "flame high in the United States." Thousands of telegrams were "pouring in" to President Roosevelt and members of Congress urging that the United States make an official protest to Germany against the Nazi persecution of Jews.[26]

Many strongly worded telegrams and letters demanding immediate action from President Roosevelt came from non-Jewish government bodies and from civic and trade groups. The city clerk of Revere, Massachusetts, notified President Roosevelt that the city council had passed a resolution at its March 13 meeting condemning the Hitler government's plans for "establishing a complete Anti-Jewish program throughout Germany on a scale as terrible as any instance of Jewish persecution in two thousand years." The resolution stated that "the entire 600,000 Jewish residents are to be subjected to many types of persecution and possible murder." The city council appealed to Roosevelt to apply pressure on the German government to end its persecution of the Jews.[27] The Johnson County, Iowa, Taxpayers' League sent a similar resolution, urging Roosevelt to use his "every power" to protect German Jewry.[28] Citizens of Erie County, Pennsylvania, "together with Americans in all parts of the country," wrote to the president to express their "horror and indignation at the brutal attacks on Jews and members of other minority groups in Germany" and at Germany's "reversion to medieval barbarism." They denounced "the policy of boycotting Jewish merchants and professional men, [and] of preventing professors, lawyers and physicians from pursuing the professions."[29] New York City's taxicab industry representatives passed a resolution calling on Roosevelt to make every effort to "once and for all end the attacks and terrorism on the Jews of Germany." The resolution declared that German government policies "threatened a return to the anti-Semitic spirit of the Middle Ages, based on tyranny, religious bigotry, and race hatred."[30]

Roosevelt almost never mentioned the issue of Nazi antisemitism publicly before the Kristallnacht in November 1938. In response to a query at his March 24 press conference about requests for him to take action "in connection with the reported persecution of the Jews over in Germany by the Hitler government," Roosevelt acknowledged receiving "a good many." He stated dismissively that the White House had sent all of them to Secretary of State Hull and made no further comment.[31]

In the week before March 27, the American press gave almost continuous coverage to the planning of the Madison Square Garden rally. On March 20, the New York Herald Tribune ran a front-page article headlined "Militant Jewish Rally Here Opens National Drive against Hitlerism/Police Called as Crowd Overflows Astor Ballroom." The next day, the New York Times published a front-page article headlined "Jews Here Demand Washington Action" against the persecution of German Jewry. The New York Evening Post on March 22 featured a story on page 1 headlined "Jews to Fast Monday in U.S. Nazi Protest/Rabbinical Groups Order Day of Prayer." The article reported that Rabbi Stephen S. Wise and other rally participants would deliver speeches "over a nationwide radio hookup" condemning Nazi antisemitism. On the same day, the Boston Herald carried a front-page story reporting American Jews' plans to stage mass protests against Nazi antisemitism in eleven cities, including Boston. On March 24, the Herald Tribune reported on page 1 that the March 27 Madison Square Garden rally would represent two million American Jews. It informed readers that simultaneous protest meetings would be held in three hundred US cities "and in virtually every European country outside Germany, as well as in Palestine."[32]

On March 27, the *New York Evening Post,* under the headline "Jews Show Solid Front," stated that the AJCongress was receiving an avalanche of messages supporting the national day of protest from Jews across the country. Rabbis announced "a day of fasting and prayer."[33] In Palestine, Jews throughout the Yishuv determined to fast on March 27 in sympathy with German Jewry.[34]

In the days before March 27, even the French press gave the New York City anti-Nazi protest considerable attention. The Paris dailies *Le Temps* and *Figaro* reported that Jewish stores throughout the city would close at 2:00 p.m. and that taxicabs would stay off the streets between 2:00 p.m. and 3:00 p.m. to express solidarity with the Madison Square Garden rally. They also noted that the governors of Pennsylvania, Massachusetts, Wyoming, and South Carolina had sent telegrams of support to the AJCongress.[35] *Le Temps* reported anti-Nazi demonstrations at the New York offices of both German shipping companies, the Hamburg-American and North German Lloyd. It added that many American Jews had canceled travel reservations on German liners.[36]

Jews across New York City worked feverishly to mobilize supporters for the Madison Square Garden rally. The Jewish Telegraphic Agency reported such passionate support in the Jewish community that it predicted a record crowd would "storm" the amphitheater. The Federation of Hebrew Schools of Greater New York called on all Talmud Torahs and yeshivas to stop classes at 6:00 p.m. so that their principals and teachers could speak to them about the Nazi threat to German Jewry. The students were then to "march in bodies" to Madison Square Garden. The federation had more than 250 school affiliates, with sixty thousand pupils. The National Federation of Orthodox Congregations, representing one thousand congregations in the United States, passed a resolution endorsing the national day of protest and asked Jews outside New York City to participate in rallies in their localities. The Orthodox resolution explicitly stated that German Jewry faced annihilation, declaring, "We must stay the hand of destruction."[37]

Many distinguished non-Jews agreed to speak at Madison Square Garden, including former New York governor and 1928 Democratic presidential nominee Al Smith, US senator Robert Wagner of New York, Mayor O'Brien, Bishop Francis McConnell, and American Federation of Labor (AFL) president William Green. Jewish speakers included Rabbi Wise, Bernard S. Deutsch, Samuel Margoshes, *Jewish Daily Forward* editor Abraham Cahan, and Morris Rothenberg, president of the Zionist Organization of America. Although the AJC had opposed a day of mass protest, James Rosenberg was a speaker at Madison Square Garden. The AJC found a rally highlighting prominent non-Jewish speakers acceptable.[38]

For the most part, the Madison Square Garden speakers, both Christian and Jewish, adopted a cautious approach, strongly condemning the Nazi leadership but minimizing the role of the German people in persecuting Jews. Al Smith, for example, compared the Nazis to the Ku Klux Klan but "absolved the German people from any wrongdoing or sympathy with anti-Semitism." Still, he emphasized the necessity of making a strong public stand against Nazism, declaring that "he had never appeared at any public gathering with greater satisfaction than at the Garden rally to protest against the persecution of Jews." Christian speakers "appeal[ed] ... to the German people to have the persecutions stopped in the name of humanity and Christian principles." None of the speakers called for an organized boycott of German goods and services. Bishop John Dunn of the Catholic Archdiocese of New York withdrew from the speakers' list the morning of the rally in deference to the wishes of the US State Department, which claimed that the "mistreatment of Jews in Germany had been stopped."[39]

The national day of protest drew enormous support, with an estimated one million Jews participating in three hundred protest rallies across the United States. Madison Square Garden was packed to its twenty-two-thousand-person capacity, with thirty-five thousand more, unable to gain entry, listening to the speeches over loudspeakers in surrounding blocks. It was reported to be the largest protest meeting in American history. The NBC and Columbia radio systems broadcast the proceedings throughout the United States.[40]

In Brooklyn's largely Jewish and working-class Brownsville section, the day of protest sparked grassroots calls for an organized boycott. Business was suspended for two hours as ten thousand people, many shouting, "Down with Hitler," marched through the streets in protest against the persecution of German Jewry. One placard carried by demonstrators announced, "The Sutter Avenue Merchants Pledge Boycott to German Products." Other placards denounced the "German Massacres." After the march ended, participants convened a mass meeting at the PS 84 auditorium, where city officials, rabbis, and others condemned the Nazis' antisemitic policies and atrocities. As in Manhattan, "throngs filled the auditorium and overflowed into the streets." Loudspeakers broadcast the speeches to those outside.[41]

The boycott garnered similarly strong support in the heavily Jewish Williamsburg section of Brooklyn. The day after the Madison Square Garden rally, three thousand Jews met at PS 168 and resolved to boycott German-made goods. The resolution had been circulated throughout Williamsburg and had the support of one hundred thousand residents.[42]

Headlines emphasized the enormous turnouts in major cities and the strong indignation expressed by both Jews and many non-Jews about Nazi antisemitic atrocities. New York's leading newspapers, the *Times* and the *Herald Tribune*, splashed news of the March 27 coordinated national demonstrations in banner headlines across their front pages, illustrated by several photographs. The articles were continued on inside pages, taking up a huge amount of space. The *Herald Tribune*'s headline, covering two articles across five columns, read, "22,000 Pack Anti-Hitler Rally at Garden/Labor and All Faiths Combine in Protest/Nazis Threaten Reprisals Against Jews." The *Times* published the full text of Al Smith's and Rabbi Wise's speeches on inside pages. The *Cleveland Plain Dealer*'s front-page article called the Madison Square Garden rally "one of the greatest mass demonstrations in [New York] city history."[43]

Massive numbers joined marches and attended rallies against Nazi antisemitism in many other large metropolises. In Philadelphia, a capacity crowd of six thousand Jews participated in the AJCongress mass protest meeting at the Metropolitan Opera House. Another two thousand, unable to gain admission, pressed against police lines outside, where they listened to the speeches over amplifiers. The speakers included leading non-Jews such as Cornelia Pinchot, wife of Pennsylvania governor Gifford Pinchot and herself prominent in labor causes, and John Phillips, the president of the Pennsylvania State Federation of Labor, as well as Jews like James Waterman Wise, a supporter of an organized boycott and the son of Rabbi Stephen S. Wise, and Harry Berger, manager of the *Jewish Daily Forward*.[44] In the spring of 1933, James Waterman Wise published one of the first books about Hitler's Germany, *Swastika: The Nazi Terror*, in which he stated that the Nazi brutality against Jews was unparalleled in human history. Cleveland's AJCongress-sponsored demonstration, attended by two thousand, was broadcast in part over the radio and similarly featured both non-Jewish and Jewish speakers.[45]

In Chicago's protest rally, "Jews packed the Auditorium theater to the top gallery [and] crowded the lobbies" to hear both Jewish and non-Jewish speakers denounce "the German government for its treatment of Jews in notes of sorrow, bitterness, wailing, and in the stern moral indignation that rivaled the ancient prophets." Thousands more heard the speakers over amplifiers in the streets outside. The principal speaker was Paul McNutt, governor of Indiana and former national commander of the American Legion, who denounced Nazi antisemitism as a "return to medieval days." Dr. Paul Hutchinson, editor of *The Christian Century*, condemned Nazi gangs' "barbarous" antisemitic violence and the "civic ostracism and economic discrimination which has as its avowed purpose the economic and spiritual strangulation of the Jews of Germany." Rabbi Solomon Goldman, who presided over the meeting, ridiculed those who warned that strident denunciations of the German government would cause it to intensify its persecution. He refused to be "diplomatic" because "Hitler and his henchmen are . . . murdering Jews." The Nazis were "the enemies of mankind."[46]

The St. Louis rally speakers were largely Christian leaders, giving the meeting a more conciliatory tone than that of other protests, where Jews had a greater voice. Moreover, the rally was held at Christ Church Cathedral, an environment in which most Jews would feel distinctly uncomfortable. According to the *St. Louis Post-Dispatch*, twelve hundred people "from every creed and all walks of life" attended. The meeting resolved to send a statement to the US State Department and the German embassy condemning "any manifestation of anti-Semitism anywhere." The Rt. Rev. William Scarlett, Episcopal bishop of Missouri, a Methodist pastor, a Catholic layman, and Rabbi Ferdinand Isserman spoke. Bishop Scarlett blamed the German situation partly on the US government, claiming that it had "saddl[ed] Germany with an unjust and unbearable treaty." He urged that attendees make "some sense of corporate repentance."[47]

Boston Jewry flocked to AJCongress-sponsored mass anti-Nazi rallies on March 26 and April 3, 1933. In contrast to the St. Louis meeting, the March 26 protest was held at Temple Mishkan Tefila in Boston's heavily Jewish Roxbury district. Upon completing their orations denouncing German "brutality and outrages" against Jews, the speakers proceeded to the Temple Mishkan Tefila school and then to the Crawford Street synagogue to repeat them to overflow crowds unable to squeeze into the Temple. Most of the speakers were Jewish. Alexander Brin gave the principal address. JWV department commander Maxwell Cohen called for an organized boycott of German goods, a tactic that had strong Jewish grassroots backing in the Hub.[48]

By contrast, two days later, Rabbi Stephen S. Wise, speaking at Temple Ohabei Shalom in Brookline, just outside Boston, declared his opposition to an organized boycott, reflecting Jewish leadership's underestimation of popular antisemitism in Germany. Wise argued that he still "ha[d] faith in the basic love for righteousness of the German people."[49]

Wise did, however, authorize the Boston AJCongress to proceed with its April 3 Faneuil Hall protest in defiance of Josef Goebbels' threat to carry out the Nazis' scheduled April 1 boycott of Jewish stores and offices with unprecedented "force and vehemence" unless Americans ended their anti-Nazi rallies. More than seven thousand Jews and non-Jewish sympathizers "rocked" the Cradle of Liberty on April 3, loudly applauding speakers who denounced the German anti-Jewish boycott and jeering Hitler's name whenever it was mentioned. The speakers included Jewish leaders like Brin and Kaletsky, along with such prominent non-Jews as Massachusetts governor Joseph Ely; Boston mayor James Michael Curley; Alice Stone Blackwell, a longtime champion of the Jewish and Armenian causes; and Boston University president Daniel Marsh. Because Faneuil Hall was crammed beyond capacity, a crowd of three thousand heard the speeches over amplifiers in the square outside the building; others listened to them on the radio. The *Boston Herald* and the *Boston Globe* both featured the Faneuil Hall mass meeting on the front page.[50]

The Boston rallies were accompanied by the hanging of effigies of Hitler in the streets, a method of grassroots protest in the city dating back to the Revolutionary War era. On the evening of April 2, a policeman discovered a life-size dummy with a sign marked "Hitler" hanging at a street corner in the Jewish working-class district of Chelsea. The *Boston Globe* reported that the Fuehrer had also been hanged in effigy a few days before in nearby Malden.[51]

SEPHARDI-MIZRAHI-ASHKENAZI
SOLIDARITY AGAINST HITLER

The American Jewish day of protest had worldwide impact. Jews from Mexico to the Middle East publicly displayed their solidarity. The US embassy in Mexico City reported to Secretary of State Hull that on the evening of March 28, the Jewish colony of the Mexican capital, numbering more than two thousand, had staged a mass meeting in protest against Nazi antisemitism. The Mexico City rally adopted several resolutions denouncing the Nazi outrages.[52] In Buenos Aires, Argentina, twenty-five thousand Jews attended a similar protest meeting on March 27. On March 30, Jewish businesses in Rio de Janeiro, Brazil, closed to express their solidarity with the March 27 demonstrators in the United States.[53]

Several of the major Jewish communities in North Africa also publicly exhibited solidarity with the American March 27 day of protest. The immediate Sephardi/Mizrahi embrace of Germany's besieged Ashkenazim clearly indicated how threatening Nazi policies and atrocities appeared to Jews of all backgrounds from the very beginning of Hitler's rule. On March 27 in Tunis, where the population was about one-fifth Jewish, Jews staged street demonstrations against the persecution of German Jewry. The American consul in Tunis informed the State Department that Jewish protestors had clashed with policemen attempting to confiscate their placards. Eighteen or nineteen Tunis Jews were arrested. *La Dépêche Tunisienne* reported on March 28, "The bad treatment meted out to Jews in Germany under the swastika has raised very intense emotions in Tunisia." It noted that "for some time already the merchants refuse to buy or sell German merchandise." Tunis's grand rabbi had Jewish restaurants close on March 27 for the protest. Tunis Jews also held a "large meeting of protest" against Nazi antisemitism on March 29. To permit the maximum possible number to attend, the Israelite Council asked Tunis's Jews to close their places of business that day at 5:00 p.m. Tunisian Jews also staged anti-Nazi demonstrations in Bizerte, Sousse, and other smaller towns where Jews resided. *La Dépêche Tunisienne* conceded that the wave of protest "from our little Tunisia" could not by itself "influence the implacable Nazis." But it was confident that Tunisian Jews' protests would nonetheless have an impact: "by joining the great movement of protest that extends from Europe to America," they would "reinforce the voices that from all places protest against the abuses of the [Nazi] regime.[54]

In Beirut, Lebanon, the Jews declared March 26 a day of fasting to protest Germany's persecution of Jews. In the synagogues, "special prayers were held . . . announced by the sounding of the ram's horn."[55]

Polish Jews organized eleven anti-Nazi protest meetings in Warsaw on March 27, but authorities prohibited street demonstrations. Police arrested a group of Jews who defied that order by marching with a placard proclaiming, "Down with Hitler!" At Lodz, Orthodox Jews fasted. The London *Jewish Chronicle*'s Warsaw correspondent reported on March 24 that the Jews of Vilna were refusing to purchase German goods and the boycott was taking hold throughout Poland. He stated, "Never has Polish Jewry shown so much unanimity as in this protest against German barbarism."[56]

The American anti-Nazi protests, triggering demonstrations around the world, caused the Hitler government great concern, and it lashed out at them even before the major mass rallies occurred. On March 25, Hermann Goering convened a meeting with the foreign press corps in Berlin to deny that the Nazis had committed atrocities against Jews. He conceded that some Jewish stores had been shut down and in "rare" instances Jews were beaten. But he claimed that the violence was mainly against Jews who had cheated "Aryans", a simple "crime of common law." The rest of the cases involved Jews "bullied" because they were socialists.[57]

Shortly before the coordinated March 27 street demonstrations and rallies began, the *New York Herald Tribune* reported from Berlin that "a steady stream of cablegrams protesting against the anti-Hitler demonstrations held tonight in Madison Square Garden in New York and against related activities hummed over the wires from Germany to the United States." *New York Times* Berlin correspondent Frederick Birchall reported that the Hitler government had concentrated its campaign of denial on the United States because reports of German anti-Jewish atrocities were having the greatest impact there. The Nazis enlisted the support of prominent German clergymen, who informed

American Christian leaders that the American press reports of antisemitic atrocities were lies. On March 27, the Lutheran bishop of Saxony, vice president of the Lutheran World Convention, cabled the convention's president, Dr. John Alfred Morehead of New York, imploring him to "take a vigorous stand against the lying propaganda against Germany." The president of Germany's Evangelical Church Committee, Dr. Kapler, appealed to Dr. S. Parker Cadman, a leading American clergyman, pleading with him "to use his influence to prevent demonstrations ... on the basis of false rumors." Kapler insisted that "the Reich Government guarantees security and order." Dr. Burghart of the Berlin Cathedral, president of the German chapter of the World Alliance for International Friendship through the Churches, cabled American clergymen "begging them" to ignore "the exaggerated or invented reports" of anti-Jewish violence.[58]

German business leaders issued similar denials of what the Hitler government labeled "Jewish atrocity propaganda." The president of Germany's national association of domestic and foreign chambers of commerce sent a cable to the Board of Trade for German-American Commerce in New York several days before the March 27 rallies stating that reports of "anti-Jewish disturbances" in the Reich were "greatly exaggerated."[59] The German transatlantic liner *Europa* arrived in the French port of Cherbourg on March 27 displaying signs denying that the Nazi government was persecuting Jews.[60]

Le Temps reported on April 14, 1933, that recently, while in Berlin, American diplomat Norman Davis had conveyed to Chancellor Hitler and Reich Foreign Minister Konstantin von Neurath President Roosevelt's "disquiet with the Jewish situation in Germany" and appeared pleased with their response. The Paris daily stated that "the satisfaction [Davis] showed upon his return" to the French capital "is interpreted as indicating that he received assurances that the antisemitic movement will cease."[61]

The US State Department responded to Jewish leaders' concerns about repeated physical attacks on German Jews by downplaying American press reports of antisemitic violence and assuring them that the Hitler government would promptly suppress any further outbreaks. On March 26, 1933, Secretary of State Cordell Hull informed Rabbi Wise that at his request the American embassy in Berlin had consulted with the principal US consulates in Germany and had reported back that there was nothing to worry about. The embassy account conceded that "there was for a short time considerable physical mistreatment of Jews" but concluded that "this phase must be considered virtually terminated." It noted—on the eve of the Nazis' nationwide April 1 boycott of Jewish stores and offices!—that there had been "some picketing of Jewish merchandising stores and [some] professional discrimination." But Hull, citing the report, emphasized that "these manifestations were viewed with serious concern by the German Government." He informed Wise that "Hitler in his capacity as leader of the Nazi party issued an order calling on his followers to maintain law and order [and] to avoid . . . disrupting trade."[62]

Some leading American diplomats stationed in Germany, deriding Western press assessments of the impact of Nazi antisemitism, expressed strong approval of the Hitler government's achievements. John Kehl, American consul general in Hamburg, Germany's largest seaport, on March 31 denounced the foreign press's "display of exaggerated news on events and conditions in Germany." The "relatively small number of really serious excesses . . . in the Hamburg district . . . were due largely to overzealous youths who . . . have since been taken in hand." The Nazis had imprisoned many people largely to prevent more "bloodshed and disorder" and for "the personal welfare of those detained." The majority of the German people had "been well and satisfactorily served" by the Hitler government's policies and actions, while the Communists and Radical Socialists had not—and that was "as it should be." Kehl concluded, "It must be admitted that the National Socialist organization before it came to power, and since then the Nazi-Nationalist government, have rendered invaluable services to the world at large in crushing Communism in Germany."[63]

Acting for the AJCongress on April 16, 1933, Rabbi Wise pleaded with Roosevelt advisor and Harvard law professor Felix Frankfurter for "some word" from the president that he was seriously concerned about antisemitic persecution in Germany, but the White House would not speak out publicly. Frankfurter could only respond that he and Justice Louis Brandeis believed that Roosevelt would "in his own way [and] at the right moment give effective evidence of his concern over the occurrences in Germany." Wise warned that the president's continued silence would result in more mass street demonstrations and stimulate organized boycotts of German goods (which Wise did not yet support). Influential senators might embarrass the White House by offering resolutions criticizing the president's inaction, particularly as several British members of Parliament were vocally denouncing the Nazis. Frankfurter asked Roosevelt for "some word of progress on a plan of admission . . . of political refugees so as to reassure Wise . . . and hold off demands for Congressional action," but the president did not comply.[64]

On May 20, Assistant Secretary of State Wilbur Carr recorded in his diary that Secretary Hull had mentioned that Justice Brandeis came to see him to discuss the persecution of German Jews. Brandeis told Hull that he was "very much concerned . . . because the U.S. makes no remonstrance." Carr could not think of anything that Hull could do to "show more consideration" about German Jewry's plight.[65]

Carr noted in a May 31 memorandum that he had discussed German Jews' situation with Secretary Hull and Undersecretary of State William Phillips two days earlier, and they all agreed "that no representations on the part of the [US] Government should be made." Carr acknowledged that there had been "considerable persecution" of German Jews after Hitler assumed power. He repeated the State Department's argument, however, that it was improper for the United States to interfere in another country's "internal matter." Moreover, the persecution of German Jews had "subsided." Directing attention to the subject "might do far more harm than good."[66]

The leading British Jewish organization, the BoD, was uncomfortable with mass rallies and street parades like those staged in the United States in March 1933. If a protest meeting were held, it should be under BoD auspices, so that British Jewry could speak with one voice. On March 29, 1933, immediately after the American national day of protest, the BoD advised British Jews that the only protest meeting "of any value" was one in which the primary speakers were prominent non-Jews who must "at all times" use "guarded and restrained language." The BoD's foreign affairs work was conducted through the JFC, which also included the AJA, an organization similarly representing more affluent British Jews. The JFC considered it inadvisable for speakers to use the word *atrocity* in describing events in Nazi Germany and urged that they not "emphasize the physical aspect"—that is, beatings and torture. Groups and speakers engaged in anti-Nazi protest should emphasize instead "the discrimination against Jews," both legal and informal.[67] The BoD secretary stated on April 6 that although the JFC did not object to "Jewish meetings," it maintained that they "can have no real effect, least of all upon the German government." BoD president and JFC chairman Neville Laski considered it preferable to have the archbishop of Canterbury speak on Nazi persecution of Jews than to stage for the Jewish community "the biggest mass meeting which any stadium could provide."[68]

Fearing that a wave of spontaneous protests would spark an antisemitic reaction in Britain, on March 15, 1933, the BoD warned Jewish youth organizations that were considering staging an anti-Nazi protest not to do so. Lavi Bakstansky, a British Zionist leader, had informed Neville Laski that representatives of British youth organizations, "not having seen any overt steps" to organize a public anti-Nazi protest, had met to consider holding a mass meeting with Winston Churchill and George Lansbury, both ardent anti-Nazis, as possible speakers. Bakstansky stated that the Jewish youth were motivated by a "sense of horror at the present situation of German Jewry." Laski replied that Jewish youth "should take no steps whatever" to organize anti-Nazi action, "and least of all to hold public meetings." The JFC was "taking every possible step and were probing every avenue." Actions not authorized by the JFC would only place German Jewry in an even more precarious position. Laski stated that if Jewish youth "took overt steps" to organize a public protest, the JFC might repudiate it.[69]

Many British Jews and part of the Jewish press condemned the BoD and the JFC for what they considered a tepid response to the Nazi persecution. On March 17, 1933, the BoD secretary informed Neville Laski that "there appears to be a growing demand amongst the Jewish community in England for an organized protest." He had learned from the secretary of Britain's Jewish Ex-Servicemen's Association that Jewish veterans were dissatisfied with what they perceived as BoD inaction and were meeting to discuss sponsoring a protest rally.[70] On March 29, a Jewish woman from Liverpool, impressed by the American mass rallies and marches of the previous week, expressed her amazement to Laski that Jewish leaders in Britain "should even hesitate to follow the splendid lead of our kinsmen overseas." She demanded immediate and forceful action against the German government, which was composed of "people who are but one step removed from savages."[71] The *Jewish Standard*, published in West Yorkshire, criticized the JFC for doing far too little to combat Nazi antisemitism. It engaged in "*haute politique*" rather than reach out to the Jewish masses. The JFC should "hand over the sacred task entrusted to it to more energetic men."[72]

In Britain, the boycott of German goods and services was initiated spontaneously by Jews in London's heavily working- and lower-middle-class East End and was in "full swing" by the end of March 1933. The London *Daily Herald*, organ of the British Labour Party, called the boycott "the dramatic reply to Hitler's brutal persecutions in Germany." Announcements chalked on pavements supported the boycott and demanded that Palestine be opened for unrestricted Jewish immigration. The London *Jewish Chronicle* reported on March 31 that the boycott was "the leading topic of conversation" in Jewish shopping districts, with shopkeepers' compliance nearly universal on many streets. Many displayed posters in their windows stating that they would not speak to agents handling German-made products. "Enthusiasm and determination" for the boycott was "running high." Many Jews in these neighborhoods expressed to the *Jewish Chronicle* their disappointment in the "milk and water" attitude some British Jewish leaders had adopted "towards those who are trying to wipe out German Jewry."[73] On March 25, 1933, the newly organized London-based World Alliance for Combatting Anti-Semitism extended the boycott to include German motion pictures and restaurants.[74]

Working-class Jews in London used military rhetoric to promote the boycott. Soon after the Nazis came to power, East End shopkeepers displayed notices in their windows proclaiming in both Yiddish and English, "Judea Declares War on Germany! Boycott German Goods!"[75] These Jews deliberately chose the word *Judea* rather than *Jewry* to link their resistance to Nazism to their forebears' three massive wars against the Roman Empire from 66 CE to 135 CE. A Jewish box manufacturer printed and distributed fliers entitled "Judea Arise," which stated, "German goods [are] soaked in Jewish blood," and urged British Jews to do battle for "our unfortunate brothers in Germany unable to strike back."[76] The London *Daily Herald* reported on March 27, 1933, that the previous night young Jewish men and women had passed out thousands of English and Yiddish boycott leaflets in the streets of the East End. The manager of one of the East End's largest movie theaters stated that Jews' militancy had caused him to cut out a section of a newsreel about Germany and Hitler. He explained, "It would be madness to show such a film with feeling running as high as it is tonight." In London's Whitechapel district, where the boycott was almost complete, "the pavements were chalked with 'Open Palestine for German refugees,' and cars dashed about bearing boycott placards."[77]

In April 1933, the British boycott movement adopted "Israel's oldest symbol, the Golden Lion of Judah," as its emblem. Jewish activists prepared to issue thousands of leaflets stamped with the Golden Lion and the slogan "The Lion of Judah Awakes," calling for a widening of the anti-Nazi boycott. A boycott organizer told the London *Daily Herald*, "We will fight poison with poison," and characterized the economic boycott as Jewry's "most potent weapon."[78]

The BoD leadership condemned the organized boycott on the grounds that it would stimulate antisemitism in Britain and provide the Hitler regime with an excuse to increase its persecution of German Jews. It strongly disapproved of the aggressive posture and intensity of the boycotters, who were overwhelmingly of East European Jewish background. In a letter to the London *Jewish Chronicle* on March 31, Neville Laski and Leonard G. Montefiore, president of the AJA, denounced the boycott in the strongest terms. Laski and Montefiore had seen automobiles in London "disfigured" with the slogan "Judea Declares War against Germany," which they called "a complete and dangerous perversion of the truth." The two leaders complained that Jewish businesses, in canceling orders with German companies, had stamped their letters with "expressions of an abusive and scurrilous character," which they labeled "gutter propaganda." The same day, Laski admonished a boycott supporter from Glasgow: "The boycott is a very dangerous weapon. . . . It only does harm and I am satisfied does no good."[79]

The launching of a grassroots Jewish boycott of German goods in Britain alarmed the Hitler regime, which immediately attempted to suppress it. The

German government sent agents to London to urge Conservative MPs sympathetic to Hitler to have the boycott posters in the East End and other parts of the city torn down on the grounds that they were "calculated to give offense to a friendly Power." These MPs persuaded Scotland Yard to send policemen into the East End on April 9 to order the removal of the posters. The policemen issued court summonses to shopkeepers who refused to comply. Police called at the home of Captain W. J. Webber, head of the newly formed Organisation for Ending Hostilities to German Jews, and informed him that his group could not send a caravan of automobiles through the city displaying boycott posters, which it was preparing to do.[80]

Scotland Yard's effort to bar the display of boycott posters precipitated a furious response in the House of Commons. Major Clement Attlee (Labour), deputy leader of the opposition, demanded to know whether Home Secretary Sir John Gilmour had ordered the police to stage the raid on the East End shopkeepers. The home secretary replied that the commissioner of police had informed him that "in view of the feeling likely to be caused by the posters, and the possibility of a breach of peace being caused," the posters should be removed. Winston Churchill (Conservative) denounced the poster removal as a denial of the "reasonable expression of free opinion" on an important subject, Nazi antisemitism. Hannen Swaffer, a non-Jewish writer for the London *Daily Herald*, announced in a column entitled "How Dare They?" that as an act of protest he would place a boycott poster in the window of his home and was awaiting a police summons. On April 11, five days after the raid, the London *Daily Herald* reported that outrage among the public and in the House of Commons had resulted in the police rescinding the ban on boycott posters.[81]

Boycotts of German goods sprang up across the world, heartening Jews organizing and participating in the movement in the United States and Britain. The boycott gathered particular strength in Poland, the country with Europe's largest Jewish population; in France; and among the sizeable Jewish communities of North Africa and the Middle East. The London *Jewish Chronicle*'s Warsaw correspondent stated on March 24, 1933, that Polish Jews were "determined to stop buying machinery, paper, electric goods, sweets, and other manufactures" from Germany. On April 7, the *Jewish Chronicle* reported that Jewish physicians in Warsaw and other Polish towns had resolved "not to prescribe any medicines imported from Germany." Jewish hospitals had ceased ordering from German firms. Many Polish Jews had canceled reservations for travel on German vessels sailing from Warsaw.[82]

The *Jewish Chronicle* reported on April 7 that never since the Dreyfus Affair had French Jewry made such a passionate protest against antisemitism as during the past few days. The boycott of German goods had spread to Paris, where shops in many quarters posted notices: "Les réprésentants allemands ne seront pas réçus" ("German agents will not be received"). By April 21, the great Paris department stores, the Galeries Lafayette and the Samaritaine, had joined the boycott. Two organizations were directing the boycott in France: the newly formed Committee for the Defense of German Jews, headed by Pierre Dreyfus, son of Captain Alfred Dreyfus, and the International League against Anti-Semitism (originally the International League against Pogroms), organized during the 1920s after the assassination of the pogromist Hetman Petlura in Paris. The latter organization had branches in many cities and towns outside Paris, including Marseilles, Lyons, Lille, and Nantes. Both groups were canvassing commercial and industrial corporations asking them to adhere to the boycott.[83]

The boycott movement spread rapidly throughout the Yishuv during March 1933. The *Palestine Post* reported on March 29 that the screening of the German film *Tango Für Dich*, scheduled in Jerusalem, had been canceled in compliance with the boycott. Shortly afterward, Jewish youths in Tel Aviv were arrested for disrupting the showing of a German film. The sympathetic audience forced the theater management to substitute an English film. At their trial, the youths' defense attorney submitted a photograph sent to Jews in Germany of a Jew being hanged. The caption threatened recipients "with the same fate" if they remained in the Reich.[84]

Le Temps reported on March 30 that among Egyptian Jews, "the boycott of German firms and products is effective and generalized." It noted that "important withdrawals had been made from the Dresden Bank. . . . Large orders of [German] industrial machinery have been canceled." Jewish physicians were no longer ordering German pharmaceutical products. By April 1933, the Jewish French-language newspaper in Alexandria, Egypt, *La Voix Juive*, was publishing an "Index" of German products to promote the boycott.[85] An American Legation official reported to Secretary of State Hull the cancelation on April 25 of the Brahms Festival sponsored by the German Colony in Cairo, because Jewish musicians refused to perform in it.[86]

In April 1933, the JFC launched numerous protest meetings across England and in Scotland and Wales that received significant press coverage in Britain. In an internal memorandum of April 13, the JFC recommended that each British city and town form a small organizing committee to arrange public meetings that featured "solely or mainly leading non-Jews." The lord mayor or mayor, or persons of equal standing, should chair these meetings. The memorandum stressed the importance of securing the attendance of "local MPs, magistrates, and leading churchmen." An "influential Jew (or non-Jew)" in each community

should call on the local newspaper editor "for the purpose of publishing a leading article" on the Nazi persecution of Jews. Meetings should pass resolutions
expressing sympathy with the Jewish plight in Germany and denouncing discrimination against Jews in the civil service, professions, and business. These
resolutions should be sent to the Undersecretary of State at the British Foreign
Office, the German ambassador to Britain, and the secretary-general of the
League of Nations.[87]

The BoD and the AJA had used this approach in organizing support for
persecuted Jews in Russia during the early twentieth century. In 1906 they had
convened a public meeting at Queen's Hall in London to raise funds for pogrom
victims at which "almost all the speakers were non-Jews." At a meeting to rally
support for Mendel Beilis, tried in Kiev for ritual murder in 1913, the speakers
were largely "[Christian] ecclesiastics and statesmen."[88]

At least eleven anti-Nazi public protest meetings were held in April 1933
under JFC auspices, starting in Liverpool and Cardiff, Wales, on April 5th.[89]
Most passed resolutions condemning Nazi persecution of Jews, but none urged
a boycott of German goods and services. A flier announcing the meeting in
Hull on April 9 to denounce Germany's "return to medieval barbarism" stated
that it had been called at the request of the Hull Jewish community with the
full support of the three principal congregations and the Hull Zionist Society.
The flier emphasized that "this meeting would be prohibited in Germany." The
meeting, however, was chaired by Canon W. Seldon Morgan, vicar of Holy
Trinity Church. The advertised speakers included two Christian clergymen and
the sheriff of Hull.[90] In Manchester on April 19, three to four thousand people
gathered at a protest rally chaired by the lord mayor, who was joined on the
platform by the bishops of Manchester and Salford and by the mayors of several
surrounding towns. The *Manchester Guardian*'s editor-in-chief, W. P. Crozier, a
non-Jew, condemned Germany for "marching back into the Dark Ages."[91]

The rallies staged by grassroots British Jewish and labor groups in the same
month adopted a more militant tone than those under JFC influence and urged
a boycott of German goods and services. At an anti-Nazi protest meeting in
Glasgow sponsored by the Scottish Socialist Party on April 16, Duncan Graham, a Labour MP, declared that he was ready "to encourage an army [from
Britain] to take the field against Germany as a reprisal for the persecution of
Jews." The audience cheered Graham's announcement that he was prepared to
vote in Parliament to expel the German ambassador. He stated that Germany
would not have achieved "its place as the seat of philosophy, music, and the
arts if it had not been for its Jewish citizens."[92] A few days later, at Glasgow's
Cromwell Road Synagogue, Rabbi S. Bloch denounced the Nazis as "modern

Torquemadas" and strongly urged Jews to boycott German goods and services. The congregation, "attired in their prayer shawls, stood up as one man as a sign of protest against the atrocious treatment of the Jews in Germany."[93]

Although British Prime Minister Ramsey MacDonald and US President Franklin D. Roosevelt refrained from publicly denouncing Nazi antisemitic policies and atrocities, several MPs in the House of Commons pressed the British government to refuse the German government any treaty adjustments because of its persecution of Jews and political opponents. Josiah Wedgwood (Labour) and James Maxton (Independent Labour) introduced a motion to break off any negotiations with the German government concerning revision of the peace treaties "until law, order, and civilized treatment of prisoners are restored to all classes in Germany."[94] Eleanor Rathbone, independent MP for the Combined English Universities, declared that although she had "steadily protested against the unfair treatment of Germany at and since Versailles," she could no longer support any concessions. The Germans had "by majority vote deliberately chosen to put themselves under an autocracy more complete, more truculent, more contemptuous of individual liberty and of minority rights . . . than any Government before the War." They had done so "in full knowledge of . . . [its] leaders maniacal anti-Semitism." Permitting "any measure of rearmament to Germany under its present Government would be lunacy."[95] Other MPs also vowed not to make any concessions on armaments to the new German regime. *Time* magazine reported on April 3, 1933, that a few days before, Colonel Josiah Wedgwood had denounced German atrocities against Jews in the House of Commons, declaring that the Nazi barbarities had "completely converted pro-German England into pro-French England!" Winston Churchill had promptly risen to support Wedgwood, asserting that "during this anxious month there are a good many people who had said what I've been saying for years: 'Thank God for the French army!'"[96]

Commander Locker-Lampson, MP (Conservative), challenged Foreign Secretary John Simon in the House of Commons to bring the persecution of German Jews before the next meeting of the League of Nations Council in Geneva. The Foreign Secretary responded that no article in the League Covenant permitted His Majesty's Government to do so.[97]

In April, Sir Austen Chamberlain (Conservative) delivered in the House of Commons what the Nazi government described as the "most anti-German outburst [in] a decade," blasting the Hitler regime for combining "the old Prussianism with an added savagery of racial pride and exclusiveness." Sir Austen asked whether Europe could afford to grant equal status to a Germany that had made it "a crime to be a Jew." Backing Sir Austen, Winston Churchill (Conservative), declared that he rejoiced in Germany's military weakness, given its ongoing persecution of the Jews.[98]

On his government's instruction, the German ambassador in London, Dr. Leopold von Hoensch, "protested immediately and emphatically" against Britain's "unwarranted meddling in the internal affairs of the Reich," a clear sign that the protests, denunciations, and boycott had rattled the Hitler regime. The *New York Times* noted that the reaction to Sir Austen's and Churchill's speeches "ranges all the way from anxiety to indignation and downright fury." Referring to the German ambassador's official protest, the *Times* reporter commented, "This unusual action would indicate that the [Hitler] government does not underestimate foreign opinion."[99]

In the House of Lords in early April, Viscount Cecil of Chelwood asked His Majesty's Government to make a statement about the Nazi persecution and outrages inflicted on German Jewry. He pointed in particular to the "wholesale dismissals of Jewish judges, doctors, and other professional men," noting that this had "caused a great deal of anxiety" among the British public. Lord Reading, a former British foreign minister and a Jew, rose to say that "he found it impossible to refrain from adding his appeal to the Government."

Viscount Hailsham, leader of the House of Lords, responded that the British government had no authority "to press the German government for justice" unless the persecution involved Jews who were British subjects. He was "happy to assure" his colleagues "that from inquiries the [British] Government had made," it had uncovered no such cases. Viscount Hailsham added that the United States government had not made any official protests to the Hitler regime over the mistreatment of German Jews. He stated that the ambassadors of both Britain and the United States had been in conversation with the German government about German Jews' situation, and he "was glad to [say] that the results were of a reassuring nature." Viscount Hailsham parroted the Hitler regime's own argument that any violence in Germany was due to the "very remarkable circumstances" that had prevailed when the country was in the throes of a revolution. He "hoped and trusted" that the Nazi government would "allow nothing to happen in Germany that would in any way increase the anxieties which had been expressed in the House."[100]

On May 10, 1933, American Jews again took to the streets in huge numbers to protest the mass book burnings of Jewish and other "un-German" books that the Nazis staged that night at universities across the Reich. Like the March 27 demonstrations and rallies, these protests received prominent coverage in major metropolitan daily newspapers. The AJC and B'nai B'rith issued a joint statement opposing the parades. The United Hebrew Trades, by contrast, announced that Jewish trade unionists would participate in the New York City mobilization. In New York City, sixty-five to eighty thousand people marched for six hours in the largest parade in the city since the Armistice celebrations in 1918. Bystanders stood seven-deep on the sidewalk along Fifth Avenue and lower Broadway, and showers of ticker tape floated down from the office towers in the financial district. Awed spectators watched a contingent of two thousand rabbis march by, making a "majestic picture with their long-flowing coats, beards . . . and eyes that glistened with sorrow at the occasion." The demonstrators included Talmud Torah students, sweatshop workers, and judges who deserted their benches to march against Hitler. Jewish collegians chanted, "2, 4, 6, 8, who would we assassinate—Hitler!" Banners bore such slogans as "Hitler—Remember What Happened to Spain," linking that nation's sharp cultural and economic decline to its expulsion of the Jews in 1492, and "Hitlerism, Germany's Yellow Badge of Shame," a reference to the medieval degradation of European Jews. A massive labor contingent participated, including a delegation from the Undertakers Union marching under the banner, "We Want Hitler!" Members of the largely Jewish Furriers' Union carried a sign proclaiming, "We Will Not Sell Any Furs Dyed with Jewish Blood." In Chicago twenty-five thousand marched, and in Philadelphia twenty thousand.[101]

In Cleveland on that day, ten thousand attended what the *Cleveland Plain Dealer* called a "gigantic" meeting against Nazi antisemitism, which was broadcast over the radio. The meeting's chair, Rabbi Barnett Brickner, reported that "the deliberate and systematic campaign of the Nazi regime to exterminate the Jewish people in Germany continues unabated." He declared that the most esteemed newspaper correspondents had "pronounced this reversion to medieval barbarism as a sinister menace to world peace." The major speaker, Rabbi Stephen S. Wise, urged all present not to go to bed that night without writing to President Roosevelt, the State Department, Ohio's senators, and Cleveland-area congressmen to demand US government action against Nazi persecution of German Jewry.[102]

The next day, fifteen hundred people crammed into the Cleveland Jewish Center to witness a mock trial of Hitler before "the court of humanity," a means of providing Cleveland residents with up-to-date eyewitness accounts of anti-Jewish persecution in the Reich. Sitting on the bench were the chief justice of the Common Pleas Court, two Common Pleas justices, and one municipal judge. Attorneys were there to prosecute Hitler on behalf of "the civilized world" for crimes against the Jews and humanity, while others defended him. Actors impersonated American Berlin correspondents H. R. Knickerbocker and Dorothy Thompson, drawing on their published reports from Germany as they testified about atrocities against Jews and Hitler's political opponents. A Cleveland resident, Max Ratner, who had been in Germany from March 28 to April 3, 1933, during the national boycott of Jewish stores and offices, exhibited signs torn from Jewish stores. Defense counsel admitted that all the charges against Hitler were justified and pleaded guilty on his behalf.[103]

In Boston, the seventh annual Jewish Book Week at the Boston Public Library opened with a strong condemnation of the Nazi book burnings. The celebration of Jews' highly significant contribution to literature was in itself a form of anti-Nazi protest. Lee Friedman, who led efforts to combat employment discrimination against Jews in Boston, speaking on "Zola and the Dreyfus Case," emphasized the critical importance and impact of personal commitment in fighting antisemitism.[104]

Other Jewish communities outside the United States followed American Jewry's lead in staging rallies in May to protest the Nazi book burnings and the continuing persecution of German Jewry. On May 21 in Alexandria, Egypt, four thousand responded to a call from the local League for Combating Hitlerite Anti-Semitism, gathering at the "spacious lecture hall" and playground of the Schools of the Jewish Community of Alexandria. Rally speakers included both Jews and non-Jews. The Rev. J. F. Anderson, chaplain of Alexandria's St. Mark's Church, denounced the persecutors of German Jews as "savages." Addressing an audience well aware of the Nazis' public burning of massive numbers of books written by Jews, he declared that the "prosperity and greatness of the United Kingdom were in great measure due to the genius of a large number of Jewish subjects." Léon Castro, a Cairo Jew, lawyer in the Mixed Tribunals, and president of the Egyptian branch of the Paris-based Ligue Internationale Contre l'Antisemitisme, denounced the book burnings in a lengthy address and informed the audience that his group had been founded to "join forces with other such organizations throughout the world in order to fight the stupid and unjustified persecution of a race which had given the world the moral laws which were the . . . foundation of every conscience."

The rally concluded at 11:30 p.m. after the grand rabbi of Alexandria, in an address that anticipated Martin Luther King Jr.'s "I Have a Dream" speech thirty years later, declared that "he saw as in a dream on the summit of a mountain Moses, Jesus Christ, and the Prophet Mohamed, united and symbolizing fraternity and unity among all the different creeds and nationalities." The audience "heartily applauded" the grand rabbi's address and "dispersed after singing the Hatikvah," the Zionist anthem.[105]

In April and May 1933, after the German minister in Cairo pressed them to take action, British officials in the Egyptian government made a concerted effort to discourage forceful Jewish anti-Nazi protest and the boycott of German goods and services. A few days after the March 27 worldwide demonstrations against Nazi antisemitism, A. W. Keown-Boyd, director-general of the European division of the Egyptian Ministry of the Interior, summoned Jacques Maleh, editor of the Cairo Jewish newspaper *L'Aurore*, and warned him that the lead article in his March 27 issue supporting the demonstrations and condemning Nazi antisemitic outrages in Germany was unacceptable. He ordered Maleh to "moderate his tone and not dress up the news in a manner calculated to excite feeling" between Germans and Jews in Egypt.[106] In early June, after the May rallies and demonstrations, Keown-Boyd denounced what he claimed were *L'Aurore*'s "flaming headlines" and the "series of wild articles" on German persecution of Jews published after March 27. Around June 4, after the Alexandria rally, he met with Léon Castro and ordered him "to abstain from the publication of further violent articles [about Nazi persecution of Jews], to discontinue public meetings, and generally to keep the movement quiet." Keown-Boyd issued a similar warning to the grand rabbi and to five Egyptian Jewish newspapers in addition to *L'Aurore*. He noted that despite his "warnings to the contrary," the Ligue Internationale Contre l'Antisemitisme had "issued and distributed a . . . pamphlet in large quantities; seizure of this has been ordered."[107]

* * *

Almost as soon as Hitler assumed power, Jews in the United States and Britain, recognizing that German Jewry was in mortal danger, held massive street demonstrations and rallies all over both countries to protest Nazi antisemitic policies and atrocities. Although the AJCongress and the JFC coordinated many of these protests, they were largely initiated by working- and lower-middle-class Jews, who also began spontaneous boycotts of German goods and services. American and British Jews' relentless challenge to the Nazis was inspired, in part, by earlier rank-and-file Jewish protests against Russian pogroms and Dreyfus's conviction. The militant American Jewish demonstrations and rallies, staged across the United States on March 27, prompted Jews from Central and South America, North Africa, and the Middle East to organize simultaneous demonstrations of solidarity with persecuted German Jewry.

The enormous wave of protests by Jews in both hemispheres, which received considerable press outside Germany, alarmed the Hitler government and caused it to launch a vigorous public relations campaign against "Jewish atrocity propaganda." From March 27, 1933, the Hitler government monitored the US protests very closely, and almost every time they occurred, the government

angrily appealed to the highest White House and State Department officials
to suppress them. This reveals the Nazi regime's great concern about the protests' impact on public opinion in the United States—and abroad. The US
State Department responded by hastening to assure American Jews and other
concerned citizens that press reports of Nazi outrages against Jews were exaggerated and that antisemitic violence in Germany was diminishing.

The mass grassroots protests had a significant long-term impact, awakening
millions of Americans and others around the globe to the dangers of Nazism.
Jewish youth who witnessed or heard about these demonstrations when they
were ten or twelve years old became eager to join the struggle to destroy Nazism
and rushed to enlist in the armed forces several years later when the United
States was at war with Germany. These soldiers' memories of masses of Jews
marching in the streets in the spring of 1933, denouncing the Nazis' antisemitic
atrocities, and demanding immediate and militant US action against Germany
led them to put their maximum effort into fighting the Wehrmacht when they
went into combat. Like the demonstrators, they understood what was at stake.

NOTES

1. Alliance Israélite Universelle to Cyrus Adler [president of the AJC],
February 2, 1932, and Le Secrétaire, Alliance Israélite Universelle, to O. E.
d'Avigdor-Goldsmid, February 26, 1932, ACC/3121/C/11/012/014, Board of
Deputies of British Jews Papers (hereafter, BoD Papers), London Metropolitan
Archives (hereafter, LMA), London, UK.

2. "Déclaration de M. Bernhard Kahn, de Berlin, Directeur du 'Joint' Sur
la Situation des Juifs en Allemagne," January 21, 1932, ACC/3121/C/11/012/014,
BoD Papers, LMA.

3. Toni Sender, *The Autobiography of a German Rebel* (New York: Vanguard,
1939), 274. Richard J. Evans stated that the results of the September 14, 1930,
Reichstag election "delivered a seismic and in many ways decisive blow to the
political system of the Weimar Republic." Evans, *The Coming of the Third Reich*
(New York: Penguin, 2003), 259.

4. "Déclaration de M. Bernhard Kahn."

5. Ibid.; Le Secrétaire, Alliance Israélite Universelle, to O. E. Avigdor-
Goldsmid, February 26, 1932; letter to Monsieur Bigart [probably from Neville
Laski], February 29, 1932, ACC/3121/C/11/012/014, BoD Papers, LMA.

6. Alliance Israélite Universelle to Cyrus Adler, February 2, 1932; Cyrus
Adler to Mr. President [of the Joint Foreign Committee], February 18, 1932,
ACC/3121/C/11/012/014, BoD Papers, LMA.

7. *Brooklyn Jewish Examiner*, August 19, 1932, 1, and August 26, 1932, 1.

8. *Jewish Exponent* (Philadelphia), March 17, 1933, 6; *New York Times*, March 20, 1933, 5; *Boston Herald*, March 22, 1933, 1; Moshe Gottlieb, "The First of April Boycott and the Reaction of the American Jewish Community," *American Jewish Historical Quarterly* 57 (June 1968): 522.

9. *New York Times*, March 13, 1933; *Jewish Exponent* (Philadelphia), March 17, 1933; *Cleveland Plain Dealer*, March 18, 1933.

10. *New York Times*, March 20, 1933, 5.

11. Minutes of Meeting of the Executive Committee of the American Jewish Committee held on March 19, 1933, www.AJC.org.

12. *New York Times*, March 20, 1933, 5.

13. Louis I. Falk to Joseph Tenenbaum, March 25, 1955, RG 21.001.01*4, Joseph and Sheila Tenenbaum Collection, US Holocaust Memorial Museum Archives, Washington, DC.

14. *New York Times*, May 22, 1919, 1.

15. *Chicago Tribune*, May 22, 1919, 5; *Boston Globe*, May 29, 1919; *Los Angeles Times*, June 11 and 12, 1919, 5, 6; *Washington Post*, June 2, 1919, 1.

16. *New York Times*, November 25, 1919, 6. In Boston, more than twenty-five thousand Jews marched in a "bitter wind" over "a long route" to protest pogroms in the Ukraine. The *Boston Globe* reported that "it was so cold, so disagreeable that few stood to watch the great parade pass." It emphasized how committed the predominantly working-class Jewish marchers were to demonstrating solidarity with their "dying kinsfolk in Europe": "thousands of ill-clad working people clattered along . . . their hands tucked into their sleeves, their faces blue. But they went through." *Boston Globe*, December 16, 1919.

17. *New York Times* March 24 and 26, 1933, 3; *Washington Post*, March 25, 1933, 1; *Daily Herald* (London), March 24, 1933, 3; *New York Evening Post*, March 24, 1933, 24.

18. "Our Protest Parade," *Jewish Veteran*, April 1933, 8–9, 24, National Jewish Military Museum Archives (hereafter, NJMMA), Washington, DC; *New York Times*, March 24, 1933, 3.

19. *New York Herald Tribune*, March 24, 1933, 1; *Daily Herald* (London), March 24, 1933, 1; "Appeal to the Jewish Youth. Stop Persecution and Legal Lynching of German Jews!," 876/2/15, Anti-German Protest and Prayer Meetings (hereafter, AGPPM) Collection, Wiener Library for the Study of the Holocaust and Genocide, London, UK.

20. "Our Protest Parade," 8–9.

21. J. G. Fredman to Friend, March 21, 1933, and Edgar H. Burman to Gentlemen, December 11, 1933 and Burman to Friend, n.d., box 1, Jewish War Veterans of the United States of America Collection, I-32, American Jewish Historical Society, Center for Jewish History, New York, NY; *New York Times*, March 25, 1933, 10; J. David Delman, "Haman, 'Yemach Shemoh!,'" *Jewish War Veteran*, April 1933, 18, NJMMA.

22. Stephen H. Norwood, *Antisemitism and the American Far Left* (New York: Cambridge University Press, 2013), 33, 35–36; *Daily Worker*, March 24, 1933.

23. *New York Evening Post*, March 25, 1933, 1, 2. Joseph Freeman, editor of the CP magazine *New Masses*, assailed "the efforts of wealthy Jews and their gentile friends in this country to obscure the real meaning of Fascism by making it an exclusively Jewish issue." *New York Evening Post*, April 6, 1933, 24.

24. *Chicago Tribune*, September 3, 1899, 2; September 11, 1899, 2, 3; and September 12, 1899, 1, 3, 4, 6; *Boston Globe*, September 12, 1899, 3; *New York Times*, September 10, 1899, 3; September 12, 1899, 2; and September 13, 1899, 3; *Washington Post*, September 13, 1899, 1; *Atlanta Constitution*, September 13, 1899. The *Tribune's* editorial noted that although it did not expect any government to withdraw from the Paris Exposition, "hundreds of thousands of people who would otherwise have gone to Paris in 1900 will stay away and their money will stay away with them." *Chicago Tribune*, September 12, 1899, 6.

25. L. Mullen, special agent, Department of State, to A. R. Burr, special agent in charge, Department of State, June 30, 1933, box 6786, Central Decimal Files (hereafter, CDF), 1930–39, Department of State General Records, Record Group (hereafter, RG) 59, National Archives, College Park, MD (hereafter, NA-CP); *Cleveland Plain Dealer*, March 28, 1933.

26. *Manchester Guardian*, March 25, 1933, 13.

27. City Clerk, Revere, Massachusetts, to President Franklin D. Roosevelt, March 15, 1933, box 6783, CDF, 1930–39, Department of State General Records, RG 59, NA-CP.

28. Clay Bowerrox, president, Johnson County (Iowa) Taxpayers' League to President Franklin D. Roosevelt, April 2, 1933, box 6783, CDF, Department of State General Records, RG 59, NA-CP.

29. "Resolutions Authorized by Mass Meeting Held in Erie, Pennsylvania, Sunday, March 26, 1933," box 6784, CDF, Department of State General Records, RG 59, NA-CP.

30. Taxicab Industry—State of New York to Franklin D. Roosevelt, March 25, 1933, Department of State General Records, RG 59, NA-CP.

31. Press conference number 6, March 24, 1933, Press Conference Transcripts, Franklin D. Roosevelt Presidential Library and Museum, Hyde Park, NY.

32. *New York Herald Tribune*, March 20, 1933, 1, and March 24, 1933, 1, 3; *New York Times*, March 21, 1933, 1; *New York Evening Post*, March 22, 1933, 1; *Boston Herald*, March 22, 1933, 1.

33. *New York Evening Post*, March 27, 1933, 1; "Prayers and Atrocities," *Time*, April 3, 1933, 17.

34. *Daily Herald* (London), March 27, 1933, 2.

35. *Le Temps*, March 26, 1933; *Figaro*, March 26, 1933.

36. *Le Temps*, March 25, 1933.

37. Jewish Telegraphic Agency, March 26, 1933; *New York Evening Post*, March 24, 1933.

38. *New York Evening Post*, March 27, 1933, 1, 2; *New York Times*, March 28, 1933, 1, 12, 13.

39. *New York Times*, March 28, 1933, 1, 13.

40. "Prayers and Atrocities"; *Hitlerism and the American Jewish Congress: A Confidential Report of Activities* (New York: American Jewish Congress, 1934), container 43, William E. Dodd Papers, Manuscript Division, Library of Congress (hereafter, LC), Washington, DC; *New York Evening Post*, March 27, 1933; *New York Times*, March 28, 1933.

41. *New York Times*, March 28, 1933, 14.

42. *New York Times*, March 29, 1933, 8.

43. *New York Herald Tribune*, March 28, 1933, 1, 3, 5; *New York Times*, March 28, 1933, 1, 12, 13; *Cleveland Plain Dealer*, March 28, 1933, 1.

44. *Philadelphia Inquirer*, March 30, 1933; *Jewish Exponent* (Philadelphia), March 31, 1933, 1, 8.

45. James Waterman Wise, *Swastika: The Nazi Terror* (New York: Harrison Smith and Robert Haas, 1933), 114; *Cleveland Plain Dealer*, March 23 and 28, 1933.

46. *Chicago Tribune*, March 28, 1933, 1, 4. Under its front-page headline, the *Tribune* stated, "New York—Sixty thousand Jews massed in Madison Square Garden and at overflow meetings in streets protest [antisemitic persecution] in Germany.... Details on page 4." It printed an enormous accompanying photograph showing the Chicago auditorium with every seat filled.

47. *St. Louis Post-Dispatch*, March 28, 1933.

48. *Boston Herald*, March 27, 1933, 7.

49. *Boston Evening Globe*, March 29, 1933, 6.

50. *Jewish Advocate* (Boston), April 4, 1933, 1; *Boston Globe*, April 1, 1933, 2, and April 4, 1933, 1; *Boston Herald*, April 4, 1933, 1, 8; *Christian Science Monitor*, April 4, 1933, 3.

51. *Boston Globe*, April 3, 1933, 2.

52. Arthur Bliss Lane, Embassy of the United States, Mexico, to Secretary of State, March 31, 1933, "Subject: Alleged persecutions against the Jewish race in Germany," box 6783, CDF, 1930–39, Department of State General Records, RG 59, NA-CP.

53. *Boston Globe*, March 28, 1933, 2; *Manchester Guardian*, March 30, 1933, 9; *New York Times*, March 31, 1933, 15.

54. Nester, Tunis, to Secretary of State, March 27, 1933, box 6782, and Alfred T. Nester, American Consul, Tunis, to Honorable Secretary of State, March 29, 1933, "Subject: Jewish Demonstrations in Tunis, Tunisia," box 6783, CDF, 1930–39, Department of State General Records, RG 59, NA-CP.

55. *Palestine Post*, March 29, 1933, 5. The next day, the *Post* cited "Arab press reports" that "the boycott by Jews of German goods ... has spread to Baghdad,

where some Jewish merchants have cancelled their orders in Germany." *Palestine Post*, March 30, 1933, 1.

56. *Boston Globe*, March 28, 1933, 2; "Foreign Reactions: Boycotting German Goods," *Jewish Chronicle* (London), March 24, 1933, 25

57. *Figaro*, March 26, 1933.

58. *New York Times*, March 28, 1933, 1, 12.

59. *New York Evening Post*, March 24, 1933.

60. *Boston Globe*, March 28, 1933. *Le Temps* reported on April 16, 1933, that Donald Frantz, director of the Berlin Daily News Syndicate, which supplied information to two hundred German and Swiss newspapers, had arrived in New York to monitor American reactions to Nazi policies. *Le Temps*, April 16, 1933.

61. *Le Temps*, April 14, 1933.

62. Cordell Hull, Secretary of State, to Rabbi Stephen Wise, March 26, 1933, box 6782, CDF, 1930–39, Department of State General Records, RG 59, NA-CP.

63. John E. Kehl to George A. Gordon, March 31, 1933, box 6784, CDF, 1930–39, Department of State General Records, RG 59, NA-CP.

64. Felix Frankfurter to President Franklin D. Roosevelt, April 16, 1933, box 6784, CDF, 1930–39, Department of State General Records, RG 59, NA-CP.

65. Wilbur J. Carr, diary entry for May 20, 1933, box 4, Wilbur J. Carr Papers (hereafter, Carr Papers), Manuscript Division, LC. Carr made antisemitic statements in his diary during this period. On February 22, 1934, describing a visit to Atlantic City, he expressed his displeasure that "along the Boardwalk we saw but few Gentiles. Jews everywhere, and of the commonest kind. Yet most of them were well dressed. Women usually wore handsome mink coats—sometimes Persian lamb. All seemed prosperous. The Claridge [Hotel] is filled with them, and few presented a good appearance. Only two others besides myself in dinner jacket." Carr, diary entry for February 22, 1934, box 5, Carr Papers, LC. In 1935, President Roosevelt by executive order waived the requirement that Carr leave the State Department at the mandated retirement age of sixty-five. Christian F. Groth to Wilbur J. Carr, October 29, 1935, box 12, Carr Papers, LC.

66. Wilbur J. Carr, "Measures Considered with Respect to the Attitude of the United States toward the Jews in Germany," May 31, 1933, box 10, Carr Papers, LC.

67. Joint Chairmen to Moses Schonfeld, March 29, 1933, ACC/3121/E/03/537, BoD Papers, LMA.

68. Secretary, Board of Deputies of British Jews, to Mr. d'Avigdor Goldsmid, April 6, 1933, BoD Papers, LMA; Neville Laski, quoted in "The Deputies," *Jewish Chronicle* (London), May 19, 1933, 22.

69. "Notes of Interview between Mr. Neville Laski and Mr. L. Bakstansky," March 15, 1933, ACC/3121/C/11/012/014, BoD Papers, LMA.

70. Secretary to Mr. Laski, March 17, 1933, ACC/3121/C/11/012/014, BoD Papers, LMA.

71. Miss A. R. Lowenthal, Liverpool, to Neville Laski, March 29, 1933, ACC/3121/E/03/537, BoD Papers, LMA.

72. "What Is the J.F.C. Doing?" (editorial), *Jewish Standard*, June 23, 1933, clipping in ACC/3121/C/11/03, BoD Papers, LMA.

73. *Daily Herald* (London), March 24, 1, and March 27, 1933, 1; "Boycott Scenes" and "Boycott German Goods!" *Jewish Chronicle* (London), March 31, 1933, 19, 39.

74. *Daily Herald* (London), March 24 and 25, 1933; *Boston Globe*, March 26, 1933, A9; "World Alliance for Combatting Anti-Semitism," *Jewish Chronicle* (London), March 31, 1933, 40.

75. "Judea Declares War on Germany! Boycott German Goods!," 876/2/5, AGPPM Collection, Wiener Library, London.

76. "Judea Arise," 876/2/6, Anti-German Protest and Prayer Meetings, Wiener Library, London.

77. *Daily Herald* (London), March 27, 1933, 1.

78. *Daily Herald* (London), April 24, 1933, 3.

79. "A Call to Self-Restraint from Messrs. Neville Laski and Leonard G. Montefiore," *Jewish Chronicle* (London), March 31, 1933, 43; Neville Laski to Fred Nettler, March 31, 1933, ACC/3121/E/03/537, BoD Papers, LMA.

80. *Daily Herald* (London), April 10, 1933.

81. *Daily Herald* (London), April 11, 1933.

82. "Foreign Reactions: Boycotting German Goods," *Jewish Chronicle* (London), March 24, 1933, 25; "The Boycott in Poland: Imports of German Goods Drop to 7%," *Jewish Chronicle* (London), April 7, 1933, 28.

83. "French Public Feeling Aroused: Many Protest Meetings," *Jewish Chronicle* (London), April 7, 1933, 27; "Germany: The Jewish Agony," *Jewish Chronicle* (London), April 21, 1933, 14; "The Boycott in France Goes On," *Jewish Chronicle* (London), May 19, 1933, 16.

84. *Palestine Post*, March 29, 1933, 5, and June 13, 1933, 2.

85. *Le Temps*, March 30, 1933; A. Hamdy to the Director General, Public Security Department, Egyptian Ministry of the Interior, April 26, 1933, The Residency, Cairo, no. 581 (part 1): Jews & Nazis, FO 141/699/17, National Archives, Kew Gardens, London, UK (hereafter, NA-UK).

86. W. M. Jardine, Legation of the United States of America, Cairo, to Honorable Secretary of State, May 18, 1933, "Subject: Further Reaction in Egypt to German Anti-Semitism," box 6786, CDF, 1930–39, Department of State General Records, RG 59, NA-CP.

87. Memorandum (private and confidential), April 13, 1933, 1658/7/1/2/3, BoD Defence Committee Papers, Wiener Library, London.

88. "The Anglo-Jewish Association," n.d., ACC/3121/C/11/08, and J. H. Hertz to the Presidents, JFC, March 22, 1933, ACC/3121/C/11/012/014, BoD Papers, LMA.

89. "Public Meetings of Protest Which Have Been Held," n.d., 1658/7/1/8/45, BoD Defence Committee Papers, Wiener Library, London. Three of these took place in London. In April 1933, in addition to Liverpool and Cardiff, there were protest meetings in Leeds, Glasgow, Middlesborough, Manchester, Swansea, and Pontypridd.

90. "Protest Meeting against the Persecution of Jews in Germany: A Mass Meeting," 1658/7/1/7/5, and *Hull Daily Mail*, April 10, 1933, 1658/7/1/13/1, BoD Defence Committee Papers, Wiener Library, London.

91. "Manchester Leaders Denounce Persecutions," *Jewish Standard and Record*, April 28, 1933, 1658/7/1/17/12, and *Daily Dispatch* (Manchester), April 20, 1933, 1658/7/1/17/6, BoD Defence Committee Papers, Wiener Library, London.

92. *Herald* (Glasgow), April 17, 1933, 1658/7/1/11/3; *The Scotsman*, April 17, 1933, 1658/7/1/11/4; and *Bulletin and Scots Pictorial*, April 17, 1933, 1658/7/1/11/2, BoD Defence Committee Papers, Wiener Library, London.

93. *Jewish Echo* (Glasgow), April 21, 1933, 1656/7/1/11/11, BoD Defence Committee Papers, Wiener Library, London.

94. "British Reactions: Protests in Parliament," *Jewish Chronicle* (London), March 31, 1933, 36.

95. Susan Pedersen, *Eleanor Rathbone and the Politics of Conscience* (New Haven: Yale University Press, 2004), 271–72; Eleanor Rathbone, letter to the editor, *Times* (London), April 11, 1933, 10.

96. "Prayers and Atrocities," 16.

97. *Manchester Guardian*, March 31, 1933, 11.

98. *Daily Herald* (London), April 14, 1933, 1; *ManchesterGuardian*, April 15, 1933, 6, 11.

99. *New York Times*, April 15, 1933, 6. The *New York Herald Tribune* placed its story on the parliamentary speeches on the front page. *New York Herald Tribune*, April 15, 1933, 1, 7.

100. "The House of Lords," *Jewish Chronicle* (London), April 7, 1933, 29–30.

101. *Jewish Ledger* (Rochester, NY), May 19, 1933, clipping in box 6785, CDF, 1930–39, Department of State General Records, RG 59, NA-CP; *New York Evening Post*, April 28, May 10, 3, and May 11, 1933, 6; *BrooklynJewish Examiner*, May 12, 1933, 1, 3; *Philadelphia Inquirer*, May 11, 1933, 3; *Cleveland Plain Dealer*, May 11, 13, 14, and 15, 1933; *Hitlerism and the American Jewish Congress*. The press emphasized the enormous numbers participating in and watching the demonstrations and the marchers' energy and commitment. The *New York Herald Tribune*'s front page headline read, "250,000 Here Join in Jewish Hitler Protest. [Mayor] O'Brien Leads 65,000 in 4-Hour Parade . . . Denunciations [of Nazis] Last 3 Hrs." The *New York Evening Post* ran a page 3 headline on May 10: "Jews Shut Shops for Parade Today/Majority Will Close at 2:30 to Give All a Chance to Protest." *New York Evening Post*, May 10, 1933, 3. The *Chicago Tribune*'s

article on May 11 was headlined "25,000 Chicago Jews Join Persecution Protest Parade." It included a large photograph of the crowd. *Chicago Tribune*, May 11, 1933, 4. *Time* magazine reported that 80,000 Jews marched in New York, 50,000 Jews in Chicago, and 20,000 Jews in Philadelphia. "Germany: Bibliocaust," *Time*, May 22, 1933, 21.

102. *Cleveland Plain Dealer*, May 11, 1933, 3, May 13, 1933, 12, May 14, 1933, 1, 3, and May 15, 1933, 1, 6.

103. *Cleveland Plain Dealer* , May 12, 1933, 7.

104. *Boston Globe*, May 15, 1933, 17.

105. "German Anti-Semitism. Alexandria Protest Meeting. Huge and Representative Gathering," *Egyptian Gazette*, May 23, 1933, 581/7/33, "Jews & Nazis: Egypt," British Foreign Office (hereafter, FO) Records, NA-UK.

106. A. W. Keown-Boyd, director-general, Cairo, to H. E. the Minister, April 2, 1933, "Jews & Nazis: Egypt," British FO Records, NA-UK.

107. A. W. Keown-Boyd, "The German-Jewish Movement in Egypt," June 9, 1933, British FO Records, NA-UK.

FOUR

——ᴍ——

THE ESCALATION OF JUDAEA'S WAR AGAINST NAZISM

May to December 1933

AMERICAN AND BRITISH JEWS DEVELOPED multifarious and highly inno-
vative forms of protest against Nazi antisemitism during the months following
the massive May 10, 1933 demonstrations against the book burnings. Grassroots
Jewish militancy, which received widespread press coverage, invigorated Jewish
defense organizations in both countries. Jews forcefully challenged the Hitler
regime and highlighted its antisemitic atrocities. They continued to stage mass
street rallies and collected huge numbers of signatures on petitions demanding that the US and British governments publicly condemn Nazi antisemitic
policies. They sponsored anti-Nazi lectures and directly confronted emissaries
whom the German government sent abroad to promote Nazi goals and policies.
From the beginning of the Hitler regime's reign of terror, major Jewish organizations and individual Jewish activists exhaustively researched and documented
German Jewry's plight in order to refute Nazi propaganda, which circulated
widely in the United States and Britain. Strong efforts were made to instill pride
in being Jewish as a means of mobilizing Jews to combat the spread of Nazism.

THE BOYCOTT AS DECLARATION OF WAR ON THE NAZIS

Among the most dramatic methods of protest was the boycott of German
goods and services, which developed significant momentum in the United
States, Britain, and many other countries after May 1933. The boycott damaged several German industries and German shipping while making both
Jews and gentiles more aware of the unparalleled degradation of Jews in Germany and the danger of German military expansionism. The boycott also
made anti-Nazi resistance more effective by forging bonds and creating new

communication networks among Jews in the many countries where the movement was active.

On May 14, 1933, 600 delegates representing 288 Jewish groups met in New York City and established the American League for the Defense of Jewish Rights (ALDJR) to coordinate the national boycott. The American Jewish Congress (AJCongress) at its May 1933 meeting continued to reject the boycott, as did the American Jewish Committee (AJC). The ALDJR grew out of a group called the Anti-Nazi League, founded in late April 1933 by AJCongress dissidents who opposed its antiboycott position, including Ezekiel Rabinowitz and Dr. Abraham Coralnik, associate editor of the Yiddish daily *Der Tog* (*The Day*). Anti-Nazi League members conferred with the Jewish War Veterans (JWV) about how to organize boycott activities. Rabinowitz and Coralnik joined with prominent Jewish attorney and Zionist Samuel Untermyer to set up the ALDJR. In a speech to the American Friends of Hebrew University the previous month, Untermyer had called on opponents of Nazism to follow the lead of London's Jewish shopkeepers and establish a boycott movement.[1]

Speakers at the ALDJR founding convention, to which the *New York Times* and the *New York Herald Tribune* gave front-page coverage, defined the boycott as "a declaration of war" against the Nazis' challenge to world Jewry. Samuel Margoshes, editor of *Der Tog*, vowed, "there will be no quarter given nor [any] received." Untermyer, who became the ALDJR's head, declared that the boycott would be a primary weapon in combatting the Hitler regime's "cruel campaign of extermination." The organization announced that it would wage its "commercial war with Germany" in cooperation with Jewish groups in Britain, France, Poland, and other countries, making the boycott a coordinated international effort.[2]

The ALDJR immediately began to organize boycott activities in New York by dividing the city into twelve districts—four in Manhattan, six in Brooklyn, and two in the Bronx. In each, a council was established to identify stores that carried German products and compile lists of suppliers of substitutes manufactured in other countries. ALDJR volunteers would present these lists to storekeepers, using them to replace the German-made goods they stocked.[3]

The JWV stepped up its boycott activities in May 1933, joining with a group of Jewish US Army officers—whose names it would not divulge—to target German ships entering and leaving New York City. The JWV committee charged with picketing the docks hoped that its boycott movement would "develop into a chain encircling the globe." Like the ALDJR, the JWV would canvass American businesses importing German goods and inform them how to substitute items from other countries.[4]

The London *Jewish Chronicle* reported on May 12 that Jews on both sides of the Atlantic were complying with the shipping boycott. Although three-quarters of Jews traveling between Europe and the United States had previously sailed on German liners, now nearly all booked passage on British ships. It noted a few weeks later that while transatlantic passenger traffic had dropped significantly over the first four months of 1933, the British Cunard line had lost only 19.8 percent of its passengers, compared to the North German Lloyd line's whopping 35.9 percent. This was particularly striking because new German liners held the Atlantic speed record, whereas the Cunard's fastest ship was more than twenty-five years old. By June 22, passenger traffic on Germany's two fastest transatlantic liners, the *Bremen* and the *Europa*, had been halved.[5]

By June 15, the ALDJR and JWV boycott campaign had sufficiently alarmed the Hitler government that its ambassador to the United States, Dr. Hans Luther, met with Undersecretary of State William Phillips in an effort to convince him to suppress it. Luther showed Phillips samples of the JWV's "Don't Buy German Goods" stamps, which, he complained, were widely distributed across the country. Phillips promised Luther that he would see if the US government could do anything about it.[6]

Two days later, George S. Messersmith, US consul general in Berlin, informed Secretary of State Cordell Hull that Hitler, Goering, and Goebbels had become seriously concerned about the impact the boycott could have on the German economy. Messersmith observed that initially the German government had believed it could disregard foreign opinion. But it now recognized "that a very effective boycott exists against German goods in many countries on account of the program against the Jews, and they now understand the disastrous effects which this boycott can have on the German economic situation and on the Nazi party."[7]

Travelers investigating the Jewish situation in the Third Reich in 1933 were appalled by what they had seen. A little more than a week after the May 10 demonstrations, Jonah B. Wise, chair of the American Jewish Joint Distribution Committee's relief campaign for European Jewry, wrote to *New York Times* publisher Arthur Hays Sulzberger that he was badly shaken by what Jews there had told him. He stated that "the leaders of German Jewry" had informed him "point blank that the Jews are finished in Germany." The vast majority of German Jews would be forced to remain there, either "to await death in childless penury" or to "eke out an existence on a social and economic level which threatens to be lower than that of any Jewish community in the world." German Jewish youth knew beyond any doubt that they would be denied "all the amenities of civilization." There was "no precedent in modern history in a civilized State" to force into "poverty and dependence . . . men who have been outstanding in the learned professions. . . . [N]o provision is made so that they be saved from starvation."[8]

NON-JEWISH SUPPORT FROM SENATORS, REFORMERS, AND JOURNALISTS

Jews at the grassroots and trade unionists in the United States and Britain initiated and provided the momentum for the mass street demonstrations and rallies against Nazi antisemitism and for the boycott. But although Jews were always more engaged than others, some prominent American and British non-Jews spoke out forcefully against the Hitler regime from the time it assumed power. This was important, because non-Jewish involvement in the struggle heightened public awareness of the desperate state of German Jewry. In both nations, many of these non-Jews were prominent in politics, reform, and the press.

Although President Roosevelt, like the British prime minister, remained publicly silent about German Jewry's plight, on June 10, US Senate majority leader Joseph Robinson (a Democrat from Arkansas) expressed "strong criticism of the persecution of Jews in Germany" on the Senate floor, denouncing the Hitler regime's antisemitic policies and atrocities as "sickening and terrifying." Robinson stated that "universities are closed to Jewish scientists and students. The right of Jewish children to attend primary schools is limited or denied." He added that the persecution was "rendered the more intolerable by decrees forbidding Jews to leave Germany." Robinson quoted passages from Hitler's *Mein Kampf* that graphically portrayed the global menace of the Jewish pestilence and suggested the solution of gassing them: on page 70 of the twelfth edition, published in Munich in 1932, "If the Jew wins his crown of victory [it] is the death wreath of humanity, and this planet will once again, float through the ether bereft of men." Then, on page 344 of the same edition: "If at the beginning of the war, 12,000 or 15,000 of these corruptors of the people [that is, Jews] had been held under poison gas . . . then the sacrifices of millions at the front would not have been in vain." Robinson quoted Josef Goebbels's statement published in a Munich Nazi newspaper in 1929, in which he compared the Jew to an insect, also pointing toward a "final solution": "Certainly the Jew is also a human being . . . but the flea is also an animal. . . . As the flea is not a pleasant animal, we do not feel any duty . . . to . . . let it thrive so that it may bite, sting, and torture us." Senator Robinson drew attention to the Nazi Party program's statement that Jews were not "persons of German blood" and therefore could not be citizens.

Several other senators then rose to condemn the persecution of Jews in Germany, just as British MPs Austen Chamberlain and Winston Churchill had in the House of Commons in April. Senator Robert Wagner (a Democrat from New York), who was born in Germany and spent his boyhood there, declared that he was "struck with horror at the reports of intolerance, discrimination, and. . . violence" in the Reich. The next day Robinson's speech and the statements of the other four senators were front-page news in the *New York Times*.[9]

The protest in the Senate stung the Hitler regime, prompting Ambassador Luther to complain once again to Undersecretary Phillips. Luther told Phillips that his government found Robinson's remarks especially offensive because he was the majority leader and a prominent member of President Roosevelt's Democratic Party. Phillips explained to Luther that the State Department had no jurisdiction over the legislative branch of government and therefore did not have the power to silence Senator Robinson.[10]

Several other prominent non-Jewish Americans protested the Roosevelt administration's unwillingness to publicly denounce Nazi persecution of Jews or to assist German Jewish refugees. On the initiative of former US ambassador to Germany James Gerard, on June 5, 1933, they convened an American National Conference against Racial Persecution in Germany in Washington, DC. The *Brooklyn Jewish Examiner* declared that never before had a "more distinguished group of Christians" gathered "for the sole purpose of giving aid to their Jewish fellow men." The conference was endorsed by Governors Gifford Pinchot of Pennsylvania and Albert Ritchie of Maryland; US senators William H. King of Utah, Millard Tydings of Maryland, and Burton Wheeler of Montana; several US representatives; Department of Labor Children's Bureau head Grace Abbott; and National Women's Trade Union League (WTUL) secretary-treasurer Elisabeth Christman. Several conference speakers "roundly condemned anti-Jewish conditions in Germany," and the conference unanimously passed a resolution calling for temporarily lowering immigration barriers to the United States. It also resolved to create a fund to "support the destitute victims of German oppression and enable them to establish homes in other lands." The conference called on the British government to allow increased Jewish immigration into Palestine. In his keynote address, former US representative Fiorello La Guardia called Hitler a "perverted maniac." John J. O'Connor, US representative of New York, denounced the Fuehrer as "the Madman of Germany." US representative Loring Black of New York urged American delegates to the upcoming London Economic Conference to refuse to negotiate with the German government's representatives.[11]

In August 1933, Carrie Chapman Catt, prominent women's suffragist, disclosed that during the previous month nine thousand women from across the

United States had signed a "letter of protest" prepared by her newly established Protest Committee of Non-Jewish Women Against the Persecution of Jews in Germany. The letter stated that "the German pogrom against the Jews" was the most shocking event since the world war. It condemned Germany's expulsion of Jews from the professoriate and the medical and legal professions. The letter also accused the Hitler regime of barring Jews from other occupations and discharging Jewish youth from schools and universities. Catt recruited several prominent women reformers to join the Protest Committee. They included Grace Abbott; Cornelia Pinchot, wife of Pennsylvania's governor and a leader of the National WTUL; settlement house leader Jane Addams of Hull House; feminist Charlotte Perkins Gilman; and Mary Woolley, president of Mount Holyoke College.[12]

From the beginning of Hitler's rule, several talented non-Jewish journalists writing for American and British newspapers were aghast at Nazi antisemitism and committed to documenting it. Pierre van Paassen, syndicated columnist for several American newspapers, contacted German Jews inside the Reich and in exile in Paris, and in 1933 and 1934 he communicated their accounts to millions of readers. He also lectured widely on the Nazi persecution of Jews and the pressing need to open Palestine to full-scale Jewish immigration. Van Paassen unequivocally warned Americans that "there was no hope for the Jews in Germany." In February 1934, the *Boston Globe* reported that the Nazis had thrown van Paassen into a concentration camp, charged with assisting Jews to escape from the Reich and "spreading atrocity propaganda in France and the United States." Soon after, they expelled him from Germany. The *Globe* noted that Palestine's Jews held van Paassen in such high regard that they had made him an honorary citizen of Tel Aviv.[13]

During the early months of Hitler's rule, Edgar Ansel Mowrer of the *Chicago Daily News* worked tirelessly to document Nazi atrocities against Jews. He "combed medical journals and provincial newspapers for possible clues or inadvertent revelations." In his autobiography, Mowrer would recall that "to discredit my reports of anti-Semitic outrages," Hitler's foreign press chief Ernst Hanfstaengl "started the rumor that I was a 'secret' Jew." In September 1933, the Nazis forced Mowrer out of Germany.[14]

In August 1934, Dorothy Thompson, who had covered the Nazis since 1931, was expelled from Germany for having written "numerous anti-German articles in the American press." Her expulsion from the Reich was front-page news in the *New York Times* and the *Chicago Tribune*. In the short time since Hitler assumed power, she had made five trips to investigate conditions in the Reich. Having served as head of the Central European Bureau for the Philadelphia

Public Ledger and *New York Evening Post* during the 1920s, Thompson was very well informed about German affairs. In May 1933, she harshly criticized Nazi policies in a series of six articles for the *Jewish Daily Bulletin* of New York, which also appeared in such metropolitan dailies as the *New York Evening Post* and the *Cleveland Plain Dealer.* In 1936, Thompson began a syndicated column, reaching eight million readers in 170 newspapers by the eve of World War II, in which she strongly and repeatedly condemned Nazi antisemitism and brutality.[15]

The Roosevelt administration was unwilling to employ the retaliatory measures that some other nations used to protect their journalists in the Third Reich from expulsion. In August 1934, Sigrid Schultz pointed out that when the Hitler government threatened to deport Camille Loutre of *Le Petit Parisien*, "the French ambassador warned the Germans that for every French correspondent ousted four Germans would be ejected from France." The Nazis were forced to back down. The Soviet and Czechoslovak governments had reacted similarly when the Nazis' threatened their journalists with expulsion.[16]

In Britain, two distinguished non-Jewish journalists with the *Manchester Guardian*—Robert Dell and Frederick Voigt—reporting from Berlin, Paris, Geneva, and London, provided regular in-depth coverage of Nazi antisemitic persecution. Dell, the son of a Protestant minister, was a convert to Catholicism. A *Guardian* colleague called Voigt "a deeply devout practicing churchman." Referring to Nazi Germany in the May 3, 1933, issue of the American magazine *Nation*, Dell concluded that "never in modern times has the government of a great country declared its intention of outlawing all its Jewish nationals and depriving them not only of the rights of citizenship but also of the means of subsistence." In a pamphlet he wrote for the AJCongress, published in late 1933 or 1934, Dell quoted foreign correspondents he had met with in Berlin in August 1933 that the Nazi treatment of Jews was "unprecedented since the 13th century." Indeed, "even the persecution of the Jews in the Middle Ages was probably less brutal and less the outcome of a sheer lust of cruelty."[17]

Frederick Voigt's obituary in the *Guardian* in 1957 explained that "he was among the first journalists to recognize the peculiar nature of Nazism and its dangers to the world." A week after the obituary appeared, two German Jewish refugees stressed that from the beginning Voigt had "see[n] the dangers existing in Germany . . . clearer than anybody else, and . . . did his best to point to and warn against them." They noted that Voigt, "unnoticed," had secured support for many refugees from the Reich.[18]

W. P. Crozier, the *Guardian's* editor from 1932 until his death in 1944, raised as a Methodist, was committed to providing in-depth coverage of the Nazi persecution of Jews. He participated in the early mass protest rallies against

Nazi antisemitism. In April 1933, addressing one of the largest gatherings in Manchester "under any auspices for many years," Crozier characterized the Nazi persecution as the worst the Jews had suffered in two thousand years. In a published tribute to Crozier at the time of his death in 1944, Harry Sacher, a Jewish *Guardian* reporter, wrote that his editor was eager to help his staff cover any of the key issues affecting the Jews, "whether it was the Nazi terror or the tepid and ineffectual work of rescue or the destiny of the Jewish National Home in Palestine." The next day, the prominent British Jewish historian Lewis Namier stated in the *Guardian* that Crozier was "one of the noblest friends of the refugees in this country from Nazi persecution."[19]

THE *BROOKLYN JEWISH EXAMINER*'S MASS PETITION CAMPAIGN

The *Brooklyn Jewish Examiner*, a leading English-language Jewish newspaper, decided to apply pressure on an indifferent Roosevelt administration. On June 2, 1933, the *Jewish Examiner* announced that it was circulating a petition to send to President Roosevelt and the US Congress "in a militant attempt" to bring to the government's attention "the urgent and imperative need for intervention on its part in behalf of the stricken Reich Jewry." By August, two hundred thousand Americans had signed the petition, including two governors, three US senators, and six US representatives.[20]

COMMENCEMENTS IN ABSENTIA

Jews in Newark, New Jersey, initiated an unprecedented form of grassroots protest by staging a commencement in absentia on July 12, 1933, to honor Jewish youth in Nazi Germany denied access to schooling and to publicize their plight. Jews from "Newark and its environs" at this ceremony passed a resolution declaring their solidarity with "those young men and young women deprived of their merited right to complete their studies ... because of the cruelly calculated policy of persecution in force by the Nazi regime."[21] During the next several years, many similar commencements in absentia were held in the United States. In May 1934, Temple Emanu-El in Manhattan awarded degrees and diplomas to German Jewish students denied them on "racial grounds." The sponsoring group, the Junior Division of the New York United Jewish Appeal, used the occasion to initiate a $1.2 million relief campaign for German Jews. Albert Einstein sent the commencement the following message: "That we Jews, a scattered people for almost two thousand years have been able to survive without . . .

physical power is due to the fact that the teachings of our forefathers have remained alive within us." These teachings included support "for our Jewish brethren who are bound to us by ties of tradition and a common destiny." He emphasized that "such help is now necessary for the Jews of Germany."[22]

JUDAEA'S WAR AGAINST NAZISM IN BRITAIN,
MAY–JULY 1933

Anti-Nazi protestors aggressively challenged Alfred Rosenberg, editor of the Nazi Party newspaper *Völkischer Beobachter* and one of Hitler's principal foreign affairs advisors, when the Fuehrer sent him to London in May 1933 to promote friendship between Britain and the Third Reich. Rosenberg was the Nazi Party's leading race theorist and head of its *Aussenpolitische Amt*, a foreign policy bureau that paralleled the German Foreign Office. He arrived in London on May 5 and returned to Germany on May 14, two days early, rattled by the sustained grassroots protests against him. Rosenberg reacted angrily to British foreign secretary Sir John Simon's statement that there was indignation in Britain over the Nazi persecution of German Jewry, issuing "a sensational warning to Britain" that Germany would "not stand for any interference in her internal affairs." In the first major street confrontation with a Hitler regime official in Britain or the United States, opponents of Nazism picketed Rosenberg's hotel on the night of May 11 during his press conference there, protesting the appearance of a Hitler emissary in Britain and his reception by British officials.[23]

After delivering a ten-minute speech in German to the reporters, many of whom did not understand the language, Rosenberg withdrew to a corner. The London *Jewish Chronicle* representative confronted him there, followed by many other journalists, and asked him whether the German government was going to allow the professors and others it had forced out of employment to starve. Upset, Rosenberg retorted, "No one worried about starving Germans." The journalists then demanded that Rosenberg's responses be translated into English and that he answer more questions. Instead, he ignored them and "entered into conversation with a lady." Rosenberg abruptly departed when a correspondent from the London *Daily Herald*, the Labour Party newspaper, showed him a photograph of a woman whom about twenty Nazis had beaten in her home, "until parts of her body were like pulp." The correspondent displayed more photographs of Nazi atrocities to the eighty reporters present. Pickets outside could be heard shouting at Rosenberg, "Go home!"[24]

The London *Jewish Chronicle* dismissed as ludicrous Rosenberg's claim that "the destruction of the Jewish intellectual and commercial classes" in Germany had been carried out to overturn a Russian Jewish immigrant monopoly of "all positions in the State." It noted that Albert Einstein, Fritz Haber, Lion Feuchtwanger, Bruno Walter, and the "thousands of Jewish professional and business men" were hardly "newcomers from another country." The *Jewish Chronicle* emphasized that the Nazis' purpose was "to root out all Jews, and not some of them, on the ground of their non-Nordic origin!"[25]

A former British army captain decorated in the world war received public support when he was arrested for hurling a wreath bearing a swastika that Rosenberg had placed on the major British world war memorial, the Cenotaph, into the Thames River. The London Trades Council immediately passed a resolution condemning the swastika wreath as "an insult to the British people and a mockery of the British soldiers" killed fighting the Germans. In an editorial entitled "Clear Out!" the London *Daily Herald* protested the "desecration" of the shrine by a representative of a government that carried out savage "political and racial murders."[26]

Anti-Nazi protestors followed Rosenberg to the docks when he returned to Germany, shouting, "Down with Hitler and the Murder Government!" The London *Daily Herald* commented that these "were the last words he heard as he left British soil—as they were the first he heard when he arrived." It emphasized that the protests showed that the British viewed Nazi antisemitism as "a reversion to barbarism" and recognized that Hitler's policies had "greatly increased" the prospects for war.[27]

While Rosenberg was in London, activists staged further anti-Nazi demonstrations. At Madame Tussaud's wax museum, a man poured red paint over the figure of Adolf Hitler and hung a sign around its neck that read, presciently, "Hitler, the mass murderer." At Rosenberg's hotel, a young man in the restaurant launched into an "emphatic speech against Hitler," as a young woman who had been sitting at his table distributed anti-Nazi leaflets to guests. She resisted efforts by hotel waiters and porters to remove her. As hotel personnel dragged her out, "she kicked over the table next to one where Lord Fitzwilliam was lunching with a party." Then "she kicked over another one" at which Lord Cadogan was sipping coffee, "which was upset all over him."[28]

Five days after Rosenberg's departure, in the principal address at an anti-Nazi protest meeting organized by University of London students, Professor J. B. S. Haldane, a prominent biologist, ridiculed a resolution passed unanimously at a heavily attended anti-Nazi meeting at London's Queen's Hall two nights before. It had been drafted by a group of mostly non-Jewish youth organizations, including the Young Friends (Quakers), the National Sunday School Union, the Young Men's Christian Association, and the British Federation of

University Women. The resolution "appealed in a spirit of friendship to the German people" to end "the present discrimination practiced against German Jewry."[29] Haldane's speech, by contrast, resembled the denunciations of Nazi antisemitism heard at grassroots Jewish rallies. He declared that the Nazis were engaged in "a systematic attempt . . . to expel everyone of Jewish origin . . . from positions of all kinds, to starve the better part of a million people to death unless they could get out of the country." This constituted, in effect, an "attempt to wipe out the entire Jewish section of the German nation." Any effort to persuade the German people to end the persecution of the Jews was "utterly futile." Strong pressure had to be applied from abroad, much like when pogroms raged in czarist Russia. To say that the British had no right to "interfere in the internal affairs of another nation" was "damned nonsense." A boycott of German goods and services was the most effective weapon available to anti-Nazis. It was also very important to fight antirefugee propaganda in England and to raise money to support German Jews and others whom the Nazis forced out of employment and into exile.[30]

In late June, the archbishop of Canterbury gave the principal speech at another almost entirely Christian Queen's Hall protest meeting. He and the others who addressed the gathering spoke "in measured and moderate terms." The archbishop claimed that there was "much, and very much" in the "present German revolution" that was "praiseworthy," particularly the efforts of German youth to "restore self-respect to a generation of Germans." At the same time, he appealed to the German government to restrain "some of these vehement emotions unleashed by the Nazi revolution." The archbishop introduced the meeting's resolution by "disclaiming any right or desire to interfere" in Germany's internal affairs. Nonetheless, he declared, the Nazis' discrimination against Jews was "contrary to the basic principles of tolerance and equality which are expected by the modern world." Lord Horder, physician for Prime Minister Ramsey MacDonald, provided the only militant voice. Unable to be there, Lord Horder sent a letter to be read aloud by the Rt. Hon. Viscount Buckmaster, who presided, in which he vowed not to attend "any medical or scientific meeting or congress at which accredited German representatives will be present."[31]

In mid-1933, grassroots British Jews' militancy escalated into a series of rallies and demonstrations, as well as aggressive efforts to enforce the boycott of German goods and services. On May 28, the Jewish community in Glasgow, Scotland, held a mass meeting to protest Nazi antisemitism at which the two principal speakers, both rabbis, called for universal participation in the boycott and a lowering of barriers to Jewish settlement in Palestine. The meeting's chair, Maurice Bloch, opened the proceedings by declaring that it was the most tragic moment in Jewish history, as "unparalleled cruelty . . . was being perpetrated against an innocent people." He stated that the German government must be arraigned before the "bar of justice in the form of the League of Nations." Bloch praised the boycott as a great spontaneous movement emanating from the Jewish rank and file.[32] The first speaker, Rabbi M. S. Simmons of Glasgow's Pollokshields Synagogue, lamented that the General Assembly of the Church of Scotland had just passed a resolution on antisemitism in Germany that was "timid and cautious." Lord Sands, in supporting the resolution, had urged the assembly to "refrain from any violence of thought or language." Simmons advised the Church of Scotland to "cast caution to the wind, and to say that we will not tolerate the death of the innocents; we shall not tolerate the 600,000-fold crucifixion of the Jew upon the Swastika."[33]

Rabbi Isadore Goodman of Glasgow's Queen's Park Synagogue followed Simmons and similarly urged massive support for the boycott to save German Jewry from "extinction." By robbing Jews of "the economic possibility of existence," the German government denied that Jews "had the right to live." Rabbi Goodman considered German Jewry's plight to be far worse than that of Jews under the Spanish Inquisition. Torquemada, the Grand Inquisitor, had given Spain's Jews a choice between "the cross or exile." But the Jew in Germany was "kept like a trapped rat with no one to appeal to and nowhere to go." They were presented with "no choice but extinction." Like Simmons, Goodman denounced the Church of Scotland for "not see[ing] itself fit to do something with regard to the [anti-Jewish] persecutions."[34]

In closing, J. Sachs declared that the Hitler government "had made war on the Jews within her borders," waging it "with unbridled brutality," committing "cruel, savage, and disgusting" atrocities. He noted that in a few days, the Germans would "celebrate in patriotic panegyrics the memory of two men, the assassins of Rathenau." He declared that there had once been a time in Europe "when gentlemen did not shake hands with murderers." Sachs ended by urging Jews to "treat Germany as a country that had declared war upon them." The meeting concluded with the singing of the Zionist anthem "Hatikvah."[35]

In early July 1933, ten thousand London Jews gathered at Albert Hall to show solidarity with "their persecuted co-religionists in Germany." Hundreds wept as the cantor of the Great Synagogue, Aldgate, "sorrowfully chanted an age-old Hebrew prayer," and London's chief rabbi, Dr. J. H. Hertz, described the desperate situation of Germany's Jews. Dr. Hertz declared that during the previous four months, German Jewry had been "battling for its very life against a tidal wave of mass hysteria and racial persecution." The Hitler regime's expulsion of Jews from the professions and state and municipal service was accompanied by "a campaign of such relentless ruin against the Jew in commerce and industry . . . tantamount to denying them the elementary right to work and live."[36]

That same month in London's Whitechapel district, an angry crowd of about one thousand Jews surrounded a truck delivering German-made toys to an importer's shop on Sydney Street. As soon as someone spotted boxes marked "Made in Germany," a cry of "Boycott German goods!" went up, and within minutes the crowd began to push the truck over. Boycotters took the boxes to a warehouse, where several smashed the china dolls they contained. Meanwhile, another truck had arrived at the shop with more German-made toys. When a demonstrator "threatened to pour a can of petrol on the goods" and "set them on fire," it drove off without unloading. As the crowd continued to shout, "Boycott German goods," the shop owner "allowed the toys to be repacked and sent away." Mounted and foot police proved unable to clear the streets around the warehouse. The crowd did not disperse until every box had been removed. Captain W. J. Webber, who had charge of the boycott in the East End, arranged for the boxes to be returned to Germany and secured a written promise from the store proprietor that he would not sell any more German-made products.[37]

In Manchester, in the north of England, Jewish youth formed a "Jewish Defence Corps," which staged a series of open-air meetings throughout the city to "spread the truth" about the Nazis' persecution of Jews. The London *Jewish Chronicle* described the "sight of Jewish stump orators" as highly unusual in Manchester, another sign of intensifying grassroots Jewish militancy. Young speakers stood on boxes flanked by a large blue-and-white Zionist flag with a small Union Jack in the corner and appealed to listeners to "institute a complete boycott of German commodities."[38]

THE ROMANCE OF A PEOPLE: JEWISH PRIDE AND THE CELEBRATION OF JEWISH RESISTANCE

The Chicago Century of Progress World's Fair, which opened in late May 1933, provided the American Jewish community with the opportunity to use public theater to instill pride in Jewishness and turn it into a weapon against the Nazis. *The Romance of a People*, with a cast of sixty-two hundred actors, singers, and dancers, presented the "struggles and triumphs" of the Jews. Beginning with the creation, it proceeded through the story of Abraham and the struggle for monotheism, the Jews' enslavement in Egypt and liberation under Moses, the Babylonian exile, and their uprisings against the Romans. The play depicted the capture of Jerusalem by the Roman general Titus "with carnage unequaled in the long history of wars." The embattled Jews "fight like lions; they die, but do not surrender." There followed a portrayal of the Jews' almost two millennia of exile and persecution, including the Spanish Inquisition. The birth of the United States offers promise, as "an exultant voice" shouts "the words of the Torah" on the Liberty Bell that "first pealed American independence: 'Proclaim liberty throughout the land to all the inhabitants thereof.'" At the end, the Jews are able "to turn thoughts once again to restoration of [their] ancient civilization in Palestine."[39]

One hundred twenty-five thousand people attended the play's opening night on July 3 in Chicago's Soldier Field. They included "Jews from every part of the United States and many from Canada." Jews of "every shade of orthodoxy and liberalism" were there. The *Chicago Tribune* called it "the mightiest pageant which this city has ever seen." It noted that the Jewish singers on stage—these "young women of regal poise," with their "dark, glowing, searching eyes" and "deep, velvet voices"—conveyed intense pride in their Jewish heritage. They sang "like the divas of grand opera." Flanking the stage, Zionist flags and the Stars and Stripes flew from thirty-two flagstaffs. Another fifty-five thousand attended a second performance two days later.[40]

The Zionist Organization of America (ZOA) began its convention at the Chicago Century of Progress fair two days before *The Romance of a People* opened. Attended by five thousand delegates and friends, it was "hailed as the largest convention in the history of the organization." ZOA president Morris Rothenberg denounced the Nazi persecution of Jews "in forcible language." He declared that German Jewry, which had made immense contributions to German culture, "stands hopeless and homeless, their life made unendurable in their own land, and the opportunity to seek refuge denied them." All five thousand came to the opening performance of *The Romance of a People* as a unit.[41]

The Romance of a People then moved to New York City, where it played nightly at a Bronx armory, the largest in the nation, in September and October 1933. Samuel Untermyer and New York governor Herbert Lehman were honorary chairs of the sponsoring committee. The *New York Times* praised the pageant in an editorial, commenting that given Hitler's effort "to stigmatize a great people as an aggregation of pariahs and public enemies, perhaps the best thing to be done is to let the historic record speak for itself." JWV chapters across New York state backed the play. Many playing Roman Legionnaires were Jewish world war veterans with combat experience in France. Former New York governor Al Smith and his wife attended a performance and congratulated the pageant's sponsors. Samuel Untermyer, addressing the twenty-three thousand at the October 3 performance, urged support for the boycott of German goods and services. He pointedly condemned the "scattered few of would-be Jews who are ashamed of their race [namely the AJC leadership]" who opposed the boycott. A few days later, a special children's performance was staged at the request of educators convinced that the pageant was the best way to provide them with "an understanding of 4,000 years of Jewish history." The Brooklyn *Jewish Examiner* on October 13 reported that more than 270,000 had seen *The Romance of a People* since it opened in the Bronx on September 24. When it closed on October 19, the *New York Times* stated that a total of four hundred thousand had attended in New York.[42]

In 1934, the pageant also played to large audiences in Philadelphia (February), Cleveland (March), and Detroit (April). In Philadelphia, ten thousand—including Albert Einstein and his wife—"braved snow and ice" for the premiere, filling Convention Hall. When the performance ended, the crowd "broke into a spontaneous demonstration lasting ten minutes, during which cheers and applause thundered throughout the great hall." The Philadelphia *Public Ledger*, which covered the opening on the front page, called it "unquestionably . . . the greatest spectacle ever presented in Philadelphia." The Jewish Telegraphic Agency estimated on August 1, 1934, that nearly one million people had seen *The Romance of a People*.[43]

RESISTANCE TO NAZI PROPAGANDIZING AT THE CHICAGO CENTURY OF PROGRESS WORLD'S FAIR, MAY–AUGUST 1933

American Jews and other antifascists disrupted Hitler regime efforts to disseminate Nazi propaganda at the Chicago Century of Progress World's Fair. In late May 1933, one thousand Communist and other anti-Nazi demonstrators prevented German Propaganda Ministry official Hans Wiedemann, whom Josef Goebbels had dispatched to serve as Germany's "good-will ambassador" at the Chicago World's Fair, from landing in Brooklyn at his assigned pier. Goebbels had also sent Wiedemann to Chicago to study American propaganda and advertising methods. The demonstrators forced Wiedemann to slip into the United States "through the back door," on a tugboat that eluded the protestors. When the demonstrators at the pier refused an order to disperse, club-swinging mounted police charged, injuring several in what became "a pitched battle," with the fighting "hand-to-hand." Demonstrators hurled bottles and bricks at the policemen, wounding four. The Associated Press reported that "a semblance of order was restored [only] after police drew their pistols and leveled them at the rioters." Fourteen demonstrators were arrested.[44]

The New York local of the Socialist Party (SP) denounced Wiedemann's visit as "a disgrace and insult" to German workers whose unions Hitler had crushed and to Jews whom the Nazis had "brutally beaten, ousted out of their occupations, and reduced to a helot class." The SP also drew attention to the Nazis' burning of "some of the world's best literature" and exile of "authors, scientists, and philosophers of world reputation." It emphasized that any representative of the Hitler government "should be met with execration and loathing."[45]

The Jewish Women's Organization of Chicago, a coalition of mainstream Jewish women's organizations, notified World's Fair administrators that it refused to participate in the large luncheon to be held in the German American building if the swastika flag flew above it. The German consul general in Chicago had hoped the Nazi flag could be hoisted over the building. A spokesperson for the German American hostess society, after conferring with an advisory committee consisting of representatives of seventy-five Chicago women's organizations, announced that the German American building would not display the Nazi flag. In addition, the German government canceled plans for an exhibit, although it had already arrived in the United States.[46]

Jewish organizations, however, were unable to prevent the World's Fair administration from according Ambassador Hans Luther a nineteen-gun salute when he toured the fairgrounds in late October. Luther was personally greeted by Century of Progress president Rufus Dawes. Speaking at a swastika-draped podium at the Union League Club, the Nazi ambassador condemned the "Jewish-American" boycott of German goods and services. His audience included prominent Chicago bankers, industrialists, and German Americans. Also present were Rufus Dawes, representing Chicago's mayor, and Rear Admiral Cluverius, commander of the Great Lakes Naval Training Station.[47]

INTERNATIONAL COORDINATION OF THE BOYCOTT: THE AMSTERDAM CONFERENCE, JULY 1933

For three days in July 1933, thirty "grimly determined" delegates from Jewish communities in sixteen nations met in Amsterdam to formulate strategies for combatting the Nazi persecution of Jews and to extend the boycott of German goods and services across the world. The countries included the United States; Britain, France, Belgium, and the Netherlands in Western Europe; Poland and Latvia in Eastern Europe; and South Africa and Egypt in Africa. In each, the boycott movement was already well developed. Jewish organizations in ten other countries informed the conference that, although they could not send representatives, they would "loyally support" any actions the conference endorsed. The delegates elected Samuel Untermyer conference president. With all delegates standing, the conference unanimously passed a resolution calling the boycott Jews' only effective weapon against Germany, whose government intended "to annihilate them economically, to deprive them of their citizenship, to reduce them to a state of pariahs and eventually to exterminate them." The conference disclosed plans to establish a Jewish Federation for International Exchange to inform importers around the world where goods could be obtained to replace those manufactured in Germany.[48]

Dutch and Egyptian delegates presented positive reports on the boycott's impact in their countries. The Dutch reported a 40 percent decline in imports of German products into the Netherlands. The Egyptians, positioned at "the gateway of Germany's former great trade in Africa and the Orient," noted that Jews in their country exercised disproportionate influence in the import trade. They announced that "Germany's share of that trade has become almost non-existent."[49]

Frederick Birchall, Berlin correspondent for the New York Times, in a front-page article on July 21, described the conference as "a thoroughly militant assembly from the moment when it was called to order." Birchall emphasized that a dynamic boycott movement had already gained considerable popular support in many nations, where it was having a sizeable impact.[50]

Untermyer castigated the League of Nations, which, "to the supreme disappointment of its friends . . . has not lifted its hands to stay this catastrophe." Unless the League acted immediately and forcefully against the Nazi menace, "it might as well fold its tents and slink away," because it would have demonstrated that it was useless, incapable of dealing with the "great issues of humanity." Untermyer proposed several measures the League might undertake, including (1) sending a League committee to Germany to investigate and fully report on the situation of hundreds of thousands of imprisoned Jews; (2) issuing internationally recognized Nansen passports to Jews denied passports by Germany, which would enable them to leave the country and take their property with them (the League had originally created Nansen passports for persons whom the Bolshevik regime had rendered stateless; it later issued them to Greek, Armenian, and Romanian emigrants); (3) enforcing the Versailles Treaty's labor provisions, which Germany was flagrantly violating by expelling and barring Jews from trade unions; and (4) invoking and immediately implementing the treaty's relief clauses to save Jews from starving to death. Untermyer emphasized that in Amsterdam itself Jewish agencies were already providing relief for twenty-six hundred German Jewish refugees.[51]

The conference revealed deep strains between the ALDJR and the AJCongress, which still refrained from endorsing the boycott. Untermyer expressed his displeasure with AJCongress honorary president Rabbi Stephen S. Wise's refusal to participate in or publicly back the conference. In a speech in Paris, Wise had dismissed Untermyer as representing a very small group. Untermyer attributed Wise's opposition to his "apparent determination to discredit any movement he cannot lead" and invited him to "tell Jewry frankly whether or not he personally favors a boycott."[52] Neville Laski, president of the Board of Deputies of British Jews (BoD) on July 23, 1933, put the boycott question to a vote of his board, which voted 101 opposed and only 27 in favor.[53]

LONDON JEWS' MONSTER DEMONSTRATION
AGAINST NAZI ANTISEMITISM, JULY 20, 1933

Working- and lower-middle-class Jews, mostly from the East End, again displayed formidable initiative and solidarity by staging a mass street parade and rally in London against Nazi antisemitism on July 20, 1933, the largest demonstration in British Jewry's history. The London *Daily Herald* called it "one of the most impressive demonstrations of mass protest ever seen in London." An estimated thirty to fifty thousand Jews paraded from Stepney Green in the East End to Hyde Park, where another forty to fifty thousand awaited the marchers. The BoD made strenuous efforts to prevent the parade and rally from taking place, to no avail.[54]

The demonstration represented a powerful display of anti-Nazi Jewish grassroots militancy, with numerous participants carrying pro-boycott banners. One "hair-raising" banner depicted Hitler as King Kong, the giant ape "clasping a swastika in one hand and crushing the Jewish race in the other." The marchers included "rabbis and ex-servicemen; factory girls and businessmen; old men with scarcely the strength to keep in the march; youngsters and even babies carried in arms; *Chassidim* in their *kaftan* and [their opponents] *Misnagdim*." Nearly all Jewish shop owners in the East End posted notices in their windows that they had shut down to observe a twelve-hour "National Day of Mourning and Protest" against Nazism and proclaiming, "Join the Jewish procession to Hyde Park." The open-air pushcart market in Petticoat Lane was closed, with guards stationed at the corners to "see that no outsider should try to do business." Automobiles patrolled East End streets bearing signs exhorting residents to boycott German goods.[55]

The demonstration was pervaded with military imagery, indicating that London working-class and lower-middle-class Jews considered themselves to be engaged in a war against Nazism. There were about eight thousand Jewish army and navy veterans in the parade, a considerable number at its head, wearing their combat medals. The veterans were accompanied by four bands and young men waving the Union Jack. They were led by Captain W. J. Webber, head of the boycott in England. Many of the marching veterans clearly showed the effects of wounds from the world war: there were "men with one arm, faces scarred and bearing testimony to plastic surgery." The veterans' banner read, "In 1914 we defended Freedom against the Huns; in 1933 we must defend Jews against Hitler's atrocities."[56]

At Hyde Park, the intently serious crowd of one hundred thousand "stood to attention in the glaring sunlight . . . as if they were in some place of worship." There were no amplifiers, so the audience had difficulty hearing what was said. Dr. David Jochelman, president of the United Protest Committee that coordinated the parade, called for all Jews to stand firmly behind the boycott. In 1919, Jochelman had organized a "huge" parade in London to denounce the pogroms in the Ukraine. Another speaker "roared out his message to the crowd," and listeners close to the podium passed his key phrases through the crowd, including his "most telling" phrase: "Every pair of German stockings your daughter buys is costing half-a-pint of Jewish blood."[57]

Dr. Jochelman announced that "news of this great gathering . . . will travel around the world, pointing to the whirring cine-cameras on the sound film vans and the batteries of Press photographers." The London *Jewish Chronicle* commented on the striking images of the procession to Hyde Park and the gathering that were shown in London's movie theaters the next week. It reported that in the East End theaters, loud applause greeted Dr. Jochelman's demand that "no Jew should shake the hand of any other Jew if he knows he is continuing to deal commercially with Germany."[58] A non-Jewish spectator told marchers that the demonstration and rally "will do more to bring your cause before the English people . . . than all the isolated speeches and letters of protest."[59]

EXPANDING THE BOYCOTT

During late summer and fall of 1933, the boycott gathered momentum in both the United States and Britain as Rabbi Stephen S. Wise and the AJCongress finally decided to back it, and both nations' leading labor organizations, the American Federation of Labor (AFL) and the British Trades Union Congress (TUC), as well as the British Labour Party, endorsed it. In August, Rabbi Wise broke his long silence on the boycott and in a speech in Prague, Czechoslovakia, hailed it as an important weapon against Nazi Germany, led by "the modern Haman" who was determined to "exterminate" the Jews. A few days afterward, in an all-day emergency session in New York, the AJCongress National

Executive Committee unanimously went on record in support of the boycott. In early September, speaking in Geneva, Wise issued an unequivocal call for "war" against the Nazi terror, "even at the cost of reprisals against Jews in Germany."[60]

The American and British labor movements announced their official support for the boycott as a protest against both Hitler's destruction of the German trade unions and his antisemitic polices and atrocities. In a speech to the AFL convention in October 1933, President William Green declared that the "utter destruction" of Germany's labor movement had been "equaled only by the ruthless persecution of Germany's Jewish population." About a week later, Green announced that the AFL was preparing circulars to send to affiliated unions across the United States calling on them to support the boycott.[61] A short time before, 250 members of the Brotherhood of Painters, Decorators, and Paperhangers, AFL, working at Radio City in New York, walked off the job when they discovered that the wallpaper they were hanging was marked "Made in Germany." The secretary of the union's district council announced that by stopping work, the paperhangers proudly demonstrated what they thought of Hitler and their solidarity with the German trade unionists and Jews.[62]

In Britain, the National Joint Labour Council, made up of the TUC and the Parliamentary Labour Party, issued a manifesto in July 1933 urging members of the Labour Movement and the public not to buy German commodities or use German services. The manifesto provided a long list of German-made products sold in Britain and also targeted German films screened in British theaters and German steamship services and holiday attractions, which were widely advertised. The Labour Party annual conference report in October denounced the Hitler regime's "disgraceful and unwarranted persecution of the Jews, Pacifists, Trade Unionists, Socialists, and Communists." It noted that "the Nazi persecution of Jewish citizens, unknown since the worst days of Russian Czardom, [had] roused the Jewish community throughout the world."[63] Former Labour Party MP Ellen Wilkinson, who had witnessed the Nazi terror while in Germany shortly after Hitler came to power, declared, "If democracy is going to win this fight [against Nazism] it must have teeth and claws."[64]

By fall 1933, the American boycott had caused several German industries to lose a significant share of the American market. In August, the *Nation* reported that the longtime chairman of the board of Germany's Hamburg-American line, one of the Reich's two leading shipping corporations, had told a stockholders' meeting on July 26 that "the boycott has severely hurt the Hamburg-American's business and is continuing to hurt it and German shipping generally." He stated that "the volume of business is constantly falling back." The *Nation* noted that the next day the meeting of Germany's other major shipping company, the North German Lloyd, "was similarly doleful." The Boston *Jewish Advocate* reported on July 28 that a dispatch from Berlin indicated that the Hamburg-American line's shipping "is at a very low ebb and that the volume of business is constantly receding."[65]

In September 1933, Ambassador Hans Luther met with Secretary of State Hull to complain about the boycott, which he wanted the US government to stop. Although not addressing the boycott directly, Hull pointed out that he and other federal officials "had been endeavoring to avoid complications with the German Government by refusing to attack it on account of this alleged mistreatment of its Jewish nationals." Hull informed Luther that "more than once" he had "sent for congressmen and senators and urged them not to go beyond the proper bounds" in criticizing Germany. But he feared that when Congress reconvened in January, "there would likely be a flood of denunciation of the German Government and nationals" because of their treatment of German Jews.[66]

The American boycott had extended to major cities beyond New York, including Chicago, Kansas City, and Boston. In the late 1890s, there had been movements in all three cities to boycott the Paris Exposition of 1900 as a protest against the conviction of Alfred Dreyfus. Now, in September 1933, Chicago activists announced that they had initiated a boycott movement in the Windy City and were receiving information about alternative sources of products from Untermyer's organization (which in December 1933 changed its name to the Non-Sectarian Anti-Nazi League, NSANL). Chicago boycott activist Max Korshak stated on September 14 that Czechoslovakia was "prepared to replace the German dye industry products on the world market." He added that "sources in other countries have been found that can entirely replace German production of chemical and drug supplies." By March 1934, Chicago boycott volunteers had embarked on a citywide survey of stores to determine where German goods were sold.[67] The Kansas City boycott committee had secured the assistance of sixteen food wholesalers in persuading eight thousand retail grocers to sign an appeal to beet sugar refineries not to buy beet sugar from Germany, a major supplier of the crop.[68]

In Boston, whose sizeable Jewish population was heavily concentrated in the Mattapan-Roxbury-Dorchester enclave, support for the boycott developed spontaneously and rapidly in 1933. *Boston Herald* editor Frank Buxton informed US ambassador to Germany William Dodd that Boston's Jewish population "reads every word that comes from Berlin." Buxton wrote of an "anti-Hitler rage" in the Jewish neighborhoods. Theodore H. White, later the chronicler and analyst of presidential elections, notified the ALDJR in New York that on October 23, 1933, a German Boycott Council had been founded in Boston, of which he was chair. White wrote that the Boston German Boycott Council intended to "prosecute a complete and active boycott of all German goods entering Boston and New England" and was using "every avenue of attack." The council was informing storeowners and consumers of the boycott, in person, through posters, and by enlisting speakers to promote the boycott around the city. White asked the ALDJR for information about German goods sold in Boston, because storeowners and chambers of commerce were not cooperating with the council, and he also requested help with poster design and the contents of circulars.[69]

Less than three weeks later, the Boston *Jewish Advocate* reported that the Boston German Boycott Council was picketing chain novelty stores in the heavily Jewish Dorchester section and had already secured the signatures of three hundred people who pledged not to purchase German-made goods. The council commented that the picketed stores lacked any sense of decency in "knowingly displaying and selling German goods in a community where 85 percent of their customers were Jewish."[70]

In the fall of 1933, the ALDJR and some Jewish newspapers vilified R. H. Macy & Co., New York's biggest department store, largely owned by the Jewish Straus family, for refusing to comply with the boycott. On September 29, the Brooklyn *Jewish Examiner* cited the comment of Richard Neuberger, recently returned from a seven-week trip to study conditions in Nazi Germany, that "there is . . . one weapon Hitler and his lieutenants . . . fear—the boycott." Neuberger contrasted R. H. Macy's policy with that of one of its Christian-owned competitors, Lord & Taylor's, which "recalled its buyers from Germany shortly after Hitler inaugurated his reign of terror, and regardless of price established the policy of not buying one pfennig's worth of Nazi goods."

A week later, both the *Jewish Examiner* and the ALDJR ridiculed a full-page advertisement that Macy's president Percy Straus had placed in English and Yiddish New York newspapers defending his store's decision not to boycott German-made goods. The advertisement not only justified selling German goods but also denied that it had often rendered illegible the "country of origin" designation the law required to be stamped on merchandise, or had disguised it by substituting "Made in Saxony" or "Made in Bavaria." The *Jewish Examiner* reported that Macy's advertisement had angered many of its readers. In a derisive front-page editorial entitled "Business Is Business: Or They Who Foul Their Own Nest," it called the advertisement "a flimsy attempt to stem the rising tide of community-wide hostile sentiment" against Macy's, "aroused by its arrogant policy with regard to the boycott of German industry." The editorial noted that because Macy's had been established by Jews and was "today operated by those who are called Jews," New Yorkers had "a legitimate right" to demand that the store stand by the Jewish cause "in one of the most crucial hours of all the history of Jewry." The editorial concluded that Macy's "has failed us in that crisis."[71]

Samuel Untermyer wrote Straus an angry letter accusing him of pressuring the New York press not to publish the ALDJR's response to Macy's advertisement. Untermyer informed him that the ALDJR had "made desperate attempts to answer your advertisement by another in the same newspapers the following morning." Because these newspapers depended on Macy's patronage, as "by far the most important advertiser" in New York City, none would accept the ALDJR response, which was presented in the form of an open letter. Untermyer informed Straus that the ALDJR was now preparing to spend $200,000 to distribute five million copies of its response to the public.[72]

The ALDJR's letter informed the public that Macy's held many American department stores in line by continuing to purchase German goods because they would give Macy's a competitive advantage if they boycotted them. Unlike Macy's, however, most American department stores no longer maintained purchasing offices in Germany. The ALDJR reminded the public that German Jewish manufacturers were "no longer permitted to function . . . except . . . in rare instances and only under the most stringent Hitler control" and that they all had been required to discharge their Jewish employees. There were many alternate sources for the "gloves, textiles, chinaware," and other German-made products Macy's continued to buy.

The open letter emphasized that "the entire German nation" was boycotting "Jewish manufacturers, shopkeepers, and professional men . . . for the avowed purpose of destroying their means of livelihood and of ruining and exterminating the German Jews." Germany's "incredible 'Crime of the Centuries'" was aimed at every person in Germany with one or more Jewish grandparent. The Nazis were also committing a "crime against all womanhood" by expelling them from "all business occupations and condemning them to the fate of breeders of children and household drudges." The open letter also noted Germany's "suppression of . . . organized labor and its rigid exclusion of Jews from labor unions."[73]

In September 1933, Lord & Taylor's publicity director, Ira Hirschmann, appealed to merchants attending a conference on retail distribution in Boston to protest Nazi policies by boycotting German goods. Hirschmann, who had just returned from Germany, reported that Hitler was "openly preparing for war."

He told the merchants that in New York, manufacturers', retailers', and customers' interest in the boycott was second in importance only to the National Recovery Administration.[74]

THE BOYCOTT: STEADY GROWTH IN BRITAIN

In Britain, the boycott movement made steady progress from the spring of 1933 onward, although it was most dynamic in places with sizeable Jewish populations, like the East End of London, Manchester, and Glasgow. In May the London *Jewish Chronicle* reported that the British boycott was already having a "deadly effect" in the fur trade, where the majority of wholesale suppliers were Jewish. The importation of German furs into England had "to all intents and purposes ceased completely." Leipzig, where the German fur trade was centered, was no longer handling the dressing and dyeing of furs for the British market. The London *Times* predicted on May 9 that the coming year would probably be the most profitable in history for the British fur trade because of the international Jewish boycott's impact on the Leipzig market. It was estimated that the boycott had diverted an annual £7 million of trade from Germany to England.[75]

The boycott's impact became quickly evident in several other industries. In May, two thousand members of the British textile trade, meeting in London, enthusiastically voted to boycott German goods. Lord Melchett, a prominent boycott leader, who presided, told the meeting that Germany had no right to plead for equality with other nations when it denied Jews the opportunity to earn a living and was "conducting the most virulent persecution that has been seen in the last 1,000 years." Lord Melchett said that if one were to take away the Jews' contribution to Germany, Germany would "*not* have made her fair contribution to civilization."[76] That spring, ten British glass importers—seven in London and the others in Liverpool, Cardiff, and Preston—announced they were boycotting German glass. The *New York Times* reported on October 10 that Sheffield's "world famous cutlery factories" were "experiencing a sudden boom, largely as a result of the anti-Nazi boycott against Germany." Cutlery and tool works were "swamped with orders," and there was not sufficient skilled labor to meet the demand.[77]

By November 1933, the boycott was "intensely organized" in Britain. More than five hundred delegates from three hundred Jewish organizations met at a Conference of British Jews at Victoria Hall in London and unanimously passed a resolution introduced by Romanian-born Moses Gaster, chief rabbi of London's Spanish and Portuguese congregation, which endorsed the boycott and called on Jews in all parts of the British Empire to comply. The delegates represented about 175,000 Jews in Britain and Ireland. In August, Captain Webber had already declared that he had received twenty thousand certificates from individuals and businesses pledging to support the boycott. In September he had addressed overflow Jewish anti-Nazi meetings in Glasgow, which burst into applause when he urged the use of the boycott as a weapon of reprisal against Germany.[78]

The Conference of British Jews established a Jewish Representative Council to administer the boycott, which the BoD still refused to sanction. It objected on the grounds that the council was an attempt to establish a rival organization "as the representative authority on all questions affecting British Jewry." The council responded that its only purpose was to promote the boycott. Sir Robert Mond, who accepted the council presidency, immediately proposed an exhibition in London where German goods and substitutes from other countries would be displayed side by side.[79]

INFORMATION AS A WEAPON

In May 1933, the AJC published a 112-page *White Book* detailing the antisemitic laws and regulations the Hitler regime had introduced and documenting the Nazis' brutal treatment of Jews and their threats against them since 1923. The *New York Times* reported the *White Book*'s publication. The *New York Herald Tribune* praised it as an account of "the Nazi effort to convert German Jews into a pariah caste." The *Herald Tribune* urged any American who doubted that this was the Nazis' objective to read the *White Book*.[80]

Soon after the Nazis assumed power, the Joint Foreign Committee (JFC) of the BoD and the Anglo-Jewish Association (AJA) initiated an even more ambitious drive to heighten awareness of Nazism's catastrophic impact on German Jews. The JFC established a subcommittee to gather and disseminate information about the Jews' persecution. It was essential that the British public be knowledgeable about the antisemitic measures and atrocities, because the Hitler regime devoted significant effort to denying and justifying them. The subcommittee collected information in several ways: obtaining and systematically filing articles from Germany's major newspapers and those of neighboring countries; reading the principal English newspapers' coverage of events in Germany, taking copious notes, and compiling an index; collecting books and pamphlets the Nazis published; examining the statistical literature on Jews in Germany; and securing "confidential firsthand accounts" from refugees in London who had been victims of or had witnessed Nazi persecution. By the end of October 1933, the JFC had amassed "a considerable body of absolutely reliable information on all phases of the persecution."

The JFC information subcommittee considered Germany's antisemitic persecution so appalling that it would be enough to "let the facts speak for themselves." In 1933, it proceeded to publish pamphlets entitled *The Persecution of the Jews in Germany*, which reprinted excerpts from British and German newspapers "on the various aspects and successive phases of the Nazi persecution, on the Terror, on the Nazi propaganda and Nazi pronouncements, and on the reaction of British opinion to the persecution of the Jews in Germany." The subcommittee distributed the pamphlets to "prominent organizations and individuals in the political, economic, academic, and religious spheres of life." They were displayed at newsstands throughout Britain and were also sent abroad. By November 1933, about fifty thousand had been printed.

The JFC subcommittee responded directly to German antisemitic propaganda, as when Goebbels' Propaganda Ministry issued a memorandum claiming "Jewish preponderance in all spheres of German life" and distributed it to British visitors to the Third Reich as well as to British businesses. The subcommittee organized correspondents who could immediately answer antisemitic attacks in the British press by writing letters to the editor. Most of these letters were published. It also arranged for speakers to lecture about the persecution of the Jews to organizations and clubs throughout Britain, as Zionist groups had done to combat pro-Arab propaganda in England during the 1920s.[81]

To more effectively monitor German Jewry's increasingly desperate plight, the AJC and BoD joined with other Jewish organizations in Western Europe, most notably the Alliance Israélite Universelle, to form a Jewish Central Information Office (JCIO) in Amsterdam. The JCIO was the first Jewish organization established to amass information about antisemitism throughout Europe and other parts of the world and to circulate it globally. It was the first attempt to forge "a permanent and close connection between all important Jewish organizations and leading personalities all over the world." Beginning preparatory work in late February 1934, the JCIO was fully operational in July. It was directed by Dr. Alfred Wiener, formerly an official of the Centralverein deutscher Staatsbürger jüdischen Glaubens, Germany's major Jewish organization, who had fled to Amsterdam when the Nazis came to power, and Professor David Cohen, who resided there.[82]

The JCIO's primary activities included combatting Nazi propaganda that the Hitler regime aggressively distributed throughout the world and assessing the development of antisemitic movements outside Germany. In 1934, it was already publishing a monthly journal, *Jüdische Informationszentrale*, also issued in English and French. The JCIO rapidly assembled a sizeable library on anti-semitism. It included all the "literature on Hitler and the Third Reich published in England and France" and numerous works in other languages. The library amassed Nazi propaganda publications in German, English, French, Dutch, Spanish, Portuguese, and Arabic. It accumulated nearly all that was printed on the *Protocols of the Elders of Zion* and "a complete collection of the Dreyfus literature in French." The JCIO also organized clipping files on antisemitism from newspapers and journals in many countries. It issued a weekly, *Presse-Materialien*, which included "the latest news" on German Jewry's situation, along with "reports on the anti-Jewish world campaign and the anti-Jewish movements" in numerous lands. AJA president Leonard Montefiore prepared a pamphlet, "The Jews in Germany," which the JCIO sent to 550 newspapers around the world. By September, the JCIO had issued thirty-two confidential reports about the persecution of Jews in Germany and elsewhere. In 1934, the JCIO's library was consulted by groups organizing the boycott of the 1936 Olympic Games in Berlin and by exiled German Jewish writers, like Emil Ludwig.[83]

Neville Laski, president of the BoD, reported in September 1934 after a visit to the JCIO, "I have never seen so many newspapers and magazines referring to Jewish questions." He noted that the JCIO staff regularly read eighty newspapers in many languages and received clippings from three hundred other newspapers. It was "clear that a most tremendous activity pervades the whole place." The staff informed Laski that the JCIO had agents in Paris who had formed contacts with journalists representing the Polish, Latvian, and Russian newspapers there. They also regularly received information from Bucharest and Constantinople about the Balkan press's coverage of Jewish affairs and antisemitism. A JCIO agent in Tel Aviv monitored the Palestinian press, and another in Cairo scrutinized the Egyptian press. The JCIO was about to establish working relations with journalists in North and South America.[84]

By the end of 1934, the JCIO could report a further expansion of its activities. Its staff was now reading 135 newspapers, magazines, and correspondence papers, including Nazi publications, European religious magazines, and the major English, American, Hungarian, Danish, and Dutch newspapers. It also regularly examined Yiddish and Hebrew publications from Egypt, Palestine, England, France, Belgium, Romania, Mexico, Argentina, and South Africa. Two JCIO pamphlets were in press: one on Nazi and antisemitic literature in Germany since Hitler's rise to power, and another on Nazi racial theory. The JCIO had also provided about fifty "important persons" with confidential research reports on Jews' situation in Germany, Austria, and Eastern Europe and on Nazi propaganda in Syria. The JCIO was receiving financial support from the AJC in New York, the Alliance Israélite Universelle in Paris, and other Jewish organizations in London, Warsaw, Johannesburg, and Belgrade.[85]

1933 ENDS WITH MASS ANTI-NAZI PROTESTS
IN BOSTON AND NEW YORK

The year 1933 closed with a mass anti-Nazi parade and rally in Boston's Mattapan district and a tumultuous anti-Nazi demonstration at Columbia University in New York, where the administration had invited Nazi Germany's ambassador Hans Luther to speak in defense of Hitler's policies. The Boston protest on November 12 began with a parade of more than seven hundred members of Jewish youth organizations, joined by Jewish war veterans, who marched through Mattapan carrying placards denouncing the Hitler government's antisemitic outrages. The *Boston Globe* described "an enthusiastic crowd of 2,000" jamming Dorchester Manor at the anti-Nazi rally after the parade. A sizeable overflow audience in surrounding streets heard the speeches through amplifiers. Jennie Loitman Barron, president of the AJCongress Women's Division, read a message to the gathering from Boston mayor-elect Frederick Mansfield, who wished to "express [his] abhorrence and condemnation" of the Hitler government's "brutal extermination policy." Other speakers included Rabbi Joseph S. Shubow, director of the AJCongress' New England Office; Captain Maxwell Cohen, JWV adjutant general; Alexander Brin; and trade union representatives. Rabbi Shubow and most of the other speakers urged everybody not to purchase anything made in Germany.[86]

Columbia's president, Nicholas Murray Butler, winner of the 1931 Nobel Peace Prize and head of the Carnegie Endowment for International Peace, welcomed Nazi ambassador Luther as "the official diplomatic representative to the Government of the United States on the part of the government of a friendly people." Butler praised Luther as "well-mannered," a "gentleman" deserving of the university's and the nation's "courtesy and respect."[87]

Less than three weeks earlier, in a speech at an ALDJR luncheon in Cleveland, Samuel Untermyer had denounced Luther as "one of the most destructive of propagandists," who was "masquerading" as an ambassador. Luther promptly called on Secretary of State Hull to ask that he repudiate Untermyer's speech and "deny the allegations in it." Hull responded by voicing "his concern that an Ambassador accredited to the United States government should be subjected to an attack of this nature."[88]

From the time Hitler assumed power, there had been a considerable amount of anti-Nazi agitation on the Columbia campus. Despite strict quotas on Jewish admissions, because of its location the university had a larger proportion of Jewish students than other elite schools. In March 1933, Columbia's Jewish Students Society collected five hundred signatures on a petition denouncing Nazi outrages, "that recall the blackest hours of the Dark Ages." Columbia had sent a student delegation to the March 27 Madison Square Garden rally against Nazi antisemitism.[89]

The Columbia Social Problems Club, a student group, and seven faculty members immediately denounced President Butler's invitation to Luther and insisted that it be rescinded. The club declared that the welcome meant university "recognition of the 'achievements' of the Nazi regime . . . and the tacit approval of Nazi barbarism." It stated that the university instead "should show sympathy for our arrested and persecuted German colleagues . . . [and] should also take active steps to rescue and help them." Many people on campus noted that the Nazis had burned the books of one of Columbia's own professors, Franz Boas, the world's leading anthropologist. The seven faculty members issued an appeal to cancel the invitation, stating, "it is the duty of members of the Faculty and the University as a whole to protest against the persecution of scientists, artists, and philosophers in Germany, against the public burning of books, 'purging' of libraries, wholesale dismissal of professors and the prostitution of such sciences as genetics and anthropology to justify the Nazi philosophy." The letter also urged that "steps should be taken to obtain [the] release of our colleagues in German prisons and concentration camps."[90]

Six days before Luther's appearance, he gave his standard Nazi propaganda speech at Madison Square Garden at a German Day celebration sponsored by the Steuben Society of America, a leading German American organization. Although the White House was fully aware of the Nazis' antisemitic policies and outrages, it assigned US Secretary of Commerce Daniel Roper to present President Roosevelt's greetings to the gathering. The Steuben Society's pro-Nazi views were patently clear. On April 3, 1933, the *New York Herald Tribune* ran a front-page story reporting on a Steuben Society message to President Roosevelt that "denied reports of atrocities in Germany and said the country was quiet."[91]

Luther's speech at Madison Square Garden provided a good indication of what Columbia could expect. The *New York Times* covered his address in a lengthy front-page article. Luther began by giving the stiff-armed Nazi salute. "To deafening cheers," he praised Hitler as "this powerful leader of the German people" who had unleashed "constructive forces now vibrating through Germany." Luther insisted that Germany "had the right to regulate her own affairs according to her own wishes." His meaning was clear: criticism of Germany's persecution of Jews was illegitimate. When Luther finished, many in the audience shouted, "Heil Hitler," gave the Nazi salute, and sang the "Horst Wessel Lied."[92]

The Columbia Social Problems Club and AJCongress president Bernard S. Deutsch both publicly condemned Luther's remarks. The Social Problems Club emphasized that "Luther's previous speeches in this country, particularly his address in Madison Square Garden last week, have been direct attempts to whitewash Nazi persecution, imprisonment, and torture of thousands of workers, Jews, and liberals." Deutsch issued an open letter challenging Ambassador Luther's claim in the speech that the American press published "incomplete reports" about Nazi Germany "whose correctness is so often contradicted and inherently questionable."[93]

The student newspaper, the *Columbia Spectator*, whose editor-in-chief was Jewish, published a stinging editorial, "Silence Gives Consent, Dr. Butler," which denounced President Butler's refusal to comment on Nazi outrages. The editorial referred to the Hitler regime as "a government . . . which has wiped out any vestige of academic freedom by the expulsion of scientists and professors; which has persecuted non-Aryans because of their race and religion; which has burned books and tracts from which Dr. Butler has quoted; and which has crushed democracy."[94]

Anti-Nazi organizations at Columbia sent a call to students of City College of New York, New York University, Hunter College, Barnard College, Brooklyn College, and Long Island University to rally in front of the hall in which Luther was to speak. Despite freezing winds, more than one thousand assembled to protest, listening to a succession of speakers who denounced the Nazi ambassador. Although police had barred the demonstrators from gathering near the building where Luther held forth, when a Columbia economics instructor, Addison Cutler, called for defying the restrictions, many attempted to cross Broadway, determined to distribute anti-Nazi fliers to those present at the speech. For several minutes Broadway was "choked," until police managed to push them back. Police arrested a young woman trying to bring her leaflets into the hall, charged her with violating an ordinance against distributing pamphlets, and took her to night court, where a judge dismissed the charge. She then led the many demonstrators who had supported her at the court in an anti-Nazi parade down Broadway to Times Square.[95]

The largely hostile audience of twelve hundred crammed into Horace Mann Auditorium, "overflowing into the aisles and jamming the galleries," greeted Luther with "derisive laughter" and hissing. Interrupting Luther several times, they demanded to know "Why have the books of Boas and other Columbia professors been burned in German universities?" and "Why have Jews been oppressed in Germany?" and denounced Nazi propagandizing in the United States. Police removed several anti-Nazi hecklers from the auditorium. The *New York Evening Post* reported that the audience "sporadically threatened outright disorder." In his address Luther denied that Hitler had abolished freedom of the ballot and claimed that Nazi Germany "had exhibited the most peaceful attitude of any nation."[96]

The next day, the *New York Times* and *New York Herald Tribune* reported the demonstrations on the front page, emphasizing the intensity of the mostly youthful protestors' anti-Nazism. The *Herald Tribune* headline read, "Crowd Storms Hall as Luther Defends Nazis." It was accompanied by two photographs, one of which showed the mass picket line and a sign marked "Columbia Professors' Books are Burned in Germany." The *Chicago Tribune* also ran a front-page story about the demonstrations, headlined "Women Jeer Berlin Envoy/Hitler Flayed."[97]

Several days after Luther's Columbia speech, Samuel Untermyer spoke at the Maccabean Festival in Madison Square Garden, sponsored by the New York Zionist Region. Accusing the German ambassador of "insincerity and hypocrisy," Untermyer once again denounced him as a Nazi "propagandist in disguise." Above all he called on American Jews to draw inspiration from the ancient Hebrews' struggle for liberation—to "revive the militant Maccabean spirit" celebrated at Chanukah to wage a "defensive war" against Nazism through enforcing the boycott and combating German propaganda.[98]

* * *

From May 1933 onward, Jews in many countries repeatedly protested Germany's antisemitic policies and atrocities, employing methods previously used in campaigns against Eastern European pogroms but also developing new ones. There were considerable differences within the American and British Jewish communities over how best to combat Nazi antisemitism. By the fall of 1933, however, most Jewish organizations in both countries had endorsed not only mass demonstrations but also the organized boycott of German goods and services, which inflicted severe damage on several German industries and caused significant decline in Germany's foreign trade. The creation of the ALDJR in May and the AJCongress's decision to support the boycott in August provided a major boost for the movement. By contrast, the AJC and the BoD, representing more affluent and acculturated Jews, continued their opposition to both an organized boycott and street demonstrations. By officially backing the boycott, the AFL, the British Labour Party, and the TUC helped extend participation

beyond the Jewish population. Like the March 27 and May 10 mass street demonstrations, the boycott helped rank-and-file Jews forge an international anti-
Nazi alliance.

Large-scale street protests and rallies continued to be staged during the
second half of 1933 in the United States, England, and Scotland. Many commentators considered London's July march from the heavily working-class
Jewish neighborhoods of the East End to Hyde Park the most powerful display of grassroots Jewish militancy in British history. The closing of nearly
all East End shops and pushcarts for the march reflected strong working-
and lower-middle-class Jewish commitment to defeat the German plan to
render the Jews helpless and starving. The participation of eight thousand
British Jewish war veterans, many maimed in combat, gave the demonstration an especially military character—this was a battle for survival. Fierce
protests, including clashes with police, by New York college students challenging the Columbia University administration's warm welcome of Nazi
Germany's ambassador to campus in December, and the sizeable march
through Mattapan the previous month in support of the boycott, broadcast the spreading rank-and-file anti-Nazi militancy. Petition campaigns
denouncing Nazi antisemitism and urging the Roosevelt administration
to intervene to protect German Jews also heightened public consciousness
about their desperate plight.

The pageant *The Romance of a People*, opening in Chicago in July before an
audience of 125,000, with subsequent performances in New York, Philadelphia,
Cleveland, and Detroit, represented a dramatic new form of Jewish resistance.
It reinforced in American Jews a deep pride in their Jewish heritage and situated the campaign against the persecution of German Jewry within a tradition
of Jewish struggle against oppression dating back thousands of years. It also
made many non-Jews aware of the imminent danger confronting German and
European Jewry.

The JFC's newly created information subcommittee made a major contribution to the struggle against Nazism by conducting research that enabled the
Hitler regime's opponents to effectively refute its propaganda, which poured
into both Britain and the United States. The thoroughness of the subcommittee's investigations and the level of international coordination achieved in its
effort to disseminate the resultant data were unprecedented. Other anti-Nazi
activists in both countries joined in the campaign, providing the press and public with devastating reports drawn from testimony of former inmates about the
torture, starvation, and degradation of Jews and other prisoners in Germany's
expanding concentration camps.

NOTES

1. Louis I. Falk to Joseph Tenenbaum, March 25, 1955, RG 21.001.01 * 4, Joseph and Sheila Tenenbaum Collection (hereafter, Tenenbaum Collection), US Holocaust Memorial Museum Archives (hereafter, USHMMA), Washington, DC; Joseph Tenenbaum, "The Anti-Nazi Boycott Movement in the United States," *Yad Vashem Studies* 3 (1959): 146; Richard A. Hawkins, "'Hitler's Bitterest Foe': Samuel Untermyer and the Boycott of Nazi Germany, 1933–1938," *American Jewish History* 93 (March 2007): 22–25. The Provisional Boycott Committee that planned the founding conference had sent out a circular letter to numerous Jewish organizations, "be it congregation, society, landsmanschaft, lodge, or branch," asking each to send two delegates. Provisional Boycott Committee, Dr. A. Coralnik, chairman, to Friend, May 2, 1933, box 114, Non-Sectarian Anti-Nazi League Papers, Rare Book and Manuscript Library, Columbia University, New York, NY.

2. Hawkins, "Hitler's Bitterest Foe," 25; *New York Herald Tribune*, May 15, 1933, 1, 5; *New York Times*, May 15, 1933, 1.

3. *New York Times*, May 16, 1933, 11; Hawkins, "Hitler's Bitterest Foe," 26.

4. *New York Evening Post*, May 4, 1933, 1.

5. "Jews Boycotting German Ships," *Jewish Chronicle* (London), May 12, 1933, 31; "More Gruesome Atrocities Revealed," *Jewish Chronicle* (London), June 9, 1933, 14; *Palestine Post*, June 22, 1933.

6. William Phillips, undersecretary of state, memorandum of conversation with German ambassador, June 15, 1933, box 6786, Central Decimal Files (hereafter, CDF), Department of State General Records, Record Group (hereafter, RG59), National Archives, College Park, MD (hereafter, NA-CP).

7. George S. Messersmith to Secretary of State, June 17, 1933, mss 0109 0195-00, George S. Messersmith Papers, Special Collections, University of Delaware Library, Newark, DE.

8. Jonah B. Wise to Arthur Hays Sulzberger, May 18, 1933, box 175, Arthur Hays Sulzberger Papers (hereafter, Sulzberger Papers), New York Public Library (hereafter, NYPL), New York, NY.

9. *New York Times*, June 11, 1933, 1, 25. Senator Robinson had been the Democratic Party nominee for vice president in 1928, on the ticket headed by Al Smith.

10. William Phillips, undersecretary of state, memorandum of conversation with the German ambassador, June 15, 1933, box 6786, CDF, Department of State General Records, RG 59, NA-CP. The Hitler regime charged that "Jewish Senators who dominate the American Senate" had instigated the protest from the floor against Nazi persecution of Jews. This accusation was "received in Washington with much amusement" because there were no Jewish US Senators

and it was doubtful if there was even "a single Senator with as much as a Jewish grandparent." "U.S. Senate Speaks," *Jewish Chronicle* (London), June 16, 1933, 19.

11. *Brooklyn Jewish Examiner*, June 9, 1933, 9; *New York Times*, May 31, 1933, 8, and June 6, 1933, 15; *Washington Post*, May 25, 1933, 5, May 31, 1933, 2, June 4, 1933, 10, and June 6, 1933, 1.

12. *New York Times*, August 14, 1933, 5.

13. *Boston Globe*, February 6 and February 9, 1934, 2.

14. Edgar Ansel Mowrer, *Triumph andTurmoil: A Personal History of Our Time* (New York: Weybright and Talley, 1968), 218–19, 226.

15. *New York Times*, August 26, 1934, 1, August 27, 1934, 8, and obituary, February 1, 1961, 35; *Chicago Tribune*, August 26, 1934, 1, and August 27, 1934, 3. Thompson's expulsion was also covered in the *Manchester Guardian*, August 27, 1934, 9, and in the London *Times*, August 27, 1934, 9. The London *Times* reported that Thompson "had a very large public in the United States."

16. *Chicago Tribune*, August 26, 1934, 1, 2; "Confidential Letter on Germany: The Visit of Under-Secretary Phillips to Berlin," n.d. but late 1935 or 1936, ACC/3123/C11/12/21, Board of Deputies of British Jews Papers, London Metropolitan Archives, London, UK.

17. Robert Dell, "Hitler over Europe," *Nation*, May 3, 1933, 497; Robert Dell, *The Truth about Germany* (American Jewish Congress, n.d.), 1; "Robert Dell," *Church Times*, July 6, 1934, box 6, Robert Dell Papers, London School of Economics and Political Science Library Archives, London, UK.

18. *Manchester Guardian*, January 9, 1957, 2, and January 15, 1957, 3.

19. *Manchester Guardian* , April 20, 1933, 11, April 17, 1944, 6, and April 18, 1944, 5. Namier praised Crozier's support during the 1930s for British rearmament and for Zionism.

20. *Brooklyn Jewish Examiner*, June 2, 1933, 1 and August 4, 1933, 1.

21. "Resolution Adopted at Commencement Exercises 'In Absentia' for German-Jewish Students—Sponsored by Jewish Youth Groups in Newark, New Jersey," July 12, 1933, box 6786, CDF, Department of State General Records, RG 59, NA-CP.

22. Jewish Telegraphic Agency, May 25, 1934; *Detroit Jewish Chronicle*, June 1, 1934.

23. Document file note from Atherton regarding: visit of Alfred Rosenberg, personal confidant and principal advisor of Hitler on foreign affairs, to London, May 8, 1933, box 61, CDF, Department of State General Records, RG 59, NA-CP; *Daily Herald* (London), May 6, 11, and 12, 1933; *Manchester Guardian*, May 12, 1933, 12, 13; Richard Griffiths, *Fellow Travellers of the Right: British Enthusiasts for Nazi Germany, 1933–39* (London: Constable, 1980), 112–13.

24. *Daily Herald* (London), May 12, 1933, 11; "The Evasive Herr Rosenberg," *Jewish Chronicle* (London), May 19, 1933, 18.

25. "Shamming Blind," *Jewish Chronicle* (London), May 19, 1933, 8.

26. *Manchester Guardian*, May 12, 1933, 8; *Daily Herald* (London), May 12, 1933; C. C. Aronsfeld, "A Refugee's Memories of London, 1933," *Jewish Frontier*, April 1980, 22.

27. *Daily Herald* (London), May 15, 1933, 2.

28. *Daily Mail* (London), May 13, 1933, 10.

29. "British Youth Appeals to Germany," Anti-German Protest and Prayer Meetings (hereafter, AGPPM) Collection, 876/2/3, Wiener Library for the Study of the Holocaust and Genocide, London, UK; "Professor Haldane Hits Out," *Jewish Chronicle* (London), May 19, 1933, 20.

30. "Professor Haldane Hits Out," 20.

31. *Palestine Post*, July 11, 1933, 3, 6, 8; *Manchester Guardian*, June 28, 1933, 15. A *Palestine Post* editorial regretted that non-Jewish religious leaders in Jerusalem had not expressed feelings of sympathy for German Jewry, as the archbishop of Canterbury had.

32. *Jewish Echo* (Glasgow), June 2, 1933, 1658/7/1/11/36, and *Glasgow Herald*, May 29, 1933, 1658/7/11/35, Board of Deputies of British Jews Defence Committee (hereafter, BoDDC) Papers, Wiener Library, London.

33. *Edinburgh Evening News*, May 29, 1933, 1658/7/1/11/34, and *Jewish Echo* (Glasgow), June 2, 1933, BoDDC Papers, Wiener Library, London.

34. *Glasgow Herald*, May 29, 1933, 1658/7/1/11/35, and *Jewish Echo* (Glasgow), June 2, 1933, BoDDC Papers, Wiener Library, London.

35. *Jewish Echo* (Glasgow), June 2, 1933, BoDDC Papers, Wiener Library, London.

36. *Daily Herald* (London), July 10, 1933.

37. *Daily Herald* (London), July 23, 1933; *Manchester Guardian*, July 22, 1933, 13; *Le Droit de Vivre* (Paris), July–August 1933.

38. *Jewish Chronicle* (London), July 7, 1933, 32–33.

39. *Chicago Tribune*, July 2, 1933, 3, and July 4, 1933, 1.

40. *Chicago Tribune*, July 4, 1933, 1, July 5, 1933, 1, and July 6, 1933, 1; *New York Times*, July 4, 1933, 16. The impact of *The Romance of a People* extended far beyond those who attended the performances, because the press gave it enormous attention. The *Chicago Tribune*'s page 1 article on July 4 was headlined "125,000 Witness Jewish Spectacle" and accompanied by photographs. Other articles on the event ran on pages 1 and 4 that day. The *Tribune* also ran front-page articles about the pageant on July 5 and July 6. The *New York Times* similarly emphasized the enormous turnout at the pageant's Chicago premiere: "125,000 see Drama of Israel at Fair." The *Times* on July 4 described the event as an impressive display of Jewish unity. It reported, "The vast audience [consisted of] Jews from every part of the United States . . . and other countries, representing every shade of orthodoxy and liberalism."

41. *New York Times*, July 2, 1933, 4, N2, and July 4, 1933, 16.

42. *New York Times*, August 27, 1933, 15; September 14, 1933, 22; September 16, 1933, 15, September 24, 1933, N1; October 4, 1933, 15; and October 19, 1933, 22; *Jewish Examiner* (Brooklyn), October 6, 1933, 2, and October 13, 1933, 2.

43. Jewish Telegraphic Agency, December 18 and 31, 1933, and August 1, 1934; *Public Ledger* (Philadelphia), February 20, 1, 10–11, February 22, and February 23, 1934; *Detroit Jewish Chronicle*, April 6, 1934, 1, 8, and April 13, 1934, 1, 3–9, 11, 14, 19, 25–26, 28–29. Philadelphia's performances used a cast of four thousand; Detroit's, and probably Cleveland's, two thousand.

44. *New York Evening Post*, May 25, 1933, 1; *New York Times*, May 18, 1933, 6, and May 26, 1933, 9; *Daily Worker*, May 26, 1933, 1, 4. The Associated Press story appeared in many newspapers, including the *Boston Herald*, May 26, 1933 and *Boston Globe*, May 26, 1933, 8. The *Daily Worker* reported that Wiedemann had recently attempted "to take over the German section of the Carnegie Exhibition of Art in Pittsburgh," scheduled for October 18, 1933, and "exclude all Jewish artists of Germany from exhibiting their work." *Daily Worker*, May 19, 1934, 1.

45. *New Leader* (US), May 27, 1933, 1.

46. *Chicago Tribune*, July 29, 1933, 7, and August 12, 1933, 4; Jewish Telegraphic Agency, August 14, 1933.

47. *Chicago Tribune*, October 25, 1933, 1, and October 27, 1933, 1.

48. *New York Times*, July 21, 1933, 1; *New York Herald Tribune*, July 21, 1933, 1, 7; Hawkins, "Hitler's Bitterest Foe," 30.

49. *New York Times*, July 21, 1933, 1, 5.

50. Ibid. The *New York Herald Tribune* also ran its article on the boycott conference that day on page 1.

51. *New York Times*, July 21, 1933, 1; *New York Herald Tribune*, July 21, 1933, 1, 7.

52. *New York Times*, July 21, 1933, 1; Falk to Tenenbaum, March 25, 1955.

53. "The Economic Boycott," Jewish Central Information Office (Amsterdam), November–December 1934, 20, 35/176–180, Central British Fund for World Jewish Relief (hereafter, CBFWJR) Records, Wiener Library, London.

54. *Daily Herald* (London), July 21, 1933, 1; "Jewish Standard Demonstration Supplement," July 21, 1933, 876, AGPPM Collection , Wiener Library, London.

55. "Monster Jewish Protest Demonstration," *Jewish Chronicle* (London), July 21, 1933, 10; *Daily Herald* (London), July 21, 1933, 1, 6; *Manchester Guardian*, July 21, 1933, 3; "Jewish Standard Demonstration Supplement," AGPPM Collection, Wiener Library, London; *New York Times*, July 21, 1933, 4; *Times* (London), July 21, 1933, 13; *New York Herald Tribune*, July 21, 1933, 7.

56. "Monster Jewish Protest Demonstration," 10; *New York Times*, July 21, 1933, 4; *Manchester Guardian*, July 21, 1933, 3.

57. *Manchester Guardian*, July 21, 1933, 3; *Daily Herald* (London), July 21, 1933, 6; Jewish Telegraphic Agency, July 10, 1941.

58. *Daily Herald* (London), July 21, 1933, 6; "Great Protest Demonstration," *Jewish Chronicle* (London), July 28, 1933, 27.

59. "Jewish Standard Demonstration Supplement," July 21, 1933, AGPPM Collection , Wiener Library, London.

60. *Jewish Exponent* (Philadelphia), August 18, 1933, 9; *New York Times*, August 21, 1933, 2; *New York Herald Tribune*, September 6, 1933.

61. *New York Times*, October 14, 1933, 1, and October 22, 1933, 28.

62. "Paperhangers Refuse to Handle German Goods," *New Leader*, October 8, 1933, 3

63. The Labour Party, "Report of the 33rd Annual Conference Held in the White Rock Pavilion, Hastings, October 2nd to 6th, 1933," 17–18, 222, People's History Museum, Manchester, UK.

64. *Daily Herald* (London), October 6, 1933; *Thameside Mail*, February 2, 1934, Reel LP, W1/5, Ellen Wilkinson Scrapbook, People's History Museum, Manchester, UK.

65. *Nation*, August 9, 1933, 142; *Jewish Advocate* (Boston), July 28, 1933, 1.

66. "Memorandum of Conversation between Secretary Hull and the German Ambassador, Herr Hans Luther," September 21, 1933, reel 29, Cordell Hull Papers, Library of Congress, Washington, DC.

67. *Chicago Tribune*, September 15, 1933, 16, and March 4, 1934, 8.

68. *New York Times*, September 16, 1933, 4.

69. Frank Buxton to William E. Dodd, July 6, 1933, container 40, William E. Dodd Papers, Library of Congress, Washington, DC; Theodore H. White to Samuel Untermyer, October 26, 1933, box 217, Non-Sectarian Anti-Nazi League Papers, Rare Book and Manuscript Library, Columbia University, New York, NY. Born in 1915, White grew up in Dorchester, the son of Jewish parents. His father was an immigrant from Russia. White graduated from Boston Latin School in 1932. His widowed mother was then on relief. At the time White was helping lead the anti-Nazi boycott movement in Boston, he was eking out a living selling newspapers on streetcars and teaching Hebrew to Jewish children at a Hebrew school. White entered Harvard as a scholarship student in the fall of 1934. Theodore H. White, *In Search of History: A Personal Adventure* (New York, Harper and Row, 1978), 38–41.

70. *Jewish Advocate* (Boston), November 10, 1933, 2.

71. Samuel Untermyer to Percy H. Straus, Esq., President R. H. Macy & Co., October 4, 1933, box 175, Sulzberger Papers, NYPL; *Jewish Examiner* (Brooklyn), September 29, 1933, 1, and October 6, 1933, 1.

72. Untermyer to Straus, October 4, 1933, box 175, Sulzberger Papers, NYPL.

73. "An Open Letter in reply to the advertisement of R. H. Macy & Co. entitled 'Three Personal Letters' concerning the continued sale by them of German goods," n.d., box 175, Sulzberger Papers, NYPL.

74. *Boston Globe*, September 19, 1933, 12.

75. "The Fur Trade Boycott," *Jewish Chronicle* (London), May 12, 1933, 30; *Times* (London), May 9, 1933, 16.

76. *Daily Herald* (London), May 19, 1933, 4; *Manchester Guardian*, May 19, 1933, 14.

77. "Glass Dealers Boycott German Goods," *Jewish Chronicle* (London), April 21, 1933, 27; *New York Times*, October 10, 1933, 10.

78. "The Economic Boycott," Jewish Central Information Office, November–December 1934, 20, CBFWJR Records, Wiener Library, London; *Daily Herald* (London), October 30 and November 6, 1933; *Times* (London), November 6, 1933, 11; *Daily Record* (Glasgow), September 25, 1933, 1658/7/1/9/20, BoDDC Papers, Wiener Library, London.

79. *Daily Herald* (London), November 14 and 18, 1933.

80. Stephen H. Norwood, *The Third Reich in the Ivory Tower: Complicity and Conflict on American Campuses* (New York: Cambridge University Press, 2009), 6–7; *New York Times*, June 19, 1933, 5; *New York Herald Tribune*, June 19, 1933, 14.

81. . "The Information Service by the Joint Foreign Committee," papers for the International Conference for the Relief of German Jewry, London, October 29-November 1, 1933, 35/258-60, CBFWJR Records, Wiener Library, London.

82. "Tasks and Aims of the Jewish Central Information Office in Amsterdam," ACC/3121/E03/261, reel 79, BoD Papers, USHMMA; "Minutes of the Executive Committee of the American Jewish Committee," June 9, 1934," ajcarchives.org.

83. Neville Laski, "Report on a Visit to JCIO, Amsterdam, September 20, 1934," September 27, 1934, ACC/3121/E03/261, reel 79, BoD Papers, USHMMA.

84. Ibid.

85. "Report about the activity of the Jewish Central Information Office for the period from June 1st to December 1st, 1934," ACC/3121/E03/261, reel 79, BoD Papers, USHMMA.

86. *Boston Globe*, November 13, 1933; *Jewish Advocate* (Boston), November 10, 1933, 1, 2, and November 14, 1933, 1.

87. *New York Times*, November 20, 1933, 6.

88. *Washington Post*, November 2, 1933, 3, and November 3, 1933, 1; *New York Times*, November 2, 1933, 11, and November 3, 1933, 10; *Washington Herald*, November 3, 1933, clipping in box 4729, CDF, Department of State General Records, NA-CP.

89. *Columbia Spectator*, March 24, 1933, 1, and March 27, 1933, 1.

90. *Columbia Spectator*, November 24 and 29, 1933, 1.

91. *New York Times*, December 7, 1933, 1; *New York Herald Tribune*, April 3, 1933, 1; Rafael Medoff, *The Jews Should Keep Quiet: Franklin D. Roosevelt, Rabbi Stephen S. Wise, and the Holocaust* (Philadelphia: Jewish Publication Society, 2019), 34.

92. *New York Times*, December 7, 1933, 1; Jewish Telegraphic Agency, December 8, 1933. Membership in the Steuben Society was open to US citizens who were wholly or partially of German descent. It announced its sympathy with the Nazi regime as early as March 1933. Jewish Telegraphic Agency, May 7, 1933. The Jewish Telegraphic Agency reported that at least six Jews in the Madison Square Garden audience "were manhandled and driven from the hall." They included Robert Rosenbaum, president of the Federation of German Jewish Societies, and Dr. Fritz Schlesinger, a prominent member of New York's German Jewish community, both of whom were "hauled out of their seats." Jewish Telegraphic Agency, December 8, 1933.

93. *Columbia Spectator*, December 12, 1933, 1, 3; New York *Evening Post*, December 8, 1933; *New York Times*, December 8, 1933, 15.

94. *Columbia Spectator*, December 12, 1933, 2.

95. *New York Herald Tribune*, December 13, 1933, 1, 10; *New York Times*, December 13, 1933, 1, 18; *Columbia Spectator*, December 5, 1933, 1, and December 13, 1933, 1, 4; Ruth Rubin, "I Heckled Luther!," *Student Review*, January 1934, 8.

96. *Columbia Spectator*, December 13, 1933, 1, 4; *New York Herald Tribune*, December 13, 1933, 1, 10; *New York Times*, December 13, 1933, 1, 18; Rubin, "I Heckled Luther!," 8; *New York Evening Post*, December 13, 1933, 2.

97. *New York Herald Tribune*, December 13, 1933, 1, 10; *New York Times*, December 13, 1933, 1, 18; *Chicago Tribune*, December 13, 1933, 1. The *Columbia Spectator* ran two articles on its front page under the four-column headline "1,000 Battle Police in Anti-Luther Protest." It reported a series of "street battles between anti-Nazi protestors and policemen" that "threatened to precipitate a riot." *Columbia Spectator*, December 13, 1933, 1, 4. President Butler was so angry at what he considered the Columbia students' discourtesy toward Hitler's ambassador that he initially planned to expel the protest organizers. Stephen H. Norwood, "The Expulsion of Robert Burke: Suppressing Campus Anti-Nazi Protest in the 1930s," *Journal for the Study of Antisemitism* 4:1 (2012): 92.

98. *New York Times*, December 17, 1933, 30.

Photo 1. Storm trooper hurling Jewish and other "un-German" books into bonfire, Berlin, May 10, 1933. (WikiMedia)

Photo 2. Jewish War Veterans protest march, New York, March 23, 1933. (United States Holocaust Memorial Museum, Courtesy of National Archives and Records Administration, College Park, MD)

Photo 3. Chicago crowd assembled at Auditorium Theater on national day of protest against persecution of Jews in Germany, March 27, 1933. (Associated Press)

Photo 4. London Jews display boycott sign. (Bettman/Getty Images)

Photo 5. Boycotters with chalked slogan, East End of London, March 1933.
(Photo by Keystone-France/Gamma-Keystone via Getty Images)

Photo 6. New York demonstrators protest Nazi antisemitism and book
burnings, May 10, 1933. (United States Holocaust Memorial Museum, Courtesy
of National Archives and Records Administration, College Park, MD)

Photo 7. Rabbis and other Jews protesting persecution of Jews in Germany, marching from the East End of London to Hyde Park, July 20, 1933. (Hulton Archive/Topical Press Agency/Stringer/Getty Images)

Photo 8. Jews march to London's Hyde Park for mass rally protesting antisemitism in Germany, July 20, 1933. (Photo by Daily Herald Archive/SSPL/Getty Images)

Photo 9. Jews rally in Hyde Park against Nazi antisemitic policies and atrocities in Germany, July 20, 1933. Sign on speakers' platform calls for restoring rights to Jews in Germany. (Photo by Miller/Topical Press Agency/Getty Images)

Photo 10. Ellen Wilkinson with Jarrow dock workers, 1936. (Associated Press)

FIVE

—ww—

EXPOSING AND BOYCOTTING
THE THIRD REICH

1934

IN 1934, AS GERMAN JEWRY'S predicament became increasingly perilous, American and British Jews and their allies intensified their struggle against Germany's persecution of Jews, expanding the boycott and forming new defense organizations. They continued to stage mass rallies against Nazi antisemitism, including one in March 1934 that again filled New York's Madison Square Garden to capacity. American and British Jews also focused on conducting a more effective global anti-Nazi campaign. Organizations in both nations coordinated and stepped up efforts to move as many German Jews as possible—especially children—to Palestine.

A boycott flier entitled "Jewry Is in Peril," issued in Britain in April 1934, expressed the growing Jewish militancy on both sides of the Atlantic. Distributed by the Jewish Representative Council for the Boycott of German Goods and Services, the flier stated that Jews were engaged in a war against a formidable enemy whose openly proclaimed goal was not only Jewry's "humiliation" but also its "extinction." It reminded British Jews that their "600,000 brethren in Germany" were "but in the front line of a savage attack directed against your own homes." All Jews were in danger—the menace was "real and imminent." Germany's "reversion to medieval barbarism openly aims at our political and economic obliteration from civilized communities." The flier called on the world's sixteen million Jews to "wield an economic weapon of devastating power" and to "meet blow for blow with honour and self-respect." They must never yield "until this onslaught on our people shall have ceased." Jews should not purchase "a single German article," travel on a German ship, use any other German service, or see a German film.[1]

LECTURE TOURS: STRIKING BACK AT THE THIRD REICH

In the pretelevision age, public lectures were an important means of drawing attention to German Jewry's desperate plight. Prominent opponents of Nazism, some of them exiled from Germany, delivered such lectures in many American and British cities and towns and on college campuses. Newspapers often covered them. The lectures served to counter the Nazi propaganda inundating the United States through short-wave broadcasts from the Reich and Nazi officials' frequent speeches to business and university audiences. In 1934, three leading anti-Nazis embarked on national lecture tours in the United States: Lord Dudley Marley, a deputy speaker of the House of Lords, Labour Party member, and chair of the World Committee to Aid the Victims of German Fascism; and exiled Social Democratic Reichstag deputies Gerhart Seger and Toni Sender, both of whom spoke fluent English.[2]

On February 6, 1934, Lord Dudley Marley arrived in New York to begin a lecture tour across the country lasting until March 2, "on behalf of the victims of the Hitler government." Lord Marley was greeted on arrival by American Jewish Congress (AJCongress) president Bernard Deutsch, who was also president of the New York City Board of Aldermen. The next day, Mayor La Guardia received him at city hall. In December 1933 in Paris, Lord Marley had presided over a panel investigating Nazi atrocities that interviewed refugees from Germany, including some recently released from concentration camps. Before leaving England, Lord Marley had also conferred with James McDonald, League of Nations–appointed high commissioner for refugees from Germany, about the suffering of Jews and others forced to flee the Reich.[3]

The day after his arrival, Lord Marley lectured on conditions in Nazi Germany to more than six hundred at a dinner at the Aldine Club in New York at which Columbia University philosophy professor John Dewey presided. Lord Marley informed the audience that German children were taught that Jews were "inherently dishonest and morally inferior." "Such 'education' had inflicted an 'intolerable wound' from which the young Germans might never recover." A week later, Lord Marley informed "a large gathering" in Los Angeles that the Nazis were torturing tens of thousands for opposing the Hitler regime, using such methods as whipping—the number of lashes equal to the victim's age. Other anti-Nazis were submerged in icy water and then interrogated naked. Lord Marley explained that he presented only evidence he had obtained through direct testimony from refugees, not from hearsay.[4]

In Boston, Lord Marley spoke to two hundred at a reception and banquet at the Somerset Hotel on February 26 and to three hundred more at the Repertory

Theatre. He declared that there were seven hundred fifty thousand people in Germany wanting to leave but lacking the funds to do so. Those attempting to get out were "hunted down and tortured horribly by Nazi storm troopers," who broke up homes, raped women, and wielded "long telescopic steel whips" that left flesh "in ribbons." The World Committee to Aid the Victims of German Fascism had created an "underground railroad," similar to that established in the United States for fugitive slaves, to smuggle the children of Jews and other opponents of Hitler from the Saar Valley to safer areas. Lord Marley stressed that to effect change it was essential to boycott German goods and services, to make the boycott "international in scope," and for the American public to constantly denounce Nazi atrocities.[5]

Having served in the Reichstag from 1930 to 1933, when the Nazis constituted a large bloc there, Gerhart Seger was well informed about their goals and methods. Seger escaped from Oranienburg in December 1933. A non-Jew, he was the first fugitive to report to Americans and the British on concentration camp conditions. Seger delivered talks in Paris, and in March 1934 he lectured "all over England." In London, he addressed a meeting of the Labour members of the House of Commons and the House of Lords. Seger also spoke before the Foreign Affairs committees of both bodies, a talk arranged by Lady Astor and Blanche Dugdale, daughter of Lord Balfour, the author of Britain's Balfour declaration promising to support a homeland for the Jews in Palestine.[6]

Seger's American tour grew out of a meeting with the militant anti-Nazi Rabbi Ferdinand Isserman, who invited him to speak after attending a lecture Seger gave in Paris following his escape. Rabbi Isserman provided Seger with a substantial check covering "more than steamship passage," as well as an honorarium to speak at his Saint Louis temple. Before Seger departed for the United States in the fall of 1934, he contacted the *New York Times*'s Paris bureau chief and arranged for the *Times* to interview him. Upon arrival in New York, Seger mailed copies of the interview to "colleges, universities, [and] Rotary Clubs," indicating that he was available to speak. Seger recalled, "Within two weeks I had thirty-seven lecture engagements."[7]

The publication in Czechoslovakia (in German) of Seger's account of his experience in the concentration camp shortly after his escape, under the title *Oranienburg*, alarmed the Hitler regime. In February 1934, an opponent of the Nazis in the Netherlands notified the US State Department that the German government had dispatched an agent, Marcel Holzer, to the United States to respond to Seger's charges and to spread "counter-propaganda" about the camps.[8] *Oranienburg* was "translated into six European languages and ha[d] a European distribution of 250,000 copies." In early 1935, an English translation,

A Nation Terrorized, was published in the United States and reviewed in the *New York Times*.[9]

In a seven months' speaking tour that concluded in May 1935, Seger delivered 153 lectures in twenty-one states, from coast to coast.[10] In November 1934, at Columbia University under the sponsorship of the socialist League for Industrial Democracy, the exiled Reichstag deputy told an audience of three hundred that "sadism and cruelty to a degree no one could expect" prevailed throughout the Nazi camp system. Conditions were so brutal and dehumanizing that had he not escaped he would have committed suicide. At the University of California at Berkeley, Seger denounced the Nazis' "insidious campaign of hate" against the Jews.[11] In a letter to the editor in the *New York Times*, Seger explained that Hitler's rearmament and expansionist designs were rooted in "the same terrible race theory as Jewish persecution—that the Aryan nations should rule the world." On the tour, Seger spoke to a wide range of groups, including the First Unitarian Church of Los Angeles, New York's Foreign Policy Association, and New York's Rand School of Social Science. Jewish Charities of Chicago sponsored his lecture at the Standard Club there.[12]

Seger's colleague Toni Sender had served in the Reichstag from 1920 to 1933 and confronted the Nazis face-to-face numerous times in Germany. As a Jew, a woman, and a Social Democrat, she was a major Nazi target in the Reichstag. Sender described the "pogrom atmosphere" the Nazis created around her name. In early 1933, the Nazis in Dresden covered the front page of their antisemitic newspaper *Judenspiegel* (*Jews' Mirror*) with her picture and recommended that she be killed. Josef Goebbels labeled her "The Little Woman with the Big Mouth." In March 1933, she escaped into Czechoslovakia a step ahead of Nazis intent on murdering her. Shortly afterward, she made her way to Antwerp. In March 1934, the *New York Times* reported that Sender was among thirty-eight Germans, including Albert Einstein, whom the Nazis had branded "undesirable" and stripped of their citizenship.[13]

In 1934 through early 1935, and again later that year, Sender conducted a coast-to-coast lecture tour of the United States, which included stops in most of the southern states, providing firsthand accounts of the Nazis' imminent threat to Jews. On New York's Jewish radio station WEVD, she condemned the Nazis' suppression of women's rights. In Chicago, she urged the formation of "a united front" to combat virulently antisemitic Nazi propaganda that Hitler's agents were disseminating in the United States. In December 1935, Sender decided to remain permanently in the United States where she continued her anti-Nazi agitation and became a citizen.[14]

Lecturing across England in 1933 and 1934, Ellen Wilkinson, Labour MP (1924–31, 1935–47), alerted the public to the looming danger the Nazis posed to democracy, Jews, and trade unionism. In its September 10, 1933 issue, the Nazi party newspaper *Völkischer Beobachter* referred to the non-Jewish Wilkinson as *Halbjüdin* (half Jewess). She had written one of the first pamphlets detailing Nazi atrocities, *The Terror in Germany*, published in 1933. In the summer of 1932, she spent two weeks in Germany as British Labour Party liaison to the Social Democratic Party in the election campaign. Upon returning to Britain, Wilkinson told trade union conference delegates that she had seen men like them whose eyes the Nazis had "smashed with steel whips."[15]

In her talks, Wilkinson gave considerable attention to Nazi antisemitism. Addressing a women's group in London in May 1933, she condemned the Nazis' "clear[ing] all Jews out of the universities" and the professions and graphically described Nazi beatings of Jewish and non-Jewish women with steel rods. To support her charges, Wilkinson spread "on the table before her . . . photos, doctors' certificates, and . . . authenticated documents that she invited the women to examine." The London *Sunday Referee* commented that Wilkinson's evidence "left no room for doubt."[16] In November 1933, speaking about the plight of German Jews to the Manchester Jewish Literary and Social Society, Wilkinson stressed that "no Jew could hold a job, for every kind of pressure was brought to bear on his employer to dismiss him," and she made the audience aware that the torture of German Jews continued.[17] In Purfleet, England, in February 1934, responding to a Nazi storm trooper's recent lecture there "on how glorious was the present regime in Germany," Wilkinson explained that the Nazis' view of "a tremendous Jewish conspiracy against the [German] nation" was a fantasy and a central part of their message. She displayed "steel springs and rubber truncheons which had been used to 'beat up' the Jews" and political opponents of the Nazis.[18]

TRANSPORTING DOOMED JEWISH CHILDREN
TO PALESTINE

By early 1934, Jewish organizations in the United States and Britain, fully aware that German Jewry was in extreme danger, were raising funds to move as many German Jewish children to Palestine as possible. In a February speech to the Greater Boston Women's Division for the Settlement of German-Jewish Children in Palestine, Pierre van Paassen, whom the Hitler regime had recently expelled for his "atrocity" articles, declared that Palestine was the only possible haven for the "doomed" children. Van Paassen emphasized the urgency of immediately sending the five thousand German Jewish children already prepared to leave Berlin to Palestine. He explained that in German schools, teachers assigned textbooks that provided "Aryan" pupils with "sixteen distinguishing marks to identify the Jew." Everywhere the Jewish child was "scorned as belonging to an inferior people." Van Paassen went on to describe "the harrowing and grueling tortures" he had observed Nazis inflicting on German Jews when he was detained in the Munich Brown House. His Boston audience "shuddered and wept at the terror he depicted." Van Paassen had concluded that Palestine was the only place where it was possible for Jewish refugees to settle permanently. He maintained that many Jewish parents, unable to get out of Germany, wanted their children relocated to Palestine rather than have them endure endless "oppression and humiliation." After the lecture many members of the audience donated funds to support one or more German Jewish children, determined to achieve the quota of $20,000 that the Greater Boston Women's Division had pledged.[19]

The next month, Greater Boston Women's Division volunteers provided a branch meeting with enthusiastic reports of their house-to-house canvass throughout the metropolitan area. They had combed every street in the Roxbury-Dorchester-Mattapan area, where most Boston Jews lived, and many in Newton, Allston, Brighton, and Brookline. They had also solicited contributions in Somerville, Cambridge, East Boston, Chelsea, and Revere. Jewish women in Boston staged bridge parties, teas, fashion shows, and other social events to raise money to send German Jewish children to Palestine. Women's Division chapters were being formed in Haverhill and New Bedford to join the fund-raising campaign.[20]

In New York, on March 4, two hundred representatives of Jewish organizations with a combined membership of two hundred fifty thousand met at the Hotel Pennsylvania in a determined effort to prevent the ruination of "a whole generation of Jewish children" in Germany by transporting many of them to Palestine. Magistrate Benjamin Greenspan (president of the Council of Jewish Organizations on Palestine, which convened the meeting) stated that German Jewish youth were denied "almost every normal activity of childhood, including the benefits of attending school." Like van Paassen, Morris Margulies (secretary of the Zionist Organization of America) told the audience that the future for German Jewish children was so bleak that many parents were willing to break up the family to allow them to escape degradation—or worse. Several days before, prominent Jewish writer Maurice Samuel, guest of honor at a Jewish Agency American Palestine Campaign luncheon in New York, informed those attending that "the rapid assimilation of German Jewish children into Palestinian life" had "taken a load off the minds of their parents."[21]

In Britain, the Manchester Women's Appeal Committee for German Jewish Women and Children held a luncheon on January 30, 1934, that raised £1,000 to move German Jewish children to Palestine. Chaired by Mrs. Anthony de Rothschild, the speakers included E. T. S. Dugdale, a niece of Lord Balfour, and Lord

Melchett. In her opening remarks, de Rothschild declared that German Jewry had been "thrown back to the condition of the Middle Ages." Dugdale observed that it was in Manchester that Chaim Weizmann had converted her uncle, Lord Balfour, to Zionism. Characterizing the treatment of Jewish children in Nazi Germany as "organized humiliation" and "the foulest crime," she told the audience that their "fate . . . literally hung on their generosity." Dugdale described a class of small children in a Berlin school in which the only Jew was forced to line up with the other pupils to get milk and then "pass on with an empty mug while the teacher explained to the other children the 'reason' for the omission."[22]

THE MANDATORY GOVERNMENT'S SUPPRESSION
OF THE *BROWN BOOK OF THE HITLER TERROR*

Zionists and their supporters in the British Parliament were deeply distressed in early 1934 when the Mandatory government banned the sale of the *Brown Book of the Hitler Terror* throughout Palestine. The result of pressure from the German consul general in Jerusalem and a clear expression of the Mandatory government's insensitivity to Jewish suffering in Germany, the ban signaled increasing British resistance to Jewish immigration to Palestine. The Mandatory government's suppression of the first systematic account of Nazi atrocities was particularly ominous, because the government continued to permit the sale of Hitler's *Mein Kampf*. The Palestine District Commissioners prohibited booksellers in Palestine from selling the *Brown Book* in all languages on the grounds that it violated Palestine's Defamation of Foreign Princes Ordinance, promulgated on February 1, 1934, which made illegal the publication or sale of any work "tending to degrade, revile, or expose to hatred or contempt any prince, ruler, potentate, ambassador, or other dignitary of any State or territory other than Palestine." Booksellers who violated the ordinance could be imprisoned for up to three years or fined up to one hundred pounds. In Jerusalem, the assistant district commissioner, Geoffrey MacLaren, ordered the city's booksellers to appear before him, warning that they would be prosecuted if they sold the *Brown Book*. Colonel Josiah Wedgwood, Labour MP, challenged the Mandatory government's ban of the *Brown Book* in the House of Commons.[23]

J. Hathorn Hall, the officer administering the government of Palestine (in the high commissioner's absence), forcefully defended the ban, insisting that the *Brown Book* defamed the head of the German government, Hitler. As an example of "defamation," he cited a photograph of Hitler in the book, captioned, "The gate of lies is wide open: Hitler speaks." Hall emphasized that the sale of

EXPOSING AND BOYCOTTING THE THIRD REICH

the *Brown Book* could increase the already "intense feeling against the German Government" among Palestine's Jews, who included "a considerable proportion of German refugees." This feeling had "manifested itself on several occasions in acts of violence against the German consulate in Jerusalem."[24]

Zionists in Palestine vigorously protested the Mandatory government's prohibiting the sale of the *Brown Book* while permitting the circulation of *Mein Kampf.* Professor Selig Brodetsky complained that it was ridiculous to ban a book that "defamed" a prince (Hitler), while allowing the distribution of a work in which that "prince" defamed an entire people, the Jews. The *Palestine Post* argued that the *Brown Book* was "a serious attempt by serious people to set forth on documentary evidence what most of the world believes to have happened in Germany in 1933." It pointed out that "there is not a newspaper outside Germany which has not reproduced in part material contained in the *Brown Book*; there is scarcely a newspaper or serious political publication ... which cannot be condemned on similar grounds as the *Brown Book*." The *Post* noted that an "extremely reputable" publisher, Victor Gollancz Ltd., had issued the London edition of the *Brown Book* and that Albert Einstein was among its "eminent editors." It accused the Mandatory government of calling those who exposed Nazi atrocities liars while denying that Hitler was one. It was appalling that Palestine should "stand forth as the champion of a system of government [Nazism] which has hounded out thousands of its citizens and driven them to take refuge in Palestine."[25]

THE TYDINGS RESOLUTION: A FUTILE APPEAL
FOR US GOVERNMENT INTERCESSION

The major American Jewish defense organizations joined with the Jewish masses in backing a resolution introduced by Senator Millard Tydings (a Democrat from Maryland) on January 8, 1934, which called on President Roosevelt "to communicate to the government of the German Reich an unequivocal statement of the profound feelings of the surprise and pain" of the American people on "learning of the discriminations and oppressions imposed by the Reich upon its Jewish citizens." Drawing on exhaustive research by New York attorney Max J. Kohler, the resolution stated that "for nearly 100 years the traditional policy of the United States has been to take official and diplomatic cognizance of 'such invasions of human rights.'" In 1934, the B'nai B'rith Executive Committee published as a booklet Kohler's documentation of precedents of official US government intercession on behalf of Jews persecuted by foreign governments.[26]

Kohler was intent on refuting the Hitler regime's claim, echoed by many in the US government, that the United States had no business interfering in

Germany's internal affairs. He began in 1840, when Secretary of State John Forsyth notified David Porter, US minister to Ottoman Turkey, that President Martin Van Buren was pained by "the atrocious cruelties . . . practiced upon the Jews of Damascus and Rhodes" inspired by the bizarre medieval blood libel. Forsyth told Porter that the president wanted him to intercede with the sultan's government "to prevent or mitigate" the antisemitic horrors, "the bare recital of which" had "caused a shudder throughout the civilized world." Kohler stated that in 1870, President Ulysses S. Grant had appointed a Jew, Benjamin Peixotto, as US consul to Romania "for the express purpose of promoting Jewish emancipation and the cessation of anti-Jewish activity." That same year, Senator Charles Sumner, chair of the US Senate Foreign Relations Committee, introduced a "resolution of inquiry into Romanian antisemitic atrocities."[27]

Kohler also emphasized that US Secretary of State John Hay had accompanied a committee to the White House that had collected "an enormous number" of signatures of prominent Americans expressing outrage to the czar at the 1903 Kishinev pogrom in Russia. Like the Tydings resolution, the Kishinev massacre petition protested atrocities against and persecution of Jews in a foreign country. After receiving the petition, President Theodore Roosevelt declared that "the whole civilized world" should express horror over Kishinev. He instructed the US ambassador in St. Petersburg to send a public and published cablegram to the Russian foreign minister presenting the petition's contents and "asking whether it would be received for submission to the Emperor himself." Although the Russian government refused to receive the petition, "its contents thus became known all over the world, and were brought home to the Emperor himself."[28]

The US State Department opposed the Tydings resolution, and Secretary Hull used his influence to keep it bottled up in the Senate Foreign Relations Committee. On January 19, Assistant Secretary of State Robert Walton Moore informed Hull that its passage would place President Roosevelt in a difficult position. If the president refused to convey to the Hitler government the American people's displeasure with its persecution of Jews, he "would be subjected to considerable adverse criticism." But complying with the resolution would anger the German government and possibly lead to "a very acrimonious discussion" about the disenfranchisement and lynching of African Americans in the South and the increased antisemitism in the United States. Moore also doubted Congress's constitutional right to "direct or request the President to take action relative to purely domestic affairs of another country."[29]

Aware of opposition from the administration and within the Senate Foreign Relations Committee, on January 24 Tydings "remodeled" the resolution to have the Senate, rather than the president, communicate to the German government Americans' "surprise and pain" about its persecution of Jews. On January 31, American Jewish Committee (AJC) president Cyrus Adler wrote to Foreign Relations chair Key Pittman urging his support for the resolution. Adler stated that "for nearly a century" the US Congress or the executive branch had declared itself in sympathy with foreign victims of "discrimination or injustice," sometimes by Senate, House of Representatives, or joint congressional resolutions. He noted that the first such occasion was in 1824, when Daniel Webster spoke in the Senate on behalf of the Greeks, who were demanding freedom from the Turks. Drawing on Kohler's work, Adler pointed to "an unbroken line of precedent of similar action ever since 1840."[30]

By its February 22 meeting, the AJC Executive Committee had determined that the Foreign Relations Committee was "hesitating" to support even the amended resolution for two reasons: the State Department's claim that there was no precedent for such action by the president, and stiff opposition in states with large German American populations. The AJC Executive Committee nonetheless vowed to continue its efforts to persuade the Foreign Relations Committee to report the resolution to the Senate floor.[31]

On February 8, Rabbi Joseph S. Shubow, director of the AJCongress's New England Office, sent President Roosevelt a statement endorsing the Tydings resolution, which one thousand representatives of nearly five hundred Jewish organizations, meeting at a conference in Boston to promote the boycott of German goods and services, had passed unanimously. Rabbi Shubow informed the president that the statement "has the support of hundreds of thousands of Jews throughout the New England states, whose leaders were present at the conference." The Boston *Jewish Advocate* urged its readers to write or telegraph members of the Senate Foreign Relations Committee to back the Tydings resolution. On February 23, the *Detroit Jewish Chronicle* published an editorial strongly endorsing the resolution and stating that "practically all Jewish organizations and movements in this country have agreed to support it."[32]

Speaking publicly on behalf of the resolution on March 7, Tydings affirmed his intention to keep "this crime," the persecution of German Jewry, "before all the world." He declared that the Hitler government had made outcasts of Germany's six hundred thousand Jews. The case "being tried before the bar of public opinion throughout the world" was whether German Jews, law-abiding people, who had died on hundreds of world war battlefields fighting for their country, should be "persecuted, deprived of their property, deprived of their lives."[33] Tydings and the Jewish organizations were unable to prevent the resolution from dying in committee, but the campaign they waged for Senate support of it helped energize the boycott movement and heightened many Americans' awareness of German antisemitic atrocities.

HITLER CONVICTED! THE MADISON SQUARE GARDEN TRIAL OF THE NAZI GOVERNMENT

On the evening of March 7, 1934, Madison Square Garden, usually a sports and circus arena, was transformed into "a huge Hall of Justice" in which Adolf Hitler, the "Torquemada of Germany," was tried for a crime against civilization before the largest jury in the world—the twenty thousand in attendance. The proceedings were broadcast over the radio. The trial, cosponsored by the AJCongress and the American Federation of Labor (AFL), was timed for one year after Hitler fully consolidated his power. The Boston *Jewish Advocate* noted that during that year Hitler had proven himself "an incorrigible and intransigent evil-doer and menace to civilization." As people took their seats, newsboys walked up and down the aisles, selling the first edition of the New York *Daily Mirror* with the banner headline "Hitler Convicted!" Twenty-two prominent Americans appeared as witnesses to present the "Case of Civilization against Hitlerism," including Al Smith, Mayor La Guardia, and AJCongress president Bernard Deutsch, representing American public opinion, and others speaking for labor, higher education, women, and religious and civil liberties groups. Witnesses included Jewish leaders like Rabbi Stephen S. Wise and Samuel Margoshes, and well-known non-Jews, including former assistant secretary of state Raymond Moley; Senator Millard Tydings; Roger Baldwin, director of the American Civil Liberties Union (ACLU); Chancellor Harry Woodburn Chase of New York University; and AFL vice president Matthew Woll. Samuel Seabury, an "outstanding leader of the American bar," gave the summation. President Wilson's secretary of state Bainbridge Colby served as presiding judge. Nazi ambassador Hans Luther was invited to act as defense counsel for Hitler but declined. A vacant chair on stage dramatized his absence. The day before the trial, the *Daily Mirror* reported that world-renowned educators, artists, reformers, and labor leaders had "added their names to the roll of honorary sponsors of the event." They included Professor John Dewey of Columbia; Alvin Johnson, head of the New School for Social Research; prominent painter John Sloan; Joseph Schlossberg, vice president of the Amalgamated Clothing Workers; and Carrie Chapman Catt.

The trial opened at 8:30 p.m. with the reading of a petition to President Roosevelt asking him to use the power of his office to stop the persecution of German Jewry. The petition also called on the League of Nations to make "every effort to restore full citizenship to the Jews in Germany" and "protect and reestablish" refugees who had fled the Reich. Jewish American Legion members then sounded taps for those murdered in the Nazi terror. Samuel Frederick, reporting for the *Jewish Advocate*, remarked that he had never seen such a large battery of reporters and photographers at an event, easily four hundred. The speeches included editor of the *Forward* Abraham Cahan's denunciation of "Hitler's gangsters and murderers," Chase's condemnation of the Nazis' "barbaric interference with intellectual freedom," and Woll's strong endorsement of the boycott of German goods and services, officially backed by the AFL. In his summation, Samuel Seabury predicted, "Public opinion as the force and the boycott as the weapon will break the power of Hitlerism." The mass meeting "rendered solemn judgment" that Hitler and his government was guilty of a crime against civilization.[34]

Newspapers ranging from the New York *Daily Mirror*, a working-class tabloid, to the "august" *New York Times* prominently featured Hitler's "conviction" on the front page. The *Times* headline was "Nazis 'Convicted' of World 'Crime' by 20,000 in Rally." The article was continued in eight columns on the inside. The *Times* published the speeches on three inside pages.[35]

Always concerned about maintaining a favorable image in the United States, the Hitler regime had tried to persuade the US State Department to stop the mock trial. Nazi ambassador Hans Luther called on Secretary of State Hull on February 20, presenting clippings from the *New York Times* and *New York Herald Tribune* from February 18 and 19 of advertisements and news accounts of the upcoming event. In a memorandum about the encounter, Hull wrote that Luther "earnestly complained against this sort of public proceeding against the Chancellor of Germany." Hull promised to give the matter "due attention."[36]

Hull was frustrated both by Luther's inability to grasp that the executive branch of the federal government lacked the authority to suppress the speech of private citizens or members of Congress and by the determination of the AJCongress and AFL to proceed with the mock trial, which he feared would damage US relations with the Hitler government. Luther again visited Hull on March 2, expressing "great concern" that he would not be able to justify to the German government his failure to prevent the mock trial. Hull responded that the organizers did not represent the US government and were not under its control. He added that he had been unable "to find any legal authority that would enable the Federal Government to instruct or order the participants to refrain from entering upon such a mock trial." The secretary of state informed Luther that he had "all the law books ransacked in an effort to find the complete international law relating to this sort of situation." He was disappointed that thus far he found no law that gave the federal government "any legal authority to compel the abandonment of the mock trial proposed." Hull assured Luther that his staff continued to examine all available law books and that "anything possible" would be done "in the light of international law."[37]

Less than a week after the mock trial, Luther appeared at the State Department for a third time to inform Secretary Hull that his government had instructed him to enter a protest on its behalf "against such offensive and insulting acts by the people of one country against the Government and its officials of another country." Hull expressed regret that such gatherings as mock trials were being held in the United States and elsewhere in the world and again emphasized that the participants were not acting as representatives of the US government. Equating the actions of Jews and their anti-Hitler allies with those of Nazis, Hull opined that the world was in ferment, "with the result that the people in more countries than one are neither thinking nor acting normally."[38]

The mock trial, with its massive Jewish grassroots support, reinforced the tactical division between its sponsor, the AJCongress, and the AJC, which refused to endorse the event. Arthur Hays Sulzberger, publisher of the *New York Times*, declined Bernard Deutsch's request to join the mock trial's Committee of Sponsors, but the *Times* did give the trial extensive front-page coverage. The AJC had "vigorously criticized" the AJCongress before the trial for launching the project without having consulted the Joint Council, which included both groups and B'nai B'rith. B'nai B'rith president Alfred Cohen declared that "such a meeting sponsored chiefly by Jewish organizations was not likely to be effective and might even have harmful repercussions." Cohen recommended, in addition, that Jewish organizations withdraw entirely from organizing the event and turn leadership over to the AFL and other non-Jewish groups.[39]

Sulzberger, whose views were close to the AJC's, made clear his strong discomfort with the AJCongress and mass Jewish-led protest. Sulzberger told a gentile anti-Hitler friend who complained to him that the mock trial "lacked dignity" and had been accorded too much space in the *New York Times* that he "disapprove[d] of most of the things" that Stephen S. Wise, Samuel Untermyer, and Bernard Deutsch had done. Sulzberger nonetheless felt obligated to give the mock trial significant coverage "in the light of the affront that civilization has received at Germany's hands." Moreover, when persons of the stature of Al Smith, Mayor La Guardia, the head of the ACLU, and so on participated, it was important news.[40]

To be sure, when Bertha Cone, a Jewish *New York Times* reader, complained to Sulzberger three weeks before the mock trial that the *Times* devoted less coverage to Nazi antisemitism than the "fearless and wonderful" *Manchester*

Guardian, he agreed. Cone argued that it was especially important for the *Times* to inform Americans about the persecution of the Jews in Germany because "neither our President nor our great newspapers" had "come out strongly against Hitler and his devilish work." Sulzberger acknowledged that his newspaper's coverage of "the outrages in Germany" had diminished, justifying this on the grounds that, unlike the *Guardian,* the *Times* was not a newspaper that "crusades for a cause." Sulzberger explained that for weeks after Hitler came to power, the *Times* did publish "many stories each day of the outrages in Germany." But the beatings, torture, and degradation of Jews and others whom the Nazis despised had gone on for so long that "they are no longer news." Sulzberger concluded, "If a German lawyer were thrown out of his practice, that was news—the fact that he is still out [of work] is no longer news."[41]

Under Sulzberger, the *New York Times,* which provided the most coverage of European affairs of any American newspaper, tended to downplay the unique nature of Jewish suffering in Germany. Like the AJC and Board of Deputies of British Jews, Sulzberger feared that if Jews assumed a high profile in the anti-Nazi campaign, it would spark an antisemitic backlash.[42]

MASS PROTESTS OF VISITS OF NAZI EMISSARIES

In May and June 1934, appearances by two important Nazi emissaries to the United States, Ambassador Hans Luther and Hitler's foreign press chief, Ernst Hanfstaengl, elicited mass protests by Jews, trade unionists, leftists, and many in the mainstream when the former visited St. Louis and the latter, Cambridge, Massachusetts. St. Louis's Central Trades and Labor Union (CTLU) initiated a protest upon learning that Luther was to be a principal speaker at the Saengerfest (May 31–June 2), a festival involving visiting German and American choirs and a seventy-six-person orchestra, including musicians from the St. Louis Symphony. The Chamber of Commerce had invited Luther to the city to meet with business leaders. The seventy-five-thousand-member CTLU passed a resolution stating that it was protesting Luther's visit because he was the ambassador of a government that had destroyed the German trade unions and democracy. The Beth Abraham synagogue passed a resolution declaring that its congregation was "deeply hurt and insulted that the representative of a government which brutally oppresses and persecutes the Jews should be given honors and welcomed to our city." Commenting on the planned protests, Mayor Bernard Dickmann declared that he hoped St. Louis residents would appeal to the German government through Ambassador Luther "to correct the injustices [in Germany] which today disturb all right-thinking people."[43]

The mayor's statement and the labor and Jewish protests deeply offended Ambassador Luther and caused the German consulate in St. Louis to cancel his participation in the Saengerfest parade through the city's downtown. The German consulate also announced that Luther would not call on the mayor at city hall to receive an official welcome, as the Saengerfest committee had arranged. When the mayor's "administrative orator," Counselor Hays, began a speech on "Hospitality" from the city hall steps, as a friendly gesture to Luther, about forty Communists, mostly African Americans, arrived, sang the "Internationale," distributed fliers protesting an official welcome to the Nazi ambassador, and marched away.[44]

Much of St. Louis's business community, by contrast, appeared highly receptive to Luther's views. Instead of attending the parade, Luther addressed a businessmen's luncheon that the Chamber of Commerce arranged at the Noonday Club. The previous night, he spoke at a reception held for him at the Hotel Jefferson, before a pro-Nazi audience of five hundred Saengerfest delegates, who greeted him with the stiff-armed salute and the German anthem, "Deutschland über Alles." The National Saengerfest president, George Voges, welcomed "the guest of honor." Speaking in German, Luther denounced the Versailles Treaty and called the Nazi government "the only salvation of Germany." Hitler's rule "meant peace, not war." His dictatorship had brought order to Germany, eliminating twenty-six squabbling political parties. The *St. Louis Post-Dispatch* commented that there was "no apparent need" for the German ambassador "to seek converts to Hitlerism" at the meeting: "The name of the Nazi leader was greeted with applause and cries of 'Heil!'"[45]

At the Saengerfest, Ambassador Luther sat in a box draped with a huge swastika banner, placed there at his request. The swastika led hundreds to protest vehemently. Local 116 of the International Ladies Garment Workers Union, with a substantial Jewish membership, added "its protest against the presence of Ambassador Luther in St. Louis."[46]

The next day, Mayor Dickmann attended the Saengerfest, where he and Luther occupied adjoining boxes. Luther invited Dickmann into his box, where the mayor sat and talked with the Nazi ambassador through several musical performances. The following day the mayor gave Luther an automobile tour of St. Louis. Luther then visited Washington University and made a formal call at city hall, where the mayor received him. Luther later held a press conference at which he reiterated that Nazi Germany was a Christian state committed to a policy of peace. Responding to the CTLU's protest, Luther commented that after the world war the German trade unions had tried to "carry out the class conflict theory through Marxian socialism." Hitler had abolished them for "the common good."[47]

The anti-Nazi protests and the revulsion that many city residents expressed about Hitler's policies resulted in a smaller attendance than expected at the Saengerfest. It was feared that receipts would not cover expenses. The *Post-Dispatch* ascribed this in part to poor weather and bad acoustics in the performance hall, but it also emphasized that Luther's presence was a significant factor: "The swastika flag which Dr. Luther required on his box, at the first two night concerts, is believed to have kept many persons away."[48]

The arrival in the United States in June 1934 of Hitler's foreign press chief, Ernst Hanfstaengl, to attend the twenty-fifth anniversary reunion of his Harvard class (1909) precipitated mass protests at the New York docks and in Cambridge, Massachusetts, which drew front-page newspaper coverage in Boston for more than a week. The Harvard administration warmly welcomed Hanfstaengl, a longtime friend of Hitler and member of his inner circle. In the assessment of Hitler biographer Ron Rosenbaum, Hanfstaengl "may have been as close to [Hitler] as anyone in the 1920s." In those critical early years, he was an important financial contributor to the Nazi Party and also provided Hitler entry into conservative upper-class circles. Hanfstaengl's loan to the party newspaper *Völkischer Beobachter* helped keep it afloat during the hyperinflation of the early Weimar period. Notably, Hanfstaengl supervised the production and composed the music for one of the most viciously antisemitic early Nazi propaganda films, *Hans Westmar*, based on the life of storm trooper Horst Wessel, the party's leading martyr, killed in a brawl with antifascist workers in 1930. The film portrayed Jews as spreaders of the viruses of Communism and "internationalism" and featured antisemitic stereotypes of cowardly, greedy, selfish, and overfed Jews. During production in late 1933, German Jews expressed fear about the danger the film posed to their safety in the Reich.[49]

Hanfstaengl's virulent antisemitism was well known in the United States long before he arrived for his Harvard reunion. On April 3, 1933, American diplomat James G. McDonald recorded in his diary that Hanfstaengl had just told him—invoking the medieval blood libel—that the Jews "are the vampire sucking German blood" and should be crushed. A month before the Harvard commencement, the British antifascist writer John Langdon-Davies in the American magazine *Forum and Century* cited an interview with Hanfstaengl in which he justified Nazi antisemitism on the grounds that Jews were parasitical, having "never produced anything at all." He claimed that Jews had "made the English and American theaters into sewers. All women and nakedness." Hanfstaengl praised the burning of the works of Albert Einstein and Sigmund Freud in what he called "the great literary *auto da fe*"—the mass book burnings staged on or near German university campuses in May 1933. On May 5, 1934, the *Boston*

Globe reported that Hanfstaengl had contributed "perhaps the most interesting" autobiography to the twenty-fifth anniversary report of the Harvard Class of 1909. In it, he boasted that in 1922 he had met "the man who has saved Germany and civilization—Adolf Hitler." Again drawing on the medieval image of Jew as bloodsucker, Hanfstaengl claimed that US Attorney General A. Mitchell Palmer, alien property custodian, had stolen his family's New York art reproduction firm and sold it at forced auction for far less than it was worth to a "Jewish firm." Hanfstaengl then repeated the vicious antisemitic slur Henry Ford had circulated during the 1920s, that Jews had caused the world war in order to enrich themselves: "This may serve as a hint as to who in reality won the war."[50]

The Harvard chapter of the National Student League (NSL), in a May 8 letter to the editor of the student newspaper, the *Harvard Crimson*, expressed outrage that any institution of higher learning would welcome a top official of a government that a year before "publicly burned 20,000 of the world's greatest books" and had "earned the hatred of the civilized world." Hanfstaengl had come to Harvard "to propagandize for murder." The *Crimson* appended an editors' note to the NSL's letter, stating that Hanfstaengl, as a member of the Harvard Class of 1909, was "perfectly justified" in returning to the campus.[51]

The Harvard administration announced on June 12 that it would welcome Hanfstaengl and impose "drastic punishment" on any student demonstrator attempting to disrupt the reunion. It insisted that he was coming to the United States only as an individual; his visit had no political significance. The administration declared that Hanfstaengl was "extremely popular with his fellow graduates of the class of 1909, and they are sure to welcome him enthusiastically." The *Harvard Crimson* urged that the university award Hanfstaengl an honorary degree as a tribute to "his high position in the government of a friendly country." The *Crimson* declared that the Nazi press chief had "all the qualifications" for an honorary degree. He had "risen to a distinguished station," was "a benefactor of the university," and was "held in high esteem by those members of his class who have, as he has, made marks in the world."[52]

By contrast, prominent *New York World-Telegram* columnist Heywood Broun on June 15 recommended that Hanfstaengl be removed from the *Europa* before landing and sent to Ellis Island as an undesirable alien. He noted that the anarchist Emma Goldman had been denied entry to the United States. Broun wrote that Hanfstaengl would "arouse more different kinds of hatred" in New York than anybody in the world except Hitler. There were hundreds of thousands of New Yorkers whose relatives and friends were victims of Nazi persecution. He maintained that Harvard's president, James Bryant Conant, should have used his influence to prevent Hanfstaengl from coming to Harvard.[53]

Leftist groups took the initiative in denouncing Hanfstaengl's visit, gathering at the New York dock to protest his arrival on June 16. The Joint Consultative Committee, representing the AJC, AJCongress, and B'nai B'rith, refrained from issuing a public statement because Hanfstaengl was allegedly coming as an individual, not as an official representative of the German government. However, many Jews at the grassroots protested strenuously. As with Hans Wiedemann's visit the year before, the authorities carried out a diversionary action to avoid a confrontation with the anti-Nazi demonstrators. Hanfstaengl was secretly transferred from the German liner *Europa* to a waiting tugboat, while a "double" resembling the Nazi press chief landed at the dock with a police bodyguard, who held back "a menacing crowd" of "thousands of yelling people."[54]

When Hanfstaengl arrived in Cambridge for his reunion, prominent members of Boston society received him, while Harvard police busily tore down fliers that anti-Nazi protestors had posted on campus. These fliers recommended that the Harvard administration bestow on Hanfstaengl a doctor of pogroms, master of sterilization, or bachelor of book burning degree. Wealthy alumni entertained Hanfstaengl at the Brookline Country Club and on the fashionable North Shore.[55]

The *Crimson* published letters to the editor condemning and supporting its proposal to award Hanfstaengl an honorary degree. Barbara Ware, who had read about the *Crimson*'s pro-Hanfstaengl stand in the *New York Post*, suggested the degree be an assistant doctor of laws "to make Torture, Starvation, Hatred, and Suffering legal in the Reich." By contrast, C. H. Ehiers, drawing on antisemitic images, excoriated the "sinister machinations . . . of self-styled groups which continue to . . . slander Ernst Hanfstaengl." He praised the *Crimson*'s "courageous attitude" in recommending that Harvard bestow the honorary degree. The Nazi press chief was "fifty percent American by ancestry" (on his mother's side), and his family had done more to unify America and make it great than the Jewish leaders Samuel Untermyer and Congressman Samuel Dickstein, who had launched a probe of Nazi propaganda in the United States. Untermyer and Dickstein were motivated by a "clannish" and "destroying" attitude and lacked any sense of "fair play."[56]

On June 18, Hanfstaengl experienced a "moment of unpleasantness" when Rabbi Joseph S. Shubow, a Harvard graduate, Boston AJCongress leader, and writer for the Boston *Jewish Advocate*, confronted the Nazi press chief in Harvard Yard and demanded to know what he meant when he said that "everything would soon be settled for the Jews in Germany." The "doughty" rabbi, later a US army chaplain in Europe in World War II, told Hanfstaengl that the Jewish people wanted to know whether it indicated that the Nazi plan for the Jews was "extermination." Hanfstaengl refused to respond. Harvard police immediately pushed Rabbi Shubow aside and ushered Hanfstaengl away. The next day, the *Boston Post* and the *Boston Herald* reported Rabbi Shubow's challenge to Hanfstaengl on the front page.[57]

President Conant's commencement remarks were interrupted by two young women Communists, who chained themselves, waists and wrists, to a railing of the grandstand in the Yard reserved for wives and daughters of the Class of 1909. They expressed their opposition to Hanfstaengl's presence by shouting, "Down with Hitler!" The *Boston Post* depicted the audience as "thunderstruck." Never before in Harvard's nearly three centuries of existence had a commencement exercise been disrupted in the Yard. The *Post* reported that "society women seated near the girl Communists gasped in surprise. Men in tall silk hats and frock coats remonstrated in urbane tones but to no avail." President Conant carried on but proved no match for the "girl Communists," who continued to cry, "Down with Hanfstaengl!" and "Down with all Nazis!" One "shrieked with a voice that seemed to be coming through a megaphone." A police detail "wrenched loose the railing of the grandstand to which the girls were chained" and arrested them. The *Boston Globe* described them as well-dressed liberated women, noting that as they sat in the women's detention cell at police headquarters in Central Square, Cambridge, "they calmly asked the officers for cigarettes and puffed away," while the "chains and clamps still dangled from their arms."[58]

The protest in the Yard was a prelude to a much larger one in Harvard Square, just outside the campus, that resembled the mass demonstration against Hanfstaengl on the New York docks the week before. This protest was initiated by young Communists and NSL members, many of whom wore shirts marked "Free Thaelmann," the German Communist leader whom the Nazis had imprisoned in a concentration camp. It was timed to coincide with the evening rush hour, forty-five minutes after the end of commencement exercises. One protestor chained himself to the heavy iron picket fence dividing the Yard from the Square and began denouncing Nazi Germany and the Harvard administration for inviting Hanfstaengl and "showering honors upon him." Policemen obtained a chain-cutting tool and arrested him. Another demonstrator climbed to the top of the kiosk adjacent to the station, a major terminus, and shouted, "Down with the Nazis!" Others moved through the swelling crowd leaving the subway station, which served two thousand people at its peak. Many commuters remained to listen to the anti-Nazi speeches. Protestors passed out anti-Nazi stickers issued by the NSL or the Boston Committee to Aid the Victims of German Fascism. Commuters were unable to board homeward-bound buses stationed in the Square. The *Boston Post* reported that "long lines of automobiles were halted for five blocks on either side of the square." The police arrested seven demonstrators as they spoke, or attempted to speak, on the charge of disturbing the peace and speaking without a permit.[59]

Although much of the protest against Hanfstaengl's appearance at Harvard was initiated by Communists or their sympathizers, important mainstream Jewish leaders, in addition to Rabbi Shubow, expressed similar outrage at the warm welcome the Harvard administration extended to him. Samuel Untermyer, the main speaker at a mass boycott meeting at Philadelphia's Metropolitan Opera House on June 27, opened his address, broadcast over CBS radio, with a stinging denunciation of Hanfstaengl. His presence at Harvard was "a disgrace ... and an insult to every one of the thousands of its distinguished Jewish and other graduates." Hanfstaengl was a "Jew-baiting ... apostle of race hatred and bigotry," a Nazi propagandist who was "abusing his privileges as a guest" in the United States. Untermyer declared him to be as responsible "as any other one man—except Hitler and Goebbels" for the atrocities inflicted on German Jews in 1933 and "many other forms of brutality . . . and persecution that have reduced [them] to their present sad plight—all with the avowed purpose of exterminating them." Joseph Tenenbaum, head of the AJCongress's boycott committee, took issue with the Harvard administration's claim that Hanfstaengl was visiting the United States as an individual. Tenenbaum maintained that the Hitler government had sent him as a propagandist to persuade Americans to view the Third Reich favorably.[60]

Shortly after his July 7 departure for Germany, Hanfstaengl published an article in an August issue of Collier's magazine, praising Hitler's vigor in eliminating Jews from the German economy and society. Once again invoking the medieval blood libel, he characterized Jews as parasites, "leeches feeding on the body politic," and demonic conspirators, the enthusiastic "pacemaker for Bolshevism." Hitler, the surgeon, knew that "to cure the body" ("Aryan" Germany), he had to "cut off the leg" (German Jewry).[61]

Pleased with the exceedingly friendly reception that prominent Harvard alumni had accorded Hanfstaengl, Hitler accorded him the honor of opening the sixth Nazi Party congress at Nuremberg in September 1934. These alumni, after all, included many of America's leading industrialists and financiers. Hanfstaengl's address, delivered in the honor court of Nuremberg's Germanic Museum, was "intended to batter down the last vestige of opposition to the Nazi program" and its commitment to "race purity."[62]

COMBATTING THE NAZI BLOOD LIBEL
AND DEICIDE ACCUSATION

Hanfstaengl's use of blood libel images occurred close on the heels of Julius Streicher's publication in May 1934 of a special issue of Der Stürmer devoted to "documenting" that since ancient times Jews had engaged in the kidnapping of Christian children to extract their blood to mix with Passover matzo. Pierre van Paassen warned that *Der Stürmer*'s special issue was "the opening signal" for pogroms, concluding, "the German Jews are doomed."[63] Reacting immediately to Streicher's special issue, Jewish defense organizations, in particular the AJC and the Board of Deputies of British Jews (BoD), labeled the blood libel vicious and baseless. AJC president Cyrus Adler and secretary Morris Waldman planned to discuss the issue with officers of the BoD and Alliance Israélite Universelle at an upcoming meeting of the three organizations in Paris. Adler proposed that the Philadelphia-based Jewish Publication Society, of which he was a trustee, issue an English translation of Aleksandr Semonovich Tager's book on the trial of Mendel Beilis, a Jewish brick factory manager in Kiev who had been framed for ritual murder in 1911 and whose plight had produced an outpouring of sympathy and outrage in Britain and the United States. Adler also advised reissuing Professor Hermann Strack's *The Jew and Human Sacrifice: Human Blood and Jewish Ritual, An Historical and Sociological Inquiry*.[64] Originally published in German in 1891 and in English in 1909, Strack's study fully exonerated the Jews of the blood libel accusation.

Using the mass protests in England in 1912 and 1913 against Beilis's arrest, imprisonment, and trial for ritual murder as precedent, the BoD attempted to enlist prominent Christian religious leaders in Britain to discredit the accusation. On May 11, only days after the ritual-murder issue of *Der Stürmer* appeared, England's chief rabbi, Dr. J. H. Hertz, referred in the London *Times* to "the protest, signed by the Archbishops of Canterbury and York, the Cardinal Archbishop of Westminster, and others, that appeared on May 6, 1912." Rabbi Hertz noted that these prominent clergymen had denounced the ritual murder accusation as "a relic of the days of witchcraft and 'black magic,' a cruel and utterly baseless libel on Judaism." Rabbi Hertz drew attention to their warning that "this unscrupulous fiction, spread among the people, has from the Middle Ages until recent times . . . incited the ignorant masses to outrage and massacre." It had "driven misguided crowds to pollute themselves with the innocent blood" of Jews. In 1912 the Christian clergymen had emphasized, "not a shadow of proof has ever been adduced to justify this crazy belief" that Jews commit ritual murder.[65]

Rabbi Hertz persuaded the archbishop of Canterbury, Cosmo Cantuar, to send a letter to the London *Times* denouncing *Der Stürmer*'s ritual murder issue. Cantuar wrote that the issue "rakes up legends and lies about the alleged custom of ritual murder by the Jews which have been over and over again exposed." Its illustrations were "gruesome and disgusting." Cantuar found it "almost incredible that such a publication recalling the worst excesses of medieval fanaticism should have been permitted in any civilized country."[66]

Rabbi Hertz expressed "profound gratitude" to the archbishop for his letter, which undoubtedly influenced some Anglican, and possibly other Christian, British subjects to question their long-standing belief about Jews. But Hertz's hope that the letter would undermine belief in the "Satanic lie of 'ritual murder'" in Germany and end the Nazis' use of it in their anti-Jewish agitation was not realized.[67]

The same month that *Der Stürmer* published its ritual-murder issue, the special tercentenary performances scheduled by the Hitler government of the Oberammergau Passion Play opened in Bavaria. Long denounced by Jews as viciously antisemitic, the play had been staged in the Bavarian village at ten-year intervals since 1634. Hitler had seen the play in 1930 and, recognizing its usefulness in fomenting hatred of Jews, scheduled a series of performances in 1934 to celebrate its three hundredth anniversary. The play emphasized Jews' collective guilt for Jesus' crucifixion and depicted them as racially distinct— dark complexioned, wearing dark clothes—while Jesus, Mary, and the apostles conformed to the Nazis' "Aryan" ideal. Judas's red hair identified him with the devil. His inner garment was yellow, the color Jews had been forced to wear in the Middle Ages. The Nazis had placed yellow circles above the Jews' stores and offices during their nationwide boycott on April 1, 1933. The actors playing Jesus and Mary, along with eight of the apostles, were Nazi Party members. Hitler met with them when he attended the play again in August 1934. Jewish priests wore tall horned hats, indicating they were the devil's allies. Residents of Oberammergau with parts in the play, bearded to resemble people of ancient Judaea, greeted one another with "Heil Hitler!"[68]

A London *Jewish Chronicle* reporter, J. Hodess, who saw the play in 1930, wrote that spectators saw the Jews of ancient Judaea portrayed as deicides, "savages of the worst kind." They saw "crowds of Jews fighting like a horde of vultures demanding their prey"—Jesus. In a section titled "Keen to Exterminate the Jewish People," Hodess described the passion play's depiction of the brutal Roman governor of Judaea, Pontius Pilate, as "battling for the life of Jesus" but "yielding finally to the insistent demand by the Jews that he should die." By portraying Jews as "barbarians gloating in the death by torture of any living being," the play defamed them and flagrantly distorted history. If, upon leaving a performance, an audience encountered a Jewish congregation coming out of a synagogue, Hodess feared it might well incite a pogrom.[69]

The Oberammergau Passion Play had long been a major tourist attraction, drawing 380,000 visitors to the village in 1930, a third from Britain and the United States. In 1934, the Hitler government aggressively promoted the play, hoping to draw large sums of money from abroad to fuel its economy and war industries, and to associate the Third Reich with Christianity. The German Tourist Information Office placed large notices in the *New York Times* proclaiming, "New Germany is on parade!" and highlighting the Oberammergau Passion Play, "a sacred drama superbly acted with simple piety by 1,000 players." The North German Lloyd and Hamburg-American Lines also advertised the play extensively. German Railways slashed fares to Oberammergau, and board and lodging charges in the village were reduced by 50 to 60 percent. The Hitler government sent British members of Parliament elaborately illustrated travel brochures of the Third Reich featuring the Oberammergau Passion Play, "offering hospitality for much less than moderate terms."[70]

Many American and British gentiles went to Oberammergau in 1934 and expressed their appreciation of the play. In May, the NBC radio network and other stations broadcast rehearsals from Oberammergau to American listeners. The Seven Sisters colleges, among the many American institutions of higher learning that maintained exchange programs with German universities throughout the 1930s, promoted European tours for their students during the summer of 1934, highlighted by attendance at the Oberammergau Passion Play. In Britain, Lord Baden-Powell (founder of the Boy Scouts), Lord Moynihan, and the bishop of Chichester signed an invitation to two thousand educators and students to attend a special performance on August 10 and "to be the guests of the villagers in their homes."[71]

By contrast, American Jewish leaders strongly denounced the Oberammergau Passion Play. In 1929, when Louis Marshall, president of the AJC, learned of plans to bring the play to the United States, he immediately protested, emphasizing that Jews would suffer "untold harm" if it were performed. Rabbi Stephen S. Wise, AJCongress vice president, publicly denounced the play in 1923 as "cruelly unjust" to the Jews. In 1930, he called it "a poisonous influence" on Christians who attended, encouraging "every manner of ill-will against the Jews." In December 1933, a few months before the tercentenary performances began, Wise condemned the play as an incitement to hatred.[72]

COMBATTING NAZISM WITH
ANTHROPOLOGICAL RESEARCH

The AJC monitored the proceedings of the first International Congress of Anthropological and Ethnological Research, held in London from July 30 to August 4, 1934, and "immediately realized the value" of some of the papers in combatting Nazi racial theories. More than one thousand anthropologists from forty-two nations attended the congress. As with the blood libel, the AJC

believed that a public exposed to serious scholarly research on race and culture would be less likely to embrace Nazi allegations about Jews' racial inferiority and demonic attributes. On August 17, Morris Waldman, who had read
the "fairly full reports" of the proceedings in the New York Times, noted that
the AJC had written at once to the Joint Foreign Committee of the BoD and the
Anglo-Jewish Association (AJA) in London, asking them to send a copy of one
paper that it considered especially valuable. This was the welcoming address to
members of the Section of Anatomy and Physical Anthropology delivered by Sir
Grafton Elliot Smith, one of Britain's most eminent anthropologists, in which
he "ridiculed" Nazi racial doctrine as delusional and in "flagrant conflict with
the generally recognized teachings of anthropological science." The New York
Times called the address "the most outspoken that had been heard at a British
scientific meeting in a long time." Cyrus Adler asked Neville Laski to send the
AJC a copy of Sir Grafton's address that it could circulate in the United States
and England. Waldman suggested that it also be translated into German and
French. In addition, he recommended to Adler the paper by J. B. S. Haldane,
professor of genetics at the University of London, which the New York Times
described as "an assault" on Nazi racial theories that supplemented Sir Grafton's.

Although Sir Grafton sponsored a resolution directed against the Nazi claim
of Aryan supremacy and two congress sections passed it, the governing committee of the International Congress "quietly killed" it. The New York Times
reported that the governing committee believed that the resolution was "tact-
less" but added that some attendees believed "it did not go far enough." The
resolution called for an impartial committee under League of Nations auspices
"to examine various facts bearing on races and the relations of races and to
condemn any distortion by science."[73]

Haldane, along with A. C. Haddon, whose impact on British anthropology
was "profound," and Nobel laureate F. Gowland Hopkins, published a letter to
the editor in the London Times on August 7 in which they expressed their deep
concern that Sir John Simon, secretary of state for foreign affairs, had stated in
a letter to Sir Archibald Hurd that he was "of Aryan stock without any Jewish
admixture whatsoever." The three anthropologists emphasized that the word
Aryan could not legitimately be "applied to race or stock." It was unfortunate,
they wrote, that a minister of the Crown should misuse a "term in a sense that
politically has done so much damage in Germany."[74]

Many advocates of appeasement had repeated the Hitler government's false
charge that Sir John Simon was a Jew or of Jewish origin. They alleged that it
was as a Jew and a dominant force in the British cabinet that he was determined
to undermine Germany's demands for rearmament, border changes in Europe,

and the return of its colonies. In November 1933, the French newspaper *Le Petit Parisien* had reported that the Hitler government had instructed its propagandists to use Sir John Simon's "Jewish origins" to explain Germany's withdrawal from the League of Nations the previous month. German propagandists were told to identify the British, not the French, as primarily responsible for denying German demands at Geneva and to attribute this to Sir John's Jewishness. Simon, the son of a Congregationalist minister, had, in fact, no Jewish ancestry. In June 1934, Sir Archibald Hurd, a friend of the British foreign secretary, asked him whether he knew "how frequently it is being stated . . . that you are a Jew and that your Jewish associations are influencing the foreign policy of this country." Sir Archibald reported that only a day or two before "a guest of ours, who is a keen Conservative, repeated this story and it has reached me from many other quarters." Sir Archibald expressed deep concern that the claim of the foreign secretary's Jewishness was "being so widely used to weaken the National Government."[75]

LABOR'S COMMITMENT TO THE BOYCOTT

In 1934, the American boycott campaign made new inroads and solidified its bonds with Jewish groups involved in the movement in other countries. The Non-Sectarian Anti-Nazi League (NSANL, formerly the ALDJR), the AJCongress, and the JWV continued to energetically promote the boycott. The NSANL expanded its grassroots activities, organizing district councils in several major cities that carefully monitored which stores were still purchasing German goods. District volunteers personally informed merchants where they could obtain alternative non-German products. In early 1934 the NSANL and the AFL agreed to cooperate in promoting the boycott. AFL president William Green, who negotiated the alliance with NSANL vice president Abba Hillel Silver, explained that organized labor desired to form a "united front with the hosts of Israel," because "every anti-Semite is, under the skin, an enemy of freedom and the working class." The two groups supported longshoremen who refused to load or unload German goods. In February 1934, the New York Central Trades and Labor Council, after an address at its meeting by anti-Nazi refugee trade unionist Martin Plettl, passed a resolution to boycott German goods and services. Plettl described German workers under Nazism as "abject slaves of their employers."[76] Organized labor's support provided additional economic leverage to the boycott campaign.

For the most part, the AJCongress, which endorsed the boycott in August 1933, several months after the ALDJR, employed similar tactics, although initially it differed on two issues. The AJCongress considered the boycott campaign a Jewish movement; the NSANL contended that it would be more effective if the public perceived it as nonsectarian (thus the name change). Joseph Tenenbaum, head of the AJCongress boycott committee, stated that his organization had always believed that Jews should be in the forefront of the movement, instead of entering "through the back-door of 'non-sectarianism.'" He identified picketing as the other major point of difference. Tenenbaum claimed that Samuel Untermyer, NSANL head and a prominent attorney, opposed picketing stores that carried German goods, fearing that it could interfere with efforts to persuade the owners and persons who shopped there from joining the boycott. Moreover, unlike in labor disputes, picketing to enforce boycotts had no legal status. Indeed, Tenenbaum acknowledged that he and other AJCongress activists spent much time in night courts bailing out pickets arrested for disorderly conduct and disturbing the peace. Still, Tenenbaum conceded, "as time went on," the NSANL had become "more predominantly sectarian (Jewish)" and the AJCongress's "'Jewish' boycott not a little non-sectarian."[77]

The JWV's demobilized soldiers, sailors, and marines, who had waged an energetic military campaign that helped defeat Germany in the world war, in 1934 planned "an extensive anti-Nazi drive to avert any possible loosening of the boycott." The JWV announced that it would convene mass meetings in every major American city to promote the boycott. The chair of the JWV Boycott Committee declared that "there is cause for a vigorous tightening of the boycott reins all along the line."[78]

A close working relationship among the AJCongress, the JWV, and the AFL was already evident by January 1934, when they cosponsored a New England boycott conference attended by one thousand representatives from several hundred Jewish and labor organizations. The conference set up a twenty-five-member committee to "vigilantly" supervise boycott activities in New England's trades, professions, industries, and communities. AJCongress speakers included Jennie Loitman Barron, president of the Women's Division, and Rabbi Shubow, director of the New England AJCongress. Commander-in-Chief William Berman spoke for the JWV, praised by the Boston *Jewish Advocate* as "in the vanguard of the boycott since Hitler's rise to power." William Dwyer, delivering a message from the AFL, assured the Jews present that they were not alone in their fight but had organized labor's fullest support in the struggle against "the enemy of civilization." The United Shoe and Leather Workers union, whose membership was largely non-Jewish, informed the conference that it was refusing to handle any German products used in manufacturing shoes. The heavily Jewish needle trades unions affirmed their solid backing for the boycott.[79]

In February 1934, the Jewish Labor Committee (JLC) was formed at a conference in New York City attended by one thousand delegates, an important step in mobilizing labor support for the boycott. The JLC represented four hundred thousand Jewish workers in New York alone and established branches in other major cities. Its organizing statement emphasized that Nazism threatened not only Jews but also organized labor and the liberal movement. Baruch Charney Vladeck, manager of the nation's most widely known Yiddish daily, the *Forverts* (*Forward*), became JLC chair, and David Dubinsky, president of the International Ladies Garment Workers Union, became JLC treasurer.[80]

In 1934 the JLC wrote numerous letters to New York City businesses that it discovered were still carrying German goods. The JLC warned each business that unless it received a definite reply within "a week, not later," it would inform the public that the business was selling German goods. Alert shoppers often provided the JLC with information about how stores were concealing the German origin of products on their shelves—for example, by removing the "Made in Germany" stamp.[81]

Needle trades unions affiliated with the JLC instructed their business agents to inspect tools and other materials used in the factories to determine whether they were German made. The unions would then pressure management to replace them with American-made products.[82]

The JLC wrote to prominent citizens planning to travel on German liners, reminding them of the "terrible persecutions of the Jewish population" under Hitler. It informed NBC broadcaster Andy Correll, who had booked passage on the *Bremen*, a vessel "absolutely controlled" by the Hitler regime, that as a member of the Actors Equity Association, an AFL affiliate, he was violating the AFL boycott resolution.[83]

The labor movements of the United States and Britain in 1934 contributed significantly to the forging of closer ties between the anti-Nazi boycott campaigns of both countries. AFL president William Green invited Walter Citrine, general secretary of the British Trades Union Congress and president of the International Federation of Trade Unions, to address the AFL's annual convention in October in San Francisco on the Nazis' destruction of Germany's trade unions and persecution of Jews. Upon arriving in the United States, Citrine traveled by train to the West Coast with Baruch Charney Vladeck and David Dubinsky, Jewish trade unionists highly active in the American boycott movement.

In his convention address, Citrine identified "the poisonous growth of Fascism" as the "one, outstanding, overriding question" commanding the attention "not only of the British Trades Union movement, but of the whole continent of Europe." The Nazis had destroyed one of the world's most long-standing, well-established, and advanced labor movements in just a few months. They had arrested Theodor Leipart, president of the German trade union association, thrown him into a cellar, and repeatedly bent his injured leg backwards and forwards, inflicting severe pain. "At the direct instigation of Nazi officials," German Jews were "brutally beaten and tortured." Citrine cited the example of an eighty-year-old rabbi whom the Nazis had dragged out of his synagogue and pummeled in the street. Citrine told the convention that the boycott of German goods and services was the most effective way to bring about the collapse of the Nazi government. The AFL delegates, highly receptive to his militant anti-Nazi message, "rose and cheered for several minutes" after he finished. His "hand was nearly wrung off by the hearty congratulations."

Accompanied by Vladeck, Citrine spoke a few days later in Los Angeles about the Nazi persecution of Jews. He noted that the audience was so moved that afterwards "even the waiters came up and contributed a couple of dollars and wanted to shake my hand."[84]

American proboycott organizations encountered opposition from the AJC and from Quaker groups. The AJC, which corresponded with the BoD and AJA and met regularly with them in London and Paris, remained firmly opposed to an organized boycott. After Morris Waldman met in Paris in June 1934 with representatives of those organizations—Neville Laski, Leonard Montefiore, and Sir Osmond Goldsmid—he reported to Cyrus Adler that the three had concluded that an official boycott (i.e., one organized and proclaimed by Jewish groups) would be counterproductive but also that nothing should be done to discourage individuals from boycotting German products.[85]

Neville Laski proffered two explanations for the BoD's opposition to an official Jewish boycott. First, because of the high level of antisemitism in Britain, it would spark a backlash against the Jews. Laski cited the boycott of Jewish stores by German American Nazi sympathizers in the United States, which, he claimed, "has already had serious economic results," driving many of them out of business. The second explanation was that it seemed overly dramatic, a "play to the gallery." He quoted the warning of Sir Robert Vansittart, Britain's permanent undersecretary for foreign affairs, that an official boycott was "fraught with grave consequences for the Anglo-Jewish community." Lord Vansittart predicted that it "would be seized upon as tantamount to admitting the existence of a quasi-Jewish State within the body politic of England." He maintained that "for a religious community composed of persons owing allegiance to the British Crown to act in this organized way would be to usurp a function which properly belonged to the government of the country." Laski acknowledged the existence of significant support for an official boycott within the British Labour Party but argued that while the party could "stand criticism," given Jews' precarious position in Britain, they needed "to avoid criticism as much as possible."[86]

CHRISTIAN MORAL SUASION VERSUS THE BOYCOTT

Quakers constituted a significant source of opposition to the organized boycott, some of it expressed in antisemitic terms. The Quakers advocated using moral suasion to persuade the Hitler government to abandon its brutality toward Jews, contrasting it with Jews' alleged vindictive approach. Quakers accused Jews who backed the organized boycott of intensifying Nazi antisemitic persecution. Henry Cadbury, professor of biblical literature at Bryn Mawr College, lectured the Central Conference of American Rabbis (CCAR) in June 1934 that Jews must not hate the Nazis but cultivate their goodwill. Cadbury, an official of the Society of Friends (Quakers), declared that war was wrong and the boycott was "simply war without bloodshed." The German Emergency Committee of the Religious Society of Friends in Great Britain shared Cadbury's outlook, advising a "positive and practical Christian attitude towards anti-Semitism and its victims" rather than Jewish-led mass rallies and boycotting of German goods and services. It cited reports that "the protests made by Jews outside Germany are proving embarrassing and in some cases dangerous to German Jews."

Rabbi Stephen S. Wise "led a wave of objection" from Jews to Cadbury's speech, which he said trivialized Nazi persecution of Jews. According to Cadbury, Wise stated, "some vulgar quarrel or street brawl had occurred between Hitler and the Jews and . . . the Jews were at fault." Wise accused Cadbury of implying that the Jews had launched an aggressive war against the Germans, when they were, in fact, employing the boycott, a moral and economic weapon, in self-defense. The CCAR's committee, headed by President Dr. Samuel Goldenson and including Rabbis Abba Hillel Silver and Wise, responded forcefully to Cadbury's speech, declaring that the CCAR supported "every manner of non-violent resistance calculated to bring to an end the regime of inequity and enslavement which today obtains in Nazi Germany"—including the boycott.[87]

William Ebor, archbishop of York, was, like the Quakers, naive in believing that his moral appeal to the Nazis could persuade them to abandon their vicious persecution of Jews. In June 1934, the same month Cadbury condemned Jewish leaders' advocacy of an anti-Nazi boycott, the archbishop asked a friend to deliver a follow-up letter he had written the Fuehrer, begging him to use his "great influence" to end the German government's antisemitic policies. The archbishop's first letter, sent through emissaries the previous month with the same request, had been signed by "a small number of persons eminent in . . . English life, who have given tangible evidence of their friendship for Germany." The Fuehrer did not grant the archbishop's emissaries a meeting, and the letter was never delivered. The archbishop's second attempt was also unsuccessful.[88]

* * *

In 1934, Jews and their allies in both the United States and Britain waged an increasingly vigorous struggle to combat Nazi Germany's cold pogrom on several fronts. The AJCongress's August 1933 endorsement of the boycott had brought the movement additional organizational expertise, funding, and press coverage. The formation of the JLC in February 1934, on the initiative of the heavily Jewish needle trades unions in New York, America's largest commercial center, provided better coordination of the boycott at the grassroots. The membership of the needle trades unions was largely female. As the household's primary shoppers, women were more familiar than men with neighborhood stores and often had daily contact with local merchants. Women's services proved critically important to the boycott. They were in the best position to compile lists of neighborhood stores selling German goods and to persuade merchants whom they knew to terminate their orders. Both American and British Jewish women also energetically raised funds at the neighborhood level to send Jewish children, doomed to misery and ultimate extinction in Germany, to Palestine.

The boycott, which included travel to Germany, was especially important in 1934 when the Hitler government was staging tercentenary performances of the Obergammergau Passion Play, among the most fiercely antisemitic dramas in theater history. When last staged in 1930, the play, which wove together theologically and racially antisemitic themes, had attracted more than one hundred thousand attendees from the United States and Britain. The more moderate BoD and AJC, which still refrained from supporting the organized boycott, nonetheless worked determinedly in 1934 to combat Der Stürmer's aggressive campaign to spread the medieval blood libel, an accusation that for centuries had precipitated large-scale violence against Jews.

The effectiveness of the developing alliance between proboycott Jewish groups and organized labor was demonstrated in St. Louis in May, where Jews joined with the city's Central Trades and Labor Council in denouncing the

Saengerfest, a primarily German American event, after they learned that Ambassador Hans Luther would be present as a speaker extolling Nazi policies and as an honored guest. Although the St. Louis Chamber of Commerce and much of the business and German American communities enthusiastically welcomed Hitler's emissary to St. Louis, the combined Jewish-labor opposition to his presence noticeably reduced attendance.

In Cambridge, Massachusetts, and on the New York docks, vociferous grassroots protests erupted when American university administrators again displayed willingness to warmly welcome a top Nazi official, Hitler's foreign press chief, Ernst Hanfstaengl, to campus. The mass protests revealed a significant division between the Jewish community and working-class and lower-middle-class Americans, on the one hand, and the nation's elite colleges and prominent alumni on the other. During the 1930s, rigid quotas drastically limited the numbers of Jewish students admitted to universities like Harvard and Columbia, and almost no Jews held faculty positions. A few months before, Columbia president Nicholas Murray Butler had praised Ambassador Hans Luther, a leading spokesperson for Nazi antisemitic policies, who had been invited to speak on campus, insisting he deserved respect. The Jewish community viewed with alarm the Harvard administration's similarly friendly welcome to Hanfstaengl, undeterred by his enthusiastic support for the Nazis' mass burnings of Jewish and other "un-German" books.

Despite the well-documented Nazi brutality toward Jews, the White House and the State Department continued to remain silent, although some prominent American politicians strongly condemned it. Al Smith, Robert Wagner, Millard Tydings, and Fiorello La Guardia, for example, participated in the March 1934 mock trial of Hitler for crimes against civilization before a capacity audience at Madison Square Garden. In November 1934, a Jewish attorney, Martin Kolbrener, wrote to Roosevelt's secretary, Louis Howe, requesting any statement the president had issued deploring Nazi persecution of Jews or other minorities in Germany, in order to respond to "people who have expressed their disappointment with the President regarding this matter." Howe's assistant responded flatly to Kolbrener, "The President has made no statements with regard to the subjects to which you refer."[89] British prime minister Ramsay MacDonald appeared just as indifferent. And in an alarming display of insensitivity to Jews suffering severe persecution in the Reich and targeted by Nazi-inspired Arab propaganda in Palestine, the British Mandatory government prohibited the sale of the Brown Book, the first published volume detailing Nazi antisemitic atrocities, while defending the distribution of Hitler's Mein Kampf.

The State Department helped stifle Senator Millard Tydings' resolution calling on the president and the US Senate to communicate to the German government their deep concern about the Nazi oppression of German Jewry. American Jews provided critical assistance to Senator Tydings by conducting research demonstrating that there had been a long tradition of US presidents making public statements denouncing the persecution of Jews by foreign governments, dating back to 1840.

Although there was considerable antisemitism in the American and British professoriates, several distinguished British anthropologists contributed significantly to the struggle against the Hitler regime by drawing on cutting-edge research to disprove Nazi claims of Jewish racial inferiority, presenting their findings at the First International Congress of Anthropological and Ethnological Research in London, in late July and early August. The AJC and the BoD cooperated in disseminating their conclusions to the public.

In 1934, many critics of the Nazis, mostly non-Jews, like Al Smith, continued to believe that a sizeable number of Germans remained unsympathetic to the Hitler government's antisemitic policies. Hitler's massive victory in the long-awaited January 13, 1935, Saar plebiscite, which provided the first opportunity since the Nazis assumed power for a German population to freely express its view of his regime and its anti-Jewish measures, shocked and terrified many in the West. But the Saar's strong endorsement and celebration of Nazism, and the subsequent forced exodus of the Jews, did not cause the American and British governments to reassess their appeasement of Nazi Germany and their neglect of German Jewry's plight.

NOTES

1. Flier, "Jewry Is in Peril," April 1934, 876/2/10, Anti-German Protest and Prayer Meetings, Wiener Library for the Study of the Holocaust and Genocide, London, UK.

2. The World Committee to Aid the Victims of German Fascism was formed in 1933 with Albert Einstein as president. It had local branches in Britain and the United States, usually called relief committees for the victims of German fascism. In Britain, most chapters consisted of left-leaning Labour Party members who were willing to work with Communists. *Manchester Guardian*, October 3, 1933, 3, 9. Many moderates, however, participated in the organization's relief work with refugees and attended its rallies.

3. *New York Times*, December 9, 1933, 8, February 4, 1934, 22, February 6, 1934, 18, February 7, 1934, 4, and March 3, 1934, 4.

4. *New York Times*, February 8, 1934, 5; *Los Angeles Times*, February 16, 1934, A1.

5. *Jewish Advocate* (Boston), February 16, 1934, 1, 4, and February 27, 1934, 1; *Harvard Crimson*, February 28, 1934.

6. "The Reminiscences of Gerhart Henry Seger," December 1950, Oral History Research Office, Butler Library, Columbia University, New York, NY, 93–94.

7. "Reminiscences of Seger," 105–7; *New York Times*, October 31, 1934, 6.

8. Anonymous to American Government Department of Foreign Affairs [sent from the Netherlands], February 20, 1934, box 4729, Central Decimal Files (hereafter, CDF), 1930–39, Department of State General Records, Record Group (hereafter, RG) 59, National Archives, College Park, MD (hereafter, NA-CP); *New York Times*, March 31, 1935, BR4.

9. *Mr. Gerhart Seger Lectures*, n.d., box 24, Non-Sectarian Anti-Nazi League Papers, Rare Book and Manuscript Library, Columbia University, New York, NY; *New York Times*, March 31, 1935, BR4.

10. *New York Times*, October 31, 1934, 6, May 28, 1935, 24, and June 4, 1935, 18.

11. *Columbia Spectator*, November 15, 1934, 1, and November 19, 1934, 1; *Daily Californian*, January 31, 1935.

12. Gerhart Seger, letter to the editor, *New York Times*, May 28, 1935, 24; *New York Times*, November 11, 1934, 25 (Rand School), and December 9, 1934, 15 (Foreign Policy Association); *Chicago Tribune*, November 22, 1934, 4; *Los Angeles Times*, December 16, 1934, D4, and December 22, 1934, A12.

13. Toni Sender, *The Autobiography of a German Rebel* (New York: Vanguard, 1939), 278–308; "Toni Sender" and "Conference on Jewish Material Claims against Germany," box 6, Toni Sender Papers, Wisconsin Historical Society, Madison, WI; Stephen H. Norwood, "Toni Sender," in *Encyclopedia of American Jewish History*, ed. Stephen H. Norwood and Eunice G. Pollack (Santa Barbara, CA: ABC-CLIO, 2008), 1:388–90; *New York Times*, March 30, 1934, 14.

14. Sender, *Autobiography of a German Rebel*, 314. Sender's WEVD address on January 4, "How Hitler's Aryan Paradise Enslaves the Women of Germany," appeared in the socialist weekly *New Leader* (US), January 12, 1935, 5. An article on the next page, headlined "Tony Sender Thrills Vast Pennsylvania Throng," reported another of Sender's anti-Nazi speeches "before a large audience" in Pittsburgh on January 6. Sender, and the American press, sometimes spelled her first name "Tony"; *Chicago Tribune*, March 11, 1935, 6.

15. *New Leader* (US), October 7, 1933; *Thameside Mail*, February 2, 1934, reel LP, W1/5, Ellen Wilkinson Scrapbook, People's History Museum, Manchester, UK; Betty D. Vernon, *Ellen Wilkinson, 1891–1947* (London: Croom Helm, 1982), 156–8, quoted. *New York Herald Tribune*, July 20, 1932, 1, 10.

16. *Sunday Referee* (London), May 21, 1933, Ellen Wilkinson Scrapbook, reel LP, W 1/5, People's History Museum, Manchester, UK.

17. *Manchester Guardian*, November 6, 1933, 11.

18. *Thameside Mail*, February 2, 1934, Wilkinson Scrapbook, People's History Museum, Manchester, UK. In January 1935, Wilkinson began an anti-Nazi

lecture tour of twenty-five US cities under the auspices of the socialist League for Industrial Democracy. *New Leader* (US), January 12, 1935, 6.

19. *Jewish Advocate* (Boston), February 16, 1934, 1; *Boston Globe*, February 9, 1934, 2.

20. *Jewish Advocate* (Boston), March 16, 1934, 4, and March 23, 1934, 2.

21. *New York Times*, February 27, 1934, 9, and March 5, 1934, 18.

22. *Manchester Guardian*, January 31, 1934, 11.

23. Le Consul Général d'Allemagne to Monsieur le Secrétaire Général, January 5, 1934, and P. Cunliffe-Lister to Colonel and the Right Honourable J. C. Wedgwood, MP, April 14, 1934, CO 733/258/13, Colonial Office Records, National Archives, Kew Gardens, London, UK; extract, *Palestine Post*, February 26, 1934.

24. J. Hathorn Hall, Officer Administering the Government, High Commissioner for Palestine, to Sir Philip Cunliffe-Lister, MP, His Majesty's Principal Secretary of State for Colonies, March 19, 1934, CO 733/258/13, Colonial Office Records, National Archives, Kew Gardens, London, UK.

25. "Nazi Propaganda in Palestine," extract from note of Lord Plymouth's discussion with Professor Brodetsky and Dr. Lourie on March 12, 1934; *Palestine Post*, February 26 and 28, 1934, CO 733/258/13, Colonial Office Records, National Archives, Kew Gardens, London, UK.

26. *New York Times*, January 9, 1934, 13; Max J. Kohler, *The United States and German Jewish Persecutions: Precedents for Popular and Governmental Action* (Cincinnati: B'Nai B'rith Executive Committee, 1934).

27. *New York Times*, January 9, 1934, 13; Kohler, *United States and German Jewish Persecutions*, 34–37. Kohler's work was originally presented as a paper to the Jewish Academy of Arts and Sciences on June 1, 1933.

28. Kohler, *United States and German Jewish Persecutions*, 28–30.

29. Sheldon Spear, "The United States and the Persecution of Jews in Germany, 1933–1939," *Jewish Social Studies* 30 (October 1968): 216; Robert Walton Moore, "Memorandum for Secretary Hull with Respect to Senate Resolution 120 Introduced by Senator Tydings of Maryland," January 19, 1934, box 6786, CDF, 1930–39, Department of State General Records, RG 59, NA-CP.

30. *New York Times*, January 25, 1934, 8; Cyrus Adler to Key Pittman, January 31, 1934, box 11, Cyrus Adler Papers (hereafter, Adler Papers), American Jewish Committee (hereafter, AJC) Archives, New York, NY.

31. AJC, "Minutes of Meeting of the Executive Committee Held on February 22, 1934," AJCArchives.org.

32. Rabbi Joseph Shubow to the President, February 8, 1934, box 6787, CDF, Department of State General Records, RG 59, NA-CP; *Jewish Advocate* (Boston), February 9, 1934, 1, 2; *Detroit Jewish Chronicle*, February 23, 1934.

33. "Speech of Senator Millard E. Tydings," March 7, 1934, box 2, series 2, Millard E. Tydings Papers, Archives and Manuscripts Department, Hornbake Library, University of Maryland, College Park, MD.

34. *New York Times*, March 8, 1934, 1; "Hitler and His Government 'Guilty!,'" *Jewish Chronicle* (London), March 16, 1934, 40; *Jewish Advocate* (Boston), March 13, 1934; Bernard S. Deutsch to Arthur Hays Sulzberger, February 12, 1934, box 175, Arthur Hays Sulzberger Papers (hereafter, Sulzberger Papers), New York Public Library (hereafter, NYPL), New York, NY; *Daily Mirror* (New York), March 7, 1934, 1, 2, 11, and March 8, 1934, 1. The *Daily Mirror* also carried an article about the trial several days before it was staged headlined "Hitler on Trial as World Menace." *Daily Mirror* (New York), March 3, 1934, 4. The mock trial was covered in major British newspapers. *Times* (London), March 9, 1934, 13; *Manchester Guardian*, March 9, 1934, 9.

35. *Daily Mirror* (New York), March 8, 1934, 1, 2, 9; *New York Times*, March 8, 1934, 1, 14, 15, 16.

36. "Memorandum of Conversation between Secretary Hull and the German Ambassador, Herr Hans Luther," February 20, 1934, reel 29, Cordell Hull Papers (hereafter, Hull Papers), Library of Congress (hereafter, LC), Washington, DC.

37. "Memorandum of Conversation between Secretary Hull and the German Ambassador, Mr. Hans Luther," March 2, 1934, reel 29, Hull Papers, LC.

38. "Memorandum of Conversation between Secretary Hull and the German Ambassador, Herr Hans Luther," March 13, 1934, reel 29, Hull Papers, LC.

39. Arthur H. Sulzberger to Bernard S. Deutsch, January 11, 1934, box 175, Sulzberger Papers, NYPL; AJC, "Meeting of the Executive Committee Held on February 22, 1934," AJCArchives.org.

40. Captain Hilton Howell Railey to Arthur (Sulzberger), March 17, 1934 and Arthur Hays Sulzberger to Captain H. H. Railey, April 2, 1934, box 175, Sulzberger Papers, NYPL.

41. Bertha L. Cone (Mrs. Moses H. Cone) to Sulzberger, February 14, 1934, and Sulzberger to Cone, February 21, 1934, box 175, Sulzberger Papers, NYPL.

42. On Sulzberger's reaction to Nazi Germany's persecution of the Jews, see Laurel Leff, *Buried by the Times: The Holocaust and America's Most Important Newspaper* (New York: Cambridge University Press, 2005).

43. *St. Louis Post-Dispatch*, May 28, 1934, 4C, May 29, 1934, 7A, May 30, 1934, 3A, May 31, 1934, 1; Jewish Telegraphic Agency, May 29 and 30, 1934. The *Post-Dispatch* covered the protests for an entire week.

44. *St. Louis Post-Dispatch*, May 31, 1934, 1; Jewish Telegraphic Agency, June 3, 1934.

45. *St. Louis Post-Dispatch*, May 31, 1934, 1.

46. *St. Louis Post-Dispatch*, May 31, 1, and June 1, 1934, 1; Jewish Telegraphic Agency, June 3, 1934.

47. *St. Louis Post-Dispatch*, June 2, 1934, and June 3, 1934, 1.

48. *St. Louis Post-Dispatch*, June 3, 1934.

49. *New York Times*, November 13, 1923, 1; Henry Ashby Turner Jr., *German Big Business and the Rise of Hitler* (New York: Oxford University Press, 1985),

55; Peter Conradi, *Hitler's Piano Player: The Rise and Fall of Ernst Hanfstaengl, Confidant of Hitler, Ally of FDR* (New York: Carroll and Graf, 2004), 52–53, 63, 134–35; Ron Rosenbaum, *Explaining Hitler* (New York: HarperCollins, 1998), 125; Stephen H. Norwood, *The Third Reich in the Ivory Tower: Complicity and Conflict on American Campuses* (New York: Cambridge University Press, 2009), 47–49.

50. Richard Breitman, Barbara McDonald Stewart, and Severin Hochberg, eds., *Advocate for the Doomed: The Diaries and Papers of James G. McDonald, 1932–1935* (Bloomington: Indiana University Press, 2007), 28; John Langdon-Davies, "Nazi Science and Ourselves," *Forum and Century*, May 1934, 310; entry for Ernst Hanfstaengl, Harvard College, 25th Anniversary Class Report, Class of 1909, 277–78; *Boston Globe*, May 5 and 18, 1934. The *Boston Evening Transcript* carried an article similar to the *Globe*'s about Hanfstaengl's class report autobiography. *Boston Evening Transcript*, May 18, 1934. Bella Fromm, German Jewish diplomatic correspondent for the *Vossische Zeitung* in Berlin, quoted Hanfstaengl in her diary on March 24, 1933, declaring at a reception at the Italian embassy that "all the rumors about the persecution of Jews . . . are cheap lies." Bella Fromm, *Blood and Banquets: A Berlin Social Diary* (New York: Harper and Brothers, 1942), 92.

51. *Harvard Crimson*, May 8, 1934.

52. *Boston Post*, June 12, 1934, 1, 15; *Harvard Crimson*, June 13, 1934, 2; *New York Times*, June 13, 1934, 13.

53. *New York World-Telegram*, June 15, 1934, 21. Broun had attended Harvard from 1906 to 1910. Hanfstaengl was there during three of those years.

54. *New York World-Telegram*, June 16, 1934. The *New York Times* estimated the crowd at fifteen hundred. *New York Times*, June 17, 1934, 1. Speakers at the dock included NSL member Joseph Cohen, Communist leader Robert Minor, Peter Cacchione of the Communist-sponsored Ex-Servicemen's League, former concentration camp inmate Hans Baer, and Joseph Lash of the socialist student organization Student League for Industrial Democracy. Lash later became a major biographer of Franklin D. Roosevelt. *Daily Worker*, June 18, 1934, 1, 2.

55. *Boston Evening Globe*, June 18, 1934, 1; *Boston Globe*, June 19, 1934, 1, 4, and June 20, 1934, 1; *Boston Evening Transcript*, June 18, 1934, 1, 2; *Boston Herald*, June 20, 1934, 1, 11; *The Day*, June 24, 1934; *New York World-Telegram*, June 18, 1934. For additional discussion and analysis of Harvard's response to Hanfstaengl's visit, see Norwood, *Third Reich in the Ivory Tower*, chap. 2.

56. *Harvard Crimson*, June 20, 1934, 7.

57. *Boston Post*, June 19, 1934, 1, 9; *Boston Herald*, June 19, 1934, 1, 6. On March 30, 1945, Rabbi Shubow conducted a Passover Seder for three hundred American soldiers in Josef Goebbels' castle, which American forces had captured a short time before. *New York Herald Tribune*), March 31, 1945, 1.

58. *Boston Herald*, June 22, 1934, 1, 15; *Boston Post*, June 22, 1934, 1; *Boston Globe*, June 22, 1934, 1, 8; *New York Times*, June 22, 1934, 1, 15; Conradi, *Hitler's Piano Player*, 156.

59. *Boston Post,* June 22, 1934, 1; *Boston Herald,* June 22, 1934, 1, 15; *Boston Globe,* June 22, 1934, 1, 8. A judge sentenced the seven arrested in Harvard Square, six men and a woman, to thirty days in jail. When they appealed the sentence, however, the Superior Court sentenced them to six months' imprisonment at hard labor in the Middlesex House of Correction. The Superior Court judge explained that he meant this to be "a deterrent to those who hold views similar to yours." President Conant intervened to have the charges against the two young women arrested in the Yard dropped, but he refused to do so for those who had demonstrated in Harvard Square, on the grounds that their actions had taken place outside university property. He termed their protest "ridiculous." The seven were released after serving thirty-six days of their sentence. Norwood, *Third Reich in the Ivory Tower,* 54–55, 267.

60. *New York Times,* June 28, 1934, 15; *Wall Street Journal,* June 29, 1934, 3; Jewish Telegraphic Agency, June 20 and 28, 1934.

61. Ernst F. S. Hanfstaengl, "My Leader," *Collier's,* August 4, 1934, 9; Conradi, *Hitler's Piano Player,* 152–53.

62. *Los Angeles Times,* September 5, 1934, 1; *Washington Post,* September 5, 1934, 26. The Germanic Museum was selected as the site of Hanfstaengl's address to emphasize his claim of Nazism's deep historical roots. Surrounded by medieval trophies, Hanfstaengl linked "the Nazi revival" to the Renaissance and the Reformation. *Manchester Guardian,* September 5, 1934, 13.

63. Pierre van Paassen, "Pogrom Ahead," *The Sentinel,* June 14, 1934, 7, box 4, Adolph Ochs Papers, NYPL.

64. Cyrus Adler to Morris D. Waldman, June 6, 1934, and Waldman to Adler, June 19, 1934, box 11, Adler Papers, AJC Archives. Tager's book, written in Russian, was published by the Jewish Publication Society in English translation in 1935 as *The Decay of Czarism: The Beilis Trial.*

65. *Times* (London), May 11, 1934, and *Evening Standard,* May 11, 1934, 882/9, Documents concerning Antisemitism and Ritual Murder, Wiener Library.

66. *Times* (London), May 16, 1934, 17.

67. J. H. Hertz to Lord Archbishop, May 16, 1934, 882/14, Documents concerning Antisemitism and Ritual Murder, Wiener Library.

68. Saul S. Friedman, *The Oberammergau Passion Play* (Carbondale: Southern Illinois Press, 1984), 86–88, 123; James Shapiro, *Oberammergau: The Troubling Story of the World's Most Famous Passion Play* (New York: Pantheon, 2000), 3, 12, 88, 165–67; Barbara E. Scott Fisher, "Notes of a Cosmopolitan," *North American Review,* March 1934, xi; *Manchester Guardian,* May 20, 1934, 8.

69. J. Hodess, "Oberammergau: An 'Evil Play,'" *Jewish Chronicle* (London), August 24, 1930, 16–17.

70. Friedman, *Oberammergau Passion Play,* 120; *New York Times,* May 2, 1934, 14 and May 16, 1934; Dr. Franz X. Bogenrieder, "The Centenary Performances of

the Oberammergau Passion Play in 1934," AR 25441, 3/29, Florence Mendheim
Collection of Anti-Semitic Propaganda, Leo Baeck Institute, Center for Jewish
History, New York, NY; Norwood, *Third Reich in the Ivory Tower*, 121–22;
"Parliamentary Notes," *Jewish Chronicle* (London), April 27, 1934.

71. Norwood, *Third Reich in the Ivory Tower*, 121–22; *Washington Post*,
October 22, 1933, and March 5, 1934; *New York Times*, May 18, 1934, 12, and July
1, 1934, 26; *Manchester Guardian*, April 10, 1934, 1, 10. The world war caused the
Oberammergau Passion Play scheduled for 1920 to be delayed until 1922.

72. Jewish Telegraphic Agency, April 24, 1929; *New York Times*, March 23, 1923,
8, and May 19, 1930, 23; *Washington Post*, December 25, 1933, 4.

73. Morris D. Waldman to Cyrus Adler, August 17, 1934, box 11, Adler Papers,
AJC Archives; *Manchester Guardian*, August 1, 1934, 12; *New York Times*, August
1, 1934, 19, August 4, 1934, 13, and August 5, 1934, 14.

74. *Times* (London), August 4, 1934, 7, and August 7, 1934, 11; Sir John
Simon to Sir Archibald Hurd, August 1, 1934, MS 79, Sir John Simon Papers
(hereafter, Simon Papers), Bodleian Library Special Collections, University of
Oxford, Oxford, UK. On Haddon, see Steve Mullins, "Alfred Cort Haddon," in
Australian Dictionary of Biography (Melbourne: Melbourne University Press,
1996). Frederick Gowland Hopkins won the Nobel Prize in Physiology or
Medicine in 1929.

75. *News Chronicle*, November 23, 1933; John Simon to Willie [Lord Tyrrel],
November 25, 1933; Lord Tyrrell to Sir John Simon, November 29, 1933; and Sir
Archibald Hurd to Sir John Simon, June 19, 1934, MS 77, Simon Papers, Bodleian
Library, Oxford. Sir John emphasized to Sir Eric Phipps, British ambassador to
Germany, that his father's family was "pure Pembrokeshire (hence the Biblical
name), i.e., Welsh and Flemish, and my mother comes of a very ancient purely
English stock, so there is nothing Hebraic about me." Simon told Phipps that
a denial should be issued and to consider speaking directly to Propaganda
Minister Goebbels about the matter. Sir John Simon to Sir Eric Phipps,
November 27, 1933, 1/11, Sir Eric Phipps Papers, Churchill College Archives,
University of Cambridge, UK.

76. "The Economic Boycott," Jewish Central Information Office, November–
December 1934, Wiener Library; *New York Times*, February 16, 1934, 5.

77. Joseph Tenenbaum, "The Anti-Nazi Boycott Movement in the United
States," *Yad Vashem Studies* 3 (1959): 144–45. Rona Sheramy stated that the
AJCongress's Women's Division assumed "primary responsibility" for picketing
stores selling German goods, in addition to "neighborhood organization" and
"consumer mobilization," in part because Tenenbaum believed that women
had more free time to devote to picketing. This may have been the case with the
AJCongress's Women's Division's middle-class members, on whom Sheramy
focused. A significant proportion of the Jewish women in the boycott movement,

however, were members of New York's needle trades unions and seasoned pickets, having participated in strikes. Rona Sheramy, "There Are Times When Silence Is a Sin": The Women's Division of the American Jewish Congress and the Anti-Nazi Boycott Movement," *American Jewish History* 89 (March 2001): 105, 113–15.

78. "United States," *Jewish Chronicle* (London), September 7, 1934, 34.

79. *Jewish Advocate* (Boston), January 30, 1934, 1, 16.

80. *New York Times*, April 5, 1934, 10.

81. Jewish Labor Committee to R. H. Macy & Co., May 10, 1934; Jewish Labor Committee to May Glove Company, August 31, 1934; Jewish Labor Committee to Hollywood Theatre, October 25, 1934; H. Raskin to R. H. Macy & Co., October 5, 1934; Sid Stark to B. C. Vladeck, May 17, 1934, reel 33, Jewish Labor Committee (hereafter, JLC) Papers, US Holocaust Memorial Museum Archives (hereafter, USHMMA), Washington, DC.

82. "Minutes of Meeting of Executive Committee of Jewish Labor Committee Held on March 9th, 1934, N.Y.C.," reel 1, JLC Papers, USHMMA.

83. Jewish Labor Committee to Andy Correll, July 16, 1934, reel 33, JLC Papers, USHMMA.

84. "Visit to America, 14th September, 1934 to 19th November, 1934," 1/17, Walter Citrine Papers, London School of Economics and Political Science Library Archives, London, UK.

85. Morris D. Waldman, Paris, to Dr. Cyrus Adler, June 19, 1934, box 11, Adler Papers, AJC Archives.

86. Neville Laski, "Memorandum Re Boycott," May 30, 1934, ACC/3121/E3/36/2, Board of Deputies of British Jews Papers, London Metropolitan Archives, London, UK.

87. *New York Times*, June 15, 1934, 15, and June 16, 1934, 16; "Report of Emergency Gathering of Friends on the Situation in Germany," March 27, 1933, German Emergency Committee, vol. 1, Minutes, March 27, 1933–December 16, 1935, reel 1, Records of the Religious Society of Friends in Great Britain: Friends Committee for Refugees and Aliens, 1933–1954, RG-59.027M, USHMMA.

88. William Ebor, Bishopthorpe, York, to Malcolm, June 19, 1934, and William Ebor, Archbishop of York, to Your Excellency, June 20, 1934, folder 30, John Wheeler-Bennett Papers, St. Antony's College Library Archives, University of Oxford, Oxford, UK.

89. Martin M. Kolbrener to Colonel Howe, Secretary to His Excellency Franklin D. Roosevelt, November 13, 1934, and Stephen Early, Assistant Secretary to the President, November 14, 1934, Official File 76—Church Matters 76c—Jewish, Documents Relating to the Holocaust and Refugees, 1933–1945, Franklin D. Roosevelt Presidential Library and Museum, Hyde Park, NY.

SIX

—〰—

DISASTER FOR THE JEWS

The Saar Plebiscite, January 1935

NAZI GERMANY'S OVERWHELMING VICTORY IN the Saar plebiscite on January 13, 1935, provided an enormous stimulus for German expansionism and underscored the indifference of the British and American governments toward European Jewry's plight, as well as the League of Nations' weakness and ineffectiveness. The Hitler regime's violent and well-financed "Victory in the Saar" campaign was conducted like an aggressive military operation to wrest territory from an enemy. To promote the Saar's reunion with Germany, the Nazis organized monster demonstrations in the Saar and in the Reich itself that resembled in size and frenzy those celebrating the beginning of the world war in August 1914. The largest of the rallies drew an estimated four to six hundred thousand participants. During their plebiscite campaign, the Nazis unleashed antisemitic terrorism in the Saar on a larger scale and level of coordination than ever before outside the Reich. In the year before the plebiscite, the Hitler regime's viciously antisemitic propaganda effort, which included persistent radio broadcasts from Germany into the Saar, drove the Jews there into a state of panic. The British and American governments and the League of Nations did nothing to thwart the widespread dispossession of, assaults on, and murders of Saar Jews that followed the German victory. This foreshadowed the Anglo-American abandonment of European Jewry during the Holocaust.

A German victory in the plebiscite meant incorporation into the Reich. This was a frightening prospect for those committed to blocking Nazism's advance, especially because the Saar had been a favored place of refuge for both Jews and non-Jews fleeing Hitler's Germany. The *New York Times* reported on March 20, 1933, that refugees from Germany were "pouring into the Saar at a rate of 250 a day," most of them arriving penniless with "distressing tales" about Nazi terrorism in Germany. They fled to the Saar because it was German speaking, was contiguous to Germany (and to France), and did not require emigrants to possess a passport. Anti-Nazi refugees from Germany who first settled in France but whom French authorities expelled also often chose to resettle in the Saar during the early months of Hitler's rule. At the time of the plebiscite, more than two thousand refugees from Nazi Germany resided in the Saar.[1]

In 1934, France, which had provided asylum for the largest number of anti-Nazi refugees from Germany, imposed severe restrictions on persons seeking entry into the country and made it very difficult for refugees already in France to secure employment. French authorities issued notices of refoulement— orders to leave France—to many refugees who had arrived after November 1933 or who had first resided in another country of refuge. Citing rising unemployment among French citizens, they denied work permits to many refugees from Germany. French police shut down small businesses that refugees had started and prohibited many from even earning a living peddling on the streets. As a result, many refugees left France for the Saar.[2]

The Treaty of Versailles had placed the Saar under League of Nations administration for fifteen years, after which a plebiscite would be held to determine the Saar's future status. The treaty specified that the Saar's Governing Commission was to consist of one representative from France, one from the Saar, and three from countries other than France or Germany. Voters would be presented with three alternatives: reunion with Germany, annexation to France, or continuation of League of Nations rule (referred to as the Status Quo). Only persons who had resided in the Saar at the time of the treaty's signing, June 28, 1919, and who were now at least twenty years old were eligible to vote.[3] Many Germans and persons of German origin living outside the Reich, including in the United States, were qualified to vote in the plebiscite.

The Saar was a valuable coal-producing region, whose mines the treaty had ceded to France during the fifteen-year period, "in full and absolute possession, with exclusive rights of exploitation," as partial compensation for the German army's destruction of coal resources in the north of France during the world war. With 816,000 people packed into eighteen hundred square kilometers, it was among the most densely populated regions in Europe. The Saar was heavily industrialized with steel factories, foundries, and brick and glass works grouped around the mines. French currency was the medium of exchange in the Saar during the fifteen-year period before the plebiscite, and the territory was included in the French tariff system.[4]

The French population in the Saar was minuscule at the time of the plebiscite, and it was understood that the Status Quo was the only realistic alternative to reunion with Germany. Status Quo supporters, who most conspicuously included Social Democrats and Communists in addition to Jews, hoped that opposition to Hitler would cause persons who had supported German annexation before 1933 to back the continuation of League of Nations administration. During the 1920s, efforts to instill in Saarlanders a sense of separation from Germany by encouraging them to display a Saar flag and a Saar coat of arms had failed. The Saar flag was flown only on government buildings. The Paris daily *Le Petit Parisien* admitted in January 1935 that the French "never truly made, during fifteen years in the Saar, any serious propaganda effort" to persuade its population to consider annexation by France.[5]

The prospect of a German plebiscite victory and annexation to Nazi Germany terrified the Saar's Jews, who numbered five thousand, 0.6 percent of the territory's population. Columbia University professor Michael Florinsky, non-Jewish author of *The Saar Struggle* (1934)—the major book published on the Saar during the campaign—who backed reunion with Germany, admitted that it would consign the Saar's Jews to "concentration camps, exile, or a miserable existence as social pariahs and second-class citizens."[6] Jews had lived in the Saar since the thirteenth century. Nearly half lived in Saarbruecken, the territory's largest city. At the beginning of 1935, there were seventeen Jewish religious congregations in the territory. Most Saar Jews were engaged in small trade or light manufacturing in the towns or cattle breeding in the rural areas.[7]

The most astute political commentators of the time realized the critical importance of the Saar plebiscite. In December 1933, *Manchester Guardian* Paris correspondent Frederick Voigt warned that "if the Germans win the plebiscite, it will be a prodigious victory for Hitler and will augment his prestige and authority immensely.... If they lose it, it will be the[ir] first serious defeat...a real defeat of far-reaching consequences." Dorothy Thompson, one of the American journalists most conversant with German affairs, stated in the *New York Times* in September 1934 that a German defeat in the plebiscite would deal a severe blow to Hitler's prestige. She reported that the Saar's five thousand Jews were "preparing for instant flight" if Germany won.[8]

The Hitler regime made its "Victory in the Saar" campaign a major priority and devoted massive energy and resources to it. The Fuehrer himself was personally involved from the beginning. On May 16, 1933, only three-and-a-half months after becoming chancellor, Hitler received in Berlin, with vice chancellor Franz von Papen and foreign minister Konstantin von Neurath, a delegation from the Saar's Christian syndicates to plan the campaign.[9] On August 27, 1933, the Fuehrer addressed an enthusiastic mass rally of one hundred fifty thousand at the monument on the mountain at Niederwald, on the Rhine, held to proclaim that "the Saar is German Forever." The monument stood opposite the French city of Bingen and commemorated the foundation of the German Empire in 1870–71. Joining Hitler at the rally were von Papen, defense minister Werner von Blomberg, and Prussian minister of education Bernhard Rust.[10]

In November 1933, the government-owned German Railways Company carried thousands of Saarlanders to the Reich frontier town of Treves to hear Prussian Premier Hermann Goering denounce the League of Nation's "alien terror" in the Saar and promise them that the Reich would "stand by them, to a man, until the Saar is restored to the Fatherland."[11] The German government established a special Saar propaganda department headed by von Papen. Von Papen owned an estate in the Saar and had served as Reich commissioner for the Saar before his appointment in August 1934 as Germany's ambassador to Austria.[12]

Michael Florinsky, who spent the summer of 1934 in Germany and the Saar conducting research on the plebiscite campaign for *The Saar Struggle*, reported that it was impossible to visit the Reich without being exposed at every turn to the Hitler regime's propaganda urging the annexation of the Saar. The propaganda appeared on "cigarette boxes, in show windows, on hotel menus, and in dining cars." Boats on the Rhine sailed by rocks on the shore on which was painted the slogan "Germans, remember the Saar!" The German government issued special postage stamps highlighting the campaign to incorporate the Saar into the Reich. It placed on sale a special Saar calendar that "measure[d] time in terms of the number of days until the plebiscite and the anticipated reunion with Germany." German newspapers and magazines were "filled with articles" calling for the Saar's annexation.[13]

By the fall of 1933, all the Saar's political parties except the Social Democrats and Communists had disbanded and joined in a Nazi-officered coalition called the Deutsche Front, which combined aggressive propaganda with violent terror and intimidation against Jews and other Status Quo supporters, often called Separatists. Within the Deutsche Front, only the Nazi Party maintained its identity. Social Democrats and Communists joined in a loose anti-Nazi coalition called the Freiheitsfront, led by Social Democrat Max Braun and Communist Fritz Pfordt. Both Braun and Pfordt supported the Saar's reunion with Germany, but not so long as the Nazis held power there.[14]

Geoffrey Knox, British chairman of the League of Nations Governing Commission, issued a report in January 1934 charging that the Nazis in the Saar had usurped the commission's power and organized a parallel government that gave orders directly to communal authorities. The Nazi storm troops, which the Governing Commission had prohibited in the Saar, were nonetheless operating and engaging in military exercises. The commission had received "almost daily complaints" of Nazi persecution of Jews in the Saar, including the boycotting of Jewish-owned stores. Jews and Social Democrats, fearing for their children's safety, had removed them from the Saar's German schools and placed them in French schools established for families of French employees of the territory's mines. The Saar's Jewish community had requested that the commission open a special school for Jewish children.[15]

In 1934, violence and threats against Jews and Status Quo supporters intensi-fied, with little or no interference by the police. The Jewish Telegraphic Agency (JTA) reported in June 1934 that the Saar Nazis were meeting frequently with Hitler, Goering, and von Papen and "carry[ing] out their orders."[16] The Nazi-led Deutsche Front ordered public rallies across the Saar that month to cele-brate the announcement on June 2 that the plebiscite was scheduled for January 13. Rennie Smith, a British Labour Party activist who arrived in Saarbruecken shortly after the plebiscite date was announced, described the city as "gay with Swastika flags and streamers . . . as if it were already part of Nazi Germany on a festival day." He listened to a sermon in a Saarbruecken Evangelical Church in which a clergyman proclaimed that "the Saar was on the threshold of pass-ing into the 'Kingdom' and that Nazi Germany was the incarnation of this Kingdom of Heaven on Earth!"[17] Saarbruecken shopkeepers were afraid to stock pro–Status Quo newspapers. Status Quo activists were unable to secure lodging because landlords sympathized with or feared the Deutsche Front. Georg Beyer, editor of the Saar Social Democratic newspaper *Deutsche Freiheit*, who had earlier fled from Cologne to the Saar to escape Nazi "brown hordes" determined to kill him, stated in early 1934 that "a Nazi reign of terror" was sweeping the Saar. In October 1933, Beyer's landlord forced him out of his lodg-ings in Saarbruecken because he was afraid the Saar Nazis would demolish his house and reduce him to penury if Beyer remained there. Beyer and his family of five moved out of the Saar to the French frontier town of Forbach, because no other homeowner in Saarbruecken would take them in.[18]

Rennie Smith concluded from his observations in Saarbruecken that the League of Nations Governing Commission ruled the Saar only on paper and was "a dangerous farce." The Deutsche Front and the German government in Berlin knew that "they have the substance of power in their hands." A League of Nations official in the Saar informed Smith that when a crowd of Nazi stu-dents from Stuttgart had invaded Saarlouis (the town in which most of the Saar's French population resided), singing, "Now we go marching into France," and proceeded to create disturbances, the police, "as usual," had "closed their eyes," as they invariably did whenever the Nazis and Deutsche Front engaged in violence. The League official emphasized that "the overwhelming majority of the police and the gendarmerie act in the spirit of the *Deutsche Front*."[19]

New York Times foreign correspondent Frederick Birchall on January 18, 1934, reported that the Saar Nazis had issued a warning, "After 1935" or "Remember 1935," directed at Jews and any others who would not join the Deutsche Front, which implicitly threatened them with physical assault, dispossession, imprisonment, exile, or murder when Germany annexed the Saar. Birchall stated that the Nazis' "threat is more terrible because everyone in the Saar knows what is meant by concentration camp, Aryan clause, [and the] boycotting of Jews." The Saar correspondent of the London *Daily Herald*, organ of the British Labour Party, stated that Deutsche Front officials went from house to house distributing membership forms and pressuring people to join. They placed a black mark next to the names of persons who refused, along with the ominous words, "Remember 1935. You will regret it then." The situation was "practically impossible" for opponents of the Deutsche Front in the smaller mining and industrial towns, "where every man is known to his neighbor." At the great steelworks at Volklingen and Neuenkirchen, workers who greeted the company official at the door upon entering the plant at the start of the work day with "Good morning" instead of "Heil Hitler!" and the Nazi salute were discharged. By May, German propaganda broadcasts transmitted from Frankfurt into the Saar concluded with the speaker exclaiming, "'Remember 1935!' all throbbing with emotion."[20]

The Copenhagen newspaper *Politiken* reported in April 1934 that a Nazi leader, Anton Scherer, had stated explicitly in a speech in the Saar town of Dilligen that the party would take "exemplary vengeance" after the plebiscite against persons who had opposed annexation to Germany. Scherer had called on members of his audience to "sharpen your knives and get ready for the job." When Conservative MP Charles Cayzer asked British foreign secretary John Simon in the House of Commons whether he planned to look into Scherer's promise to retaliate, Simon brushed the matter aside, replying that it was "entirely within the competence of the Saar Governing Commission."[21]

A JTA correspondent reported in June 1934 that Saar Governing Commission representatives with whom he had spoken deplored the Nazi terrorism against Saar Jews and Status Quo supporters, but the League of Nations was not prepared to take any serious steps to protect these groups, either before or after the plebiscite. The JTA's reporter stated that the Saar Nazis had "amassed complete archives" against those opposed to the territory's annexation to Germany, which were "full of photographs showing a Saarlander in conversation with a Jew or a Frenchman, the latter seated during the singing of the Horst Wessel [Lied] while all else are standing at attention."[22]

Rennie Smith reported that Max Braun, upon returning to the Saar from Geneva, had informed him that he was "bitterly disappointed" with the League of Nations, which had set the earliest possible date for the plebiscite, an important concession to Hitler. As a result of the rampant Nazi terrorism in the Saar, the Freiheitsfront had hoped to postpone the plebiscite "until the end of 1935 at the earliest." Braun described the French government as "lethargic" regarding the Saar and considered Britain the only hope for those attempting to stave off Nazi Germany's annexation of the territory. But Braun was "in despair" of British foreign secretary Simon, who "had shown himself inaccessible" to the anti-Nazis hoping to meet with him in Geneva.[23]

The League of Nations' announcement in Geneva on June 2 that it had set a definite date for the plebiscite sparked a new round of Nazi terror in the Saar. Municipal officials in towns across the Saar encouraged residents to display the swastika and imperial German flags. Nazi bands roamed the streets, ostentatiously recording the addresses of homes without flags and "shouting loud threats against the 'traitors.'"[24]

In the spring of 1934, the leading British Jewish defense organizations, the Board of Deputies of British Jews (BoD) and the Anglo-Jewish Association (AJA), deeply alarmed by Nazi antisemitic violence and intimidation in the Saar, asked His Majesty's Government to press the League of Nations to guarantee Saar Jews' rights and security should Germany annex the territory. The AJA's Leonard Stein told the League in April that it had to implement protective measures for Saar Jewry because the Reich was ruled by a "gang of savages."[25] But the British Foreign Office believed that calling attention to Nazi persecution of Jews in the Saar would exacerbate Franco-German tensions, which might lead to war. For the Foreign Office, the plebiscite's best outcome would be "an overwhelming victory for Germany," which it thought would remove the Saar as a European trouble spot.[26] The Foreign Office informed the Joint Foreign Committee (JFC) of the BoD and AJA that although His Majesty's Government sympathized with its request, it did not consider a League guarantee of Jewish rights in the Saar to be "a practical possibility." There was "considerable doubt" that the League Council was empowered to "make any decisions as regards the return of the Saar to Germany conditional on the German Government's acceptance of minority obligations."[27] The League's Comité des Trois, which had direct responsibility for the Saar in Geneva, informed Nahum Goldmann, leader of the Comité des Délégations Juives, who was lobbying there for a League protective guarantee for Saar Jewry, that the matter did not "come within its competence."[28]

Hitler signaled the official opening of Germany's Saar electioneering campaign in an address before a massive rally at the fortress of Ehrenbreitstein, near Coblenz, on August 26, 1934, attended by 300,000 to 600,000 Germans. The audience included 150,000 from the Saar, many arriving on 130 special excursion trains that the German government provided. Hitler's speech was preceded by an outdoor mass and an evangelical service. The crowd exceeded the 150,000 assembled at the April 1933 rally at the Niederwald monument. Before traveling to the fortress, Hitler attended the opening of a Saar exhibition in Cologne, "Queen City of the Rhine," where Propaganda Minister Josef Goebbels spoke. Traveling by steamboat up the Rhine, Hitler was cheered by thousands of Germans on shore waving swastika flags. Bands played on village landings as the Fuehrer's steamboat passed. His appearance at Ehrenbreitstein was greeted "with frenzied heils" and "a colossal ovation." Before Hitler spoke, he was handed messages of loyalty to the Saar brought by ten runners, completing relays staged by 150,000 athletes from all parts of the Reich. In his address, Hitler claimed that the Reich's annexation of the Saar would remove any reason for conflict with France, producing "a sincere peace." He also placed great emphasis on the Reich being a Christian state, citing the thousands of priests cooperating with the Nazi government. No work was more Christian, Hitler declared, than the Nazi struggle against "cultural bolshevism," against "the godless movement, criminality, and social degeneration of our time."[29]

On September 1, the Associated Press reported that the Hitler government was making efforts to send every former Saar resident eligible to vote in the January 13, 1935, plebiscite back to the Saar to cast ballots. In November, the *New York Times* informed readers that the German government was spending hundreds of thousands of marks "to bring back from every corner of the world every man and woman who lived in the Saar territory up to June 28, 1919, and is therefore entitled to vote in the plebiscite." The German government estimated that there were about two thousand qualified Saar voters in foreign countries, with the greatest number in the United States. Saar voters abroad arriving for the plebiscite were assured of "a triumphant reception by the Saar Verein and Nazi party organizations, sightseeing trips through Germany and a guest of honor status."[30]

By December, hundreds of former Saarlanders residing in the United States were crossing the Atlantic to participate in the plebiscite. This transatlantic movement, covered on newsreels across the United States, reinforced the Nazi contention that strong ties of blood bonded all persons of German ancestry throughout the world to Germans in the Reich. German and German American contingents from various points in the United States met in New York in early December, preparing to cross the ocean on the German liner *Bremen.* Gustave Brand, leader of the Chicago group, organized a benefit concert and ball in that city to cover travel expenses for voters' families making the trip to the Saar. Attending the benefit were three thousand members of German American organizations, their friends, and Germany's consul general in Chicago, Rolf Jaeger. The *Chicago Tribune* estimated that about eleven hundred persons from the United States would vote in the plebiscite.[31]

On December 26, the departure of Saar voters from Chicago as well as from Hoboken and Weehawken, New Jersey, "and other German sections" of the New York metropolitan area from the West Forty-Fourth Street pier "took on the appearance of a Nazi demonstration in Germany." The group traveling to the Saar marched along the pier behind the swastika flag, the German imperial flag, and the Stars and Stripes. Relatives seeing them off gave the Nazi salute as they passed. On board the ship, Carl Froehlich, president of the United German Societies in New York, praised the voters' loyalty to the Fatherland, and "lusty Sieg Heils, for Germany, the Saar, and Adolf Hitler rang through the air." The ceremony on board ended with the singing of "Deutschland Uber Alles" and the Nazi anthem, the "Horst Wessel" song.[32]

US Representative Samuel Dickstein of New York, chair of the House Immigration Committee and an ardent anti-Nazi, introduced a bill shortly after the Seventy-Fourth Congress opened on January 3, 1935, requiring any naturalized American citizen who participated in the Saar plebiscite to forfeit his or her citizenship. The bill failed to secure passage. The US Labor Department insisted that because participation in the plebiscite did not require an oath of allegiance to a foreign government, it would not jeopardize a naturalized American's citizenship. Secretary of State Cordell Hull refused to take action on a request from a New York attorney to warn naturalized German Americans that they would lose their US citizenship "under presumption of expatriation."[33]

During the fall of 1934, prominent anti-Nazis from Germany who had taken refuge in the United States attempted to raise public awareness of the dangers of a German victory in the Saar plebiscite. They joined socialists and Jewish trade unionists in staging mass rallies and lectures around the slogan "Never to Hitler!" On October 28, anti-Nazi groups held a street counterdemonstration in front of the St. Nicholas Arena on New York's Upper West Side against a German American Nazi mobilization there for German annexation of the Saar. They distributed fliers warning that a German victory in the plebiscite would transform the Saar "into a huge concentration camp."[34] In New York in November, former Prussian minister of justice Kurt Rosenfeld, an exiled Jewish Social Democrat; Professor Julius Lips, an anthropologist forced to leave the

University of Cologne because of his opposition to Nazism; and George Med-alie of the Federation of Jewish Philanthropies spoke at a luncheon conference convened to "organize American support for Saar forces opposing Hitlerism."[35]

By December, American antifascists had formally organized a Committee for the Status Quo in the Saar Territory that raised funds to help the Freiheits-front publish fliers for its plebiscite campaign. It also shipped canned goods and clothing to the Freiheitsfront so that its activists and their families could "eat and live" while facing Nazi terror gangs. The committee warned that Nazi agents in the United States "spar[ed] no effort or expense" to bring Germans and German Americans back to the Reich "to cast their votes for Hitler." In December it reported that Jewish organizations in New York, Boston, Philadel-phia, Pittsburgh, Cleveland, Detroit, Chicago, and Milwaukee were sponsoring mass meetings to hear Kurt Rosenfeld speak in support of the Freiheitsfront that month and during the first ten days of January.[36]

The BoD and the AJA declined to become engaged in the Saar Status Quo campaign for the same reason that they refused to back mass demonstrations against Nazi antisemitism: fear of precipitating an antisemitic backlash. In November, Saarbruecken's rabbi, Dr. Ruelf, appealed to the BoD for money to print pro–Status Quo propaganda, which he considered Saar Jews' "most important and urgent task." Rabbi Dr. Ruelf informed BoD head Neville Laski that there was no doubt that if the Reich annexed the Saar it would immediately mobilize the population against the Jews.[37] But the JFC's Joint Chairmen argued that because Status Quo forces had no chance of winning the plebiscite, the JFC's financial resources could be better used to aid Jews in Germany, Poland, and Austria. Although the JFC would render assistance to oppressed foreign Jews, it was uncomfortable financing propaganda de-signed to "achieve a particular form of government or territorial status" in a foreign state. Doing so "would give color" to antisemites' long-standing charge "that the Jews are a world political entity, that there is an interna-tional Jewry."[38]

The League of Nations gave its approval to a Franco-German agreement, reached on December 3, 1934, in Rome, which promised minorities in the Saar protection from reprisals for one year after the plebiscite. The one-year promise of protection applied only to persons who had lived in the Saar for three years at the time of the plebiscite. This left at the Nazis' mercy thousands of refugees who had fled Germany when Hitler assumed power. As early as May 1934, the Hitler government had defined Saar refugees from Germany as traitors who had fled there to conspire against the Reich. They "deserved the heaviest penalties Nazi law could impose on traitors."[39] The Deutsche Front leadership similarly vowed that it would not permit the Saar to become "a place of refuge for the criminals of the entire world."[40]

The agreement precipitated outrage in the American Jewish press. The Boston *Jewish Advocate* denounced it in the strongest terms: "That the League of Nations gave its approval to . . . such barbarous terms passes understanding." American Jewish leader Samuel Untermyer, head of the Non-Sectarian Anti-Nazi League to Champion Human Rights, called the League of Nations action "the most amazing surrender and breach of trust of which a great international body was ever guilty." The Philadelphia *Jewish Exponent* quoted his assessment: Hitler had "terrorized" a craven League of Nations "into perpetrating one of the greatest wrongs of modern times." The *Advocate* editorialized that if Germany won the plebiscite, "the League of Nations will have doomed thousands of Jews" and other Status Quo supporters "to a fate worse than death." The *American Israelite* similarly stated that the League was handing over the Saar's Jews and other anti-Nazis "to whatever fate the Nazis choose."[41]

The BoD expressed concern about the one-year time limit Germany promised to observe before engaging in retaliatory action against Saar Jews and about Saar Jews' prospects after the plebiscite. It noted that the funds of the major organizations providing relief for refugees from Nazi Germany—the Central British Fund for German Jewry, the HICEM, and the Jewish Colonisation Society—were nearly depleted. At the same time, it implied that international law prevented the League or other nations from overturning the time limit.[42]

The JFC's Joint Chairmen acknowledged that working- and lower-middle-class Jews in Britain disapproved of its unwillingness to make the time limit a public issue. They expressed frustration over their failure "to persuade the Jewish masses of difficulties [in international law] they neither see nor understand." The Joint Chairmen derided the "Jewish masses" as "easily inflamed by speakers and ill-informed paragraphs in the press."[43] The "Jewish masses" had the backing of Nahum Goldmann's Comité des Délégations Juives, whose delegate pleaded unsuccessfully with the League in Geneva to reconsider its position that "the sovereign rights of Germany preclude[d] any permanent arrangement with her as to how she should treat her citizens in the Saar."[44]

Citing strong support for Saar annexation to Germany by persons of German ancestry the world over, Hitler declared in his New Year's proclamation that the Saar would be returned to Germany on January 13, 1935, through a "voice of blood." Massive pro-German crowds singing the "Horst Wessel Lied" and "Deutschland Uber Alles" enthusiastically welcomed the Saar voters from the United States at the railroad station in Saarbruecken, where balloting was to take place.[45]

On New Year's Eve, the Saarbruecken correspondent of the Paris daily *Le Petit Parisien* noted residents' zeal for a Nazi Saar. Young women in evening dress and their escorts, who had been dancing and smoking in the Café Kieffer, stepped outside at the stroke of midnight and began to loudly sing the "Horst Wessel Lied." They yelled, "Heil! Heil!" vigorously and menacingly above the sound of exploding firecrackers and cheered for the German Saar. Stores in Saarbruecken's main streets had removed their Christmas and New Year's displays by January 5 and, looking to January 13, replaced them with swastika flags and streamers, mugs and lamps bearing swastikas, dolls in swastika-decorated uniforms, and lead and wooden soldiers that gave the Hitler salute. Store walls were covered with portraits of the Fuehrer, framed with oak leaves and laurels, and inscribed "Heil Hitler!" and "The Saar is German."[46]

Saar Jews' awareness that a Nazi "wave of terror, retaliation, and persecution" would erupt the day after a German victory in the plebiscite precipitated a "mass exodus" from the territory in the days leading up to it. The *American Israelite* reported that "every road leading to Alsace-Lorraine and Luxembourg is jammed with cars, trucks, and people on foot." Jews not yet on the roads "were packing and preparing for flight." The JTA estimated, however, that 80 percent or more of Saar Jews lacked sufficient capital to gain admission to foreign countries.[47] Rabbi Dr. Ruelf called on Western countries to lower their immigration barriers, because the League of Nations would be turning Saar Jewry over to "a system where Jews are persecuted and find no justice." He appealed to "the civilized nations of the world" to persuade the League that "5,000 Jews of the Saar must not perish." Ruelf proposed that the League divide the Saar into two districts if Germany won the plebiscite, with one remaining under League administration so that Jews and other anti-Nazis would have a place of refuge.[48] This proposal found no support at the League of Nations or from the British, French, or US governments.

Mary Ferguson, reporting from Saarbruecken for the London *Daily Herald*, described the atmosphere for Jews there in the days before the plebiscite as extremely menacing. Four days before the plebiscite, she observed that it was not possible to walk down the street without encountering young men giving the Nazi salute. Ferguson found that "even young shop girls give the salute to strange customers." When she walked into a hairdresser's shop, the first thing she saw was the proprietor "making the Nazi sign to me." The *Manchester Guardian*'s Saar correspondent stated that in Saar towns Jewish shops were systematically boycotted. Persons canvassing for the Status Quo were blockaded in their homes.[49] The day before the plebiscite, the *Völkischer Beobachter* arrived in Saarbruecken from Germany "announc[ing] gleefully" that Jews in the Saar would be "entirely liquidated" after the plebiscite.[50]

The London *Jewish Chronicle* on January 4 expressed dismay at the indifference of the British government and press toward the fate of Saar Jewry. It condemned the "obstinate and unbroken silence of the Prime Minister," Ramsay MacDonald. Stanley Baldwin, who succeeded MacDonald as prime minister later that year, announced that Britain was "ready to help [Germany] in regard to trade." The *Chronicle* ridiculed British foreign minister Anthony Eden as "the ostrich of Geneva" for claiming in a speech there that Germany's promise not to persecute Saar Jewry for one year was a sufficient defense against the "already existing" antisemitic terror. With the exception of the *Manchester Guardian* and London *Daily Herald*, the British press had not "dropped a tear" over the Saar's Jews.[51]

On January 13, Germany won an overwhelming victory in the plebiscite, polling 477,119 out of 525,756 votes, more than 90 percent of the total. The Status Quo received 46,513 votes, and annexation to France 2,124, with slightly more than two thousand disqualified. Nearly all those registered to vote cast ballots. During the night preceding the balloting, the Nazis had scattered millions of one-inch-square papers on which were printed swastikas in red and black all around the voting stations. Immediately after the polls closed, a crowd of forty thousand Nazis gathered around the Rathaus in Saarbruecken, shouting, "Heil Hitler!" and singing the "Horst Wessel Lied" and "Deutschland Uber Alles." Many among them "raised the cry 'Down With the Jews,' and threatened to wreck a Jewish-owned café." Voters who had come to the Saar from the United States celebrated the result by marching through Saarbruecken carrying the Stars and Stripes and the swastika flag side by side. From 6:00 p.m. until midnight, thirty thousand Deutsche Front members and their children paraded through the Saarbruecken streets, shouting, "Heil Hitler!" and giving the Nazi salute as they passed. In tens of thousands of homes and shops across the territory, Saarlanders celebrated by lighting candles under portraits of Hitler. The League of Nations Council decided within four days of the plebiscite that the Saar would be officially transferred to Germany on March 1, 1935.[52]

The US State Department and the British and French governments expressed pleasure over the plebiscite result, believing that it greatly reduced the possibility of serious Franco-German conflict. The overwhelming German victory meant that the "dangerous question" of partitioning the Saar, as Rabbi Ruelf had proposed, would not be considered. The British expressed confidence in Hitler's declaration that Germany now had no further grievance against France. French premier Pierre-Étienne Flandin stated that he was confident the German government would "take all possible measures to demonstrate to the whole world that it knows how to respect the rights of minorities." He did not anticipate, therefore, any significant emigration from the Saar.[53] Sarah Wambaugh, American adviser and deputy to the Saar Plebiscite Commission who had personally observed the balloting, declared that the plebiscite was a great success that "increas[ed] confidence in peace."[54]

In the aftermath of their plebiscite victory, the Nazis unleashed a torrent of antisemitic invective. Hermann Roeschling, leader of the Saar Nazis, announced that Jews would be treated "like people with a contagious disease."[55] In Germany, Der Stuermer editor Julius Streicher celebrated by ranting about a global Jewish conspiracy, claiming that "World Jewry had failed . . . to tear the Saar away from Germany." He condemned Max Braun, the non-Jewish Status Quo leader, as "belong[ing] to that race and that nation, which declared through the mouth of Walther Rathenau: 'three hundred men, who know each other and are linked by blood, govern the world.'" Although attributed to Germany's former foreign minister, assassinated by antisemitic terrorists in 1922, this quote had long been exposed as a forgery. Josef Goebbels's Der Angriff joined Der Stuermer in "rejoicing at the 'Exodus of Israel from the Saar.'"[56]

The New York Times reported on January 18 that Saarlanders opposed to German annexation were in a state of alarm because the Saar police force was now "avowedly Nazi" and would offer them no protection. Le Petit Parisien stated that Saarbruecken police had spread out a swastika flag in their barracks and some were wearing swastika armlets. The Nazis proceeded to humiliate Status Quo supporters by forcing them into carts and attaching placards around their necks identifying them as enemies of the Reich. They then drove them unimpeded through the streets before jeering crowds. When Nazis sacked the trade union offices in the Saar towns of Puttlingen and Sulzbach and threw furniture and books out the windows into the streets, the police did not intervene.[57]

The Nazis stepped up their threats against Jews and Status Quo supporters in the weeks after the plebiscite. Jews were dragged through the streets, insulted, spat on, and beaten. Along with other Status Quo supporters, they were subjected to the "torments of the pillory." Nazis crept up to the homes of Jews and opponents of German annexation after dark by torchlight and dangled a straw doll under a window, shouting, "Quack, quack." The Nazis' insinuation was that "the pillory" would be followed by a hanging after the Saar officially returned to Germany on March 1, 1935. "The pillory" often drove the wife and children of the targeted Jew or Separatist to hysteria. In one Saar village, the Nazis suspended a one-armed straw doll from "a kind of gallows" in front of the house of a pro–Status Quo ex-serviceman who had lost an arm in the world war. In another village, the Nazis, all the time shouting, "Quack, quack," dug a deep grave for four effigies in the garden of a house inhabited by a pro–Status Quo family of four. The message was clear: on March 1, all four members of the family would be buried in the grave.[58]

The *Manchester Guardian* noted that the Saar was so dangerous after dark for Jews and Separatists that many dared not return home after work but took shelter in the evenings and slept in sheds or other structures that belonged to the French mines and remained French property until March 1. The police dared not protect these people, for fear of sharing their fate after the official return of the Saar to Germany.[59]

After the plebiscite, jeering crowds repeatedly harassed and threatened Saar Jews walking in the streets. It was common for persons accosting Jews in the Saar to pretend they were making a slashing motion with a knife across the throat. Nazi slogans were painted on Jewish shops. The Reuter press agency reported that Jews did not dare complain to the police "for fear that they will be beaten as atrocity propagandists" when they left the police station.[60]

The small international force supplied by the League of Nations, largely from Britain and Italy, proved useless in defending Jews and other opponents of the Nazis. The *New York Times* reported that the troops did no police work: "Their job is to remain at their quarters ready for call if a serious emergency arises." The force's "gorgeously appareled commanders," especially the British, "hate to be bothered." The *Manchester Guardian* accused the British officers in the Saar of helping legitimize Nazism: "When British officers return the Hitlerite salute and when local Nazi leaders are welcome guests in the officers' mess, it is not surprising that simple folk in the Saarland . . . should believe that England—and therefore the League of Nations and the [Western] Powers—are on the side of Hitler."[61]

Rabbi Ruelf informed the JTA a few days before the plebiscite that Jews in the Saar were in a desperate plight. He explained that most of them would lose their immovable property because Germans knew they could easily take it from them after the one-year limit on persecution expired. Therefore, no German was willing to buy it, even for far less than it was worth.[62] Many Saar Jews, already in flight, had left their immovable property behind.

Nearby countries imposed tight restrictions on the entry of Saar refugees. France, the destination most preferred, announced that no refugee from the Saar would be allowed to enter Alsace-Lorraine or Paris or remain along the frontier. Only refugees with a consular visa attached to their passports were allowed into France, although this had been not required before the plebiscite. Saar refugees would first be taken to Strasbourg for "strict investigation" before being sent to the southwest of France. The Netherlands, Belgium, and Czecho-slovakia sealed their borders to the refugees. About one hundred Saar Jews, from the wealthiest stratum, were able to settle in Luxembourg. Some Jews of Polish origin made their way to Poland.[63]

The French government expressed strong concern about the expense it might incur in harboring Saar refugees and tried unsuccessfully to persuade the League of Nations to take responsibility. France argued it should do so because the cause of the refugees' flight from the Saar was their having voted for continuing League administration over the territory. Shortly after the plebiscite, James McDonald, League of Nations–appointed commissioner for refugees from Germany, informed BoD head Neville Laski that the League's "anxious desire" to bring Germany back into membership made it exceedingly unlikely that it would risk offending Hitler by taking on responsibility for Saar refugees.[64]

Many pro–Status Quo Saarlanders, Jews and non-Jews, were afraid to ap-ply for visas at the French consulate in Saarbruecken because Nazis circulated among the crowds standing in line outside and demanded to see their identi-fication cards, recording their names. The French consul had to open a special visa office immediately across the frontier so that refugees did not have to show any papers until they were outside the Saar. By January 18, the French frontier town of Forbach, the principal crossing point from the Saar, was "filled with refugees," and there were no more accommodations.[65]

The Saar refugees faced a difficult journey in the middle of the winter, slog-ging along muddy or snow-covered roads carrying their meager possessions in an effort to reach railroad stations. Many walked the roads in family groups. Frederick Birchall of the *New York Times* reported four days after the plebiscite that the movement of Saar refugees resembled "a wartime exodus." At frontier towns French policemen sometimes allowed refugees to rest on straw in cus-tom house sheds. Max Braun, in an appeal to the British Labour Party from Forbach, wrote that the emigrants were "as poor as a church mouse" and that Status Quo forces were unable even to supply them with "a shirt or any article of clothing to take with them."[66]

On March 1, the Hitler government celebrated the Reich's formal annexation of the Saar with "a staging without precedent": all-day parades, marches, and concerts, culminating in massive evening torchlight processions in major cities. The *New York Times* reported that Berlin's "entire population appeared to have joined storm troopers and Reichswehr forces in tramping through the streets." All over Germany, church bells were rung all day, and factory sirens "were sent shrieking." Munich celebrated the Saar's "deliverance" by placing at least one

burning candle in nearly every window in the city. Ninety special trains took
five hundred thousand Germans to the Saar for the occasion. The *Manchester
Guardian*'s correspondent in the Saar stated that "the impression was as though
the Germans had entered the Saar after a military victory." In Saarbruecken,
huge photographs of Hitler were installed. A commemorative postcard series
had been printed, depicting the Fuehrer in various poses: "smiling, saluting,
shaking hands, kissing infants, and even laughing." From 6:30 a.m. on March 1
until 3:00 a.m. on March 2, German radio broadcast programming concerning
the Saar and its annexation by the Reich without interruption.[67]

The festivities were climaxed by speeches in Saarbruecken by top Nazi
leaders, including the Fuehrer. Hitler's deputy Rudolf Hess declared that the
plebiscite result proved that Germans wanted to be governed by Nazis. He recalled "the shame of a period when Germany had renounced being a power" but
boasted that Saarlanders now returned to a country worthy of them. Josef Goebbels delivered a violent polemic against adversaries of the Hitler regime who
had taken refuge in the Saar, accusing them of plotting against it. He praised
Hitler for pursuing a policy of peace and understanding. Hitler's unannounced
arrival put Saarbruecken in a frenzy. He rode through Saarbruecken standing
in an automobile, through "a forest of raised arms." From the moment he appeared, "the day belonged to him." The lines of black-uniformed special guards
and brown-shirted storm troopers, attempting to keep order in the streets with
interlocked arms, "broke like ropes of straw" under the pressure of throngs
of Saarlanders rushing to touch the Fuehrer or see him close up. A delirious
crowd, standing in the rain under the balcony from which Hitler spoke, chanted
the same refrain uninterruptedly: "*Wir wollen unseren Führer sehen! Wir wollen
unseren Führer sehen!*" ("We want to see our leader!") Hitler declared to his audience, many of whom were weeping hysterically, that the Reich's annexation
of the Saar paved the way for peace.[68]

A day after the Saar was annexed to Germany, William Shirer, one of the
American journalists most conversant with German affairs, reported that the
new Nazi regime was already severely persecuting Saar Jews. The Nazis posted
signs in front of Jewish stores telling "Aryans" to boycott them. Storm troopers
covered the windows of many Jewish stores with antisemitic caricatures drawn
with soap. Special copies of Julius Streicher's viciously antisemitic *Der Stuermer*,
which the League of Nations Commission had banned from the Saar, were
already selling briskly on the streets on March 2.[69]

Saar Jews and other anti-Nazis who managed to find refuge in France experienced a range of treatments. According to a *Manchester Guardian* report on
March 9, refugees in the Midi, where many were taken, experienced "genuine

hospitality." This was especially the case in Toulouse, where the Socialist mayor housed them in schools, hospitals, and public buildings. For the majority of refugees in the Midi, however, who had not found jobs, "the future seem[ed] rather hopeless, even if their barest immediate necessities [were] provided for." In the intensely nationalist French frontier region near the Saar and Germany, the refugees, viewed as German-speaking and often Jewish foreigners, were the objects of some hostility. In the Lizé Nord refugee camp, in Strasbourg, Alsace, the 750 refugees were confined in prisonlike barracks "under military discipline." The camp entrance, an iron gate, was "always strongly guarded by armed sentries." Rooms were poorly heated. Families were broken up, with women and children housed separately from men. Those who violated regulations or otherwise angered camp authorities were placed in "cold punishment cells" or sent back to the Saar. The *Guardian* noted that French officials had turned back many Saar refugees at the frontier.[70]

In late January 1935, Nahum Goldmann asked the help of BoD head Neville Laski in lifting Britain's severe restrictions barring Jews' access to Palestine. Goldmann stated that Rabbi Ruelf, who had fled to Palestine after the plebiscite, informed him that the British Executive authority there had no immigration certificates left and that none would be available until April 1936. Goldmann asked Laski to appeal to the British Foreign Office to persuade the Colonial Office to issue extra certificates to Saar Jews. Goldmann emphasized that "a considerable number of Saar Jews" lacked passports and therefore could not gain admission to France or any other country. He reminded Laski that because the Saar would officially come under Nazi rule on March 1, it was essential to make this request to the Foreign Office immediately.[71]

By September 1935, it was obvious that the Saar's Nazi rulers had no intention of honoring their promise to the League of Nations to refrain from persecuting Jews for a year. Already in February 1935, the city of Saarbruecken had put up a sign: "Jews Go Back." On September 13, the London *Jewish Chronicle* reported that two large placards were posted in front of the synagogue in Saarbruecken "calling on the population to rid the Saar of the Jews." The town of Merzig displayed a sign at its outskirts inscribed, "Jews are not tolerated here." Nazi authorities warned the town's hotelier that unless he observed their order to deny access to Jews, his license would be revoked. In the steel-manufacturing center of Voelklingen, the hotels posted announcements that "Jews are not wanted here." In Dillingen, Jewish department store employees were dismissed by order of the Nazi officials.[72]

Shortly afterward, three prominent writers the Nazis had exiled from Germany—Heinrich Mann, Lion Feuchtwanger, and Ernst Toller—submitted a memorandum to the League of Nations Council protesting the "reign of terror" in the Saar. The memorandum stated that Jewish shops were being boycotted throughout the territory and "smeared with insulting notices." Nazis photographed customers who entered Jewish shops. The exiled writers charged that there were antisemitic demonstrations in Saarbruecken nearly every day. Jews who were beaten and resisted were immediately arrested and imprisoned without charges. The memorandum also called attention to the forcible expulsion of fifty Jews from the municipal baths in Deutschmuehlen.[73]

The JTA reported on September 25 that "nearly all" the Saar's Jewish communities were "being dissolved." The exodus of Jews from the Saar was so vast that there were no longer sufficient numbers to support synagogues and other Jewish institutions. The Saar's Nazi governor promised that soon after March 1, 1936, the territory would "become the most Jewless part of Germany."[74]

On January 13, 1936, the Hitler government celebrated the first anniversary of its Saar plebiscite victory by declaring a holiday in the territory, with "much marching and singing" and mass meetings to celebrate the occasion as a victory for Nazism, not just for Germany. Church bells rang across the Saar at noon to mark the holiday. All of Germany was "bedecked with swastika flags." In a ceremony presided over by the Nazi minister of the interior Wilhelm Frick, the name of the town of Saarlouis, honoring French king Louis XIV, and center of the Saar's small French population, was changed to the German Saarlautern.[75]

Hitler entered the Saar on March 1, 1935, "suddenly, dramatically—and . . . memorably," like a military conqueror, and one who was "only at the beginning of his conquests." The Freiheitsfront's "thin, poverty-stricken ranks" had "broke[n] pitiably beneath [his] final offensive."[76] Having achieved victory on the Saar "front," Germany launched its "bleeding borders" campaign, designed to absorb territories outside the Reich inhabited by significant numbers of ethnic Germans. Such territories included the Baltic port of Memel; the Eupen-Malmédy district of Belgium; Denmark's Southern Sleavig section; the "free city" of Danzig, whose foreign policy Poland controlled; Czechoslovakia's Sudetenland; France's Alsace-Lorraine; and the Polish Corridor. In late January 1935, the New York Times reported that since its Saar victory the Hitler government had "opened an intensified drumfire about the wrongs suffered by German minorities" in neighboring countries.[77]

The first fronts opened in the "bleeding borders" campaign were Memel, which the Nazis called "the Saar of the East," and the "free city" of Danzig. The Versailles Treaty had shifted Memel from German control to nominal autonomy within Lithuania. On February 12, 1935, several thousand students and faculty at Berlin University staged a massive demonstration, which the

New York Times called "a spectacular manifestation of the Nazi drive for the unification of all Germans" into one empire. The demonstrators sang the Nazi battle song, "The Nation to Arms." Then Hans Gerd Techow, who had been sentenced to four years and one month in prison for assisting in the assassination of Walther Rathenau in 1922, addressed them. He denounced "twelve years of slavery" of Memel's Germans by Lithuania and identified the protestors' goal: "penetrat[ing] the East with the ideas of the Third Reich." The demonstration ended with the singing of the "Horst Wessel Lied." The League of Germanism Abroad had set up an exhibition at the university on "the oppressed Memel Territory," under the rector's patronage.[78]

The American vice consul in Danzig, Ellis Johnson, reported that Danzig's citizens had given Josef Goebbels a "rousing welcome" when he visited the "free city" in late August 1933. Johnson called Goebbels's travel through the approaches to Danzig "a tour of triumph." In the city itself, Goebbels was accorded "a tremendous ovation and welcome." In his speech, before ten thousand Danzig residents, Goebbels declared that Germans everywhere formed part of the German nation. He warned against "the world-wide complot of international Jewry."[79]

On March 2, 1935, Nazis posted notices throughout Danzig announcing "in huge letters," "The Saar is free—Danzig will become so." That day, Arthur Greiser, a Nazi Party leader and president of Danzig's Senate, declared to that body that Danzig's citizens "remain forever faithful to the German people and their chief, Adolf Hitler." Jews had already been forced out of Danzig's trade unions.[80] The London *Jewish Chronicle* had reported on February 1 that the Danzig Senate was removing Jewish judges from the bench. The Danzig Medical Chamber, consisting entirely of Nazis, was refusing to authorize Jewish physicians to practice. The *Chronicle*'s Warsaw correspondent, who made periodic visits to Danzig, reported that "no 'Aryan' schoolchild will dare to play with a Jewish schoolchild." The Nazis' boycott of Jewish stores was "strong and gaining strength."[81]

In August 1935, "savage anti-Jewish demonstrations" were staged in Danzig, as fifty trucks filled with Nazis and SS men from Prussia arrived bearing banners with antisemitic slogans. The streets were filled with cries of "We must kill the Jews." The Nazis set up straw effigies of Jews, which the welcoming crowds proceeded to whip and cut apart with knives and bayonets.[82]

The Nazi takeover of the Saar, with its population's enthusiastic support, and their systematic degradation of Jews during the plebiscite campaign signaled that Jews had no future in any territory the Reich acquired. In its first test from an ethnically German population outside the Reich's borders, Nazism had received a ringing endorsement. The plebiscite campaign and its immediate aftermath made clear that the Western powers were unwilling to intervene on behalf of Jews viciously persecuted by the Nazis. Indeed, the British and US governments considered the plebiscite's outcome highly desirable. The warning issued by the *Manchester Guardian* the day after Hitler took control of the Saar, however, was chilling and prescient: Nazism was "a movement that cannot live without advancing from victory to victory."[83] The horrific antisemitic manifestations in Memel and Danzig were only a portent of what was to come.

NOTES

1. *New York Times*, March 20, 1933, clipping in box 6782, Central Decimal Files (hereafter, CDF), 1930–39, Department of State General Records, Record Group (hereafter, RG) 59, National Archives, College Park, MD (hereafter, NA-CP); Norman Bentwich, *The Refugees from Germany: April 1933 to December 1935* (London: Allen and Unwin, 1936), 50–51, 123.

2. Bentwich, *Refugees from Germany*, 109–110.

3. *Le Petit Parisien*, January 12, 1935; Michael Florinsky, "The Lesson of the Saar," *Hungarian Quarterly* 2 (Autumn 1936): 13.

4. *Washington Post*, September 2, 1934, B2; *Le Petit Parisien*, January 12, 1935; *New York Times*, June 19, 1933, 1, 6. *Le Petit Parisien* noted that the Saar's coal fields had extracted fifteen million tons a year before the world war and could furnish coal at the present rate of extraction for another 675 years.

5. *Palestine Post*, January 13, 1935, 4; *Le Petit Parisien*, January 12, 1935; Michael Florinsky, *The Saar Struggle* (New York: Macmillan, 1934). The 1910 census, the last before the Versailles Conference, recorded only 239 people in a population of 652,000 giving French as their mother tongue. *Palestine Post*, January 13, 1935.

6. Florinsky, *Saar Struggle*, 178–79. Reviewers in American Jewish periodicals strongly condemned *The Saar Struggle*. Edward Dahlberg, in *Opinion: A Journal of Jewish Life and Letters*, called it a "dangerous book" that denied the Nazis were conducting a terror campaign in the Saar. Florinsky was "an unconscious Fascist." Edward Grusd in *B'nai B'rith Magazine* denounced Florinsky for his lack of concern for Saar Jewry. Edward Dahlberg, "Hitler over the Saar," *Opinion*, January 1935, 33–34, and Edward E. Grusd, "The Plebiscite Approaches," *B'nai B'rith Magazine*, January 1935, n.p., box 8, Michael Florinsky Papers (hereafter, Florinsky Papers), Rare Book and Manuscript Library (hereafter, RBML), Columbia University (hereafter, CU), New York, NY.

7. Jewish Telegraphic Agency, January 2, 1935; *Jewish Exponent* (Philadelphia), January 18, 1935, 1.

8. Frederick Voigt to W. P. Crozier, December 15, 1933, 210/172–288, *Manchester Guardian* Archives (hereafter, MGA), John Rylands Library

(hereafter, RL), Deansgate, Manchester, UK; *New York Times*, September 16, 1934.

9. *Figaro*, May 17, 1933.

10. *Manchester Guardian*, August 28, 1933, 13; *New York Times*, August 28, 1933, 1.

11. *New York Herald Tribune*, November 6, 1933, 5.

12. C. A. Lambert to W. P. Crozier, February 25, 1934, 211/86–136, MGA, RL; Michael Florinsky to H. S. Latham, November 2, 1934, box 8, Florinsky Papers, RBML, CU; Jewish Telegraphic Agency, August 13, 1934.

13. Florinsky, *Saar Struggle*, 125–26.

14. Ibid., 138.

15. *Manchester Guardian*, January 9, 1934, 4; *New York Times*, January 15, 1934, 6; *Baltimore Sun*, January 17, 1934, 11.

16. Jewish Telegraphic Agency, June 22, 1934.

17. Rennie Smith to Willie, June 15, 1934, box 8, William Gillies Papers (hereafter, Gillies Papers), People's History Museum Archives (hereafter, PHMA), Manchester, UK.

18. Georg Beyer to Comrade Morrison, n.d., but early 1934, box 8, Gillies Papers, PHMA.

19. Smith to Willie, June 15, 1934, and the Labour and Socialist International Local Organization and International Federation of Trade Unions, "The Situation in the Saar," April 30, 1934, box 8, Gillies Papers, PHMA.

20. *New York Times*, January 18, 1934, 1, 9; *Daily Herald* (London), April 26 and May 2, 1934.

21. The *Politiken* account was cited in the London *Jewish Chronicle*, April 27, 1934, 16, and in Jewish Telegraphic Agency, June 22, 1934.

22. Jewish Telegraphic Agency, June 22, 1934.

23. Smith to Willie, June 15, 1934.

24. *Daily Herald* (London), June 4, 1934, 1.

25. "The Deputies," *Jewish Chronicle* (London), April 20, 1934, 26, 34.

26. C. J. Hill, "Great Britain and the Saar Plebiscite of 13 January 1935," *Journal of Contemporary History* 9 (April 1974): 128–29.

27. R. F. Wigram, Foreign Office, to the Joint Chairmen, Joint Foreign Committee, April 3, 1934, ACC/3121/C/11/12/128, Board of Deputies of British Jews (hereafter, BoD) Papers, London Metropolitan Archives (hereafter, LMA), London, UK.

28. Nahum Goldmann, interview with M. Bianchieri, May 15, 1934, ACC/3121/C/11/12/128, BoD Papers, LMA.

29. *New York Times*, August 27, 1934, 1, 6; *Manchester Guardian*, August 27, 1934, 9; *Washington Post*, August 27, 1934, 1, 2; "Hitler and the Saar," August 26, 1934, box 8, Gillies Papers, PHMA; Florinsky, *Saar Struggle*, 124.

30. *Washington Post*, September 1, 1934, 1, 3; *New York Times*, September 1, 1934, 6, and November 18, 1934, 7. The *Times* stated that Saar voters from China

and South America were already en route "after receiving rousing farewells from German colonies in Shanghai and South American ports." On December 22, the *Times* reported the arrival in Hamburg of thirty-two German Saar voters from South America, including persons "from Buenos Aires, Montevideo, Rio de Janeiro, and even from settlements on the fringe of the Gran Chaco." *New York Times*, December 22, 1934, 5.

31. *Chicago Tribune*, December 8, 1934, 1, and December 9, 1934, 14.

32. *New York Times*, December 27, 1934, 8.

33. *Chicago Tribune*, January 4, 1935, 6; *New York Times*, December 28, 1934, 13, and January 4, 1935, 12.

34. "Workers, Intellectuals, and Students Demonstrate against Nazi Terror in the Saar!," reel 33, Jewish Labor Committee Papers, US Holocaust Memorial Museum Archives, Washington, DC.

35. Jewish Telegraphic Agency, November 6, 1934; *New York Times*, November 11, 1934, 25.

36. "Saar Status Quo (What Does It Mean?) Never Back to Hitler (That's What It Means)," "Committee for the Status Quo in the Saar Territory," and "Support the Campaign for Status Quo for the Saar!," December 18, 1934, box 20, General Records Seized from the German-American Bund, Office of Alien Property, Department of Justice, RG 131, NA-CP.

37. Rabbiner Dr. Rülf to Neville Laski, November 6, 1934, ACC/3121/C11/12/129, BoD Papers, LMA.

38. "Note of Conference at House of Sir Osmond d'Avigdor Goldsmid," October 14, 1934, ACC/3121/C11/12/129, BoD Papers, LMA.

39. Hill, "Great Britain and the Saar Plebiscite," 128.

40. *Le Petit Parisien*, January 7, 1935.

41. *Jewish Advocate* (Boston), December 11, 1934, 2; *Jewish Exponent* (Philadelphia), December 7, 1934, 10; *American Israelite* (Cincinnati), January 10, 1935, 1.

42. "Note of Conference at House of Sir Osmond d'Avigdor Goldsmid," October 16, 1934, ACC/3121/C11/12/129, BoD Papers, LMA. The HICEM, headquartered in Paris, was a combined office of the New York–based Hebrew Immigrant Aid Society and the London-based Jewish Colonisation Society.

43. Joint Chairman to Professor D. Cohen, December 17, 1934, ACC/3121/C11/12/128, BoD Papers, LMA.

44. "Germany: The Saar," *Jewish Chronicle* (London), January 25, 1935, 14.

45. *Palestine Post*, January 4, 1935, 1; *Le Petit Parisien*, January 6, 1935; *New York Times*, January 9, 1935, 9.

46. *Le Petit Parisien*, January 4 and 6, 1935.

47. *American Israelite* (Cincinnati), January 10, 1935, 1; Jewish Telegraphic Agency, January 14, 1935.

48. Jewish Telegraphic Agency, January 13, 1935.

49. *Daily Herald* (London), January 12, 1935; *Manchester Guardian*, January 12, 1935, 13.

50. *Jewish Exponent* (Philadelphia), January 18, 1935, 1.

51. "Where Is That World-Conscience?," *Jewish Chronicle* (London), January 4, 1935, 8; "Germany: The Saar," January 25, 1935, 14.

52. *Washington Post*, January 16, 1935, 1; *Daily Herald* (London), January 14, 1935, 1, 2, and January 16, 1935, 1, 2; *New York Times*, January 16, 1935, 1, 13; Guenter Lewy, "The German Roman Catholic Hierarchy and the Saar Plebiscite of 1935," *Political Science Quarterly* 79 (June 1964): 203; Hill, "Great Britain and the Saar Plebiscite," 141.

53. *New York Times*, January 16, 1935, 13; *Chicago Tribune*, January 16, 1935, 4.

54. *New York Times*, February 8, 1935, 5. Michael Florinsky considered Wambaugh, whom he consulted while writing *The Saar Struggle*, "America's leading authority on the Saar." In an address to the Foreign Policy Association in Boston shortly after the plebiscite, Florinsky similarly claimed that the German victory had removed "one of the greatest obstacles to Franco-German cooperation." In his view, "the next obvious and logical step [is] the [West's] recognition of Germany's complete equality in all respects, including equality in armaments." Michael Florinsky to Sarah Wambaugh, October 28, 1935, and "Abstract of Dr. Florinsky's speech to be given at the luncheon of the Foreign Policy Association, Boston, January 19, 1935," box 8, Florinsky Papers, RBML, CU.

55. *Jewish Advocate* (Boston), January 18, 1935, 1.

56. "Jews' Hopes Shattered," *Jewish Chronicle* (London), February 1, 1935, 18; "Germany: The Saar," 13.

57. *Daily Herald* (London), January 17, 1935, 1, and January 18, 1935; *New York Times*, January 18, 1935, 2; *Le Petit Parisien*, January 20, 1935.

58. *Manchester Guardian*, January 22, 1935, 12.

59. *Manchester Guardian*, January 23, 1935, 9.

60. "Germany: The Saar," 13.

61. *New York Times*, January 18, 1935, 2; *Manchester Guardian*, January 23, 1935, 9.

62. *Jewish Exponent* (Philadelphia), January 18, 1935, 1.

63. Ibid.; *Baltimore Sun*, January 13, 1935, 1; *Le Petit Parisien*, January 14 and 17, 1935.

64. *New York Times*, January 20, 1935, E2; James G. McDonald to Neville J. Laski, January 22, 1935, ACC/3121/C11/12/129, BoD Papers, LMA.

65. *Chicago Tribune*, January 19, 1935, 7.

66. *New York Times*, January 18, 1935, 2; Max Braun to Stevenson, January 26, 1935, box 8, Gillies Papers, PHMA.

67. *Le Petit Parisien*, March 1, 1935; *Manchester Guardian*, March 2, 1935, 13, 17; *Chicago Tribune*, March 1, 1935, 1, 2; *Daily Herald* (London), March 2, 1935; *New York Times*, March 2, 1935, 5.

68. *Le Petit Parisien*, March 2, 1935; *Manchester Guardian*, March 2, 1935, 13; *Daily Herald* (London), March 2, 1935, 1, 2; *New York Times*, March 2, 1935, 1, 5.

69. Shirer's report appeared in the *Los Angeles Examiner*, March 3, 1935.

70. *Manchester Guardian*, March 9, 1935, 17.

71. N. Goldmann to Neville Laski, January 31, 1935, ACC/3121/E03/531, BoD Papers, LMA.

72. "Jewry's New Courage," *Jewish Chronicle* (London), February 22, 1935, 13, and "Nazis Flout Saar Pledges," *Jewish Chronicle* (London), September 13, 1935, 16.

73. "Saar Terrorism Protest," *Jewish Chronicle* (London), September 17, 1935, 24. The *New York Times* ran an Associated Press report that thirty Nazi youth had forced Jews using the public baths at Saarbruecken into cabins, ordered them to dress, and then chased them out of the facility. *New York Times*, August 1, 1935, 6.

74. Jewish Telegraphic Agency, September 25, 1935; *New York Times*, March 2, 1936, 10.

75. *New York Times*, January 14, 1936, 8.

76. *Manchester Guardian*, March 2, 1935, 12.

77. *New York Times*, January 27, 1935, E4.

78. *Manchester Guardian*, January 28, 1935, 8; *New York Times*, February 13, 1935, 7.

79. Ellis A. Johnson, American Vice Consul, Danzig, to Secretary of State, September 5, 1933, "Subject: Visit of Dr. Josef Goebbels," box 61, CDF, Department of State General Records, RG 59, NA-CP.

80. *New York Times*, March 3, 1935, 8. Danzig's population was 97 percent German. The Versailles Treaty removed it from Germany to provide Poland with access to the Baltic. The treaty placed Danzig under League of Nations administration but included it in Poland's customs union. In elections in early April 1935, the Nazis won 60 percent of the seats in Danzig's parliament, expanding their majority achieved in the previous election, in May 1933. This was still short of the two-thirds majority they needed to achieve incorporation into the Reich. *Palestine Post*, April 7 and 9, 1935.

81. "The Jews in Danzig: Persecution Intensified," *Jewish Chronicle* (London), February 1, 1935, 14.

82. "Prussian Nazis Invade Danzig," *Jewish Chronicle* (London), August 9, 1935, 19.

83. *Manchester Guardian*, March 2, 1935, 12.

SEVEN

—ന—

ENTERTAINING NAZI WARRIORS IN AMERICA AND BRITAIN

1934–1936

WINSTON CHURCHILL, IN ASSESSING THE West's disastrous appeasement policies of the 1930s in his memoirs, condemned British lack of wisdom and French "weakness," but he also noted that the United States cannot "escape the censure of history." Churchill emphasized that if the US government had exerted its influence to discourage Nazi Germany's rearmament and expansionism, it might have "galvanized the French and British politicians into action."[1]

From the earliest months of Nazi rule, journalists well informed about German affairs expressed alarm about Germany's rapid militarization and the increasing belligerence of its population. On June 28, 1933, the anniversary of the signing of the Treaty of Versailles, German schools suspended regular classes so pupils could spend the entire day listening to "teachers' diatribes against France and the Entente Powers" and singing the Nazi anthem, the "Horst Wessel Lied." By August 1933, several German universities had established chairs in military science.[2] *Manchester Guardian* foreign correspondent Robert Dell wrote to his editor from Berlin on October 3, 1933, that the German capital was preparing for war. Dell noted that "even the toy-shop windows are full of nothing but soldiers, tanks, guns, etc. and the dolls are in uniform." He concluded, "The young people are all lapping it up like milk."[3]

In early February 1934, *Manchester Guardian* Paris correspondent Frederic Voigt, who had formerly been based in Berlin, stated that the Western powers had allowed the Nazi regime during its first year of power "to rearm without any hindrance save the hindrance imposed by discretion." Germany already had nearly enough military strength to make it dangerous for France or any other League of Nations power to apply sanctions against it. Germany could soon proceed with "full-blown rearmament." Voigt was certain that once sufficiently

armed, Germany would go to war. He asked, "And why shouldn't she?" The Western powers were not willing to confront Germany; all that stood in its way was
"insufficient armament," an obstacle it was working speedily to overcome.[4] A
year later Voigt reported over the BBC that the Germans had built "a vast number" of new armament factories, many of which were "concealed in the forest
depths." They were swiftly erecting barracks, fortifications, and coastal defenses.[5]

In March 1934, Dell argued that France should have launched a "preventive
war" against Germany the previous May when the Germans "could have made
no effective resistance." The Germans were in "revolt against western civilization," determined to "return to ... the 10th century at [the] latest." Dell believed
that "at least half the German nation had gone mad." Ferdnand Caussy, Berlin
correspondent for the Paris daily *Le Temps*, and H. R. Knickerbocker, European
correspondent of the *New York Evening Post*, shared this view. Dell maintained
that it was now too late for preventive war. German militarism and expansionist
designs and the British government's unwillingness to stand up to the Germans
made a general European war inevitable within a few years.[6]

The Nazi government had signaled its intention to rearm almost immediately upon assuming power by appointing military and naval attachés to serve
in its embassies abroad. The German embassy in Washington, DC, received
its first military attaché since World War I in April 1933 and its first naval attaché in September 1933. German embassy officials explained that there had
been no need for military and naval attachés before because of the small size
of Germany's army and navy.[7]

During the 1930s, much of the American public shared the "revisionist"
view that the Allied powers were at least as responsible as Germany for causing
World War I and viewed the Versailles Treaty as harsh and vindictive. Many
influenced by World War I revisionism became convinced that German rearmament and expansionism were at least partially justified. The most prestigious US foreign policy symposium in the 1930s, sponsored by the University
of Virginia's Institute of Public Affairs, invited German government officials
to speak in defense of Hitler's policies and gave them a respectful hearing.[8]
Antisemitism and appeasement sentiment pervaded the upper echelons of the
State Department and the US Army and Navy.[9] The same was true of the British
Foreign Office and the Royal Army and Navy.

CARRYING THE NAZI SPIRIT TO AMERICAN SHORES:
THE GERMAN NAVY'S PROPAGANDA MISSION

From the time he became chancellor, Hitler made a rapid naval buildup an
important priority of his rearmament program. A strong navy would not only

guarantee German supremacy in the Baltic and reduce the effectiveness of a British blockade of German ports in the next war but also help the Nazis achieve political and economic domination outside Europe. US naval intelligence officer Commander H. D. Bode stated on May 29, 1933, that the Germans believed "the ultimate decisions between nations in world affairs lie upon the seas. World power follows sea power."[10] German naval strength could also disrupt French and British transport of colonial and dominion troops and supplies from Africa and Asia for use against German forces in Europe.

The Hitler regime considered a powerful navy an important propaganda instrument as well. From 1934 to 1936, it sent the cruisers *Karlsruhe* and *Emden* on round-the-world goodwill tours with US ports as the major stops. These voyages were designed to promote "the New Germany" in the United States, and they provided an opportunity for German diplomats and naval officers to spread antisemitism among Americans. Another objective was to encourage German Americans to identify with a German "Volk" that transcended national boundaries. The US Navy high command formed friendly ties with its German counterpart during these tours. Governors and mayors warmly welcomed German vessels displaying the swastika. The widespread public fraternization of American naval personnel, business and society leaders, and members of veterans' groups with German naval officers, cadets, and crewmen during the German vessels' visits generated support for appeasing Hitler.

Hitler was intent on preventing US involvement in the next European war. Having served in the German army during World War I, he was well aware that US military and naval intervention in that conflict had proved a major factor in causing the Central Powers' defeat. Hitler also perceived the United States as a formidable industrial power and agricultural producer that could provide the British and French with vital war matériel and foodstuffs in the next war.

Almost immediately after Hitler became chancellor, US naval intelligence and the American press noticed that his regime had embarked on significant naval construction. Only two months after the Nazis assumed power, Germany launched the cruiser *Admiral Scheer*, described by the *New York Times* as "more heavily armed than any other cruiser of its size."[11] At the launching, Hitler's defense minister General Werner von Blomberg, flanked by high-ranking navy and army officers, complained about Versailles Treaty "dictates" that restricted German rearmament and claimed that Nazi Germany and "her peace-loving people" had "no other aim than to regain [on] land and sea the same security that every honor-loving sovereign nation claims as a matter of course." Six weeks later, Commander Bode reported that Hitler, accompanied by Minister of Prussia Hermann Goering, Propaganda Minister Josef Goebbels, General von Blomberg, and Navy Department head Admiral Erich Raeder, were visiting Kiel to observe the German naval war games between "blue" and "yellow" fleets. These war games were timed to coincide with British naval war games in the North Sea. The German fleets engaged in maneuvers that "demonstrate[d] every kind of naval warfare, including defense against airplane attacks."[12]

As the newer and more technological military service, and because entry into its officer corps was less socially restricted, Germany's navy was particularly popular with the middle class. The heavily Prussian army leadership was traditionally more aristocratic and less geographically representative than the navy's.[13]

On May 15, 1933, Commander Bode reported that the *Karlsruhe's* captain, Erwin Wassner, had delivered a series of public lectures in Germany in which he emphasized "the new enthusiasm in the German navy under the stimulus of the present [Nazi] regime" and the "hope in the restoration of Germany to the German conception of its rightful position of power and honor among nations." Bode noted that after one of Wassner's lectures the president of the Association of Germans in Foreign Lands made "an impassioned appeal" about the importance of stimulating pride in the Third Reich among Germans and persons of German descent living abroad. He stated that visits of German vessels to foreign ports would arouse such pride.[14]

On October 14, 1933, as the *Karlsruhe* prepared to leave on its round-the-world voyage from Kiel, its new captain, Freiherr Harsdorf von Enderndorf, spoke at a farewell banquet for the ship's company and emphasized that the warship would "carry into the outside world something of the spirit of the New Germany." In visiting foreign ports, the *Karlsruhe* would "end once [and] for all the rumors and propaganda which had been spread abroad," meaning the accusations in the Western press and by Jewish and labor groups about Nazi persecution of Jews and political dissidents.[15]

The *Karlsruhe* provided a showpiece for the modern navy Nazi Germany was building. It was the third of the 6,000-ton cruisers Germany was allowed under the Versailles Treaty. According to the *Los Angeles Times*, the *Karlsruhe*, because of "German engineering genius," was "comparable in fighting strength to 8,000-ton cruisers of other powers."[16] Many naval experts considered the cruiser the warship of the future, destined to replace the battleship as the most important fighting vessel. US Navy Rear Admiral Yates Stirling, in a February 1934 *New York Times* article, asserted that naval warfare would no longer culminate in a "decisive sea battle of concentrated fleets" centered around battleships. Instead, navies would focus on destroying the enemy's "life blood," its merchant marine, and disrupting its communications lines. They would rely on cruisers, swift and able to travel vast distances without refueling, to seek out and sink enemy cargo ships. Aerial bombardment and submarines' torpedoes rendered the ponderous, highly expensive battleship obsolete.[17]

The *Karlsruhe*'s 1933–34 round-the-world voyage brought it to four US ports—Honolulu, Tacoma, San Diego, and Boston. It carried almost 600 men, including 119 naval cadets, the equivalent of US Naval Academy midshipmen, for whom the voyage was a training cruise.[18] The *Karlsruhe*'s officers forged friendly ties with the US Navy high command, which were solidified during the 1935 and 1936 voyages. The American press and business and civic organizations provided opportunities for the *Karlsruhe*'s officers to propagandize for Nazism and for American civilians to fraternize with the Germans.

The US and German navy high commands shared some similarities that help explain the Americans' friendliness toward the Germans and willingness to assist them in carrying out naval exercises. The ship's insularity reinforced awareness of rank. Navies traditionally emphasized "discipline and blind obedience." The US Navy officer corps was more socially exclusive than the US Army's. It had always been overwhelmingly Protestant at the highest levels, where antisemitism was pervasive. Jews were almost never given command of ships of any kind.[19] During the 1930s, the US Naval War College, whose purpose was to prepare officers for high command, helped legitimize racial antisemitism and appeasement of Hitler by sponsoring several lectures by Lothrop Stoddard, "arguably America's foremost racist intellectual," on "The Racial Factor as a Determinant in National Policies." In his writings Stoddard maintained that Eastern European Jews were biologically inferior, a partly "Mongolian" and "negroid" race that threatened to mongrelize the allegedly superior "Nordics." During the interwar period, his works "exercised continuous influence on the thinking of American military officers." Stoddard endorsed Nazi efforts to "weed out the unfit" and sympathized with Hitler's expansionist aims in Central Europe.[20]

In contrast to the army, nearly all the top-ranking officers—admirals, vice admirals, and rear admirals—were graduates of the service academy, which admitted very few Jews and left its students ignorant of and unprepared to grasp political issues. In 1936, a recent Naval Academy graduate published a magazine article charging that the school was academically inferior. Its curriculum offered only "the most elementary courses in English, history, economics, and government." The few midshipmen displaying interest in these fields were "subjected to a great amount of scorn." Midshipmen rarely used the library, and few read newspapers.[21]

Germany's press portrayed the *Karlsruhe*'s visit to Honolulu, lasting from February 17 to March 5, 1934, as a public relations triumph for the Third Reich.

It highlighted the "hospitality" and "courtesy" that Americans in Honolulu extended toward the *Karlsruhe*'s officers, cadets, and crewmen. The German press also emphasized the "freedom with which the German officers were shown the various Army posts and Naval stations" near the port.[22] The German newspapers covering the warship's visit considered it an excellent opportunity for its officers, cadets, and crew "to meet many of their 'comrades' of the U.S. Army and Navy" at the largest US military base in the Pacific Ocean.[23] The US naval commandant at Honolulu detailed US naval officers to give *Karlsruhe* officers and cadets tours of the "U.S. Navy Yard, the Fleet Air Base, and the Submarine Base." The US Navy used its District Communications Service to set up target practice in the ocean for the *Karlsruhe*.[24]

When the *Karlsruhe* steamed into port at Honolulu, shore batteries at Fort Armstrong fired a salute, which the German vessel returned. In an editorial entitled "Willkommen, Karlsruhe," Honolulu's major daily newspaper, the *Advertiser*, joined "the entire community" in greeting "the gallant vessel and her gallant company." It condemned "the present agitation in certain quarters" against providing a friendly welcome to "the representatives of the great Nazi republic beyond the seas."[25]

Honolulu's *Karlsruhe* entertainment committee, which included appointees of the territorial governor and mayor, arranged a daily program of dances, parties, and concerts. Honolulu's mayor and board of supervisors sponsored a lavish hotel ball attended by three thousand in the *Karlsruhe*'s honor. Immediately before the ball, a socially prominent couple staged a special dinner in the hotel's gold room for Captain von Enderndorf and three of his officers. US Navy rear admiral Harry Yarnell and Honolulu's mayor joined them at the table. The Honolulu Chamber of Commerce entertained von Enderndorf and fifteen of his officers at a luncheon earlier that day.[26]

Captain von Enderndorf, in entertaining prominent Honolulu residents on board the *Karlsruhe*, expressed hope that his vessel's visit had "clear[ed] away misunderstandings" about the Third Reich. He assured his guests that "the German Government and its leaders don't wish anything except to give work and bread to the German people and to live on peaceful conditions and equality of rights with every other nation."[27]

When the *Karlsruhe* departed for Tacoma, Washington, on March 5, "her bow decorated with a giant flower lei," thousands of Honolulans "lined the waterfront to cheer aloha." The *Honolulu Advertiser* commented that "it seemed that all Honolulu was present to bid godspeed to the popular Karlsruhe 'boys.'"[28]

The *Karlsruhe* received as enthusiastic a welcome in Tacoma from Washington's governor, city officials, and business leaders as it had in Honolulu.

Tacoma's mayor and the president of its Chamber of Commerce personally greeted Captain von Enderndorf when the *Karlsruhe* came into port for its week's visit (March 15–22). The city's American Legion members openly fraternized with the German warship's crewmen. The American Legion's drum and bugle corps joined the *Karlsruhe*'s band in a military parade.[29]

The Tacoma Chamber of Commerce and the Young Men's Business Club feted the *Karlsruhe*'s officers at a hotel luncheon open to the public, in a packed ballroom. Promoting fraternity between the United States and the Third Reich, the *Karlsruhe* band played the German and American national anthems. All those in attendance stood for both, and the German officers gave the Nazi salute. German national colors and the Nazi swastika flag were placed next to the Stars and Stripes. The Chamber of Commerce president welcomed the German officers "on a mission of peace" and then introduced the major guest speaker, the German consul for the Pacific Northwest and Alaska, Walther Reinhardt. Reinhardt criticized "the false conception and interpretations" of the Third Reich that he claimed prevailed in the United States.[30]

The *Karlsruhe*'s officers reciprocated by hosting a reception and dance aboard their warship to honor Americans who had entertained them and their crew, including US naval officers. The governor of Washington and his wife were Captain von Enderndorf's luncheon guests on the ship and stayed for "the gay afternoon festivities." The *Tacoma Daily Ledger* reported that German "national banners and symbols of the Nazi movement served as screens and decorations for those portions of the ship reserved for dancing."[31]

The *Karlsruhe*'s appearance in Tacoma did precipitate a mass Communist-led street demonstration in Seattle. The fierce clashes between the police and anti-Nazi protestors there foreshadowed an even larger-scale confrontation two months later in Boston. Hundreds of demonstrators gathered around Seattle's Masonic Temple during a concert there for visiting *Karlsruhe* officers and seamen. They carried banners marked "Down with Bloody Hitler!" and "Join the Communist Party!" When protestors pressed against the temple's doors, policemen arrived with submachine guns and tear gas and dispersed the crowd. Pamphlets left in the street bore the slogan "Smash the goodwill tour of the German Fascists."[32]

When the *Karlsruhe* arrived at its next stop, San Diego, it exchanged twenty-one-gun salutes with US shore batteries at Fort Rosecrans in another display of American-German fraternity. The *Los Angeles Times* noted that the *Karlsruhe* was "the first Nazi vessel to enter port" in San Diego. The US Eleventh Naval District headquarters announced that because of "fear of Communistic activities" the *Karlsruhe* would dock "away from harbor piers."[33] Rear Admiral William Tarrant, commandant of the Eleventh Naval District; San Diego's mayor; the president of the city's Chamber of Commerce; and Georg Gyssling, German consul at Los Angeles, all met Captain von Enderndorf to pay their respects. *Karlsruhe* officers informed the *San Diego Union* that "Nazism had given Germany a new hope and new lease on life."[34]

A US naval intelligence report revealed that the *Karlsruhe* displayed Nazi expansionist propaganda. Swastika emblems had been installed on either side of the stern. In addition, a large colored chart was mounted in the warship's main deck passageway that showed Germany and the countries that surrounded it. Germany's pre- and postwar boundaries were marked. Superimposed over each neighboring country were sketches of aircraft in V formation headed toward Germany. The intelligence report concluded that "the apparent defenselessness of Germany from an aerial standpoint under present treaty limitations was thus forcibly . . . indicated."[35]

San Diego's Chamber of Commerce hosted Captain von Enderndorf and forty of his officers at a dinner dance. Seated with von Enderndorf were San Diego's mayor, Rear Admiral Tarrant, and Consul Gyssling. The *Karlsruhe* captain later reciprocated by staging a small luncheon on board the warship to honor US Navy rear admiral Alfred Johnson and US Navy captain N. H. White. They were joined by Consul Gyssling and Captain Robert Witthoeft, German naval attaché in Washington, DC, "a feted visitor" in San Diego during the previous few days. On Easter Sunday, San Diego's German residents gave a dance for the *Karlsruhe* men.[36]

A hundred officers, cadets, and crewmen from the *Karlsruhe* spent two days in Los Angeles to take part in several gala social events in honor of Captain von Enderndorf, including a "brilliant" formal afternoon reception at Consul Gyssling's home. Germany's consul in San Francisco and his wife attended, along with "200 socially prominent Angelenos." *Los Angeles Times* society columnist Alma Whitaker noted that "everyone seemed to be there," including "bankers, university professors, doctors, [and] judges . . . together with their ladies." She reported that at a naval ball held for the *Karlsruhe* officers and cadets that evening in a private home, the American "maidens" ignored the local boys and danced instead with "the visiting Karlsruhe Adonises."[37]

On March 30, a riot broke out in Los Angeles when more than one hundred anti-Nazi protestors, whom the *San Diego Union* described as Communists, allegedly "attempted to storm" the building in which the *Karlsruhe's* men were dining. A street battle with the police lasted nearly an hour and resulted in several injuries.[38]

The *Karlsruhe* met its fiercest opposition in Boston, which it reached on May 12, 1934, after steaming through the Panama Canal and the West Indies and up the Atlantic coast. The official welcome that Boston mayor Frederick Mansfield and Massachusetts governor Joseph Ely's secretary extended to the *Karlsruhe* precipitated a "storm of protest" from leaders of Boston's Jewish community, who called it "an insult to every Jewish citizen in Boston and the commonwealth." Jennie Loitman Barron, director of the Women's Division of the Boston American Jewish Congress, expressed shock that public officials would endorse Nazi "persecution and barbarism" by greeting the German warship displaying the swastika, officered by men who wore the swastika on their caps. Another Boston Jewish leader, attorney Samuel Finkel, voiced his disgust that city officials would permit the *Karlsruhe*, "a symbol of oppression," to dock in Boston.[39]

Although Boston's leading newspapers reported the vociferous Jewish protest on their front pages, it had only a limited effect. Mayor Mansfield told the press that the *Karlsruhe* was visiting the city because the Boston Port Authority had invited it in 1932, before Hitler came to power. He was willing, however, to receive the *Karlsruhe*'s officers at Boston City Hall, and boarded the German warship to return their call. The front page of the *Boston Herald* on May 13 showed Mansfield, wearing a top hat, walking on the *Karlsruhe*'s deck, as the German sailors stood at attention. The *Herald* did comment that "perhaps because of the protests of Jewish leaders" neither the state's governor nor its lieutenant governor was present at the State House when the *Karlsruhe*'s officers called. The governor's secretary and a US army brigadier general received them instead. The *Boston Evening American* revealed a few days later, however, that Governor Ely planned "to appropriate $400 for the entertainment of the *Karlsruhe*'s complement."[40]

The US Army and Navy commands in Boston gave what the *Herald* called "their distinguished visitors . . . their full due of welcome." When the *Karlsruhe* steamed into Boston harbor, it fired a twenty-one-gun salute, to which Fort Banks responded with its own. Captain von Enderndorf visited the Boston Navy Yard soon after his arrival to pay his respects to US rear admiral Charles Hough.[41]

Boston's Germans and German Americans greeted the *Karlsruhe*'s arrival with an outpouring of enthusiasm. Soon after the warship docked, a "sizeable crowd" of them boarded it. When Captain von Enderndorf appeared on deck, the German and German American visitors "rose to their feet as if a single man and spontaneously raised their right hands in the Nazi salute." Captain von Enderndorf returned the Nazi salute.[42]

Captain von Enderndorf traveled from Boston for two days to attend a dinner and luncheon at the German embassy in Washington, DC. The German naval attaché, Captain Witthoeft, who hosted the luncheon, was joined by US rear admiral Hayne Ellis. The next day Witthoeft entertained von Enderndorf, German naval officers, and members of Washington society at a tea, where the guests gathered around a buffet table with a swastika centerpiece.[43]

The Associated German Societies of Massachusetts and the German and Austrian War Veterans sponsored a banquet on May 17 to honor the *Karlsruhe's* personnel at Boston's luxurious Copley Plaza Hotel at which one thousand people, according to the *Boston Post*, "rose to their feet and paid tumultuous acclaim to Adolf Hitler." The acting chairman of the Steuben Society of America, a leading German American organization, received an ovation "when he issued a clarion call to German sympathizers" in the United States "to get together and oppose" what he termed "the vicious propaganda being promoted throughout this country against Germany" and mobilize against the boycott of German goods and services. The *Boston Post* reported that "excitement reached its highest pitch" during Captain von Enderndorf's speech "when he called upon the 1,000 men and women present for a salute to Hitler, and issued a stirring defense of the Nazi government." The Stars and Stripes hung between the Nazi swastika and German imperial flags, and a band played both the "Star Spangled Banner" and the "Horst Wessel Lied." Mayor Mansfield sent a personal representative to the dinner, and American veterans' organizations extended friendly greetings to the German officers and seamen. The commander of the Massachusetts department of the Veterans of Foreign Wars was seated at the head table. The department commander of the Disabled American War Veterans and the past commander of the Legion of Valor sent greetings to the *Karlsruhe's* men.[44]

That afternoon, several hundred anti-Nazi demonstrators clashed with what the *Boston Herald* described as "one of the most formidable police forces ever concentrated in the city," which blocked their attempt to reach the Navy Yard in Charlestown where the *Karlsruhe* was docked. The demonstration was sponsored by the Boston Committee to Aid Victims of German Fascism. Many participants were affiliated with the Communist-inclined National Student League chapters at Harvard and the Massachusetts Institute of Technology and with the Communist-affiliated Marine Industrial Workers Union. The protestors carried banners marked "Drive out the Hitler Warship" and "No Welcome for the Persecutors of the Jews." The policemen confronted the demonstrators before they had even begun to march and drove them back "in a wild slugfest." The *Herald* reported that "police orders to give no quarter to the communists were followed to the letter." Policemen, some of whom were mounted, charged repeatedly into the crowd, using their clubs "freely." They arrested twenty-one demonstrators. Twenty of them were arraigned on charges of inciting to riot, violating a city ordinance by distributing handbills, and disturbing the peace. Several defendants and witnesses claimed that the arrests were indiscriminate. They described startling police brutality, with "persons crowded to the wall by horses [and] small children knocked down."[45] One patrolman told the court of arresting a Jewish protestor after he saw him carrying two anti-Nazi placards, one of which stated, "No Welcome to the Persecutors of the Jews."[46]

The Boston court took a very harsh view of the anti-Nazi demonstration and sentenced seventeen of the twenty defendants to prison terms of six months or more. The judge barred photographs of police violence that defense attorneys attempted to introduce as evidence, as well as their references to Nazi persecution, on the grounds that neither the police nor Hitler was on trial. US naval intelligence was equally unsympathetic, claiming that the demonstration's "true objective" had been "to magnify the importance of Communism and to exaggerate the number of its adherents." It claimed that "stories of police 'brutality' are mere publicity stunts on the part of Communists and affiliates."[47]

Denunciation in Boston of the Nazi warship's visit extended beyond the Jewish community and trade union and student activists. The *Boston Evening Transcript*, favorite newspaper of Boston Brahmins, ran a page 1 article on May 15 reporting Alice Stone Blackwell's announcement that the Boston Women's International League for Peace and Freedom (WILPF) had passed a resolution of protest against the *Karlsruhe*'s visit. The article stated that Maria Halberstadt, a refugee from the Reich and former teacher in Hamburg, had addressed the WILPF meeting. According to the *Evening Transcript*, Halberstadt had "escaped from Germany on the eve of her arrest for opposition to Nazi policies."[48]

Nazi Germany's ambassador to the United States, Dr. Hans Luther, made an official visit to the *Karlsruhe* on May 20 and gave the Nazi salute from its deck. The next day he delivered what the *Boston Post* called "a stirring speech" to the German Educational Societies in Roxbury, praising Hitler's efforts "to regain for Germany her old dignity among nations." He denounced the boycott of German goods and services. When they rose to cheer the speech, many of the five hundred people in attendance gave the Nazi salute.[49]

When the *Karlsruhe* returned to Kiel from Boston after a voyage of eight months, German defense minister von Blomberg and Admiral Raeder were on hand to welcome it. Speaking on Hitler's behalf, von Blomberg made clear the regime's appreciation for the *Karlsruhe*'s propaganda mission. He thanked the warship's officers, cadets, and crewmen for "aid[ing] the cause of the new Germany throughout the world."[50] US Naval Intelligence reported five months later that the *Karlsruhe*'s engineering officer, Lieutenant Commander Schreiner, had delivered a lecture to the Society of German Naval Architects convention about its round-the-world cruise. One of his themes was how the *Karlsruhe*'s visits to foreign ports had stimulated enthusiasm for the Third Reich in Germans and persons of German ancestry living abroad. He lamented that the *Karlsruhe*'s personnel had arrived in the mainland US ports "at the height of an anti-German Press campaign by which they were greatly surprised and not a little hurt." Schreiner insisted, however, that this was more than offset by the "graciousness of their reception by various federal and local officials and by the friendship manifested by . . . Americans of all stations." He concluded that it was very important for the German government to send warships abroad on "good-will" tours so that foreigners "could see for themselves what type of German was being developed by the Third Reich."[51]

The *Karlsruhe* received as warm a welcome from the US Navy high command, city officials, business leaders, and German American organizations when it returned to the United States on another round-the-world voyage in 1935. During this second extended Nazi propaganda campaign, it made stops of a week or more in Los Angeles, San Francisco, and Oakland on the Pacific Coast, Houston off the Gulf of Mexico, and Charleston, South Carolina, on the Atlantic Coast. It also visited Vancouver, British Columbia, for seven days. As in Boston in 1934, the *Karlsruhe*'s arrival in San Francisco precipitated anti-Nazi street protests. The US Navy, with US State Department cooperation, again eagerly assisted the German warship to improve its combat readiness. The US Navy high command also sponsored and participated in gala social events to honor the German officers and cadets.[52]

In late February, as the *Karlsruhe* approached Los Angeles for a three-day visit, the *Los Angeles Times* reported that US Navy vessels would assist it in day-and-night "battle practice firing." The US State Department arranged for the US Navy to provide vessels, personnel, and equipment to assist the *Karlsruhe* in these exercises. In what the *Los Angeles Times* called an "extraordinary example of international naval courtesy," US Navy mine sweepers and tugboats towed target rafts to the navy's San Clemente Island drill grounds for gunnery practice. It noted that this collaboration between the US and German navies was "unique in international naval annals."[53]

Admiral Joseph Reeves, commander-in-chief of the US Fleet, and Captains Wilbur van Auken and George Baum of the battleships *Oklahoma* and *Arizona*, received the *Karlsruhe*'s new captain, Guenther Luetjens, in formal calls. The *Oklahoma* was paired with the *Karlsruhe* "for social contacts." Captain Baum of the *Arizona*, formerly a US naval attaché in Berlin, was an old friend of Captain

Luetjens. Luetjens also made a formal visit to Los Angeles's acting mayor at city hall.[54]

A society columnist reported that a Los Angeles socialite had invited sixteen young *Karlsruhe* officers, "very tall, very blond, and very handsome," to her salon to meet a group of young American women for tea. The young women were "all eyes" for the German officers' "gold braid."[55]

The *Karlsruhe* next stopped for ten days in the San Francisco Bay Area, where longshoremen staged a fierce protest against it that received national press coverage. Rank-and-file members of the International Longshoremen's Association announced they would strike for half an hour at the dock when the German warship arrived, in "protest against the visit of Hitler's armed forces to San Francisco." In response to the strike call, US undersecretary of state William Phillips authorized the *Karlsruhe*'s personnel to wear sidearms while visiting the Bay Area.[56]

Violence broke out almost immediately after the *Karlsruhe* arrived in San Francisco, as the crowd at the pier booed a US naval officer descending its gangplank. When a woman bystander objected to booing an American officer, a female anti-Nazi protestor slapped her. Policemen arrested a male anti-Nazi longshoreman for allegedly knocking down the slapped woman's husband and brother when they came to her defense, and dispersed the crowd.[57]

In an editorial, the *Bakersfield Californian* condemned the crowd's jeering the *Karlsruhe* as it docked and even denounced anti-Nazi protest in the United States. It maintained that "the place to show . . . resentment to Nazism and Hitler is in Germany, and not from the safe vantage ground of another country, which maintains friendly relations with it." The *Californian* insisted that if "the disturbers" were refugees from Nazi Germany, they were "abusing the privilege of residence in the United States."[58]

Unlike the longshoremen, official San Francisco welcomed the *Karlsruhe* with "full naval and civic honors." The city government, high US Navy, Army, and Marine Corps officers, and local business leaders honored the cruiser's officers, cadets, and crewmen at city hall. The city hall rotunda was decorated with the Nazi swastika, German imperial, and American flags for the occasion. Participating were San Francisco's mayor, who gave a welcoming speech; Admiral Thomas Senn, commanding the US Twelfth Naval District; a US Marine Corps general; Nazi Germany's consul for San Francisco, Gustav Heuser; and a San Francisco Chamber of Commerce representative.[59]

In yet another public display of American-German military friendship, San Francisco's Army and Navy Club hosted the *Karlsruhe*'s officers at a reception, at which the Nazi swastika, German imperial, and American flags again hung side by side. German consul Heuser and leaders of San Francisco German organizations were also honored at the reception.[60]

The Stanford University newspaper, the *Daily*, interviewed Captain Luetjen's public relations officer, Lieutenant Harald Grosse, who enthusiastically praised Hitler for ending political chaos in Germany and uniting the people behind a great ideal. He claimed that Hitler's goal was "peace" and "a respected place in the family of nations."[61]

Karlsruhe personnel spent two days in Oakland, where a band composed of members of the Friends of the New Germany, a pro-Nazi organization in the United States, bearing swastikas, led them in a parade to city hall. As in San Francisco, the mayor and high-ranking US Army and Navy officers welcomed the German warship's officers, cadets, and crewmen.[62]

In Oakland, Consul Heuser, speaking for Captain Luetjens and the *Karlsruhe*'s personnel, maintained that Chancellor Hitler was a peacemaker who had "sent the Karlsruhe to America on a mission of goodwill and friendship." Peacemaking, he claimed, was "the essence of [Hitler's] foreign policy." Heuser emphasized that "any statements to the contrary are malicious propaganda."[63]

A week's stop in Vancouver provided the *Karlsruhe*'s officers and Germany's consul for western Canada, Dr. H. Seelheim, with an opportunity to disseminate Nazi antisemitic propaganda, which received favorable comment from the city's leading newspaper. Local rabbis forcefully challenged Seelheim's defamation of German Jewry. Canadians' enthusiasm in greeting the *Karlsruhe* resembled that of Americans in the West Coast ports. As in the United States, non-Jewish veterans' organizations joined in welcoming Nazi Germany's warship.

Four days before the *Karlsruhe* docked in Vancouver, the *Vancouver Sun* published a front-page interview with Consul Seelheim, which amounted to an antisemitic rant. Seelheim had traveled from Winnipeg, where he was stationed, to greet the *Karlsruhe* and propagandize for Hitler. The *Sun*'s interviewer, Pat Terry, framing Seelheim's remarks, stated that the Nazi consul had provided "a picture of Hitler and modern Germany which I find it difficult to disbelieve."

Seelheim depicted Hitler as Germany's savior, rescuing a nation where Jews were poised to assume control of vital institutions—"the schools, the hospitals [and] the legal profession." Weimar's republican government had produced chaos. Germans "wanted a pure-blooded Germany, with opportunity for Germans." Jews, because they were racially different, could not be true Germans. When Jews obtained administrative positions, they only hired other Jews. The Jews concentrated in the "higher professions," propagating "anti-German sentiment," and showed no interest in agriculture. Seelheim claimed that Jews were heavily engaged in the white slave trade.[64]

In a page 1 letter to the editor in the *Sun*, two Vancouver rabbis expressed profound disappointment that "one of the leading newspapers in Canada" had given approval to "these vilest accusations hurled against [the Jews] by the official representative of the Hitler government." The rabbis felt it was beneath their dignity to respond to Seelheim's "insidious and base allegations" but noted that Jews, who had lived on German soil for more than fifteen hundred years, had earned for both Germans and Jews "world renown for culture and enlightenment."[65]

After the *Karlsruhe* arrived in Vancouver, the *Sun* published a front-page interview with its public relations officer, Lt. Harald Grosse, whose celebration of the Nazi regime was similar to Seelheim's. The *Sun*'s interviewer, Bob Bouchette, was impressed by Grosse's account of Hitler's achievements, including the Fuehrer's instilling love for the Fatherland and restoring order through a one-party dictatorship. Grosse emphasized that Hitler had "crystallized our idea.... of a Germany reborn and standing on its own feet. Every cadet on this ship feels it." Bouchette believed that there was good reason, therefore, why "Mr. Grosse and all the people that Mr. Grosse represents, love Hitler."[66]

Vancouver's acting mayor officially greeted Luetjens and assured him of "the public's esteem," and military dignitaries, business organizations, and churches joined in welcoming the *Karlsruhe*'s personnel. The Canadian Army and Navy Veterans arranged smokers to promote fraternization with the seamen from the Third Reich. The Naval Officers Association and Navy League of Canada sponsored a naval ball for the German warship's men. The Vancouver Board of Trade Council hosted a luncheon for Captain Luetjens and several of his officers. Vancouver's Lutheran and Catholic churches invited the German officers, cadets, and crewmen to attend their Sunday church parades. The *Karlsruhe*'s chaplain preached the sermon at the Lutheran church. More than twenty-five thousand persons visited the *Karlsruhe* during the hours it was open for public inspection, determined, according to the *Vancouver Sun*, to "extend friendship" to the German navy men.[67]

Vancouver's Canadian Club invited Consul Seelheim to address "a huge meeting," where he praised the Fuehrer for defeating Communism and saving Christianity. Seelheim explained that before Hitler assumed power, "Godlessness was rampant and the church was in the discard." He claimed that "school boys and girls had burned straw effigies of the members of the Trinity." Nazism had drawn the German people "back to the churches."[68]

Captain Luetjens staged a dance on board the *Karlsruhe* for several hundred Vancouver residents who had extended courtesies to his men. Many Canadian army and navy officers, "prominent citizens," and members of Vancouver's

German colony attended. Portraits of Hitler and swastikas were conspicuously displayed.[69]

The German warship received very friendly receptions in the two final US cities it visited, Houston (April 26 to May 4) and Charleston (May 10 to May 18). In Houston, the officers of a US destroyer that was serving as a training vessel for the local US naval reserves unit took "a prominent part" in entertaining the Karlsruhe's personnel and honoring its officers. Captain Luetjens made a side trip to San Antonio, where the commander of Fort Sam Houston received him.[70]

The mayors of Houston and the nearby port of Galveston, the president of Galveston's Chamber of Commerce, German naval attaché Witthoeft, and the German consuls in New Orleans and Galveston were all on hand to warmly welcome the Karlsruhe when it arrived in Houston. Houston's mayor announced that he was particularly pleased that the German government had chosen Houston as one of the US ports the Karlsruhe would visit. The warship received German American delegations on board to celebrate the German national holiday of May Day.[71]

At the Texas state legislature's invitation, Captain Luetjens delivered an address to it in Austin, in which he claimed that Nazi Germany and the United States shared the same ideals. He expressed the hope that the Karlsruhe's visit would strengthen American understanding of German aspirations. In Austin, Luetjens also made an official call on Governor James Allred.[72]

The Karlsruhe's final stop in the United States on this voyage was Charleston, where it received a twenty-one-gun salute from Fort Moultrie. The Karlsruhe followed with a thirteen-gun salute to US rear admiral Edward Fenner, commandant of the US Sixth Naval District and of the Charleston Navy Yard, which responded with its own thirteen-gun salute.

US military endorsement of the Karlsruhe's visit was evident in the composition of Charleston's welcoming committee, which included three US Navy officers and a representative of the German consulate in Charleston. The US Navy high command again communicated its desire to forge bonds of friendship with Nazi Germany's naval officers when Rear Admiral Fenner hosted a dance at Charleston Navy Yard to honor Captain Luetjens and members of his staff. Charleston's mayor welcomed Captain Luetjens and members of his staff at city hall and staged an official luncheon for them.[73]

The city's churches invited the Karlsruhe's offices, cadets, and crewmen to attend religious services. At St. Matthew's Lutheran Church, the Karlsruhe's own clergymen presided at Sunday services held in German, assisted by the church's pastor. The Cathedral of St. John the Baptist hosted the Catholics serving on the German warship.[74]

In March 1935, about the time the *Karlsruhe* was visiting California, Hitler signaled the navy's growing importance as a propaganda instrument by establishing a National Socialist Navy League (Nationalsozialistischer Deutscher Marinebund) to instill the Nazi outlook within the German fleet. Its membership included all former German naval officers and seamen. About the same time, Hitler introduced a People's Navy Week to stimulate public interest in the German navy among citizens of the Reich and persons of German descent in foreign countries. Vice Admiral Conrad Albrecht, chief of the Baltic naval station, stated that the purpose of People's Navy Week was "to impress upon all our racial comrades" that the navy, "like other parts of our armed forces is a visible symbol of our National Socialist Third Reich."[75]

The Hitler regime achieved a major diplomatic and military triumph in June 1935 when it persuaded the British government to sign the Anglo-German Naval Agreement, which allowed it to significantly escalate the pace of naval construction and divide Britain from its wartime ally France. The historian Martin Gilbert called the agreement "appeasement's most dramatic success" and a herald of the Munich pact to come. The British made the agreement with the Germans without consulting the French, who opposed it. It swept aside the Versailles Treaty limitations on German naval construction, permitting Germany to build a navy with 35 percent of the tonnage of Britain's. The agreement also allowed the Germans to begin submarine construction, forbidden under the Versailles Treaty, so long as they promised not to use U-boats to attack merchant ships. Winston Churchill noted in his memoirs that the agreement set Germany's navy yards "to work at maximum activity" for years.[76]

The Anglo-German Naval Agreement, which the US government favored, greatly enhanced the German navy's potential impact in a future war. It significantly reduced the Royal Navy's advantage, because Britain required many more vessels to defend its far-flung colonial empire, stretched across several oceans. Moreover, many Royal Navy ships were antiquated. The agreement not only weakened British prospects for successfully blockading Germany's Baltic and North Sea ports in a future war but also gave the German navy the capability to seriously threaten British and American shipping in the Atlantic.[77]

Lord Lloyd, denouncing the Anglo-German Naval Agreement in the British House of Lords, called it "a tremendous stimulus of German militarism" and warned that Hitler would adhere neither to the 35 percent provision limiting German naval construction nor to the promise not to use submarines against merchant shipping. He added, "Anyone who has read *Mein Kampf* . . . and the absolutely frank avowal therein of the Nazi attitude toward treaties will find it very hard to believe that . . . [the Germans] will consider themselves nailed down."[78]

By the time the *Karlsruhe* and *Emden* made their goodwill visits to US ports in 1936, US naval intelligence had recognized that "there is growing as fast as [German] naval construction will permit, a powerful and important navy," which already controlled the Baltic. Sigrid Schultz, the *Chicago Tribune*'s Berlin correspondent, reported in March 1936 that German navy yards were "working day and night" building naval vessels. She noted that the Hitler regime was strongly encouraging naval recruitment: "Newspapers and billboards call upon the nation's youth to serve in the navy." The *Washington Post* had reported in March 1935 that the Germans had already set up fortifications that made their coasts "virtually invulnerable."[79]

In April 1936, the *Karlsruhe* received the same enthusiastic reception in San Diego from US military, civic, business, and society leaders as it had on its previous two Nazi-era trips to the United States. Neither the Hitler regime's imposition of the Nuremberg laws depriving Jews of their citizenship in September 1935 nor the July 1935 pogroms in Berlin (discussed in the next chapter) made any difference. US vice admiral H. V. Butler hosted a luncheon on a US naval vessel for the *Karlsruhe*'s new captain Leopold Siemens and Germany naval attaché Witthoeft. US rear admiral C. H. Woodward (commander of destroyers, battle force) held still another luncheon for them on board ship. The commandant of the US Eleventh Naval District and Captain Siemens exchanged official calls. Witthoeft visited the US Naval Training Station, where he was received "with full honors," and made an official call at the local US Marine Corps base.

The City and County of San Diego and the Chamber of Commerce sponsored a dinner for Captain Siemens and his officers and a dance for the *Karlsruhe*'s crew. At a Chamber of Commerce luncheon, San Diego's mayor and the county supervisor extended "felicitations" to Witthoeft and the *Karlsruhe*'s officers, cadets, and crew. US rear admiral W. T. Tarrant did the same for the navy.[80]

Captain Siemens, several of his officers and cadets, and Witthoeft made a side trip to Los Angeles, where society leaders and prominent German residents entertained them at lavish social functions, including a dinner, a tea, a luncheon, and a cocktail party. Consul Gyssling hosted a garden party for the *Karlsruhe* contingent at his home, attended by the British, French, Japanese, Italian, and Swiss consuls and Los Angeles and Hollywood debutantes.[81]

The Hitler government sent a second six-thousand-ton cruiser, the *Emden*, flying the swastika flag from bow and stern, on an eight-month goodwill and training tour in 1936 that included stops in Portland, Oregon (January 19–29); Honolulu (February 8–17); and Baltimore (April 21–May 2). American military, political, and business leaders gave the *Emden* an enthusiastic welcome. The US Navy Department in Washington, DC, US Navy admirals, state and municipal officials, and chambers of commerce used the visit to proclaim their determination to forge even friendlier relations between the United States and the Third Reich. The US Naval Academy underscored its strong commitment to this goal by inviting the *Emden*'s officers and cadets to its campus in Annapolis as honored guests. They were joined there by Nazi Germany's ambassador Hans Luther, whom the Naval Academy received with "full military honors." Maryland's governor and Baltimore's mayor exchanged official calls with the *Emden*'s captain.[82]

By contrast, Baltimore Jewish and civil rights organizations, the International Ladies Garment Workers and Amalgamated Clothing Workers locals, and Communist groups vigorously protested the *Emden*'s presence, in part through a mass demonstration on the waterfront. Baltimore rabbi Edward Israel denounced the governor and mayor for welcoming the swastika-bedecked warship rather than taking "a stand in behalf of humanity and democracy."[83]

At the *Emden*'s first American stop (Portland, Oregon), its captain, Johannes Bachmann, hosted a tea dance for the US Army officers stationed at Fort Stevens and their wives. Officers of the fort reciprocated with a supper dance for the *Emden*'s officers.[84]

When the *Emden* docked in Honolulu, the city's military and civilian dignitaries made clear their desire for friendly ties with the nation it represented. Hawaii's territorial governor's aides, Honolulu's mayor, US Navy rear admiral Yarnell, and US major general Hugh Drum, commander at Fort Schafter, exchanged official calls with Captain Bachmann. General Drum accorded Captain Bachmann an honor guard when he visited the fort. Drum had twelve hundred US troops parade for the German warship's captain, who was joined on the reviewing stand by the governor, the mayor, and Rear Admiral Yarnell. Honolulu's extensive entertainment program included a Chamber of Commerce luncheon for twenty of the *Emden*'s officers and cadets, which the governor, the mayor, and the German consul in Honolulu also attended.[85]

The *Emden* received a far less friendly reception in Kingston, Jamaica, where it docked for a week from March 23 to 30, 1936, before proceeding to Baltimore, than it had in US ports. The US consul in Kingston, who detested Nazism, reported that although "the usual formalities were scrupulously observed by German and Briton," there had been "no general entertainment and no cordiality." He described the *Emden*'s officers, cadets, and crewmen as "a splendid looking lot of Nazis." The consul was amazed that even five thousand miles from its German base the *Emden's* personnel continued to receive "its daily quota of [Nazi] propaganda direct from home." The warship's personnel assumed that the entire world shared its adulation of Hitler.[86]

As the *Emden* arrived in Baltimore, Captain Bachmann gave an address on board to celebrate Hitler's birthday. When he finished, the warship's personnel gave the Nazi salute and shouted, "Heil Hitler!" three times.[87] While the *Emden* was in Baltimore, the US Navy Department hosted a reception for Captain Bachmann and his officers and cadets in Washington. Admiral William Standley, chief of US naval operations, also held a luncheon there to honor Bachmann.[88]

US secretary of state Cordell Hull ignored the plea of Emanuel Gorfine, Speaker of the Maryland House of Delegates, and four other House members to rescind the permission he had granted for the *Emden* to dock in Baltimore. The *Baltimore Sun* reported that "thousands of [their] constituents had expressed deep resentment" that Secretary Hull had allowed the German warship to visit the city.[89]

In Baltimore, German consul Frederick Schneider hosted a dinner for Captain Bachmann and the *Emden's* officers, attended by the presidents of the city's German American organizations, at which the mayor made an appearance. The pastor of Baltimore's Zion Lutheran Church gave the invocation, and Adolf Hitler was toasted.[90]

Captain Bachmann, several of his officers, and 150 *Emden* cadets visited the US Naval Academy as guests of its superintendent, Rear Admiral David F. Sellers. Sellers had been Nazi ambassador Luther's dinner guest in Washington a few days earlier. Sellers hosted a luncheon at the Naval Academy for the *Emden* officers, at which they were joined by Luther and Witthoeft. The Naval Academy greeted Luther's arrival with a nineteen-gun salute. The German visitors watched drills, a dress parade, and several athletic contests.[91] In July, Sellers embarked on a trip of nearly two months in Europe that included more than two weeks in Nazi Germany. Between July 27 and August 13, he visited Hamburg, Hanover, Hildesheim, Kassel, Weimar, Dresden, Nuremberg, Ulm, Constance, Heidelberg, Wiesbaden, Cochem, and Cologne.[92]

On April 29, an Emergency Committee for an Anti-Nazi Protest that had been established to protest the *Emden's* visit to Baltimore sponsored a public meeting at which Gerhart Seger, former Social Democratic Reichstag deputy and anti-Nazi refugee, spoke on "Hitler, a Menace to World-Wide Civilization." The Emergency Committee announced that it was sponsoring Seger's lecture to "counteract Nazi propaganda" circulating through Baltimore as a result of the *Emden's* visit. Its members included Rabbi Israel and the president of the Baltimore Federation of Labor. Five hundred persons attended Seger's lecture.[93]

BRITAIN WARMLY WELCOMES NAZI WARSHIPS, 1934

In 1934 the German cruisers that the Hitler regime sent on goodwill missions to Britain were received with equal fervor. Sizeable crowds lined the docks to welcome the *Königsberg* and the *Leipzig*, which arrived in the English town of Portsmouth forty-five minutes apart on July 11. They were the first German warships to visit a British naval port since the world war. The Royal Navy high command lavishly entertained the officers during their five-day stay. Portsmouth shore batteries greeted the German vessels with a twenty-one-gun salute, which they returned. The Portsmouth batteries responded with a seventeen-gun salute to the flag of Rear Admiral Koble, the German squadron's commander. The Germans replied by saluting British admiral Sir John Kelly's flag. Determined to impress on the Germans their desire to forge strong bonds of friendship, the British even moved the king's yacht from where it was moored so that the *Königsberg* and *Leipzig* could occupy the best berth in the dockyard.[94]

The German officers' entire visit to England was consumed with "official dinners, receptions, and garden parties." The British naval commander-in-chief in Portsmouth hosted a party for the German officers on the day they arrived. The next day, Rear Admiral Koble and the captains of the German cruisers traveled to London, where they called on the First Lord of the Admiralty in full dress uniforms and wearing Iron Crosses. The German embassy in London held a luncheon reception for them. At Portsmouth, the British arranged for German and Royal Navy officers to get together for tennis, golf, and tea. The Royal Navy arranged daily motor coach trips for the German "lower deck," with British seamen and warrant and petty officers entertaining Germans of corresponding rank from the *Königsberg* and *Leipzig*. Men from the German vessels played a water polo match against a team of Royal Marines.[95]

US naval intelligence reported that the German press was delighted with the reception that the British accorded the German cruisers and noted the "appreciable amount of space" they devoted to the visit. Newspapers in the Third Reich were excited that "great crowds of visitors" had "lined the docks and entrances to Portsmouth's harbor." They also were thrilled by the enthusiastic reception that the British commander-in-chief in Portsmouth and other British officers extended to the Germans and "the comradeship and good feeling . . . manifested between the enlisted men of the German and British navies." The German press praised the British for their friendliness to the officers and men of the navy of the Reich "when they appeared in uniform in London." It expressed pleasure that many German crewmen "had been entertained in private British homes."[96]

Three months later, the German cruiser *Deutschland* received a similarly fervent welcome on its five-day goodwill mission to the Scottish port of Leith, serving Edinburgh. The warship, commissioned the year before, could travel ten thousand miles without refueling. The Edinburgh newspaper the *Scotsman* observed that the *Deutschland* did not need such an "enormous cruising radius" for the role the German defense minister claimed for it, guarding Germany's communication lines with East Prussia in the Baltic: "Her business must be on the high seas." Germany's construction of such high-speed, long-range cruisers suggested preparation for a large-scale offensive naval war in which they would "get to and attack ships or ports defended by cruisers, and accomplish her object before she can be overtaken by a battleship." The *Scotsman* emphasized that "the *Deutschland* is proportionately more dangerous as a raider than anything that went before her."[97]

The British naval high command in Edinburgh, as in Portsmouth, went to great lengths to encourage its seamen and the Scottish public to fraternize with the German warship's personnel. The commander-in-chief of the British Home Fleet, Admiral the Earl of Cork, invited Rear Admiral Carls of the *Deutschland* and several of his officers to a luncheon on board the British Home Fleet's flagship, HMS *Nelson*. They were joined by the naval attaché of the German embassy in London, the German embassy councilor, and the German consul in Edinburgh. The *Scotsman* reported "extraordinary scenes" at Leith, as "huge crowds," estimated at thirty thousand, assembled at the dock to greet the *Deutschland* on its arrival, and ten thousand lined up to board the warship.[98]

* * *

The German cruisers were diverted from goodwill missions to the United States and Britain for service in the Spanish Civil War after Hitler's military intervention in July 1936. Warships not engaged in Spanish waters guarded Germany's Baltic and North Sea coasts. After the Spanish Civil War ended in 1939, the ships were redeployed for service in World War II. Both sides in the Spanish Civil War relied heavily on shipping to import necessary war matériel, food, and foreign troops. By June 1937, 60 percent of Germany's newer naval vessels were in Spanish waters. The *Karlsruhe* and *Emden* both patrolled the Spanish coast, and the *Karlsruhe* participated in the blockade of Loyalist-held Bilbao, which helped force its capitulation to the Fascists.[99]

By sending modern, well-equipped cruisers on goodwill trips to US and British ports, the Hitler regime intended to project an image of respectability and military strength. The visits also provided the opportunity to disseminate Nazi propaganda in both countries. The German government hoped to ensure the neutrality of the United States, and perhaps even Britain, in the next European war by convincing the people of both nations that Germany had been unfairly victimized by the Western powers, had legitimate reason to expand, and was misrepresented in the Western press.

The German navy's goodwill voyages helped legitimize Hitler's rearmament program in the United States at a time when it was still possible to block it. The US Navy, with the cooperation of the State Department, even assisted German cruisers in carrying out target practice and maneuvers. The navy was especially important in Germany's war plans as the instrument to prevent its enemies from securing war matériel and food. The German cruisers sent to US ports were modern, well-equipped long-distance raiders designed to devastate the merchant marines of Germany's enemies.

The US Navy high command's fraternization with its counterparts from the Third Reich and the assistance it provided the German warships in conducting military maneuvers off American shores were consistent with the Roosevelt administration policy in the 1930s to consider Nazi Germany a friendly nation. The US Navy carried out the president's foreign policy; it did not make its own. During the 1930s, President Roosevelt remained largely indifferent to calls for US naval rearmament as a means to counter the German naval buildup. He focused instead on persuading other nations to cooperate in reducing naval armaments. Historian John Walter noted that through the 1940 presidential election, Roosevelt's naval policy was characterized by "vacillation and uncertainty."[100]

Their round-the-world voyages helped the Nazi government solidify bonds between the German and American navy high commands. German naval officers, cadets, and crewmen were also able to fraternize with US Navy, Army, and Marine Corps servicemen, civic and business leaders, and civilians. The German naval visits were an important part of Hitler's propaganda campaign in the United States and Britain, promoting sympathy for appeasement and presenting Nazi Germany as a respectable member of the community of nations.

Officers on the visiting German cruisers and German embassy and consular officials promoted the Nazis' virulently antisemitic ideology and policies in press interviews, conversations with US Navy officers, and speeches to business and civic groups. On its 1935 world tour, the *Karlsruhe* carried with it two thousand copies of Hitler's *Mein Kampf*, mostly for distribution in the United

States.[101] American newspapers were full of praise for the German navy's efforts to forge friendly ties between the United States and the Third Reich. American veterans' groups, many of whose members had fought the Germans during World War I, joined in hailing the officers and men of the swastika-bedecked warships. US and British military officers had no qualms about fraternizing with Nazi Germany's naval officers and diplomatic officials. Although the American press in December 1935 and January 1936 had widely reported the Nazi government's systematic eviction of Jewish war widows from low-rent municipal apartments built specifically for war widows, during the 1936 visits of German warships American officers showed no concern.[102]

American Jews were largely on their own in challenging the German navy's visits to US shores. On occasion Jewish anti-Nazi protestors were joined by non-Jewish trade unionists, and Communists sometimes staged their own demonstrations, but few mainstream Americans publicly denounced the Nazi vessels' presence in their country's ports. The consistently friendly reception accorded the German warships visiting US (and British) ports to promote goodwill toward the Third Reich reflected the widespread insensitivity toward Jews among mainstream American citizens and British subjects; US and Royal Navy officers, including those at the highest levels; and government officials at all levels. This foreshadowed what David Wyman called "The Abandonment of the Jews" during the Holocaust: the unwillingness of the United States and Britain to undertake serious rescue efforts to save European Jews.[103]

NOTES

1. Winston Churchill, *The Gathering Storm* (Boston: Houghton Mifflin, 1948), 77–78.

2. E. L., letter to the editor, *Manchester Guardian*, August 21, 1933, 16.

3. Robert Dell to [W. P.] Crozier, October 3, 1933, 210/1–86, GDN Foreign Correspondence, *Manchester Guardian* (hereafter, MG) Archives, John Rylands Library, Manchester, UK (hereafter, Rylands Library).

4. [Frederic] Voigt to Crozier, February 9, 1934, 211/1–85, GDN Foreign Correspondence, MG Archives, Rylands Library.

5. F. A. Voigt, BBC commentator, "Arms Factories Hidden in Forests," March 18, 1935, 213/112–189, MG Archives, Rylands Library.

6. Dell to Crozier, October 3, 1933.

7. Jacob W. S. Wuest, US military attaché, Berlin, "Germany (Military). Subject: Newly Appointed German Military Attachés," February 10, 1933, G-2 Report, box 3665, Central Decimal Files, 1930–39, Department of State General

Records, Record Group (hereafter, RG) 59, National Archives, College Park, MD (hereafter, NA-CP); *Washington Post*, September 22, 1933, 3.

8. Stephen H. Norwood, *The Third Reich in the Ivory Tower: Complicity and Conflict on American Campuses* (New York: Cambridge University Press, 2009), 133–57.

9. Martin Weil, *A Pretty Good Club: The Founding Fathers of the U.S. Foreign Service* (New York: W. W. Norton, 1978); Joseph Bendersky, *The "Jewish Threat": Anti-Semitic Politics of the U.S. Army* (New York: Basic Books, 2000).

10. H. D. Bode, Commander, US Navy, "Naval Attaché's Report: Further Manifestations of Re-awakened Interest in Naval Affairs—Germany," May 29, 1933, Naval Attaché Reports, 1886–1939 (hereafter, NAR), box 1191, Office of Naval Intelligence Records, RG 38, National Archives, Washington, DC (hereafter, NA-DC).

11. *New York Times*, April 2, 1933, 29.

12. H. D. Bode, Naval Attaché's Report, May 15, 1933, NAR, box 1191, Office of Naval Intelligence Records, RG 38, NA-DC; *New York Times*, May 24, 1933, 4.

13. Robert L. O'Connell, *Sacred Vessels: The Cult of the Battleship and the Rise of the U.S. Navy* (New York: Oxford University Press, 1991), 155–56.

14. Bode, Naval Attaché's Report, May 15, 1933.

15. *Times* (London), October 16, 1933, 12. Before reaching Honolulu, the *Karlsruhe* visited Palermo and Syracuse in Sicily; Port Said, Egypt; Calcutta, India; and ports in Ceylon, the Dutch East Indies, Java, Australia, and Samoa. *Honolulu Advertiser*, February 17, 1934; *San Diego Union*, March 28, 1934.

16. *Los Angeles Times*, February 27, 1935, A1.

17. *New York Times*, February 11, 1934, XX2.

18. *Boston Herald*, May 13, 1934, 1, 10.

19. O'Connell, *Sacred Vessels*, 18–19; Ira Berkow, *Maxwell Street: Survival in a Bazaar* (Garden City, NY: Doubleday, 1977), 289.

20. Bendersky, *"Jewish Threat,"* 23, 260–62 (quotes); John Higham, *Strangers in the Land: Patterns of American Nativism, 1860–1925* (New York: Atheneum, 1970), 272.

21. Morris Janowitz, *The Professional Soldier* (New York: Free Press, 1971 [1960]), 58, 81, 97, 100, 138. As late as 1950, 100 percent of admirals and vice admirals and 95.5 percent of rear admirals were Annapolis graduates. Janowitz, *The Professional Soldier*, 59; James Oliver Brown, "Annapolis—Stronghold of Mediocrity," *Forum and Century*, October 1936, 153–57.

22. C. H. J. Keppler, Captain, USN, Naval Attaché's Report, April 9, 1934, box 884, NAR, Office of Naval Intelligence Records, RG 38, NA-DC.

23. H. D. Bode, Naval Attaché's Report, March 16, 1934, box 884, NAR, Office of Naval Intelligence Records, RG 38, NA-DC.

24. T. M. Leovy, Lt. Commander, USN, Naval Attaché's Report, March 17, 1934, box 884, NAR, Office of Naval Intelligence Records, RG 38, NA-DC.

25. *Honolulu Advertiser,* February 17, 1934.

26. *Honolulu Advertiser,* February 24, 1934.

27. *Honolulu Advertiser,* March 2, 1934.

28. *Honolulu Advertiser,* March 6, 1934.

29. *Tacoma Daily Ledger,* March 16, 1934, 1.

30. *Tacoma Daily Ledger,* March 17, 1934, 1, 3, 10.

31. *Tacoma Daily Ledger,* March 21, 1934.

32. *Seattle Post-Intelligencer;* March 20, 1934, 1, 2; *Daily Chronicle* (Centralia, WA), March 20, 1934; *Los Angeles Examiner,* March 20, 1934, 1.

33. *Los Angeles Times,* March 27, 1934, A8, and March 28, 1934, 4.

34. *San Diego Union,* March 28, 1934.

35. W. G. Child, Commanding Officer, to Office of Naval Intelligence, "Subject: Intelligence Report on German Cruiser KARLSRUHE," April 5, 1934, box 1190, NAR, Office of Naval Intelligence Records, RG 38, NA-DC.

36. *San Diego Union,* March 28, March 29, and March 31, 1934.

37. *Los Angeles Times,* April 1, 1934, 14, and April 3, 1934, A6. Members of Los Angeles's German-American Alliance met the *Karlsruhe* visitors at the train station and held an informal luncheon for them. *Los Angeles Times,* March 31, 1934, A3.

38. *San Diego Union,* March 31, 1934, 1.

39. *Boston Herald,* May 12, 1934, 1, 2.

40. *Boston Herald,* May 13, 1934, 1; *Boston Evening American,* May 16, 1934, clipping in box 901, NAR, Office of Naval Intelligence, RG 38, NA-DC.

41. *Boston Herald,* May 13, 1934, 1, 2; *Boston Post,* May 12, 1934, 1, 7.

42. *Boston Herald,* May 13, 1934, 1, 10.

43. *Washington Post,* May 13, 1934, 7, and May 16, 1934, 11.

44. *Boston Post,* May 18, 1934, 15; *Boston Globe,* May 18, 1934, 8.

45. *Boston Herald,* May 18, 1934, 1, 16; *Boston Post,* May 18, 1934, 1, 15; *Boston Globe,* May 18, 1934, 1, 8; *Boston Evening Transcript,* May 18, 1934; *Harvard Crimson,* May 19 and May 22, 1934, 1, 4. Several arrested demonstrators charged that in the police stations policemen beat them severely without provocation. *Harvard Crimson,* May 22, 1934, 1, 4.

46. *Boston Post,* May 24, 1934.

47. *Boston Herald,* May 30, 1934; *Boston Post,* May 25, 1934, 6; *The Tech* (MIT), June 5, 1934, 3; *Harvard Crimson,* June 6, 1934; *Daily Worker,* June 9, 1934; H. L. de Rivera, Lieutenant, USN, to the Intelligence Officer, First Naval District, "Subject: Communistic Demonstration in Charlestown, Massachusetts, May 17, 1934," report on June 8, 1934, box 901, NAR, Office of Naval Intelligence Records, RG 38, NA-DC.

48. *Boston Evening Transcript,* May 15, 1934, 1.

49. Jewish Telegraphic Agency, May 21, 1934; *Boston Post,* May 22, 1934.

50. *New York Times,* June 19, 1934, 7; H. D. Bode, June 25, 1934, box 1191, NAR, Office of Naval Intelligence Records, RG 38, NA-DC.

51. H. D. Bode, November 26, 1934, box 884, NAR, Office of Naval Intelligence Records, RG 38, NA-DC.

52. On its 1935 round-the-world voyage, the *Karlsruhe* steamed west instead of east, traveling to the Azores and then to South America. The German cruiser visited Brazil and Uruguay, navigated around Cape Horn, and made stops in Chile, Peru, and Colombia. The *Karlsruhe* then headed up North America's Pacific Coast to Los Angeles, San Francisco, and Vancouver. From Vancouver, it reversed direction and steamed southward to Mexico's Pacific port of Acapulco and then through the Panama Canal to Houston and Charleston, South Carolina. *Houston Post,* April 27, 1935, 1, 6.

53. *Los Angeles Times,* February 26, 1935, A1, 2, and March 1, 1935, 2. The *Times* reported that US naval officers who watched the *Karlsruhe*'s firing at eleven thousand and three thousand yards complimented its (new) Captain Luetjens on the accuracy of its fire. *Los Angeles Times,* March 1, 1935, 2.

54. *Los Angeles Times,* February 27, 1935, A1, and March 1, 1935, 2.

55. *Los Angeles Times,* February 28, 1935, A5.

56. *New York Times,* March 3, 1935, 1; *San Francisco Examiner,* March 2, 1935.

57. *New York Times,* March 3, 1935, 1; *Oakland Tribune,* March 2, 1935; *San Francisco Chronicle,* March 3, 1935, 1, 3; *Los Angeles Times,* March 3, 1935, 1, 12.

58. *Bakersfield Californian,* March 4, 1935.

59. *San Francisco Chronicle,* March 3, 1935, 1, 3; *San Francisco Examiner,* March 3, 1935.

60. *San Francisco Chronicle,* March 5, 1935.

61. *Stanford Daily,* March 4, 1935.

62. *Oakland Tribune,* March 8, 1935, 1, and March 9, 1935, 5.

63. *Oakland Tribune,* March 9, 1935, 5.

64. *Vancouver Sun,* March 11, 1935, 1, 3, NAR, clipping in box 884, Office of Naval Intelligence Records, RG 38, NA-DC.

65. *Vancouver Sun,* March 13, 1935, 1.

66. *Vancouver Sun,* March 15, 1935, 1.

67. *Vancouver Sun,* March 13, 1935, March 15, 1935, 1, March 16, 1935, and March 18, 1935.

68. *Vancouver Sun,* March 19, 1935.

69. *Vancouver Sun,* March 20, 1935.

70. *Houston Post,* April 26, 1935, 1, 8, and April 30, 1935, 1, 2.

71. *Houston Post,* April 25, 1935, 1, 9, April 26, 1935, 1, 8, and May 1, 1935, 1, 11.

72. *Houston Post,* April 30, 1935, 1, 2, and May 1, 1935; *Austin American,* April 29, 1935, 1, and April 30, 1935.

73. "Visit of German Cruiser *Karlsruhe* to Charleston, SC, April 10th–18th as submitted by J. A. Von Dohlen," NAR, box 884, Office of Naval Intelligence Records, RG 38, NA-DC; *Charleston News and Courier,* May 9, 1935.

74. "Visit," NAR, box 884, Office of Naval Intelligence Records, RG 38, NA-DC; *Charleston News and Courier,* May 9, 1935.

75. [William E.] Dodd, "Regarding Naval Affairs—Germany. Formation of a New National Socialist German Navy League, Plans for," March 26, 1935, box 6779, Central Decimal Files, 1930–39, Department of State General Records, RG 59, NA-CP; *New York Times,* June 12, 1935, 9.

76. Martin Gilbert, *The Roots of Appeasement* (London: Weidenfeld and Nicholson, 1966), 150; Churchill, *Gathering Storm,* 137–38. William L. Shirer wrote that the British government accepted Hitler's offer of the agreement "with incredible naiveté and speed." Shirer believed that the agreement gave Hitler "free rein to build up a navy as fast as was physically possible." Shirer, *The Rise and Fall of the Third Reich* (New York: Simon and Schuster, 1960), 288–89.

77. J. C. White, counselor of [US] embassy, to Secretary of State, "Subject: Anglo-German Naval Agreement," June 26, 1935, and Lord Lloyd, "Naval and Military Situation," June 26, 1935, box 36, Norman Davis Papers, Library of Congress, Washington, DC.

78. Lord Lloyd, "Naval and Military Situation," June 26, 1936, box 36, Norman Davis Papers, Library of Congress, Washington, DC.

79. NAR, "Subject: Germany's Naval Position at the End of the Third Year of the Third Reich," February 7, 1936, box 1191, Office of Naval Intelligence Records, RG 38, NA-DC; *Washington Post,* March 23, 1935, 4; *Chicago Tribune,* March 29, 1936, 20.

80. Commandant, Eleventh Naval District, San Diego, to Chief of Naval Operations (Director of Naval Intelligence), April 22, 1936, and Paul P. Blackburn, Commanding Officer, US Naval Training Station, San Diego, April 16, 1936, box 884, NAR, Office of Naval Intelligence Records, RG 38, NA-DC; *San Diego Union,* April 7 and 10, 1936. The *Karlsruhe* on its 1935–36 round-the-world voyage left Kiel on October 21, 1935, and made its first stop at Santa Cruz de Tenerife. It then steamed down Africa's west coast and around the Cape of Good Hope to Durban. The warship then proceeded to Seychelles, Batavia, Iloilo, Hong Kong, and Nagasaki and Kobe in Japan. From Japan it headed to San Diego. After leaving San Diego, the *Karlsruhe* passed through the Panama Canal to St. Thomas and then to Spain, returning to Kiel in June 1936. *San Diego Union,* April 8, 1936, 1, 2.

81. *Los Angeles Times,* April 4, A8, April 13, A1, and April 19, 1936, C5, C6.

82. *Baltimore Sun,* April 18, 1936, 4, 20, April 19, 1936, 18, and April 30, 1936, 4; *Washington Post,* April 26, 1936, S8. The *Emden* on its voyage traveled to Central and South America, Portland, Honolulu, and Mexico, and then through the

Panama Canal to the Dominican Republic and Jamaica, Baltimore, Montreal, and Spain.

83. *Baltimore Sun*, April 19, 1936, 18, and April 20, 1936, 1; *Washington Post*, April 23, 1936, 7.

84. "Emden at Ft. Stevens," *Army and Navy Journal*, February 1, 1936, 440.

85. *Honolulu Advertiser*, February 8, 1936, 1, 2, and February 11, 1936, 1, 7.

86. George Alexander Armstrong, American consul, Kingston, Jamaica, to the Honorable Secretary of State, March 31, 1936, box 884, NAR, Office of Naval Intelligence Records, RG 58, NA-DC.

87. *Baltimore Sun*, April 21, 1936, 20, 24.

88. "German Vessel Visits Baltimore," *Army and Navy Journal*, April 25, 1936, 746.

89. *Baltimore Sun*, April 21, 1936, 20, 24.

90. *Baltimore Sun*, April 22, 1936, 24.

91. *Baltimore Sun*, April 18, 1936, 4; *Washington Post*, April 26, 1936, S8; *New York Times*, April 26, 1936, N8; *Chicago Tribune*, April 26, 1936, 6; Hans Luther to David Foote Sellers, "To Meet the Captain of the Cruiser 'Emden,'" box 19, David Foote Sellers Papers, Library of Congress, Washington, DC.

92. "Itinerary of Rear Admiral D. F. Sellers, U.S. Navy—1936" and Robert Witthoeft to Admiral Sellers, September 9 and 11, 1936, box 4, David Foote Sellers Papers, Library of Congress, Washington, DC.

93. *Baltimore Sun*, April 27, 1936, 4, April 29, 1936, 11, and April 30, 1936, 4, 24.

94. *New York Times*, July 11, 1934, 10; *Daily Herald* (London), July 12, 1934; *Times* (London), July 11, 1934, 12; Victor Perowne, Foreign Office, to Cmdr. C. M. R. Schwerdt, June 4, 1934, ADM 1/8777/156, Admiralty Records, National Archives, London, United Kingdom (hereafter, NA-UK).

95. *Times* (London), July 11, 1934, 12, and July 14, 1934, 18; *New York Times*, July 11, 1934, 10, and July 13, 1934, 3; John D. Kelly, Admiral, "Portsmouth General Orders," July 9, 1934, Visit of German Cruisers "Konigsberg" and "Leipzig" (G.O. 858), ADM 1/8777/156, Admiralty Records, NA-UK.

96. H. D. Bode, NAR, July 13, 1934, box 884, Office of Naval Intelligence Records, RG 38, NA-DC.

97. *The Scotsman*, October 24, 1934, clipping in box 884, NAR, Office of Naval Intelligence Records, RG 38, NA-DC.

98. Ibid., October 22, 1934.

99. *New York Times*, December 31, 1936, 8, April 14, 1937, 1, 5, and June 24, 1937.

100. John C. Walter, "Congressman Carl Vinson and Franklin D. Roosevelt: Naval Preparedness and the Coming of World War II, 1932–40," *Georgia Historical Quarterly* 64 (Fall 1980): 294–305.

101. *Manchester Guardian*, October 28, 1935, 15.

102. *Chicago Tribune*, December 31, 1935, 7; *Washington Post*, January 5, 1936, B2.

103. David S. Wyman, *The Abandonment of the Jews: America and the Holocaust, 1941–1945* (New York: New Press, 2007 [1984]).

—\\\\\—

EIGHT

DEGRADATION, APPEASEMENT, AND LOOMING CATASTROPHE, 1935

THE MASSIVE GERMAN VICTORY IN the January 13 Saar plebiscite heightened the Nazi threat to European Jewry as the Hitler regime accelerated its rearmament program, staged horrific pogroms in Berlin in July, and in September instituted the Nuremberg race laws. The lurid antisemitic propaganda campaign intensified. Britain's *New Statesman* reported that no sooner had the Saar plebiscite's results been announced than "the Streicher press launched a new anti-Jewish drive, which surpasses in blood-thirstiness and obscenity" its previous efforts. *Der Stürmer* charged that Jews sold wine mixed with Christian blood, that "the Talmud condones murder and advocates homosexuality," and that "Jewish families entice blond Aryan girls into their houses to minister to the sexual needs of their young boys." "A host of other Nazi newspapers," including those published by top-level party leaders (such as Goebbels's *Der Angriff* and race ideologist Alfred Rosenberg's *Weltkampf*) made similar claims.[1]

Anti-Jewish terrorism escalated. In June, Julius Streicher began a major tour, delivering antisemitic speeches across the Reich. He addressed large, enthusiastic crowds in Berlin, Hamburg, and Saxony. He continued his harangues in Munich, Magdeburg, Cologne, Hanover, and many other cities and towns. The Board of Deputies of British Jews (BoD) reported that "in each case a violent antisemitic campaign preceded and followed the meeting."[2]

German municipalities throughout the Reich increasingly segregated Jews. In early August, the London *Daily Herald* stated that "cafés, restaurants, and hotels are closed to Jews. They are not allowed to enter swimming baths, and they are being driven from the seaside resorts. They may not even enter the sea, where 'Aryans' bathe." The same month, the London *Jewish Chronicle* reported that notices had been placed on all the streetcars in Magdeburg announcing that Jews' presence was "unwanted." Antisemitic slogans were also "prominently display[ed]" on the streetcars. Non-Jewish shops in Frankenthal posted signs warning away Jews. Youth hostels in the Mittelelbe-Harz district barred Jews. In Oestrich, the Rhine river steamers would not sell tickets to Jews. Movie theaters in the Thuringian towns of Apolda, Bad Berka, and Blankenhain denied entry to Jews, and Weimar's largest cinema was closed to them. Many hotels refused to accept Jewish guests.[3]

Increasingly, Jews were prohibited from even entering towns, and municipalities expelled their Jewish residents. By the end of 1935, whole areas of Germany were *Judenrein* including Franconia and much of East Prussia, Mecklenburg, Pomerania, the Palatinate, Hessia, Silesia, and Baden.[4] A notice in the Pomeranian town of Ratzebuhr warned, "Jews, moths, and bugs enter at their own risk." The August 23 issue of the London *Jewish Chronicle* listed several "Jew-purged" towns and villages, adding, "Instances of this sort could be multiplied to fill several pages of the *Jewish Chronicle*, and then merely the fringe would be touched of what is only one of many lines of the Nazis' attack on the Jews."[5]

Anti-Jewish boycotts proliferated, and German Jews' economic situation deteriorated markedly. In August, the London *Jewish Chronicle* reported that Jews were being boycotted everywhere in Germany. Toward the end of the year, the Jewish Telegraphic Agency (JTA) stated that the economic boycott in provincial cities was so stringent that Jews were "virtually terrorized, to such an extent that it is virtually impossible for them to continue in business." Not only local Nazi authorities but also municipal governments enforced the boycott, which elicited mass support. Municipal administrations in "almost every city and township in the Reich" were "removing from the relief lists any 'Aryan' seen patronizing Jewish stores or Jewish doctors." They also "canceled contracts with firms . . . buy[ing] supplies from Jews." Municipal officials spotted making purchases in Jewish-owned stores were discharged. "Doomed to bankruptcy," Jewish storeowners in provincial cities had "no alternative" but to sell their stock to non-Jews, generally receiving about one-third of what it was worth. The JTA concluded that "the small Jewish business man of the provinces faces a future in which starvation and dependence on charity loom large."[6]

German children boasted of their fierce antisemitism and commitment to boycotting Jewish stores. A thirteen-year-old Mannheim girl bragged to *Der Stürmer* that she and her ten-year-old sister, members of the Nazi Girls' League, "hate the Jews like the devil." Another nine-year-old girl from Roth, near Nuremberg, sent *Der Stürmer* an essay she wrote entitled "The Jews as

Parasites." The nine-year-old described how she and other Roth children were combatting the "parasite" by intimidating anyone attempting to shop in Jewish-owned stores. "Several of our class often stand in front of the Baer department store, and when would-be customers seek to enter, they shout: 'Shame on you for dealing with Jews!'" She concluded, "Then the customers turn red and walk away."[7]

Every day this "cold pogrom" "add[ed] more victims to the rolls of already heavily overburdened Jewish organizations." Their resources diminished greatly as the number of Jews capable of making donations steadily declined. Wealthier Jews emigrated, and middle-class Jews were driven into penury.[8]

By rapidly rearming on a large scale, Germany was positioning itself to achieve control of Central and Eastern Europe over the next few years. In December 1935, British ambassador to Germany Sir Eric Phipps informed British foreign secretary Anthony Eden that all observers in Berlin believed that "German military plans are being laid with a view to operations in the East."[9] This would put the large Jewish populations there at severe risk. In Germany, the Nuremberg laws stripped Jews of their citizenship and prohibited intermarriage and sexual relations between Jews and "Aryans." This placed German Jews in what amounted to a social ghetto. The London *Times* declared that "nothing like the complete disinheritance and segregation of Jewish citizens, now announced has been heard since medieval times." The London *Jewish Chronicle* emphasized, however, that the Nuremberg laws had merely formalized "a system already existing" in Germany. The Jews had already been reduced to pariah status. In many places the German judiciary had long pronounced "mixed" marriages illegal. From the time the Nazis came to power, storm troopers and many ordinary Germans had violently attacked or publicly humiliated Jews and gentiles in "mixed" amorous relationships and sometimes even in friendships. Jews were already virtually excluded from the German army and navy.[10]

In 1935, Jews and non-Jewish opponents of Nazism in the United States staged mass demonstrations against antisemitism in Germany, which were once again initiated at the grassroots. Alarmed, the Hitler regime filed official diplomatic protests with the US State Department. In Britain, an estimated twenty to forty thousand Jews and other anti-Nazis rallied to denounce Nazi antisemitism in London's Hyde Park. American and British Jews intensified their boycott of German goods and services in 1935. By contrast, the British and American governments remained largely complacent about the pace and scale of German rearmament, although some high British officials expressed concern. Nor did either government appear troubled by German Jewry's plight. And the major British military veterans' organization, the British Legion, made a concerted effort to forge friendly ties with Nazi-controlled German veterans' groups.

GERMAN MILITARISM AND REARMAMENT

In 1935, Nazi Germany's stunning successes in the Saar plebiscite and in over-turning the Versailles Treaty's military clauses, along with its rapid rearmament, made it highly likely that in the near future Hitler would press for territorial expansion in Central Europe and even Eastern Europe. He would then be in a position to destroy Jewry not only in Germany but also outside it. The Versailles Treaty had prohibited Germany from making military service compulsory and limited its army to one hundred thousand men. But in March 1935, Hitler reintroduced conscription and announced the formation of a German army of five hundred thousand men, organized in twelve corps, or thirty-six divisions. British foreign secretary John Simon noted in his diary that Germany, "instead of rearming secretly, is rearming openly, and is demonstrating that in this respect the Versailles Treaty is a dead letter." Phipps remarked to Eden that the magnitude of Germany's Saar victory had "turned Hitler's head." A few days after the plebiscite, the Fuehrer had told Phipps that if given the opportunity, the Austrian people would vote to join the Reich by the same overwhelming majority. Phipps commented that citizens of the Reich were highly enthusiastic about Hitler's unilateral repudiation of the Versailles restrictions on the size of Germany's army and the ban on conscription: "There are few Germans who deny that Herr Hitler has 'delivered the goods.'"[11]

Since the spring of 1933, American and British journalists conversant with German affairs had been reporting that Germany was secretly re-arming on a large scale, in violation of the Versailles Treaty. On April 28, 1933, Frederick Birchall, Berlin correspondent of the *New York Times*, sent the paper's managing editor, Edwin James, eight photographs of well-coordinated German military maneuvers, which had been concealed on hills and wooded terrain, and whose publication Goebbels's Ministry of Propaganda had prohibited, both in Germany and abroad. Birchall warned James, "I cannot sufficiently emphasize that any publication whatever of these photographs or any published reference to their existence" would make it impossible for the *Times* to obtain photographs from its supplier in Germany, Wide World Photos, ever again. Birchall wrote on the backs of the photographs, "Must be destroyed after perusal." Anyone taking such photographs without the German authorities' permission was subject to arrest and imprisonment.

Birchall informed James, "If any evidence is needed that the Versailles Treaty and Germany's pledge to abide by it until amended are dead letters in Germany, here it is." He explained, "[German] disarmament is a fraud, the Hitlerites are *not* peaceable; it is the same old Germany."[12]

In August 1933, Robert Dell, *Manchester Guardian* Geneva correspondent, observed in Berlin the Hitler regime's "deliberate attempt to militarize the German people and prepare them for war." Military ceremonies were staged every day. The police solemnly goose-stepped during their daily changing of the guard as groups of onlookers gave the Nazi salute. Dell reported that a foreign consular official had seen German boys, aged fourteen to sixteen, under adult supervision, "throwing dummy hand grenades at pasteboard figures of soldiers in a dummy trench." Presumably, this had become part of "the ordinary school curriculum."[13]

Lord Robert Vansittart, British undersecretary of state for foreign affairs, emphasized in April 1934 that the Hitler regime's large-scale military training programs for youth were designed to instill bellicosity in boys and prepare them for war. Lord Vansittart referred to an April 1933 report from Britain's military attaché in Berlin, which stated that Hitler Youth and members of *Wehrsport* (Military Sport) associations were participating in regular military drill, pack marches, and miniature rifle shooting. They were taught to read maps and guide themselves by compass on long marches, scouting, "attack and defense, withdrawal and pursuit, [and] surprise and ambuscade." The military training, begun at age twelve, continued until a man "became too old for service in the field." When war broke out, Germany would possess a very large reserve of men who would require little or no training to assume their place in the armed forces.[14]

In November 1934, US ambassador to Germany William Dodd expressed his alarm to Assistant Secretary of State R. Walton Moore about Germany's "preparation for war." He had recently traveled from Berlin to Constance through Wittenberg, Leipzig, and Nuremberg, returning by way of Stuttgart, Erfurt, Bitterfeld, and Leipzig. Dodd had driven through part of this area only one year before when "most of the smokestacks showed that nothing was being done." Now, however, "almost every smokestack showed great activity." Dodd suspected that much of this recent industrial activity, which he estimated was comparable to Chicago's in 1928 and 1929 before the crash, was related to military production. Dodd informed Moore that consular reports showed that some German industrial centers were manufacturing great amounts of poison gas and explosives.[15]

GERMAN PREPARATIONS FOR AIR WAR

In June 1933, Sir Horace Rumbold, who was about to step down as Britain's ambassador to Germany, notified Foreign Secretary Sir John Simon that

Germany was openly building military aircraft, even though the Versailles Treaty prohibited it from having an air force. In September, Leon Dominian, American consul at Stuttgart, Germany, reported to Secretary of State Cordell Hull that the German press was emphasizing the need for an air force. He reported that Germany's numerous newly founded air protection societies were training the public to defend against air attacks. The Germans were building an air protection school in Stuttgart with a model bomb- and poison-gas-proof cellar and a museum depicting Allied air attacks on Germany during the world war. The school would train emergency medical teams for rescue work during air raids. Dominian told Hull that the Germans would press vigorously for the abrogation of the Versailles Treaty's air clauses.[16]

By early 1934 the Germans had opened flying schools under camouflaged names near Berlin, in Württemberg, and in Würtzberg and were propagandizing for the air buildup with the slogan "every village its aeroplane." Bomb-proof airplane sheds were under construction. German schools were holding drills for defense against aerial gas attacks, from which Jewish children were excluded. In an air-raid exercise in Munich, eight thousand paper bombs were dropped.[17]

By April 1934, Eric Phipps had become greatly alarmed by Germany's progress in building up an air force. He feared that Germany might already enjoy air superiority over Britain and France. Phipps wrote in his diary that "a very large proportion of the French air force consisted of [antiquated] 'tin kettles.'" By contrast, Germany was rapidly producing military planes that were "highly up to date and in every way efficient." This was especially distressing because Britain "had reduced her air force to an elaborate minimum."[18] Lord Vansittart was aware that Germany was also producing sports and commercial aircraft that in time of war could easily be converted into military airplanes.[19] In November 1934, Winston Churchill, at that time a backbencher in the House of Commons, warned that Germany would achieve air parity with Britain by 1935 and would have twice as large an air force by 1937. Similarly, Sir John Simon wrote in his diary on May 2, 1935, that Germany had attained air parity with Britain, with a "first-line strength of 800 to 850 aircraft." Lord Vansittart recalled in his memoirs, however, that the British government remained indifferent and Churchill's warnings were "all to no purpose."[20] The Germans had also begun manufacturing a fleet of zeppelins capable of crossing the Atlantic and convertible to war use. Germany had used these "air monsters" in the world war to bomb London and Antwerp.[21]

The US government was also well informed about Germany's air war preparations. On November 5, 1934, Ambassador Dodd told Assistant Secretary of State Moore that on November 1 the US consul in Dresden had reported the presence of one thousand airplanes in that district. When Dodd had stopped for lunch on October 28 at a hotel in Hechingen, the hotel keeper told him that a great many Germans were learning to fly. He stated that there were twenty expert flyers in Hechingen, a small town, and two thousand registered flyers in Stuttgart. Dodd emphasized to Moore that the reason so many Germans were taking up flying was "to put France out of business." He concluded, "The result of all this, if allowed to go through, will of course mean annexations and [German] predominance in the whole of Europe."[22]

In December 1935, after a two-week study of military aviation in the Reich, Lieutenant Commander Wyatt, assistant naval attaché for aviation, notified the US ambassador to France, Jesse Isadore Strauss, "Germany intends to build up her air fleet to that of the combined strength of Germany's possible enemies." The Germans were also establishing numerous antiaircraft stations and listening posts along their Baltic and North Sea coastlines. Wyatt observed that "throughout the [German] air corps there is a strong feeling of loyalty and respect for Hitler." The aviation and naval personnel with whom Wyatt spoke credited their Fuehrer with accomplishing more than any other man in German history, including Bismarck "or any of their great [German] heroes," in uniting the nation and giving it purpose.[23]

The Hitler regime clearly announced the identity of the menace Germany faced to its air squadrons. Speaking at the inauguration of the Air Protection School in Nuremberg in 1935, Julius Streicher cited the *Protocols of the Elders of Zion* "to prove that the Jews of the world intend to instigate a war against the people of Europe."[24]

GERMANY THOROUGHLY MILITARIZED

In November 1935, Eric Phipps informed Britain's new foreign secretary, Sir Samuel Hoare, that the most striking feature of "German social, economic, and political life" was "the reconstruction of the armed forces." It was apparent from driving along "any road in this country" that Germany was thoroughly militarized: "On every side giant military establishments are springing up." Army barracks and military schools were being built in nearly every town of importance. Huge aerodromes extended often for miles along many of the main roads. Many factories were surrounded by high barbed-wire fencing and protected by armed SS sentries, indicating that they were manufacturing war matériel. The streets of provincial towns were "gay with uniforms" and full of camouflaged military vehicles. The unending drone of airplanes overhead "[bore] witness to the expansion of the German air force."[25]

Lord Vansittart reported that the German government was importing huge amounts of copper from the Katanga mines in the Belgian Congo and making sizeable purchases of scrap metal to manufacture munitions for the next European war. He stated that in the summer of 1933 several German industrialists had told Britain's acting consul in Pittsburgh on his visit to the Reich that "if Germany had had the necessary raw materials for the manufacture of munitions during the past war, her position would have been impregnable." Germany planned to enter the next war in a commanding position by purchasing all available scrap metal.[26]

The German press stimulated public enthusiasm for Hitler's military buildup by celebrating the departure of recruits and publishing numerous photographs of "smiling soldiers" in their barracks, underscoring "the jollity of military life." Newspapers emphasized how soldiers' presence brought prosperity to the garrison towns and their surrounding areas. They described farmers, shoemakers, butchers, barbers, and other tradesmen "gleefully welcom[ing] the incoming troops." They viewed "the armed forces and their creator, Hitler, as the heroes of the day."[27]

Ambassador Phipps attended the opening of Leni Riefenstahl's film *Triumph des Willens* (*Triumph of the Will*) in Berlin in March 1935 and concluded that it showed how "the idea of robot militarism has now possessed itself of the German nation." The film highlighted Hitler's dramatic descent from the sky to the September 1934 Nazi Party Nuremberg rally. Phipps described it as "alarming." SS guards and police lined the streets leading to the theater for half a mile. Rows of SS stood at attention from the theater entrance all the way to the grand tier, where Hitler and other top Nazi leaders, including Josef Goebbels, Rudolf Hess, Baron von Neurath, and General von Blomberg were seated. The proceedings began "with stirring military marches played by massed bands of the SS on the stage." Phipps found it chilling when at times the Berlin audience's cheers mixed with those of the Nuremberg crowds on film. He stated that the film's purpose was to stir up German militarism "to a fever heat." There was no better way to "bring home to the British public the true state of affairs in Germany" than to show them this film.[28]

BRITISH APPEASEMENT

The British government, under Prime Ministers Ramsay MacDonald (1929–35) and Stanley Baldwin (1935–37), along with much of Britain's educated public, believed that the League of Nations should be the primary instrument for alleviating conflict among European nations, and did not grasp the consequences of failing to implement a serious rearmament program. The government ignored warnings from such high officials as Lord Vansittart and Eric Phipps, and from Winston Churchill and a few other MPs. As Martin Gilbert noted, "vacillation and indecision were frequently the dominant features of [British] policy." It was commonly believed that wars started as a result of one nation misreading another's intentions or because arms manufacturers encouraged them in order to sell their wares. By facilitating communication among countries, the League of Nations would prevent such misunderstandings. By promoting disarmament, the League would sharply reduce the prospect of war. To this end, in February 1932, the League convened a sixty-nation conference. Germany, however, left the conference on October 14, 1933, and shortly afterward withdrew from the League. The day Germany pulled out of the conference, Foreign Secretary John Simon declared that "the policy of conciliation is the only policy to pursue." He maintained that the German resignation was due in part to "reasonable and just" claims. In 1935, the British continued their effort to persuade Germany to return to the League, assuming that in that environment it could be convinced to adopt a more moderate foreign policy.[29]

A significant segment of British opinion also considered the Versailles Treaty unduly harsh toward Germany, which harbored "legitimate" grievances that the League of Nations could resolve. Harold Macmillan, British prime minister from 1957 to 1963 and a member of the House of Commons from 1924 to 1929 and from 1931 to 1964, recalled that until just before the outbreak of World War II much of the British public believed that the German people had not wanted to go to war in 1914. They assumed that it was "just the Kaiser and the militarists" who had wanted this, forgetting "how easily the Germans have succumbed to such leadership throughout history, and how readily they have applauded wars."[30]

The British had no interest in developing their army into a force that could fight effectively on the European continent. Britain would rely on its navy, which it considered the finest in the world, to patrol the sea lanes and protect its colonial interests. Many both within and outside the British government shared the view that a British naval blockade "would stop any aggressor in his tracks." This belief was shaped in part by relentless postwar German propaganda, which claimed the German army "never really broke" during the last stages of the world war and "that only the [British naval] blockade had beaten the Fritzes."[31]

The US government displayed little concern about Germany's rapid rearmament during the early years of Nazi rule, remaining convinced that Hitler's Germany could be persuaded to join other nations in disarming to acceptable levels. In his 1958 memoir *The Mist Procession*, Lord Vansittart highlighted President Roosevelt's naivete, recalling that in May 1933, during the Geneva Disarmament Conference, Roosevelt sent a round robin letter to the heads of state of every participating country proposing "that all the nations of the world should enter into a solemn and definite pact of non-aggression."[32] Asked at his March 20, 1935, press conference to comment about "the German arms situation," Roosevelt expressed hope that America's "good neighbor" principle would "be extended to Europe" and suggested that all European powers reduce their armaments.[33]

In 1935 Britain's major veterans' organization, the British Legion, assumed a prominent role in legitimizing the Hitler regime in the United Kingdom. In July it sent a delegation on a ten-day visit to the Reich for the announced purpose of forging friendly ties between Britain and Germany. In return, the British Legion hosted and paid tribute to representatives of German veterans' groups in England. British Legion leaders who visited the Reich praised Hitler as a man sincerely committed to achieving peace in Europe. During their stay in Germany, savage, anti-Jewish pogroms broke out in Berlin that received extensive coverage in the British, American, and French press. Upon the British Legion delegation's return to England, however, its spokesmen announced that they had "no first-hand knowledge of any anti-Jewish incident."[34]

At the request of Joachim von Ribbentrop, a leading foreign policy advisor to Hitler, T. Corder Catchpool, director of the Religious Society of Friends (Quaker) Berlin office, proposed to former British Legion chairman Colonel George Crosfield that reciprocal visits be arranged between British and German veterans' delegations. In his speech at the British Legion annual conference in London on June 11, 1935, the prince of Wales, a Nazi sympathizer, gave his "warm approval" to the proposal that British Legion members, as representatives of British servicemen, offer "the hand of friendship to their former foes" in Germany. That night, the prince's speech "was the main news" in the Nazi-controlled German press, which received it enthusiastically. German officials immediately transmitted "the relevant passages" in the prince's speech to Hitler and top-level advisers Hermann Goering and Rudolf Hess. Richard Griffiths, in his study of "British Enthusiasts for Nazi Germany," stated that "the propaganda value to Germany" of the prince of Wales's speech "was enormous."[35]

Coming only four days after the formation of the new Stanley Baldwin government in Britain, the prince's declaration of support for the proposal that British Legion representatives meet German ex-servicemen in the Reich and in England caused considerable uneasiness at the French and Soviet embassies in London. Diplomats at those embassies feared it signaled a major British rapprochement with Nazi Germany.[36]

The British Legion's decision to cultivate friendly relations with German war veterans was almost immediately denounced in the House of Commons by Labour MP Aneurin Bevan. Bevan demanded that Foreign Secretary Sir Samuel Hoare disclose whether His Majesty's Government had approved the visit, which, having been publicly endorsed by the prince of Wales, had "diplomatic significance." Hoare replied that the Foreign Office should not interfere in a matter that was "entirely one for the servicemen's organizations." When Bevan asked the foreign secretary whether he considered it proper for the prince of Wales to have proposed such a visit, he refused to answer. Bevan then asked if Hoare had instructed the British Legion delegation to visit a concentration camp. He replied that it was not a matter with which the Foreign Office should be concerned.[37]

The Anglo-German fraternization began on June 20, when the mayor of Brighton, a town on England's southeastern coast, received with civic honors a delegation of twenty-nine German war veterans wearing swastika armbands. The Germans had been prisoners of war in Britain during the world war. This was the first visit to Britain by an organized group of German veterans since the war. The *New York Times* noted that the prince of Wales's recent call for meetings between British and German veterans gave the visit "an importance in national and international politics that transcends its local significance as a bit of comradeship." A spokesman for the German delegation, responding to the mayor of Brighton's welcoming address, paid tribute to the prince of Wales as "the man of the moment, not only in his own country, but throughout Germany."

The next day the mayor of the nearby town of Hove officially welcomed the German veterans as "Britons and Germans alike gave the Nazi salute." Presiding at a reception dinner at the town hall, Brigadier General F. C. Lloyd, president of the British Legion's Hove branch, declared that this first visit of German veterans to England "would be the beginning of an important movement" that would improve Britain's relations with Germany.[38]

Three days later, Prince Otto von Bismarck, an ardent supporter of Hitler, addressed the German veterans at Brighton cemetery, where the delegation laid wreaths on the graves of German, British, and Dominion soldiers buried there. Each German then gave the Nazi salute at the cemetery memorial. At the graveyard ceremony, von Bismarck expressed the "great wish ... that peace and friendship shall reign between the two countries."[39] The British Legion's Brighton branch conferred honorary membership on the leader of the German veterans' delegation. The German veterans' last act before returning to the Reich was to place a wreath on the Cenotaph in London, after which they gave the Nazi salute.[40]

As the British Legion's reciprocal voyage to Nazi Germany neared, Labour MP Frederick Seymour Cocks asked Foreign Secretary Hoare in the House of Commons whether the delegation planned to meet with the leaders of German peace organizations, since it claimed the visit's purpose was to promote peace. Cocks asked if the foreign secretary was aware that all the leaders of German peace organizations were imprisoned in concentration camps. Was it His Majesty's Government's desire that the delegation meet only with "General Goering and other Nazi propagandists?" Hoare replied that the British government was not involved in the visit. He was confident that the British Legion had made "satisfactory arrangements."[41]

Harold Laski, a prominent Jewish political scientist and a Labour Party leader, complained in a letter to the editor in the *Manchester Guardian* shortly before the British Legion delegation's departure for Germany that British appeasers returning from visits to the Reich had been assuring the public "that belief in Hitler's pacifism is the key to European peace." Laski emphasized that "no diminution of [Nazi] brutality has taken place.... The atrocities against the Jews increase if anything, in volume."[42]

The day before Laski's letter was published, the Kyffhäuser League, one of Germany's leading veterans' organizations, with three million members, sponsored a rally at Kassel with a demonstration of the Reich's modern weapons. More than two thousand soldiers of Germany's new, vastly expanded army employed them in military maneuvers that climaxed in a battle for a village. The weapons displayed included tanks, antitank artillery, antiaircraft batteries, and mine sweepers. The head of the Kyffhäuser League, Colonel Reinhard, "delivered a panegyric upon Herr Hitler, the Nazi movement, and the restoration of Germany's national sovereignty." He also praised the recently signed Anglo-German Naval Agreement.[43]

From the beginning of the British Legion's visit, the *Manchester Guardian* reported that it was being "exploited by the German press in favor of the Nazi dictatorship," which stood for everything Britain's war veterans "were supposed to have fought against from 1914 to 1918." The *Guardian* could only hope that the British press and public would not forget German veterans like the anti-Nazi Schumacher, who was wounded seventeen times in the world war and had lost his arm. The Nazis had imprisoned Schumacher in a concentration camp, where he was in danger of going blind.[44]

On July 15, two days after the British Legion delegation arrived in Germany, Adolf Hitler personally received five of its members at the Chancellery in Berlin. Hitler made a special trip from Nuremberg to meet with the delegates and spoke with them for two hours. The delegation also visited General Goering at his mountain home at Obersalzberg. All the speeches during the British Legion's stay in Germany, on both sides, "stressed the close blood ties between the British and German people." The *Washington Post* commented, however, that just as the British Legion delegates "were being elaborately entertained in Berlin," German mobs were violently attacking Jews in the city's streets. The *Post* called the pogroms "the sour fruits of [Hitler's] medieval policy."[45]

On July 22, Nazi officials gave Colonel Crosfield, British Legion chairman Major Fetherston-Godley, and at least one other British Legion delegate a tour of the Dachau concentration camp. Upon their return to London, the British Legion men declared that they were favorably impressed with conditions at Dachau and by the inmates' health. Fetherston-Godley informed the London *Daily Herald* that the concentration camp "was well laid out with trees and flowers. There were sports grounds, excellent workshops, and vegetable gardens," and the food served to the inmates was "excellent." All the inmates were "extraordinarily fit." Fetherston-Godley alleged that Jews' lack of patriotism during the war explained German hostility to them. He claimed that in any event the Jews that the Germans "were after" were "those who came to Germany after the war." The chairman of the British Legion also implied that the inmates were unsavory people.

The *Daily Herald* concluded that Fetherston-Godley's "almost enthusiastic praise of Hitler's concentration camps, the total indifference to persecution of the Jews, the uncritical acceptance of Hitler's peace declarations," made the British Legion look ridiculous. It noted that many rank-and-file British Legion members were "up in arms" at their chairman's pro-Nazi views and were inundating the *Daily Herald* with letters denouncing him.[46]

ACADEMIC APPEASEMENT: INTERNATIONAL ACADEMIC CONFERENCES, 1935

Nazi Germany achieved major propaganda successes in 1935 by securing Western participation in what it promoted as scholarly conferences, staged in Berlin: the International Penal and Penitentiary Congress (IPPC), held from August 18 to 24, 1935, and the World Population Congress (WPC), which met from August 27 to 30, 1935. These were, in fact, forums to disseminate Nazi race doctrine and justify antisemitic terror. Both received daily coverage in the British and American press.

The Nazis used the IPPC as a platform to associate criminality with Jews and to justify Germany's concentration camp system and use of sterilization as a penal measure. The conference's "official thesis" was that the criminal was "a racial type." Conference hosts distributed literature to the delegates claiming that "the international criminal language draws much of its vocabulary from the Jewish Ghetto." Delegates from Western countries often challenged German prison policies in the floor debates, but the Nazis dominated the proceedings, speaking in German, often without providing translations for foreign participants. The German delegation of more than 400 was about 150 larger than those of the other fifty countries combined. By the fourth day, American delegates were protesting that they were being used as "pawns in the Nazi propaganda game."[47]

The Germans boasted of their break with Western approaches to imprisonment. They called for longer prison sentences and were dismissive of rehabilitation as a goal. Dr. Franz Gürtner, Reich minister of justice, informed the conference that Nazism considered "any attack on the interests of the national community" punishable by German courts even when no law defined it as a criminal offense.[48]

On August 21, German delegates brushed aside a French delegate's claim that the concentration camps were repressive. Sanford Bates, director of the US Bureau of Prisons, who chaired the session, denied requests from Belgian and Spanish delegates to open the floor for a discussion of the camps. Two days later, Josef Goebbels explained to an audience at Berlin's Kroll Opera House, which included the foreign delegates attending the IPPC, that the concentration camps were necessary to protect sixty-six million Germans from "individuals hostile to society."[49]

In a lecture to the delegates on "International Penal Policy," Dr. Hans Frank, head of the National Socialist Jurists Association and minister without portfolio, denounced the international boycott of German goods and services as "a menace to international juridical peace." He also condemned the "mock trials" of the Nazi government and leaders staged by the Hitler regime's "emigrant political opponents" outside the Reich. This was further indication of the Hitler regime's deep concern about anti-Nazi protest in foreign countries. Frank expressed the German government's wish that the IPPC work to prevent any more mock trials.[50]

Although a number of Western delegates attempted to challenge Nazi penal policies, the IPPC in Berlin was a significant propaganda triumph for the Hitler regime. The final session passed by an overwhelming majority a resolution endorsing "compulsory sterilization on grounds of eugenics" as a method of combatting crime, because "it would reduce in the future the number of inferior people from whom criminals are largely recruited."[51] Upon his return to the United States on a German liner, an American delegate to the Congress, Sing Sing prison warden Lewis Lawes, declined to talk about the German prisons he had visited but told the *New York Times* that "conditions in Germany were better than he had expected to find them." George Messersmith, US minister to Austria and former consul general in Berlin, told Undersecretary of State William Phillips that the Nazi government had scored "a great victory" by attracting "distinguished lawyers and jurists from all over" to Berlin, "even though Germany is no longer a state in which there is any real justice." This had helped the Reich project an image of respectability in the West.[52]

The WPC, held at the University of Berlin to promote Nazi eugenics, opened on August 27 with "a prayer of Thanksgiving to Providence for having given Adolf Hitler to Germany." The two hundred foreign scientists and three hundred Germans attending as delegates then joined WPC president Eugen Fischer, University of Berlin professor of anthropology, in hailing Hitler. As was the case at the IPPC, the Nazis controlled the conference, with German delegates constituting a majority. The Germans chose most of the foreign delegates. In 1931, the International Union for the Scientific Investigation of Population Problems (IUSIPP), an international association that drew together demographers, eugenicists, and anthropologists, had agreed to hold the WPC in Berlin. IUSIPP president Raymond Pearl, a biology professor at the Johns Hopkins University School of Medicine, was unwilling to change the conference site after the Nazis came to power in Germany.[53]

Three Americans were officially registered as delegates: Dr. Clarence Campbell of New York, president of the Eugenics Research Association; Columbia University anthropology lecturer Bruno Oetteking; and Harvard University School of Public Health biostatistician Carl Doering, although the latter two could not attend. Another American, the prominent eugenicist Harry H. Laughlin, unable to go to Berlin, accepted the honorary position of conference vice president, also accorded to Campbell. Campbell, whom the Germans considered "enthusiastic for the Nordic race theory," presented Laughlin's paper on the "History and Legal Development of Eugenic Sterilization in the United States" to the conference. Laughlin argued that the US Congress had based its 1924 immigration restriction act on "biologic principles."[54]

Campbell delivered an address to the delegates praising the Nazis' "comprehensive racial policy of population development and improvement," which "promise[d] to be epochal in racial history." He denounced Western nations that based their political systems and demographic policies "upon the patent fallacy of human equality," ignoring "obviously biological realities."[55] Such speeches led the *New York Times* to describe the WPC as "another example of a staged [Nazi] propaganda assembly."[56]

"THE BEST JEW IS A DEAD JEW!" THE
BERLIN POGROMS, JULY 1935

On July 15, 1935, Nazi mobs numbering in the thousands began pogroms that turned Berlin's West End, in the words of the London *Daily Express*, into "one great anti-Jewish battlefield" that for several days resounded "with the ominous war cry 'Germany Awake! Perish Judaea!'" The pogroms were widely covered in the British, American, and French press. The *New York Times* reported in a front-page story that they "gave every evidence of careful planning." They were directed from the start by Nazi activists wearing civilian clothes over their brown shirts. The rioting began on the Kurfürstendamm, a major shopping boulevard, lined with sidewalk cafés. The *Daily Express* called it the worst mass anti-Jewish outbreak in Berlin since the April 1, 1933, national boycott of Jewish stores and offices. Mobs blocked traffic and "freely" smashed car windshields. Jewish men, women, and children were savagely beaten in the streets, shops, and cafés. The pogromists identified Jewish-owned businesses by plastering signs on them stating, "This is a Jewish shop," and warning, "To buy from Jews is treason." Policemen made no serious effort to intervene.[57]

Varian Fry, editor of the American magazine *Living Age*, who witnessed the July 15 pogrom on the Kurfürstendamm, testified that the pogromists were in a "holiday mood" as they brutally beat Jews they encountered on the streets or dragged out of passing automobiles. Men and women of all ages encouraged the pogromists, who periodically chanted, "The best Jew is a dead Jew!" Fry noted that many women in stylish evening gowns assisted the pogromists by pointing out persons they believed to be Jewish.[58]

The pogromists caused massive property damage, targeting Jewish-owned cafés, ice cream parlors, confectionaries, and other stores, smashing plate-glass windows and systematically destroying tables, chairs, and crockery. A pogromist hurled a stone at a girl working at the Jewish-owned Bristol Café, knocking her unconscious. At least one Jew died from injuries inflicted during the pogrom, and several were badly injured. Further attacks on Jews took place on the Kurfürstendamm and other Berlin streets, including some outside the West End, over the next several days.[59]

While the pogroms on the Kurfürstendamm were at their height, Joachim von Ribbentrop was "wining and dining" five members of the British Legion delegation to Germany, whom the German press had hailed as "messengers of a new era in British feeling toward the Third Reich." Concerned that the violence and bloodshed might tarnish the foreigners' favorable image of Nazi Germany, the Hitler government canceled a scheduled luncheon for them with the Steel Helmet League, a German veterans' group. The regime instead arranged for the delegates to be taken to Hermann Goering's shooting lodge, twenty-five miles outside Berlin. Goering was away at the time. His newspaper, the *National Zeitung* of Essen, assigned responsibility for the pogroms to Berlin's Jews, whose "insolence" in openly congregating in sidewalk cafés, as they had before the Nazis assumed power, angered the German people.[60]

Julius Streicher's antisemitic battalions, who had been hard at work disseminating defamatory propaganda against Jews in Berlin during the previous few weeks, helped maintain a pogrom-like atmosphere in Berlin during the weeks after the mob attacks. They put up signboards advertising *Der Stürmer* on the Kurfürstendamm and other Berlin streets, using medieval images of Jews' sexual depravity and greed. One, which depicted a Jewish man stripped naked and deprived of his possessions, promised, "This is how the Jews will be forced to leave Germany."[61] Another, captioned, "Wasteful Jewish sow," showed "an ugly, naked, pot-bellied man with a huge nose, thick lips, covering his genitals with his hands."[62] Berlin's only remaining Jewish-owned department store, Israel Brothers, was covered with hideous caricatures of Jews from *Der Stürmer* and the inscription "Whoever enters this place does so at his own risk."[63]

Pogromists also desecrated Berlin's synagogues. In the Prinzregentenstrasse, for example, they painted on the doors, outside walls, and steps of synagogues such inscriptions as "We hate you Stink-Jews" (*"Wir hassen euch StinkJuden"*), "Pig-Jews" (*"Sau-Juden"*), and "Out with the Jews!" (*"Juden Heraus"*).[64]

On July 19, as Berlin's street violence began to subside, the Hitler regime signaled that antisemitic persecution would intensify as it appointed Count Wolf von Helldorf, "whose hands," the French anti-Nazi newspaper *Le Droit de Vivre* declared, were "full of the blood of Jews," as Berlin's new police prefect. The article was entitled "Von Helldorf, Killer of Jews" (*"Tueur des Juifs"*). In the 1920s, von Helldorf had headed Freikorps assassination squads, and *Le Droit de Vivre* considered him possibly a more fanatical hater of Jews than even Julius Streicher. In 1931, von Helldorf had led the pogroms in Berlin, and in 1933 he had commanded the Berlin storm troopers when they tortured Jews, Social Democrats, and Communists in the Brown Houses. The London *Daily Telegraph* called him "one of the most sinister figures in the Germany of today." Josef

Goebbels's newspaper *Der Angriff* announced von Helldorf's mission in Berlin in a four-column headline: to cleanse the city of Jews and Communists.[65]

Le Droit de Vivre commented that what had just transpired in Berlin "was nothing compared to the news coming from the provinces." But the London *Daily Herald* recognized that von Helldorf's appointment telegraphed that he would bring "the capital into line with the terror-stricken cities of the provinces."[66]

Neither British nor American Jewry had much success in persuading their governments to protest the July Berlin pogroms. After receiving firsthand information about the pogroms from friends in Germany, American Jewish Committee (AJC) secretary Morris D. Waldman telephoned Neville Laski in London and asked that the BoD try to convince the British government to intercede with the Hitler regime to call a halt to them. Waldman reported to AJC president Cyrus Adler that Laski and Leonard Montefiore had tried to organize a deputation of "outstanding personalities representing the three major religious groups"—Protestant, Catholic, and Jewish—to meet with Prime Minister Baldwin for this purpose. Despite Laski and Montefiore's "strenuous efforts," however, they were unable to form such a deputation.[67]

British Jewish leaders did, however, make "vigorous and successful" efforts to press English newspapers to cover the Berlin pogroms. As a result, the highly influential and usually proappeasement London *Times*, which initially had "virtually ignored the events of the Kurfuerstendamm," now devoted fuller attention and produced "satisfactory editorials." Leonard Montefiore, speaking for the Joint Foreign Committee, maintained that it was only because the British press had fully reported the Berlin pogroms "that graver crimes had not taken place."[68]

Deeply alarmed by the Berlin pogroms, four of the leading American Jewish organizations—the AJC, the American Jewish Congress (AJCongress), B'nai B'rith, and the Jewish Labor Committee (JLC)—joined in forming a delegation to press the US government to officially condemn them. The AJCongress also proposed a protest at the German consulate in New York, but the AJC and B'nai B'rith continued to oppose street demonstrations. With Secretary of State Hull absent from Washington, Undersecretary of State William Phillips, serving as acting secretary, received the delegation. Phillips gave "assurances of sympathy" but made no promises of official US government action.[69] Waldman informed AJC president Adler that the situation in Berlin "was so serious as to warrant approach to a higher personage than the Under Secretary of State"—namely, President Roosevelt. To Waldman's great disappointment, however, despite AJC executive committee member Sol Stroock's strenuous effort to persuade the Roosevelt administration to intervene, "nothing was done at the White House."[70]

A few days after the Berlin pogroms began, the AJCongress and the JLC convened an emergency conference, held in the Grand Ballroom of the Hotel Pennsylvania in New York City, to express outrage at the attacks and the lack of response by the US government. Although the conference was called with only five days' notice, the turnout was enormous, with hundreds of people turned away after the ballroom had filled to capacity. Principal speakers included Louis Lipsky, AJCongress acting president, who presided; JLC chair Baruch Charney Vladeck; *Tog* editor Dr. Samuel Margoshes; *Vorverts* editor Abraham Cahan; *Jewish Morning Journal* editor Jacob Fishman; and Amalgamated Clothing Workers secretary Joseph Schlossberg. The speakers expressed their "disappointment over the reticence of the President of the United States" concerning the Berlin pogroms. Lipsky condemned "the strange reluctance on the part of the Government of the United States, in any of its branches, to align itself with humanitarian sentiments, to denounce wrong, to . . . make a gesture even of public sympathy" for Berlin's Jews. Margoshes denounced President Roosevelt for failing to speak out about the pogroms, despite having issued a strong declaration of concern the previous week about the persecution of Catholics in Mexico. Fishman "deplored the silence of official Washington," stressing that "neither the White House nor the State Department has as yet uttered a word of displeasure at the renewed Nazi outrages." He contrasted Roosevelt's inaction with previous administrations' public condemnation of and sanctions against European nations for persecuting Jews: "Within our memory, the late Secretary Hay dispatched a stinging note to Rumania for its mistreatment of the Jews, and the late President Taft abrogated a commercial treaty with Russia for similar acts." The conference determined to fight Nazism through the boycott of German goods and services and the forthcoming Olympic Games in Berlin and demanded the termination of student and faculty exchanges with German universities.[71]

AMERICAN GRASSROOTS ANTI-NAZI PROTEST PROVOKES HITLER REGIME OUTRAGE

In 1935, large-scale grassroots protests against antisemitism in the Third Reich were staged in New York and Minneapolis. The New York demonstrations precipitated fierce German diplomatic protests. The first occurred in a socialist May Day parade in New York City, in which more than half the sixty thousand participants were needle trades workers. The Ladies Neckwear Union, part of the heavily Jewish International Ladies Garment Workers Union, marched alongside a float on which was mounted a gallows in the shape of a swastika. Hanging from the gallows was a brown-shirted effigy of Hitler. Under the effigy the Neckwear Workers Union had placed the statement "We'll supply the neckwear."[72]

On May 23, an angry Hans Luther, German ambassador to the United States, called on Secretary of State Hull, presenting him with pictures of the hanging Hitler effigy clipped from the *New York World-Telegram* and New York *Daily News*. Hull told Luther that he found the incident "disagreeable" and "would see what could be done, if anything." Dr. Rudolf Leitner, chargé d'affaires at the German embassy in Washington, on July 29 informed James Clement Dunn, of the State Department's Division of Western European Affairs, that before his recent departure for Germany, Ambassador Luther had pressed Secretary Hull "on more than one occasion," about the May 1 hanging of Hitler in effigy. Hull had promised to report back to Luther but had not yet done so. Dunn promised Leitner he would look into the matter.[73]

On July 26, a "wild anti-Hitler demonstration" by two thousand persons protesting the presence in New York harbor of the German liner *Bremen* climaxed with some storming the ship, tearing the swastika flag from the pole on the bow, and throwing it in the Hudson River. New York policemen repeatedly charged the anti-Nazi crowd gathered on or near the docks, freely swinging their clubs for at least half an hour before succeeding in dispersing it. Five demonstrators were arrested on the charge of unlawful assembly and one for striking a police detective with brass knuckles. The attack on the swastika flag provoked a furious response from the Hitler government and a public expression of regret from Assistant Secretary of State Wilbur Carr.[74]

The week of the demonstration against the *Bremen*, in a step toward breaking diplomatic relations with the Reich, Senator William H. King (a Democrat from Utah) introduced a resolution directing the Foreign Relations Committee to investigate religious persecution in Germany. The *Washington Post* commented that "it is expected that the State Department will have it pigeon-holed."[75]

In early September, Magistrate Louis Brodsky, who was Jewish, dismissed the charges against the five defendants accused of unlawful assembly. Brodsky equated the swastika banner torn from the *Bremen* with "the black flag of piracy." He compared the men who ripped it down to the heroes of the Boston Tea Party. Brodsky declared from the bench that the swastika flag represented "war on religious freedom; the disenfranchisement of nationals solely on religious or ethnological grounds; the debasement of the learned professions; the deprivation of the right to education and the earning of a livelihood, [and] the enslavement of women and workers." Brodsky denounced Nazism as a "revolt against civilization . . . an atavistic throwback to pre-medieval . . . social and political conditions."[76]

Sir Eric Phipps notified the British Foreign Office that upon learning of Magistrate Brodsky's release of these men, Hitler "exploded" and immediately had his Cabinet give him sanction "to put the swastika out of reach of insult by Galician Jews of the Brodsky type in New York or anywhere else." Hitler had the Reichstag pass the Reich Flag Law, making the swastika flag the national flag. The German press explained Brodsky's dismissal of the charges with the claim that Jews, as wanderers without a country, had no understanding of or sympathy for patriotism. Some German newspapers described him as "a tool of dark Jewish Bolshevik powers."[77]

Hitler instructed the German embassy in Washington, DC, to lodge an official protest against Magistrate Brodsky's release of the five defendants and his statements about Nazism and the German government. Hull invited Rudolf Leitner to call at the State Department to discuss the protest, because Luther was away from Washington at the time. Hull told Leitner that he regretted that Brodsky had made a point of criticizing the Hitler government when announcing his decision. The Secretary of State informed Leitner, however, "that so long as wild news reports" about anti-Jewish violence and persecution in Germany continued to reach the United States, some Americans would continue to use what Hull considered heated rhetoric in discussing the Reich.[78]

Hitler was pleased that the State Department had, in his words, "disavowed" Magistrate Brodsky's dismissal of charges against five defendants. He declared that the US government's expression of regret to Germany over the actions of a Jewish judge showed that the Nazis were justified in suppressing "Jewish influence."[79]

In a Rosh Hashanah sermon at the Free Synagogue in New York on September 27, Rabbi Stephen S. Wise, president of the AJCongress, denounced the US government for "apologizing with exaggerated profuseness and abjectness to the Nazi regime" for Magistrate Brodsky's reference to the Nazi banner as a pirate flag. Wise lamented that the US government had failed to use the *Bremen* incident to utter even "one brave word in condemnation of the program and practices of the Nazi regime." It appeared to share the Hitler government's objection to Brodsky's labeling the swastika banner a "pirate flag." Wise thought Brodsky had been unfair to pirates. He had never "heard of pirates who rob and maim and slay their own neighbors and countrymen."[80]

Brodsky was guest of honor at a reception held on December 2, 1935, in Paris, attended by lawyers from many nations who were in the city to attend the conference of the International Juridical Association. The conference had been convened to discuss juridical issues relating to Nazi Germany, including political prisoners and the legal status of German Jews.[81]

In November, seventy Jewish organizations in Minnesota released a joint statement that denounced Ambassador Hans Luther's upcoming appearance in Minneapolis to address the Civic and Commerce Association as "an affront to all-freedom loving citizens" and called on city residents to boycott it. Policemen had to escort Luther through an anti-Nazi picket line in front of the hotel at which he delivered his speech praising the Hitler regime to a friendly audience of businessmen. Alarmed by the vigor of the protest, the University of Minnesota administration made sure that Luther's scheduled visit to campus would be limited to an invitation-only tea sponsored by the sympathetic German department. The administration barred from the tea fifty uninvited anti-Nazi students who planned to question Luther about Nazi antisemitic policies.[82]

OFFICIAL CONDEMNATION OF NAZI PERSECUTION BY THE MASSACHUSETTS HOUSE OF REPRESENTATIVES

Less than a month after the *Bremen* demonstration, the Massachusetts House of Representatives passed without debate a resolution condemning the Hitler regime's persecution of "certain inhabitants of Germany . . . on account of their religious faith and nationality to an extent abhorrent to modern civilization." The Massachusetts House became the first state legislative body to officially condemn the Hitler regime. No one could miss the legislature's intent in denouncing Nazi antisemitism. The State Department expressed its displeasure. Representative Thomas Dorgan of Boston, one of the resolution's cosponsors, called on all legislative bodies to lodge similar protests with the German government.[83]

The Hitler regime was outraged at the resolution and at Massachusetts governor James Michael Curley, who "refused to back down an inch" on the House's right to pass it. Governor Curley made it clear that the resolution represented "a formal expression of the opinion of the public as a whole." The German consul general in Boston, Baron von Tippelskirch, immediately wrote to the Massachusetts House of Representatives to "mind its own business" and not interfere in Germany's internal affairs. The German press used blatantly antisemitic terminology in condemning the House of Representatives as the "Pharisees of Boston." As the scholars of antisemitism Marvin Perry and Frederick Schweitzer noted, "anti-Pharisaism has been virtually synonymous with antisemitism and a source of inflamed hatred of Jews." Boston Jewish leaders—Samuel Kaletsky, president of the Boston AJCongress; Rabbi Joseph Shubow, also an AJCongress leader; and JLC chair Leon Arkin—praised the House of Representatives resolution as "statesmanlike" and denounced von Tippelskirch as a spokesman for a regime that stood for "criminality, murder, kidnapping, and arson."[84]

The US State Department's response differed markedly from that of the Jewish leaders. The *Christian Science Monitor* reported that the State Department, concerned with maintaining amicable relations with Germany, "wished to avoid all unnecessary or undignified provocation." It "regard[ed] the whole situation with considerable regret."[85]

BRITISH ANTI-NAZI PROTEST

In Britain, the BoD found it increasingly difficult to persuade prominent Christians to speak out against Nazi antisemitism. On July 23, 1935, Neville Laski, its president, called on the Reverend Alan Don, chaplain and secretary to the archbishop of Canterbury, leader of the Church of England, and proposed that the archbishop, representatives of the Free Churches, and the chief rabbi join in asking for an interview with the prime minister to discuss the subject. Don emphasized to Laski that the archbishop "would take no part in protest meetings, and indeed would strongly dissuade them." After conferring with the archbishop, Don informed Laski that although "His Grace fully shares your misgivings at the recrudescence of anti-Jewish and anti-Christian propaganda and persecution in Germany" he "has not a moment of time between now and his departure on August 5 for his much-needed holiday."[86]

The most significant outdoor mass rally against Nazism in Britain in 1935 was staged on October 27 in London's Hyde Park by an estimated twenty to forty thousand people. It was organized in July, in response to the Berlin pogroms. The rally was one of the largest demonstrations against the Hitler regime that had been held in England. It was sponsored by the British Non-Sectarian Anti-Nazi Council, a coalition of Jewish and non-Jewish antifascists, including Labour Party leaders and activists, Trades Union Congress head Walter Citrine, and feminist activists. The BoD, still opposed to public street demonstrations, declined the Anti-Nazi Council's invitation to cosponsor the rally, and Neville Laski refused its request to be one of the speakers. Anti-Nazi street processions from several parts of London, displaying banners and accompanied by bands, converged at Hyde Park, joining crowds already assembled there. The *Manchester Guardian* reported that "nearly all the marchers were young, the great proportion were Jews, and many men wore war medals." Most of the Jews had trudged five miles from the East End.[87]

Rally speakers, who included members of Parliament from all three parties, addressed audiences from six platforms. Labour Party leader Clement Attlee declared that what was at stake was whether the world would move forward to civilization or backward to barbarism. Labour MP Josiah Wedgwood, high-lighting German Jews' desperate predicament, "was almost tempted to say that it would have been better for [them] to have gone through the quick terror of a pogrom than to undergo this slow, silent agonizing extermination by economic strangulation." Lord Marley called the boycott the best weapon against "the steel whip and the concentration camp." Independent MP Eleanor Rathbone told the crowd that "it was deplorable that British people should travel in Ger-many since when there they become . . . guests of the German Government." Professor J. B. S. Haldane asked the demonstrators the next time they saw a British woman wearing German-made clothes to "tell her she is paying for a bomb to blow her children to bits." Sylvia Pankhurst, "fiery suffragist of former years," and ninety-one-year-old Charlotte Despard, another veteran of that movement, who traveled to the rally from Belfast, also gave speeches.[88] At the rally's end, the sounding of a bugle signaled the taking of the vote on endorsing the boycott of German goods and services. The "great gathering" passed the resolution with "a great unanimous shout of approval."[89]

PROGRESS WITH THE BOYCOTT

In the United States, the boycott campaign was very well organized and effec-tive in New York and was conducted in several other major cities. It remained, however, primarily a Jewish movement. Abraham Goldberg, vice president of the Zionist Organization of America, acknowledged that the campaign had arisen from the Jewish masses and enjoyed their wide support. The AJCon-gress remained concerned, however, about "the lukewarm response of the non-Jewish population of the United States." When the American Non-Sectarian Anti-Nazi League (NSANL) established a chapter in Philadelphia in 1935, all seventy-five of the women willing to serve on its organizing committee were Jewish. In the months before the Christmas season of 1935, the NSANL dis-tributed 360,000 leaflets in New York and "throughout the country," appealing to shoppers not to purchase German toys and Christmas tree ornaments. The Baltimore chapter made a concerted attempt to hand boycott leaflets to gentile shoppers. The NSANL also received "good reports" of its chapters' work to promote the boycott in Pittsburgh and Cleveland.[90] The American role in the boycott campaign became increasingly important as European governments, especially in Poland and other Eastern European countries, clamped down on their Jewish communities' boycott efforts.[91]

The boycott movement made some headway in 1935 in forging alliances with labor organizations. The American Federation of Labor and its affiliates, particularly those with heavily Jewish memberships, such as the needle trades unions, began to cooperate with the AJCongress and the NSANL. In New York City, the AJCongress formed a united boycott front with the Central Council of Trades. After an anti-Nazi speech by JLC chair Leon Arkin at its annual convention in August, the Massachusetts State Federation of Labor passed a resolution calling for a boycott of German goods. The federation asked local unions to appoint committees "to visit merchants and ask them not to stock their shelves with such goods."[92]

To carry out the tasks necessary to enforce the consumers' boycott, the New York NSANL divided the city into districts and established a committee in each to determine which stores displayed German merchandise. Committee members warned every owner who continued to sell German goods that he or she would be boycotted. The NSANL's Legal Committee handled cases where goods were mislabeled to disguise their German origin. The Research Division provided consumers with names and addresses of enterprises that stocked non-German goods. For suppliers, it identified alternate sources of the desired products not only in the United States but also in Czechoslovakia, Poland, and other countries.[93]

As concern over Germany's rapid arms buildup mounted, the NSANL joined with the American Federation of Labor in a mass protest meeting at New York City's Hippodrome around the rallying cry "The Economic Boycott Is the Answer to the Nazi War Menace." The two thousand persons in attendance endorsed a resolution that warned that German rearmament was increasing the probability of "catastrophic war" and called on the League of Nations to support the boycott by imposing economic sanctions on the Reich. Speakers included NSANL vice president Rabbi Abba Hillel Silver and—reflecting close Anglo-American cooperation in the boycott—Helen Bentwich, wife of Norman Bentwich, prominent Zionist and former attorney general of Palestine. Helen Bentwich was herself a Labour candidate for Parliament.[94]

Similarly, the AJCongress established vigilance committees that visited stores, both retail and wholesale, determining if they were selling German goods. The AJCongress often picketed businesses stocking German products, including the "billion dollar chain stores," and it submitted lists of those firms to the press for publication. It also examined every shipment of goods coming into New York from Germany and appealed to importers and buyers to stop handling them.[95]

A testimonial dinner that the AJCongress arranged at the Hotel Commodore in New York in May 1935 for its outgoing president, Bernard Deutsch, provided the occasion to rally the American public behind the boycott. Chaired by motion picture executive Harry Warner, the dinner was attended by one thousand people. Rabbi Stephen S. Wise, the new AJCongress president, characterized the boycott as a display of "moral firmness and great resistance." In his address, Deutsch "outlined the development of the boycott and reiterated its importance." He used the dinner as an opportunity to praise the contribution of Samuel Untermyer and the NSANL to the boycott movement. The audience heartily endorsed this "gesture of harmony" between the two largest proboycott organizations.[96]

Over the year, the American boycott movement scored some notable and well-publicized successes. In July, the Chemnitz correspondent of the London *Times* reported that American buyers were placing most of their orders for gloves in Czechoslovakia, even though they acknowledged that German gloves were "better finished in every way." The buyers were determined to boycott the German-made gloves as long as the German government held to its antisemitic policies. In August the London *Jewish Chronicle* found that the American boycott movement had delivered another blow to German shipping. The American Organization of Buyers of Dresses threatened to cancel their orders with all French dressmaking firms shipping their products on German vessels. The Hotel Astor, one of New York's best-known hotels, cancelled reservations for a German-American Technologists' convention, after it received numerous complaints that its organizers insisted on displaying the swastika flag. The New Yorker Hotel, one of the city's largest, would not permit a similar German-sponsored convention for the same reason.[97]

In April 1935, British ambassador Sir Eric Phipps informed Foreign Secretary John Simon that Germany's foreign trade outlook was "not so rosy," suggesting that the boycott was having a serious impact. He noted a "retrogression of about 25 percent in the rate of exports of manufactured goods," even as Germany's industrial productivity had increased significantly. Phipps pointed out that Germany was dependent on export trade, "not merely for an adequate supply of foodstuffs and raw materials for its workers, its industries, and rearmament, but for the satisfaction of foreign financial claims upon it." The Hitler regime therefore had to view Germany's decline in exports "with great alarm." On July 11, Phipps told Leonard Montefiore that German trade, especially with the United States, had been "severely hit" by the boycott.[98]

THE NUREMBERG RACE LAWS: THE
SOCIAL GHETTO COMPLETED

On September 15, the Hitler government passed the "long-expected" Nuremberg laws, which stripped Germany's Jews of their citizenship and "formally . . . proscribed the whole Jewish community of the Reich." German Jewry was placed in a "social ghetto." Jews were not allowed to marry or have sexual relations with "Aryans" or to employ "Aryan" women younger than forty-five as domestic servants. As the London *Jewish Chronicle* observed, the denial of citizenship to Jews and the formation of a "social ghetto" had been a prime Nazi Party objective since its formation in 1920. The Nuremberg laws, in large part, just legalized a system that already existed in practice. The *Jewish Chronicle* noted that in many parts of Germany the judiciary had already issued rulings against marriages between Jews and "Aryans," forced Jewish children out of German schools, and "virtually excluded" them from the army. It added that in Breslau, the courts had "recently decided that even friendship" between a Jew and an "Aryan" "amounts to 'racial desecration,' to be punished apparently with arrest and the concentration camp."[99]

Newspaper reports and editorials across the United States viewed the Nuremberg laws with foreboding. On September 17, the *New York Herald Tribune* ran a front-page article headlined "Nazis Restore Ghetto . . . Jew-Less Nation Their Ultimate Goal." It stated that the Nazis' aim appeared to be the "elimination of all Jews from Germany." From Nuremberg, Otto Tolischus began his report for the *New York Times*, "National Socialist Germany definitely flung down the gauntlet before the feet of Western liberal opinion tonight when the Reichstag, assembled for a special session here . . . decreed a series of laws that put Jews beyond the legal and social pale of the German nation."[100]

The tone of the coverage in small and medium-sized towns was just as ominous. The Richmond (VA) *Leader*'s editorial, published the same day as Tolischus's article, was entitled "Worse than Kishinev." It declared that "in the great Russian pogroms of 1903, made memorable by mass murders at Kishinev, 810 persons lost their lives and 1,700 were injured. The German [Nuremberg] decrees, sharpened by the new denial of citizenship, outlaw close to two million people." The Nashville *Tennessean* editorial, published the next day, stated that the Nuremberg laws had "legislated [the Jew] into . . . a place similar to that he held in the Middle Ages." The *Pottsville* (PA) *Journal*'s editorial on September 18, 1935, called the Nuremberg laws "a startling innovation, because up to now the alien in a foreign land has had the protection of his home government, whereas the Jews in the Reich have no home government except that of Germany."[101]

The Nuremberg laws "created a panic among German Jewry." The JTA declared that "more than ever German Jews feel . . . their only chance is to emigrate." It was "difficult to visualize the misery of the Jews in Germany." The London *Jewish Chronicle* reported that in villages around Frankfurt, the announcement of the new laws "was taken as a signal for an organized onslaught on the Jewish inhabitants." Antisemitic mobs broke all the windows of every Jewish house or shop. Jews attempting to resist the mobs were "met with brutal maltreatment." The mobs burst into Jewish homes and dragged all "Aryan" house servants from their beds, ordering them never to return to their jobs, even though the ban on their employment did not take effect until January 1, 1936. The JTA stated that in Barth, Pomerania, a crowd gathered around the municipal building, demanding the "immediate expulsion" of the only two remaining Jewish families. It dispersed only when Barth's mayor announced that one of the families, which had Polish citizenship, had contacted the Polish consulate about leaving Germany, and the other had applied for permits to immigrate to Palestine.[102]

In the absence of any firm response by the British and American governments to the Nuremberg race laws, the boycott was the only weapon the Jews had with which to fight back. Upon the September 15 passage of the Nuremberg laws, British Labour Party activist A. L. Easterman wrote that world Jewry was "preparing to meet the challenge of this new[est] peril" by intensifying the boycott campaign. He declared that the Nuremberg "Jewish outcast law" was "the climax of Nazi persecution, short of mass massacre." Rabbi Stephen S. Wise denounced "the crime of Nuremberg, a crime that was to be expected." He demanded to know why the "civilized world" did not "intervene and protest against its destroying enemies." Wise cabled Edouard Benes, president of the League of Nations General Assembly, that the Nuremberg laws "destroy the basis of modern civilization and of the League of Nations."[103]

The London *Jewish Chronicle* maintained that German Jewry's condition was already so miserable that the Nuremberg laws "add[ed] little, beyond the stamp of officialdom, to [its] present disabilities." It mattered little to the German Jew whether he was "bullied and hounded" legally or arbitrarily. The Jew's life was unbearable either way, and the purpose was the same: "the elimination of a community of half-a-million souls."[104]

After the passage of the Nuremberg laws, the BoD came under immediate pressure to reconsider its position on the boycott. On July 22, the London *Daily*

Herald had reported that "a fierce struggle" over endorsing the boycott was taking place within the BoD, with "a large number of members" challenging the leadership's opposition to officially backing the boycott. On September 16, the day after the Nuremberg laws were passed, Sidney Salomon, editor of the *Yorkshire Post*, told Neville Laski' that the BoD's failure to give the boycott official support gave "the impression of weakness." He charged that the BoD had adopted its position under pressure from the Foreign Office. The boycott was the only effective weapon against the newly enacted legislation "that threatens to recreate the Ghetto."[105]

The BoD responded to the Nuremberg "outcast" laws by convening an emergency meeting on October 2 to address "the new peril facing German Jewry." The London *Daily Herald* reported that the gathering, attended by two hundred deputies, was "the most solemn . . . since the anti-Jewish terror in Germany began over two and a half years before." Those present "listened in tense silence to the . . . indictment of Nazi Germany delivered by the president, Mr. Neville Laski." Laski declared that the Nuremberg laws "gave the sanction of law" to "the insanity" of Nazi racial ideology, which caused Jews to be treated like lepers. The meeting unanimously passed a resolution expressing the BoD's "deep sense of outrage" at this "latest stage" in the "public degradation" of German Jewry. Although still unwilling to call for an official boycott, the emergency meeting reaffirmed a resolution the BoD had passed on November 18, 1934, "that no self-respecting Jew will handle German goods or utilize German services."[106]

The AJC, AJCongress, and B'nai B'rith joined in signing a strongly worded condemnation of the Nuremberg laws, which stated, "This debasement of the Jews was not the result of a sudden decision." These laws had been "pledged by the National Socialist Party at its foundation" and "were only the official culmination of a series of measures degrading and oppressing German Jews."[107]

THE ANGLO-GERMAN FOOTBALL MATCH:
PRELUDE TO THE NAZI OLYMPICS

The year 1935 closed with large-scale labor and grassroots Jewish protests against a December 4 football (soccer) match at Southampton, England, between teams from Britain and the Reich, which proappeasement circles in Britain exploited to promote Anglo-German fraternity. The protests were part of the larger, very bitter controversy that erupted in both Britain and the United States over the summer 1936 Olympic Games in Berlin. Nazi sports officials Hans von Tschammer-und-Osten and Dr. Frein, president and secretary, respectively, of the Olympic Games Committee in Berlin, were prominently involved in planning the December 1935 football match between a British and a German team. The British government showed no sympathy for those who challenged the visit of the German team and the ten thousand Nazis who accompanied them, traveling under the auspices of the Nazi Party "Strength through Joy" organization. About eight thousand of these Nazis made the Channel crossing in eight specially chartered boats. Nineteen trains were hired to bring the Germans to Southampton, the site of the match, after their arrival in England.[108]

The British Trades Union Congress (TUC) and Jewish grassroots protestors strongly objected to representatives of the Nazi regime being received in Britain as honored guests. Joseph Toole, a British trade union protestor, wrote a letter to the *Manchester Guardian* taking issue with Sir William Edge, a Liberal member of Parliament, who charged that the TUC had "covered itself with ridicule" in challenging the match. Toole noted that the TUC's position was consistent with its long-standing support of the boycott of German goods and services and denunciation of Hitler's "murder, butchery, and wanton destruction," all of which the *Guardian* had documented. Toole stated that a year ago in London he had met Dr. Rudolf Breitscheid, former Social Democratic Reichstag deputy. Breitscheid told him that the Nazis had confiscated his life savings, his business, and his home and had forced his wife and son to flee Germany. The Nazis had driven Breitscheid into exile in Prague.[109]

Neither the TUC nor grassroots Jews had any success in persuading the British government to cancel the match. The TUC formally protested to Home Secretary Sir John Simon, who responded that the football match had "no political implications." British ambassador to Germany Sir Eric Phipps told Foreign Secretary Anthony Eden that the TUC was "wrong in protesting against an Anglo-German football match" and that "Sir John Simon had good reason to rebuke them." Phipps did concede, however, that the TUC was right in pointing out that "there was no such thing as sport for sport's sake in Germany." There was "only sport for the sake of war . . . to increase physical fitness with an ultimate view to prowess on the field of battle."[110]

English sporting officials worked with von Tschammer-und-Osten and Frein in arranging Britain's participation in the upcoming Berlin Olympics and strongly condemned the protestors. The Rev. Herbert Dunnico, former Deputy Speaker of the House of Commons and chair of the Counties Association of Football Clubs, denounced the TUC for what he called its "gratuitous and impertinent interference" with the German team's visit. He ridiculed the anti-Nazi protestors as a "small but noisy section of people . . . incapable of living up to the high traditions of British sportsmanship"—implying that the trade unionists and Jews were incapable of conducting themselves as gentlemen. The London *Times* disparaged the protestors as anti-German bigots bent on sabotaging a prime opportunity for "promoting international good feeling."[111]

BoD president Neville Laski resented that Barnett Jenner, Labour MP for heavily Jewish Whitechapel in London's East End, had assumed a prominent role in the protests without having consulted "responsible people" like himself and Leonard Montefiore. Laski complained to AJC secretary Morris Waldman that the "aggressive conduct of Jews in the forefront of the matter" was a grave mistake, likely to precipitate an antisemitic backlash. He believed that Jenner was pandering to his proboycott working- and lower-middle-class Jewish constituents. Laski was relieved that the TUC, rather than Jewish leaders, had "tak[en] . . . .the limelight" by appealing to the Home Secretary to cancel the game.[112]

British sports officials and fans began fraternizing with the German athletes and visitors immediately upon their arrival, even as the latter openly displayed their ardent support for Nazism. A large crowd enthusiastically welcomed the German football team at Croydon Airport, as its trainer and the players gave the Nazi salute. Walter Citrine was able to extract a promise from the Home Office that the Germans would not march in procession through the London streets, sing Nazi songs, or wear swastika badges. Many British anti-Nazis had feared that the Germans would make a "triumphal progress" through the city. Some of the players, however, wore "gold badges in a modified form of the swastika design." The German and English teams attended the theater in London together.[113]

The Anglo-German football match itself provided the Germans the occasion to stage a highly visible Nazi demonstration, which most of the British spectators appeared to find acceptable. Despite the Home Office's assurances, some of the German visitors sang Nazi songs and waved swastika flags before the contest, and hundreds waved these flags during the game as well. The seventy thousand in attendance greeted both teams "with tremendous and impartial applause." When the band played the German national anthem, "Deutschland über Alles," the Germans in the stands, "like a huge, well-trained choir," rose and sang it with right arms outstretched in the Nazi salute. The British spectators removed their hats and stood at attention. The Germans then joined the British in singing "God Save the King," still giving the Nazi salute.[114]

The Nazi press in Germany considered the game a great success, even though England had by far the better team and won 3 to 0. Hitler's Chancellery and Goering's office closely monitored the game and were impressed by the warm

British reception for the Germans. The official Reich news agency expressed delight over what it called "a game of friendship in the true sense of the word."[115]

After the game, British sports officials sponsored a dinner for the German team at London's Victoria Hotel at which Sir Charles Clegg, president of the English Football Association (FA), apologized for the "annoyance" the TUC had caused by meddling in "a matter absolutely outside their business." "Amid thunderous applause," Clegg declared that he hoped it would be the last time the TUC would ever interfere. The Germans present "stood smartly at attention" when Clegg toasted King George V and as "God Save the King" was played. Then, as the FA's vice president, W. Pickford, gave the toast for Adolf Hitler, the Germans "as one" gave the Nazi salute and sang the Nazi Party anthem, the "Horst Wessel Lied." In remembrance of what he called "the momentous and happy visit," Clegg presented a silver rose bowl to Dr. W. Erbach, leader of the German visiting party. The Germans in turn gave the English athletes and officials a "beautiful porcelain cup." Von Tschammer-und-Osten spoke of the strong fraternal bonds that Britain and Germany had forged through sports.[116]

*   *   *

In 1935, the US and British governments looked away as Nazi Germany worked tirelessly to increase its military power on the ground, at sea, and in the air in order to realize its expansionist goals, including gaining control of the Jewish populations to its east and south and preparing for the next war, when it would destroy them. Lord Vansittart recalled that the "British thought wishfully, the Americans not at all." On December 10, 1935, Ambassador Phipps expressed his concern to Foreign Secretary Eden that Germany was "fast becoming the most powerful military nation in Europe." Phipps emphasized that German youth were being "trained from childhood to regard war as inevitable."[117]

The British Legion, the nation's leading veterans' organization, which shared the government's appeasement outlook and publicly promoted it, enthusiastically spearheaded efforts to forge friendly bonds with German veterans' groups. After a visit to Dachau, the British Legion leadership also helped disseminate Nazi propaganda by presenting a roseate view of camp conditions and prisoners' health. Similarly, the Anglo-German football match promoted friendly relations between Britain and the Third Reich and helped pave the way for the Hitler regime's propaganda triumph in the 1936 Berlin Olympic Games.

Despite significant Jewish and labor grassroots protest in the United States and England, neither the American nor the British political leadership warned about the impact of Germany's rapid rearmament on European Jewry or publicly expressed concern about the Hitler regime's intensely antisemitic measures. Neither government publicly denounced the savage July pogroms in Berlin. In September 1935, the Nuremberg laws made Jews' status as a pariah caste fully legal, again without public protest from the American or British government. Lord Vansittart noted that "the passing of the Nuremberg Laws made no impact" in Britain.[118]

In his 1966 memoir of the interwar period, Harold Macmillan, an antiappeasement MP during the 1930s, lamented that when Hitler assumed power nobody in the West had "bothered to read *Mein Kampf*." Certainly, the widespread familiarity with *Mein Kampf* would have allowed Western statesmen and political commentators to grasp Hitler's foreign and domestic policy intentions. As Saul Friedländer pointed out, *Mein Kampf* depicted the Jews as both "a superhuman force driving the peoples of the world to perdition" and "a subhuman cause of infection, disintegration and death."[119] In it Hitler also outlined his plans for German expansion and conquest throughout Central and Eastern Europe. The British ambassador to Germany in 1935, Sir Eric Phipps, was among the few in high government posts who were recommending *Mein Kampf* as a guide to Germany's objectives. Even Phipps, however, did not accord much attention to the impact of German military expansion on European Jewry. Still, he did point out in a December 1935 letter to Foreign Secretary Anthony Eden that the Nuremberg laws were foretold in *Mein Kampf*. He also noted that Nazi racial theories in *Mein Kampf* called for a union of all Germans in Europe "on account of the affinity of blood." This could be achieved only through German expansion eastward "at the expense of Russia and the Baltic states."[120] Yet in the next several years, both the British and American governments failed to take steps to prevent this eastward expansion, which would, within the decade, result in the annihilation of most of Eastern European Jewry and its thousand-year-old culture.

NOTES

1. "Frustrated Jewish Hopes in Germany," *New Statesman*, April 20, 1935, 545.

2. "Julius Streicher," November 28, 1935, ACC/3123/C11/12/21, Board of Deputies of British Jews (hereafter, BoD) Papers, London Metropolitan Archives (hereafter, LMA), London, UK.

3. *Daily Herald* (London), August 8, 1935, 1, 2; "The Ghetto Walls Contract: Jews Barred from Trams, Cinemas, and Shops," *Jewish Chronicle* (London), August 30, 1935, 16.

4. *The Yellow Spot: The Extermination of the Jews in Germany* (London: Victor Gollancz, 1936), 186.

5. "Jews Not Wanted," *Jewish Chronicle* (London), August 2, 1935, 13; "Jews Expelled from Villages: A Countrywide Campaign; Towns Refuse Aid," *Jewish Chronicle* (London), August 30, 1935, 15.

6. "Extremists in the Saddle: Jews Boycotted Everywhere," *Jewish Chronicle* (London), August 30, 1935, 16; "Confidential Report Issued by the Jewish Telegraphic Agency, Inc.," December 16, 1935, no. 3, box 174, Arthur Hays Sulzberger Papers (hereafter, Sulzberger Papers), Archives and Manuscripts Division (hereafter, AMD), New York Public Library (hereafter, NYPL), New York, NY.

7. "Teaching the Children to Hate," *Jewish Chronicle* (London), September 6, 1935, 18.

8. "Confidential Report," December 16, 1935.

9. Sir Eric Phipps to Sir Anthony Eden, December 10, 1935, 1/15, Sir Eric Phipps Papers (hereafter, Phipps Papers), Churchill College, University of Cambridge, Cambridge, UK.

10. *Times* (London), September 17, 1935, 15; "Nazis Proclaim a Ghetto," *Jewish Chronicle* (London), September 20, 1935, 9.

11. Sir John Simon, diary entries for March 18, 1935, and May 2, 1935, MS-7, Sir John Simon Papers, Bodleian Library Special Collections, University of Oxford, Oxford, UK; Sir Eric Phipps to Sir John Simon, April 1, 1935, 1/14, and Phipps to Sir Anthony Eden, January 6, 1936, 1/16, Phipps Papers, Churchill College, Cambridge.

12. Frederick T. Birchall to Edwin L. James, April 28, 1933, box 175, Sulzberger Papers, AMD, NYPL.

13. Robert Dell, *The Truth about Germany* (New York: American Jewish Congress, n.d.), 6/6, Robert Dell Papers, London School of Economics and Political Science Library Archives, London, UK.

14. Lord Robert Vansittart, "The Future of Germany," April 9, 1934, 1/10 Cabinet, Lord Robert Vansittart Papers (hereafter, Vansittart Papers), Churchill College, Cambridge.

15. William E. Dodd to R. Walton Moore, Assistant Secretary of State, November 5, 1934, box 32, series 3, Diplomatic Correspondence, Franklin D. Roosevelt, Papers as President: The President's Secretary's File, 1933–1945, Franklin D. Roosevelt Presidential Library and Museum, Hyde Park, NY.

16. Martin Gilbert, *Sir Horace Rumbold* (London: Heinemann, 1973), 384; Leon Dominian, American Consul, Stuttgart, to Honorable Secretary of State, "Subject: Increased Activity in Air Protection Movement in the Stuttgart Protection District," September 18, 1933, box 6779, Central Decimal Files (hereafter, CDF), 1930–39, Department of State General Records, Record Group (hereafter, RG) 59, National Archives, College Park, MD (hereafter, NA-CP).

17. German Armaments, Die Deutsche Aufrüstung, memorandum on the "German League for the Rights of Man," April 1934, 2, 8/4, Vansittart Papers, Churchill College, Cambridge.

18. Gaynor Johnson, ed., *Our Man in Berlin: The Diary of Sir Eric Phipps, 1933–1937* (London: Palgrave Macmillan, 2008), 52.

19. Vansittart, "Future of Germany."

20. Lord Robert Vansittart, *The Mist Procession* (London: Hutchinson, 1958), 497–98; Sir John Simon, diary entry for May 22, 1935, MS-7, Sir John Simon Papers, Bodleian Library, Oxford.

21. *Daily Herald* (London), June 3, 1935.

22. Dodd to Moore, November 5, 1934.

23. Lt. Commander Wyatt, "General Comments on German Aviation following a Two-Week Inspection of Aviation Activities in Germany," December 18, 1935, box 6779, CDF 1930–39, Department of State General Records, RG 59, NA-CP.

24. "Julius Streicher," November 28, 1935, ACC 3123/C11/12/21, BoD Papers, LMA.

25. Sir Eric Phipps to Sir Samuel Hoare, November 13, 1935, no. 19, C7647/55/18, "The German Danger. A Collection of Reports from the Accession of Herr Hitler to Power in the Spring of 1933 to the end of 1935," CP 13 (36), Cabinet Office Records, National Archives, London, UK.

26. Vansittart, "Future of Germany."

27. Phipps to Hoare, November 13, 1935.

28. Sir Eric Phipps to Sir John Simon, March 29, 1935, 1/14, Phipps Papers, Churchill College, Cambridge.

29. Martin Gilbert, *Britain and Germany between the Wars* (London: Longmans, 1964), xi; A. J. P. Taylor, *English History, 1914–1945* (New York: Oxford University Press, 1965), 361, 365–66; Sir John Simon, diary entry for October 14, 1933, MS 7 and Simon to S. M. Berry, April 5, 1935, MS 82, Sir John Simon Papers, Bodleian Library, Oxford.

30. Harold Macmillan, *Winds of Change, 1914–1939* (New York: Harper and Row, 1966), 346–47.

31. Taylor, *English History*, 369 (first quote); Gilbert, *Britain and Germany*, 2 (second and third quotes, from British writer and world war veteran Robert Graves).

32. Vansittart, *Mist Procession*, 486.

33. Press conference number 192, March 20, 1935, Press Conference Transcripts, Franklin D. Roosevelt Presidential Library and Museum, Hyde Park, NY.

34. *Manchester Guardian*, July 27, 1935, 14. The British Legion, composed primarily of world war veterans, was founded in 1921. Its membership was 342,000 in 1934 and 375,000 in 1936. Graham Wootton, *The Official History of the British Legion* (London: MacDonald and Evans, 1956), 29, 162, 203.

35. Richard Griffiths, *Fellow Travellers of the Right: British Enthusiasts for Nazi Germany, 1933–39* (London: Constable, 1980), 128–29; *Manchester Guardian*, June 12, 1935, 9.

36. *New York Times*, June 21, 1935, 1, 7.

37. *Manchester Guardian*, June 20, 1935, 14.

38. *New York Times*, June 21, 1935, 1, 7; *Manchester Guardian*, June 22, 1935, 13.

39. *Manchester Guardian*, June 24, 1935, 14.

40. Ibid.; *New York Times*, June 26, 1935, 12.

41. *Manchester Guardian*, June 25, 1935, 9.

42. *Manchester Guardian* , July 9, 1935, 20.

43. *Manchester Guardian* , July 8, 1935, 13.

44. *Manchester Guardian* , July 15, 1935, 10.

45. *New York Times*, July 16, 1935, 7; *Daily Herald* (London), July 16, 1935; *Observer* (London), July 21, 1935, 8; *Washington Post*, July 18, 1935, 8; *Manchester Guardian*, July 16, 1935, 6; *Chicago Tribune*, July 16, 1935, 5.

46. *Daily Herald* (London), July 25 and 27, 1935; *Manchester Guardian*, July 25, 1935, 8. Graham Wootton noted that most of the Dachau "prisoners" with whom the British Legion delegation was allowed to speak were SS men in disguise. Wootton, *British Legion*, 185.

47. "Nazi Justice in Speech and Action," *Jewish Chronicle* (London), August 30, 1935, 17; *Times* (London), August 19, 1935, 9, August 22, 1935, 11, and August 26, 1935, 9; *Manchester Guardian*, August 21, 1935, 4; *New York Times*, August 22, 1935, 11.

48. *Times* (London), August 20, 1935, 11; *Manchester Guardian*, August 21, 1935, 4; *New York Times*, August 21, 1935, 7.

49. *New York Times*, August 22, 1935, 11; *Manchester Guardian*, August 22, 1935, 4, and August 24, 1935, 17.

50. *Times* (London), August 22, 1935, 11; *Manchester Guardian*, August 22, 1935, 4; *New York Times*, August 22, 1935, 11.

51. *Manchester Guardian*, August 26, 1935, 12.

52. *New York Times*, August 30, 1935, 9; George S. Messersmith to William Phillips, August 27, 1935, 0558-00, George S. Messersmith Papers, Special Collections, University of Delaware Library, Newark, DE.

53. *New York Times*, August 28, 1935, 4; Stefan Kühl, *The Nazi Connection: Eugenics, American Racism, and German National Socialism* (New York: Oxford University Press, 1994), 32–33.

54. Kühl, *Nazi Connection*, 33–34; *New York Times*, August 29, 1935, 4, and August 30, 1935, 8.

55. *New York Times*, August 29, 1935, 5.

56. *New York Times*, August 30, 1935, 8. In June 1936, the Hitler regime staged another international academic gathering, with support from leading American institutions of higher learning, to celebrate Heidelberg University's

550th anniversary. The festival, at the site of a major 1933 book burning, proved another Nazi propaganda coup. Twenty American colleges and universities sent delegates, including Harvard, Yale, and Columbia. Top Nazis attended, and Goebbels' Ministry of Propaganda tightly controlled the festival. Hitler's education minister, Bernhard Rust, delivered a featured speech assailing Jews as an "alien race" that did not belong on university faculties. In her nationally syndicated column, Dorothy Thompson wrote that the only justification for American universities' sending delegates to Heidelberg would be to see "how in three years five centuries can be destroyed." Stephen H. Norwood, *The Third Reich in the Ivory Tower: Complicity and Conflict on American Campuses* (New York: Cambridge University Press, 2009), 61–70, 93–99, 125. Dorothy Thompson in *The Oklahoman* (Oklahoma City), July 9, 1936, 8.

57. *Daily Express* (London), July 16, 1935, and *Le Temps* (Paris), July 17, 1935, clippings on microfilm P.C. 3, reel 31, Wiener Library for the Study of the Holocaust and Genocide, London, UK; *New York Times*, July 16, 1935; "Translation of Report on July Antisemitic Riots in Berlin," n.d., ACC/3121/C/11/012/014, folder 2, BoD Papers, LMA; "Anti-Jewish Riots Sweep Berlin," *American Hebrew*, July 19, 1935; *Manchester Guardian*, July 16, 1935, 6. The *New York Times* and the *New York Herald Tribune* placed their articles on the pogrom on page 1 during its first two days. *New York Times*, July 16 and 17, 1935; *New York Herald Tribune*, July 16 and 17, 1935.

58. *New York Times*, July 17, 4, and July 26, 1935, 8; Moshe Gottlieb, "The Berlin Riots of 1935 and Their Repercussions in America," *American Jewish Historical Quarterly* 59 (March 1970): 302–6.

59. *Times* (London), July 16, 1935, 16; *Manchester Guardian*, July 16, 1935, 11; "Germany: The Berlin Riots," *Jewish Chronicle* (London), July 19, 1935, 15; "Anti-Jewish Riots," *American Hebrew*, July 19, 1935; "These Jews Are Dead," *Jewish Chronicle* (London), August 16, 1935, 13; "Translation of Report," ACC/3121/C/11/012/014, folder 2, BoD Papers, LMA.

60. *Daily Herald* (London), July 18, 1935; *Manchester Guardian*, July 17, 1935, 14, and July 18, 1935, 10; *New York Times*, July 17, 1935, 1, 4.

61. "Decorating the Kurfuerstendamm," *Jewish Chronicle* (London), November 1, 1935, 16.

62. "Sample of Stickers Still Being Posted All Over Berlin a Week after the Riots without any Interference by the Police," July 25, 1935, box 175, Sulzberger Papers, AMD, NYPL.

63. "Germany:Boycott of Jews in Berlin," *Jewish Chronicle* (London), July 19, 1935, 16.

64. Frederick Birchall to Arthur Hays Sulzberger, note with four enclosed photographs, n.d., box 175, Sulzberger Papers, AMD, NYPL.

65. Jean Denis, "Tueur des Juifs," *Le Droit de Vivre*, July 1935; *Daily Telegraph*

(London), July 20, 1935, and *Morning Post* (London), July 20, 1935, microfilm P.C. 3, reel 31, Wiener Library for the Study of the Holocaust and Genocide, London, UK.

66. *Daily Herald* (London), July 20, 1935; "Bilan d'Une Semaine," *Le Droit de Vivre*, July 1935.

67. Morris D. Waldman to Dr. Adler, September 24, 1935, box 11, Cyrus Adler Papers, American Jewish Committee (hereafter, AJC) Archives, New York, NY.

68. Ibid.; *Daily Herald* (London), July 22, 1935.

69. Gottlieb, "Berlin Riots," 313–19; Sheldon Spear, "The United States and the Persecution of the Jews in Germany, 1933–1939," *Jewish Social Studies* 30 (October 1968), 215 (quote).

70. Waldman to Adler, September 24, 1935.

71. "Report on July 23, 1935 Anti-Nazi Mass Meeting, under JLC Auspices," reel 34, Jewish Labor Committee Papers, US Holocaust Memorial Museum Archives (hereafter, USHMMA), Washington, DC.

72. *New York Herald Tribune*, May 2, 1935.

73. W. P. [William Phillips], Undersecretary of State, to Mr. Moffat, May 23, 1935, with attached clippings from *New York World-Telegram*, May 1, 1935, and New York *Daily News*, May 2, 1935; Cordell Hull, Secretary of State, "Memorandum of Conversation between Secretary Hull and the German Ambassador, Herr Hans Luther," May 23, 1935; and James Clement Dunn to Dr. Rudolf Leitner, July 29, 1935, box 4730, CDF 1930–39, Department of State General Records, RG 59, NA-CP.

74. *New York Times*, July 27, 1935, 1, July 28, 1935, 1, 2, and September 7, 1935, 1; *Washington Post*, July 27, 1935, 1, and July 28, 1935, 2; *Times* (London), July 29, 1935, 11.

75. *Washington Post*, July 28, 1935, 1, 2.

76. *New York Times*, September 7, 1935, 1.

77. Sir Eric Phipps to Foreign Office, September 18, 1935, 1/15, Phipps Papers, Churchill College, Cambridge; *Chicago Tribune*, September 8, 1935, 1; Saul Friedländer, *Nazi Germany and the Jews* (New York: HarperCollins, 1997), 1:142; *Washington Post*, September 8, 1935, M1. The Reich Flag law also prohibited Jews from displaying the swastika flag. Hermann Goering, whom Hitler assigned to explain the law to the Reichstag, told its members that this was because the swastika symbolized the Nazi "struggle against the Jews as racial wreckers." Referring to Magistrate Brodsky, Goering declared, "When an impudent Jew" denounced the swastika flag, "he insulted the whole [German] nation." Richard Evans, *The Third Reich in Power, 1933–1939* (New York: Penguin, 2005), 544.

78. "Memorandum of Conversation between Secretary Hull and the Counsellor of the German Embassy, Herr Rudolf Leitner," September 14, 1935, reel 29, Cordell Hull Papers, Library of Congress, Washington, DC.

79. *Daily Herald* (London), September 16, 1935, 1, 3.

80. *New York Times*, September 28, 1935, 18.

81. "Extracts," RG 11.001M.0218 134/2331, reel 218, Ligue Internationale Contre L'Antisemitisme Papers, USHMMA.

82. Norwood, *The Third Reich in the Ivory Tower*, 163–64.

83. *Boston Globe*, August 13, 1935, 5, and August 14, 1935, 1, 24; *New York Times*, August 13, 1935, 6, and August 14, 1935, 1, 4; *Christian Science Monitor*, August 14, 1935, 1, 5; *Jewish Exponent* (Philadelphia), August 16, 1935, 4; *Washington Post*, August 13, 1935, 1.

84. Marvin Perry and Frederick M. Schweitzer, *Antisemitism: Myth and Hate from Antiquity to the Present* (New York: Palgrave Macmillan, 2002), 23; *Boston Globe*, August 14, 1935, 1, 7; *Boston Herald*, August 14, 1935, 1, 24; *Jewish Exponent* (Philadelphia), August 16, 1935, 4.

85. *Christian Science Monitor*, August 14, 1935, 5.

86. Neville Laski, "Interview with the Rev. Alan C. Don, July 23, 1935," and Alan C. Don to Mr. Laski, July 26, 1935, ACC/3121/C/11/012/014, BoD Papers, LMA. Laski told Cyrus Adler that he had "tried tremendously hard to get the Archbishop of Canterbury to organize a deputation to the Prime Minister." N. J. Laski to Cyrus Adler, August 12, 1935, box 11, AJC Archives.

87. P. Horowitz to A. G. Brotman, July 24, 1935, and Secretary to P. Horowitz, July 26, 1935, ACC/3121/C/11/012/014, folder 2, and Frank Rodgers to Neville Laski, September 25, 1935, ACC/3121/E3/36/2, BoD Papers, LMA; *Times* (London), October 28, 1935, 16; *New York Times*, October 28, 1935, 10; *Manchester Guardian*, October 28, 1935, 18. The London *Times* provided the low crowd estimate at twenty thousand; the *New York Times* estimate was forty thousand.

88. *Manchester Guardian*, October 19, 1935, 16, October 23, 1935, 13, and October 28, 1935, 18; *Times* (London), October 28, 1935, 16; *New York Times*, October 28, 1935, 10; "Anti-Nazi Demonstration in Hyde Park," *Jewish Chronicle* (London), November 1, 1935, 24.

89. *Daily Herald* (London), October 28, 1935.

90. *Jewish Daily Bulletin*, March 25 and July 15, 1935, and Joseph Tenenbaum, letter to the editor, *Jewish Daily Bulletin*, March 31, 1935, clippings in Scrapbook 2, 1934–37, Joseph and Sheila Tenenbaum Collection (hereafter, Tenenbaum Collection), RG 27.007.03*02, USHMMA; Carrie M. Springer to Mrs. Mark Harris, June 13, 1935, box 105, Edward L. Israel to G. E. Harriman, November 20, 1935, and G. E. Harriman to Edward L. Israel, November 21, 1935, box 91, and G. E. Harriman to Samuel Untermyer, September 20, 1935, box 111, Non-Sectarian Anti-Nazi League (hereafter, NSANL) Papers, Rare Book and Manuscript Library (hereafter, RBML), Columbia University (hereafter, CU), New York, NY.

91. *The Day*, June 21, 1935, clipping in Scrapbook 2, 1934–37, Tenenbaum Collection, RG 27.007.03*02, USHMMA.

92. Tenenbaum, letter to the editor, *Jewish Daily Bulletin*, March 31, 1935, Tenenbaum Collection, RG 27.007.03*02, USHMMA; *Boston Globe*, August 7, 1935, 6.

93. G. E. Harriman, Executive Secretary, to David K. Niles, January 22, 1935, box 91, and Mrs. Mark Harris to Mrs. Eugene Springer, June 21, 1935, box 105, NSANL Papers, RBML, CU.

94. *New York Times*, April 11, 1935, 9; G. E. Harriman to R. H. Sakal, April 23, 1935, box 111, NSANL Papers, RBML, CU.

95. Joseph Tenenbaum, *Three Years Anti-Nazi Boycott* (New York: Joint Boycott Council of the American Jewish Congress and Jewish Labor Committee, 1936), 11, reel 18, World Jewish Congress Office Papers, H15 File 18, USHMMA.

96. *Jewish Daily Bulletin*, March 25, 1935, Scrapbook 2, 1934–37, Tenenbaum Collection, RG 27.007.03*02, USHMMA; *New York Times*, May 8, 1935, 12.

97. "The Boycott in America," *Jewish Chronicle* (London), July 12, 1935, 14; "The American Boycott," *Jewish Chronicle* (London), August 16, 1935, 21; "New York Hotels Bar German Assemblies," *Jewish Chronicle* (London), August 30, 1935, 20.

98. Phipps to Simon, April 1, 1935; L. G. Montefiore, "Interview with Sir Eric Phipps," July 11, 1935, ACC/3121/C/11/012/014, folder 2, BoD Papers, LMA.

99. "Germany: Disgraceful Jew-Laws," *Jewish Chronicle* (London), September 20, 1935, 16; "Nazis Proclaim a Ghetto," *Jewish Chronicle* (London), September 20, 1935, 9; *Yellow Spot*, 231.

100. *New York Herald Tribune*, September 17, 1935, 1; *New York Times*, September 16, 1935, 1; *Daily Herald* (London), September 17, 1935.

101. "Comments on Nuremberg Laws from American Press," ACC/C/11/12/21, folder 1, BoD Papers, LMA.

102. "Confidential Report," December 16, 1935; "Nazis Defy Hitler: More Anti-Jewish Terrorism," *Jewish Chronicle* (London), September 20, 1935, 16.

103. Jewish Telegraphic Agency, September 18, 1935; *Daily Herald* (London), September 20, 1935 and October 3, 1935.

104. "Nazis Proclaim a Ghetto," 9; "Germany: Disgraceful Jew-Laws," 16; "Confidential Report," December 16, 1935.

105. *Daily Herald* (London), July 22, 1935; Sidney Salomon to Neville J. Laski, September 16, 1935, ACC/3121/C/11/012/014, folder 2, BoD Papers, LMA.

106. *Daily Herald* (London), October 3, 1935; "The Deputies: Special Meeting of Protest," *Jewish Chronicle* (London), October 4, 1935, 18; *Manchester Guardian*, October 3, 1935, 2; *Times* (London), October 3, 1935, 14.

107. Cyrus Adler to Mr. Schneiderman, October 19, 1935, attached statement, box 11, Cyrus Adler Papers, AJC Archives.

108. *New York Times*, November 29, 1935, 16; *Manchester Guardian*, November 29, 1935, 6; *Times* (London), December 3, 1935, 11.

109. *Manchester Guardian*, December 3, 1935, 18.

110. *Times* (London), December 3, 1935, 15; Phipps to Eden, December 10, 1935.

111. *Manchester Guardian*, December 2, 1935, 13; *Times* (London), December 3, 1935, 15.

112. President [Nathan Laski] to M. D. Waldman, October 30, 1935, and Laski to Waldman, December 9, 1935, ACC/3121/E01/001, reel 31, BoD Papers, USHMMA. Laski claimed that Jenner raised the football match issue "obviously with his election in mind." Laski to Waldman, December 9, 1935.

113. *New York Times*, December 3, 1935, 17; *Times* (London), December 3, 1935, 11; Cyril Henriques to G. E. Harrison, December 27, 1935, box 111, NSANL Papers, RBML, CU.

114. *Chicago Tribune*, December 5, 1935, 23; *Manchester Guardian*, December 5, 1935, 9; *New York Times*, December 5, 1935, 20; "The Anglo-German Football Match," *Jewish Chronicle* (London), December 6, 1935, 16.

115. *Manchester Guardian*, December 5, 1935, 3, 12.

116. *Manchester Guardian*, December 5, 1935, 12; *Times* (London), December 5, 1935, 18.

117. Vansittart, *Mist Procession*, 484; Phipps to Eden, December 10, 1935.

118. Vansittart, *Mist Procession*, 476.

119. Macmillan, *Winds of Change*, 347; Friedländer, *Nazi Germany and the Jews*, 1:100.

120. Phipps to Eden, December 10, 1935.

—m—

EPILOGUE

Defeats, 1936–1939

FROM THE PASSAGE OF THE Nuremberg laws in September 1935 to the German invasion of Poland that triggered World War II four years later, American and British opponents of Nazism suffered repeated defeats on the diplomatic, propaganda, and military fronts. Jews in both countries continued openly and vigorously to oppose Nazi Germany and raise public awareness of the unprecedented threat it posed to Jewry and Western civilization, but they proved unable to influence either the American or British government significantly. Although some members of Parliament and the US Congress grasped what was at stake, appeasers wielded considerable power and antisemitism permeated both bodies, reaching a peak during World War II. In 1935 Britain's decision to unilaterally sign the Anglo-German Naval Agreement ended Hitler's isolation and prevented the forging of an Anglo-French coalition against Nazi expansion. Mussolini's invasion of Ethiopia the same year, and its conquest in 1936, drew Italy and Germany together and revealed the inability—and the unwillingness—of the League of Nations to make a stand against fascist aggression, which permanently shattered its prestige. British Labour Party leader H. N. Brailsford declared in March 1936 that "all Europe" was watching the "organized destruction" of the Jews, which proceeded in Germany, "unmoved, without an effort to help."[1]

News of Nazi atrocities against German Jews continued to flow into the United States and Britain in the remaining years before the outbreak of World War II. In March 1936, a major British publisher, Gollancz, released *The Yellow Spot: The Extermination of the Jews in Germany*, a volume that the *New Statesman* reported "must make the most insensitive reader gasp with horror." A New York publisher issued an American edition with the same text the same year. The title referred to the degrading badge medieval Jews were forced to wear, which the Nazis resurrected to mark Jewish stores and offices for the April 1, 1933, boycott. The *New York Times* called *The Yellow Spot* "the first complete documentary study of the extermination of German Jews," which described how that process was proceeding. In his *Manchester Guardian* review, Professor Gilbert Murray explained how the Nazis and their collaborators were in the process of denying to Jews "all ways of earning a living," pushing them to starvation.[2]

Neither the Roosevelt administration nor the British government made any serious effort to isolate Nazi Germany because of its persecution of the Jews, and their response to Hitler's relentless military buildup was tepid at best. James MacGregor Burns, Roosevelt's biographer, described his conduct of foreign policy during his first term, March 1933 to January 1937, as more that of a "pussyfooting politician than [a] political leader." He "allow[ed] himself to be virtually immobilized by isolationist feeling" and did not attempt, "through words or action," to "change popular attitudes" about the need to stand up to fascist aggression. Burns noted that "the awful implications" of Roosevelt's "policy of drift would become clear later on," by the late 1930s.[3]

As long as Roosevelt was president, he showed no interest in lowering immigration barriers that allowed only a small number of German refugees into the United States. The national origins quotas that Congress introduced in the early 1920s restricted annual immigration from Germany to a maximum of slightly less than 26,000. After Germany annexed Austria in March 1938, the quota was only raised to 27,370. The Roosevelt administration and US consular officers added further restrictions so that in most years the number of immigrants from Germany did not come close to the ceiling. Rafael Medoff noted that "the actual number admitted was just 1,324 in 1933, 3,515 in 1934, and 4,891 in 1935," and during "the entire period of the Nazi regime, 1933 to 1945, more than 190,000 quota spaces from Germany and Axis countries sat unused."[4]

PRELUDE TO DISASTER: BRITISH AND AMERICAN ACQUIESCENCE IN GERMANY'S SEIZURE OF THE RHINELAND

On March 7, 1936, about thirty thousand German troops invaded and took back the Rhineland, a blatant treaty violation that remained unopposed by the British and French. Hitler's occupation of the Rhineland opened the way for a German invasion of Western Europe. The Versailles Treaty had demilitarized the Rhineland to provide France with a territorial buffer against another German attack. The Locarno Treaty of 1925, which the German government signed, had reaffirmed this. Now, however, German forces could be positioned directly along the French frontier. The Rhine River, a formidable barrier, would no longer impede German troop movements. *New York Times* correspondent Otto Tolischus reported that the Germans had carried out the invasion "with an astonishing bravado that . . . left the world breathless." Foreign military analysts were impressed by the efficiency with which it was executed. Tolischus warned that the invasion placed both Britain and France in a potentially dangerous position: "The German army is again stationed not only at France's frontier but also on the fateful river [the Rhine] which [Prime Minister] Stanley Baldwin proclaimed the British frontier as well." The Rhineland occupation "look[ed] like a dress rehearsal for more serious business."[5]

Harold Macmillan, then a Conservative antiappeasement MP, called the German occupation of the Rhineland "an unprovoked act of aggression, requiring immediate counter action." Macmillan described the British, however, as "confused" and the French as "hesitant and fumbling." In the British House of Commons, discussion of the invasion was "feeble and lifeless." At that time, German armed forces would not have been able to effectively resist French or British military intervention, but each lacked the will to block Hitler's advance. Recognizing this, the Germans immediately began to build a new Hindenburg line at the French border. Two days after the invasion, Harold Nicholson, MP, noted in his diary that the general mood in the House of Commons was fear and a determination to do anything to keep Britain out of war. The next day he wrote, "On all sides one hears sympathy for Germany." Winston Churchill, then a backbencher in Parliament, considered the British government's failure to act when Germany invaded the Rhineland "the final and fatal step which made war inevitable."[6]

Robert Dell, the *Manchester Guardian*'s Geneva correspondent, declared that the British government "had behaved abominably" in allowing the Germans to seize the Rhineland, but he considered the British public's reaction "still worse." He lamented that "the King and the Court are pro-German and so are the enormous majority of the upper classes." Even more alarmingly, "the 'people' are too." Dell reported that "in the London cinema films of the German troops entering the demilitarized zone have been applauded." He noted that an official from the US embassy in Paris visiting Geneva after a stay in London told him he had witnessed a movie audience there burst into cheers when German troops were shown marching into the Rhineland. Dell observed that "the *Manchester Guardian* is the only English paper that has not bowed the knee to Hitler."[7]

Jewish refugees from Germany, by contrast, reacted with horror at the German occupation of the Rhineland. British Zionist leader Norman Bentwich, who was heavily engaged in efforts to rescue Jews from the Reich, reported that the refugee community in Luxembourg, which he visited in April 1936, was appalled by the lack of response to the invasion in the West. The community, which had been augmented by Jews and other anti-Nazis who had fled the Saar after the plebiscite, watched "in baffled amazement . . . [British] acquiescence at the German militarization of the Rhine Province." Bentwich wrote that the refugees "could not make out what we were doing: it seemed to them, with some prevision, surrender to Nazi plans to dominate Europe, and a prelude to disaster."[8]

The American government made no official statement about Germany's invasion of the Rhineland. The *Chicago Tribune* reported the next day that the United States "stood cooly aloof on the sidelines." The *Washington Post* quoted Secretary of State Cordell Hull's statement that because the United States had signed neither the Versailles nor the Locarno Treaty, it was "not involved in any way" in the matter.[9]

On March 13, 1936, Sir Eric Phipps, British ambassador to Germany, notified British foreign minister Sir Anthony Eden that the American embassy in Berlin was taking a position on the Rhineland invasion sympathetic to Germany. It had sent a telegram to the State Department in Washington claiming that the French, "twenty years after the War," were "still clamoring for a one-sided demilitarized zone." The American embassy complained that since the world war "there has been no attempt to negotiate with Germany on a genuine footing of equality." It was distressed that since Hitler had assumed the chancellorship, the Western powers had made no effort "to take him at his word and consider his disarmament and other proposals, or . . . to take advantage of the sentimental side of his character." The American embassy acknowledged that France and Britain might defeat Germany "in a fresh resort to arms" over the Rhineland but emphasized that "the French would prove no more reasonable at a fresh Peace Conference than they were at Versailles." Fearing Anglo-French armed intervention, the American embassy urged the German government to send the high Foreign Office representative Hans-Heinrich Dieckhoff to London "to state the German case."[10]

Celebrating a major victory, the Hitler government staged a dramatic torchlight parade of fifteen thousand brown-clad storm troopers in Berlin. The storm troopers marched down major boulevards and passed in review before the Fuehrer and cabinet members at the chancellery. Otto Tolischus noted that the storm troopers sang a song that included the line, "For today we own Germany and tomorrow the entire world." Propaganda Minister Josef Goebbels implied that the successful invasion marked a step toward Germany's achieving its

World War I expansionist objectives in the West. He announced that Germans would fly flags to demonstrate their "intimate unity" with Germany's world war dead, whose sacrifice "was no longer in vain."[11]

In June 1936, Sir Horace Rumbold, Britain's ambassador in Berlin from 1929 to 1933, wrote to London *Times* editor Geoffrey Dawson that Hitler did not believe he could achieve equal standing for Germany in Europe by merely occupying the Rhineland. Just as he had "consistently applied the principles of *Mein Kampf* within Germany," he would now enact them in his foreign policy. Once Hitler began to embark on his planned expansion in Central and Eastern Europe, war became "a dead certainty."[12]

THE BERLIN OLYMPICS OF 1936: SHOWCASING NAZISM AND FUNDING GERMAN REARMAMENT

The Hitler regime used the 1936 Olympic Games, which the International Olympic Committee had awarded to Berlin in 1931, to showcase the Reich's power, the mass support for Nazism in Germany, and the vigor and ascendancy of fascism. American and British Jews, with support from organized labor and anti-Nazi refugees, waged an intense campaign to block their nations' participation in the games, scheduled to take place from August 1 to 16. As Gerhart Seger warned, holding the Olympic Games in Berlin would provide Nazi Germany with large amounts of the foreign currency it needed to import raw materials for its rearmament program. Similarly, the *Boston Evening Transcript* noted that "every foreigner who comes to Germany helps to improve the Reich's balance of international payments. . . . [Its] need in this regard is pressing." The Jewish Telegraphic Agency observed that the Hitler regime planned to use the Olympics to recruit foreign propagandists from among the visiting athletes and spectators. And it would use contacts made at the games to secure much-needed foreign loans.[13]

Reporting on the Berlin Olympics to Foreign Secretary Anthony Eden shortly after they ended in August 1936, a British embassy official stressed that the Germans had spared "no trouble or expense . . . to make them an advertisement of the National Socialist regime." For two years the German government had scoured the Reich for talented athletes and trained them at state expense. Hitler was present at the games every day "and followed Germany's fortunes with the closest attention."[14]

In June 1933, George Messersmith, US consul general in Berlin, had informed Secretary of State Hull that Germany's Jews were being banned from all sports competition. He believed that it was therefore inadvisable to hold the

Olympics in Berlin "where real difficulties could arise on racial grounds." By 1935, the German government had closed all thirty-six of Germany's stadiums to Jews.[15]

In an August 1935 article about the upcoming Olympics, the *Boston Evening Transcript* warned that American visitors to the Reich capital might experience "unpleasantness" because of the fiercely antisemitic atmosphere there. It reported, "Tourists and foreign residents of Berlin with a dark complexion have begun to wear their national flags prominently displayed in their clothing to avoid . . . being taken for German Jews."[16]

Before the 1936 Summer Olympics began, US undersecretary of state William Phillips visited the US embassy in Berlin for two days to learn more about conditions in the Reich, especially the "Jewish and Catholic situation." When he met representatives of the *New York Times, New York Herald Tribune, Chicago Tribune, Chicago Daily News*, Jewish Telegraphic Agency, Associated Press, United Press, and International News Service in a private conference to discuss these matters, the correspondents were unanimous in alerting him that after the Olympic Games ended "the persecution of Jews . . . will become even more intense." One informed Phillips of "the hopes . . . the Jews had laid on America's abstention from the Olympiad."[17]

American Jewish groups presented a solid front against US participation in the Berlin Olympics, from the more conservative American Jewish Committee (AJC) to the militant Jewish War Veterans of the United States (JWV). The AJC considered making the prevention of holding the Olympic Games in Germany, along with the boycott of scholarly conferences there, a very high priority. Consistent with its past approach, fearing an antisemitic backlash, it favored using Christians as the principal public spokespersons for these causes.[18] Addressing a meeting of the American Jewish Congress's (AJCongress's) National Boycott Committee in New York in October 1935, Rabbi Stephen S. Wise warned, "If Hitler can bring civilized nations to Berlin it will be his crowning victory." At its convention in New York in January 1936, the Federation of Jewish Women's Organizations passed a resolution opposing American athletes' participating in the Berlin Olympics. In Boston, an August 1935 meeting of fifteen hundred, representing two hundred Jewish groups, over which New England AJCongress president Samuel Kaletsky presided, called on the United States to rescind its conditional acceptance of Germany's invitation to the Olympics. The prominent Jewish writer Ludwig Lewisohn delivered one of the principal speeches urging a boycott. The JWV national convention later that month unanimously called for the United States not to send a team to the Berlin Games. Addressing the convention, New York governor Herbert Lehman declared that six hundred thousand German Jews had been "marked for destruction." The JWV then launched a "monster petition" campaign to secure one million signatures calling for a boycott of the 1936 Olympic Games if they were held in Berlin. The Non-Sectarian Anti-Nazi League was also actively engaged in the boycott.[19]

In Britain, the movement to boycott the Olympics attracted less support. The proappeasement British Olympic Council, which selected Britain's team, insisted that the Berlin Games would promote "harmony and reconciliation between nations." Britain's failure to send a team to the games "would be nothing short of calamity."[20]

By contrast, Britain's Non-Sectarian Anti-Nazi Council waged a campaign to keep Britain out of the games. It contacted several thousand British sporting organizations, urging them to protest participation in the games.[21] Britain's leading Jewish newspaper, the London *Jewish Chronicle*, and the *Manchester Guardian* also pressed for a boycott, as did many trade unions. Cyril Q. Henriques, honorary secretary of the British Non-Sectarian Anti-Nazi Council, expressed disgust in January 1936 that the International Olympic Committee considered Germany's discrimination against Jewish athletes "an internal matter," of no concern to the outside world.[22] Henriques was a member of the Board of Deputies of British Jews and had campaigned for the boycott of German goods and services within that organization since 1933.

In a letter to Henriques, G. E. Harriman, executive secretary of the Non-Sectarian Anti-Nazi League in the United States, praised the British movement's campaign against the Anglo-German soccer match in December 1935. Harriman credited that protest with preventing "a triumphal Nazi march through London," which he called "a real moral victory." Now, in targeting the Berlin Olympics, the boycott movement was "going after an actual one."[23]

The Olympics boycott movement received some support in the House of Commons. During a parliamentary debate about Germany, Commander Oliver Locker-Lampson, antiappeasement Conservative MP, told the chancellor of the exchequer that the revenue from the Berlin Games would provide Germany with "several million pounds in foreign currency, and that such currency was now being used to finance German armaments." He asked the chancellor to prohibit the use of British funds for that purpose. The chancellor responded that he could not do so. Ellen Wilkinson, Labour MP from Jarrow, then challenged his office to "suggest to the present Government in Germany that, on the lines of their elections, there should not be more than one competitor for each event."[24]

In October 1935 the American Federation of Labor (AFL), with a membership of 2.6 million, adopted a resolution calling for a boycott of the Berlin

Games. It denounced the Hitler government for "stamping out 'in blood and fire' the German trade union movement." The AFL prohibited its members from competing in the Berlin Games.[25]

Both the United States and Britain ignored the protests and sent national teams to the Berlin Games. Peter Gay, who as a youth resided in Berlin and attended the games, recalled that the American Olympic team had "played the political game, on their [Nazi] hosts' terms and to their hosts' advantage." The head of the US Olympic Committee, Avery Brundage, a member of the proappeasement America First Committee, and the track coach, Dean Cromwell, both antisemites, bowed to Nazi pressure and "cravenly denied places [in the four-hundred-meter relay] to the only two Jews on their team, both 100-meter specialists, Marty Glickman and Sam Stoller." Glickman and Stoller were "as fit as the two sprinters who replaced them."[26]

The failure to block American and British participation in the 1936 Olympic Games was a major setback for the anti-Nazi campaign. The British embassy official monitoring the Berlin Games described them to Sir Anthony Eden as "an extraordinary success for Germany and for National Socialism."[27] The United States' rejection of the boycott confirmed to Hitler that it would continue to "adhere to [its] noninterventionist behavior."[28] As Germany accumulated more points than the United States, Italy garnered more than France, and Japan surpassed Britain, many concluded that fascist nations were thriving and dynamic and Western democracies had become decadent.[29]

ADDING MUSCLE TO THE BOYCOTT, 1936–1939

Boycott activities intensified in 1936 as the AJCongress Boycott Committee joined with the Jewish Labor Committee to form the Joint Boycott Council (JBC), forging a Jewish-labor partnership that added more muscle to the campaign. What had been largely a consumers' boycott was transformed into a movement that gave more attention to damaging the Reich's economy through work stoppages. In New York City, the JLC persuaded the Central Trades and Labor Council to participate more actively in the movement to boycott German goods and services. In June 1937, JBC chair Joseph Tenenbaum demanded that the Brooklyn and Queens Transit Corporation immediately stop using German-made steel rails. The JBC secured the cooperation of the Transport Workers Union, representing the city's subway and surface transit workers, which made clear that its members would not work with materials made in Nazi Germany. Tenenbaum noted that as a result, the "insidious practice" of using German-made rails "was stopped in its tracks!" He reported that "time and again" the Longshoremen's Union disrupted German trade by refusing to unload German-made goods from ships docking in New York.[30]

Boycott picketing became more common, and its likelihood led the Hitler government to withdraw its application to participate in the 1938–39 New York World's Fair, where it had rented one hundred thousand square feet of space for a German Pavilion celebrating Nazi achievements. The JBC had threatened to put up a "Walking Chamber of Horrors," depicting Nazi atrocities against Jews and other opponents of the Hitler regime, outside the fair gates after Grover Whalen, the World's Fair Corporation president, denied it permission to mount the exhibit on the fairgrounds. In refusing the JBC request, Whalen explained that the fair's rules did not allow "exhibits devoted to political propaganda."[31]

On the fifth anniversary of Hitler's becoming chancellor, the JBC held a mass rally in New York to excoriate the Nazis and promote the boycott. William E. Dodd, the main speaker, who had just stepped down as US ambassador to Germany, declared that "the situation for the Jews in Germany was worse than at any time in the last hundred years."[32]

CAPITULATION

The British and French capitulation to Hitler's annexation of Austria (*Anschluss*) on March 13, 1938, and to his demand for the Sudetenland at the Munich Conference on September 28–29 opened the way for Nazi domination of Central and Eastern Europe, where the vast majority of Europe's Jews resided. Immediately after the *Anschluss*, the antisemitic measures in place in Germany were implemented in Austria. The *Anschluss*, in turn, greatly facilitated the German takeover of Czechoslovakia, the only remaining democracy in Central or Eastern Europe.

The American and British press described the treatment of Austria's Jews after the *Anschluss*—the savage beatings, public humiliation, looting of their stores, and seizure of homes and property, as well as the offices of Jewish organizations. The Associated Press compared the non-Jewish Austrians' frenzied excitement over the *Anschluss* to Americans' celebration of Armistice Day in 1918. The London *Times* reported that "Vienna, as it awaited the arrival of Herr Hitler, resembled a town which has just received news of a great victory and is preparing to welcome the returning troops." It appeared that "every Viennese" wore "a swastika brassard or … carr[ied] a swastika flag." As in the Saar after the 1935 plebiscite, the church enthusiastically celebrated the annexation of Austria to the Reich. The cardinal archbishop of Vienna ordered every church to ring its bells to cheer the Fuehrer's arrival.[33] William L. Shirer, Berlin correspondent from 1935 to 1937 and then head of CBS Radio's office in Vienna, recalled that in the first weeks after the *Anschluss* "the behavior of the Nazis was worse than anything I had seen in Germany." He described "an orgy of sadism," as "day after day large numbers of Jewish men and women" were forced to scrub side-walks "on their hands and knees with jeering storm troopers standing over them, [and] crowds gathered to taunt them." The Nazis seized Jewish men and women on the streets and "put [them] to work cleaning public latrines and the toilets of the barracks where the SA and SS were quartered."[34]

G. E. R. Gedye, Vienna-based correspondent for the *New York Times* and London *Daily Telegraph*, reported in the *Times* on April 3, 1938, that "over-night, Vienna's 290,000 Jews were made free game for mobs, despoiled of their property, deprived of police protection, ejected from employment and barred from sources of relief." He added that the Austrian frontiers "were hermetically sealed against their escape." Gedye provided an eyewitness description of the Nazis driving Jews out of a synagogue and, to the amusement of the crowd outside, forcing them to "sweep the streets of the rubbish which the grinning storm-troopers kept throwing out of the windows." He persuaded several of his fellow journalists to write about the incident. Gedye also reported walking by a shop "labelled in huge yellow letters 'JEW,'" in front of which a young girl was forced to repeatedly kneel down and rise, wearing a large sign around her neck stating, "Please do not buy from me—I am a Jew sow."[35]

The *Anschluss* precipitated mass arrests of Jews and widespread plunder-ing of Jewish assets. Gedye described "a long string of lorries" parked outside Schiffman's, a Jewish-owned millinery store, into which storm troopers placed all the store's stock and equipment. They had first arrested the proprietors.[36] On March 15, the London *Times* reported that a train containing Austrian Jews attempting to flee to Poland was stopped in the provinces and sent back to Vienna, where authorities robbed the Jews of the money and property they had with them. On June 3, the *Times* calculated that during the previous two weeks four thousand Jews had been arrested in Vienna alone and that a special train had departed for the Dachau concentration camp in Germany carrying seven hundred prisoners, most of whom were Jewish.[37] Jewish teachers were dismissed from Vienna's public schools and ordered not to return.[38]

On June 18, 1938, the London *Times*, whose chief editor, Geoffrey Dawson, had long been sympathetic to appeasement, reported that after the *Anschluss* the Nazis in Austria had initiated "an unbroken orgy of Jew-baiting such as Europe has not known since the darkest days of the Middle Ages." In Vienna they had "rapidly forced" the Jews "out of every economic activity." As a result, "what was once a community outstanding in intellect and culture is being turned into a community of beggars." In addition, the Nazis had instituted a policy of the "systematic maintenance of panic for the whole Jewish population." This meant that there "can be no Jewish family in the country which has not one or more of its members under arrest." The Nazis made a special effort to humiliate and demoralize Austrian Jewish children. The *Times* reported that "the segregation of the Jewish children from the 'Aryans' is complete. Not even the very youngest were spared. . . . the infants of the kindergarten can no longer play in the public parks; and on the door of their school the legend is painted, 'Cursed be the Jew.'" Thousands of Austrian Jews were lined up at the American and British consulates waiting desperately "through the night for admission," hoping to procure immigration papers. In August 1938, *Life* magazine published a photograph of Austrian refugees awaiting the "next move by democratic Czechoslovakia's anti-Semitic, conservative Interior Minister Josef Czerny who has pigeon-holed some 50,000 applications by Austrian Jews for official permission to enter Czechoslovakia."[39]

British and French acquiescence at Munich to Hitler's taking the Sudetenland six months after the *Anschluss* left a rump Czechoslovakia without effective fortifications, surrounded by German armed forces on three sides. The Western powers handed over the Sudetenland without Czechoslovakia even being present at the conference. Not since the partition of Poland in the eighteenth century had a nation been dismembered by powers that had recognized its independence. Access to new raw materials and military manpower in Austria and Czechoslovakia provided a further boost to German rearmament. Hitler's seizure of all of Czechoslovakia in March 1939, a few months after Munich, reduced British and French prestige and made German military penetration deep into Eastern Europe possible.[40]

Sudetenland Jews were placed in an even more dangerous predicament than the Saar's Jews after the January 1935 plebiscite. The Nazis portrayed the alleged Czech persecution of the Sudeten Germans as part of a larger Judeo-Bolshevik conspiracy. On September 10, 1938, Hermann Goering declared at the Nazi Party rally in Nuremberg that "this miserable pygmy race [the Czechs] is oppressing a cultured people [the Sudeten Germans], and behind it is Moscow and the eternal mask of the Jew devil." As British prime minister Neville Chamberlain was preparing to concede the Sudetenland to Germany, William Shirer reported that Prague's railroad station and airport "were full of Jews scrambling desperately to find transportation to safer parts."[41]

Jewish and anti-Nazi German refugees, numbering about twenty-five thousand, found no welcome in Czechoslovakia. The *Manchester Guardian* stated that they were "caught in a trap," either forced back into the Sudetenland to face arrest or living in privation and barely tolerated in Czechoslovakia. The *New York Times* reported that in Czechoslovakia there was "a general unwillingness to accept any Germans or Jews, whatever their politics and however loyally they may have stood shoulder to shoulder with the Czechs in the defense of the republic and democracy." The Czechs insisted that the refugee problem grew out of Britain's agreement with Hitler at Munich, in which France acquiesced, and the refugees were therefore those nations' responsibility. They were determined to be "as hard as the countries" who had created the Sudetenland refugees.[42]

The Roosevelt administration was unwilling to become involved in the Munich crisis. As James MacGregor Burns commented, it did little but "watch and worry." Secretary of State Hull had repeatedly denounced "international lawlessness" but without specifically referring to Germany. When concern developed over Hitler's aggressive posture toward Czechoslovakia, Hull was capable only of "solemnly call[ing] attention to the Kellogg anti-war pact signed a decade before." (Signed by forty-six nations, including the United States, Britain, France, Germany, Italy, and Japan, the Kellogg pact, "officially declared in force" in 1929, had renounced war "as an instrument of national policy" but did not provide for sanctions.) In Europe, "men of power . . . laughed off America's moral protestations." President Roosevelt failed to respond to Czechoslovakian president Benes's "plea that he urge Britain and France not to desert the Czechs." Roosevelt only issued an appeal to all the nations for peace—"to potential aggressor, bystander, and victim alike."[43]

Roosevelt's insensitivity to the Jewish plight in Central Europe was reflected in his offering Hugh Gibson the post of ambassador to Germany when William Dodd resigned at the end of 1937. Gibson had served as the first US minister to Poland during the postwar pogroms. Accepting the claims of Polish antisemites, he argued in his reports to the State Department that Jews had provoked the pogroms by assuming prominent roles in Bolshevik agitation and as traders who "hoarded food" during the famine "to drive up prices." Moreover, Gibson claimed that American Jews trying to build support for Zionism had exaggerated the scale of the killings. Felix Frankfurter charged that Gibson "had done more mischief" to Jews "than anyone who had lived in the last century." He and Louis Brandeis demanded that Gibson stop filing reports on the Jewish situation in Poland. Roosevelt would probably have known about Gibson's antisemitism from Frankfurter, who served as an informal advisor to the president and likely warned him about it. It was not important enough to Roosevelt to deny Gibson the appointment.[44]

When Gibson declined the ambassadorial appointment, Roosevelt chose Hugh Wilson, who "applauded" the Munich agreement. In his study of the

US Foreign Service in the first half of the twentieth century, Martin Weil noted Ambassador Wilson's "warm admiration for Hitler's pacification of the German working class." Like most of the State Department's Europeanists, Wilson considered Nazi Germany a bulwark against the spread of Communism in Europe. He and other prominent State Department officials believed that Hitler's acquisition of the Sudetenland and other territory to Germany's east could block Soviet expansion. Wilson feared that "animosity toward Germany in the United States" might ruin the prospects for achieving peace in Europe.[45]

ANTISEMITIC TERROR IN DANZIG

Even before Germany invaded Poland in 1939 and absorbed Danzig, designated by the Versailles Treaty as a Free City, technically under League of Nations jurisdiction, Jews' situation there was desolate. A port city with a largely German population, Danzig was situated in the Polish Corridor, created after World War I to provide Poland with an outlet to the Baltic. By the time Hitler annexed the Sudetenland, seventy of the seventy-two deputies in Danzig's parliament were Nazis. William Shirer noted that in late 1938, "local Nazis controlled Danzig and they took their orders . . . from Berlin." In March 1939, the New York Times reported that Danzig was celebrating Germany's takeover of the rest of Czechoslovakia "with parades and swastika decorations." Signs in many Danzig restaurants and stores forbade Jews to enter.[46]

The antisemitic terror that engulfed Danzig was presaged in the Saar. In August 1938, the New York Times stated that the Free City's Jews "have been reduced to a status like that of German Jews," with "beatings, imprisonments and confiscations of property" every day. On August 29, forty uniformed Nazis invaded a synagogue near police headquarters, "threw the holy scrolls on the floor and danced on them and then tore them." Danzig police positioned nearby refused to intervene. The Nazis proceeded to vandalize other Jewish institutions. The Manchester Guardian described how the Gestapo in Danzig, "obviously acting on orders from Berlin . . . raided a Jewish hotel, restaurants, and cafés," searching for and arresting Jews, including refugees from Germany and Austria. Many of the Jews seized were transported to concentration camps in Germany.[47]

The Guardian also reported that as of October 1, 1938, "on express orders from Berlin," Jewish physicians would be denied the right to practice medicine in Danzig. Jews needing medical treatment would have to go to non-Jewish physicians, "who, as is known, often refuse to attend Jewish patients."[48]

The *New York Times* reported on August 31, 1938, that the Nazis had driven 30 percent of Danzig's Jews out of the Free City after confiscating their money and property. Less than two weeks later, *Time* magazine found that four hundred Jews owning houses in Danzig had been notified "that next month Aryans will 'purchase' their property.... at Nazi-dictated prices."[49]

KRISTALLNACHT: THE GOVERNMENTS' TEPID RESPONSE

Prime Minister Neville Chamberlain proclaimed that the Munich Agreement ensured "peace in our time," but on the night of November 9–10, 1938, barely a month after its signing, the Nazis launched nationwide pogroms, known as the Kristallnacht, which destroyed nearly all Germany's synagogues (along with massive amounts of Jewish property), killed about one hundred Jews, and resulted in the arrest and imprisonment in concentration camps of thirty thousand more. The *New York Journal-American* described the Kristallnacht as a night of bloody diabolical revelry. It quoted the eyewitness testimony of an American woman in Berlin on a Guggenheim fellowship, "horror struck" by the rampaging Germans' sadism and their delight in publicly humiliating Jews. She told of seeing a crowd chasing a Jew through the streets, "like a pack of hungry wolves closing in on a rabbit." The crowd seized "the poor man," who "was not a fast runner," and smashed his head against the sidewalk. For fourteen hours, the young woman wandered Berlin's streets, constantly hearing "the ax falling on glass and wood," watching Jewish men and women being beaten. She saw Germans who had just wrecked a Jew's notion shop, forcing the "poor old man" to his hands and knees and ordering him to "pick the pieces of glass . . . from his own store window," one by one, "out of the street." As he did so, the Germans laughed and jeered. The American eyewitness, "sick at heart . . . left Germany the next day."[50]

Peter Gay called Munich "father to the Kristallnacht," an agreement that opened the way for massive warfare and the annihilation of the Jews in Europe. The Western powers' "craven conduct" and the Nazis' "complete diplomatic victory" gave the Hitler government "a giddy sense of being at liberty to do anything they liked abroad and at home." And although the press in the United States, Britain, and other European countries covered the November 9–10 pogroms extensively, Gay observed bitterly that the Western powers "did almost nothing."[51] There were mass grassroots protests against the Nazis' brutal antisemitism in the United States and sharp condemnation from some members of Parliament but only a limited response by the British or American government.

To express disapproval of the pogroms, President Roosevelt recalled his ambassador to Germany, Hugh Wilson, for consultations and issued a verbal condemnation, without mentioning Jews, Nazi Germany, or Hitler by name. He put no economic pressure on the Reich and continued to make it nearly impossible for Jewish refugees from Germany and Austria to enter the United States. The immigration quota for Germany and Austria of twenty-seven thousand had already been filled through 1939. Roosevelt rejected American Jewish organizations' request to combine the immigration quotas for 1940 to 1942, which at least would have permitted an additional eighty-one thousand German and Austrian Jews to enter.[52] In 1939, the US Senate refused to pass the Wagner-Rogers bill, which would have allowed the admission of twenty thousand Jewish refugee children above the quota. The bill did not have Roosevelt's support, even though it involved young children who did not threaten Americans' jobs.[53]

As in the spring of 1933, Roosevelt turned a deaf ear to grassroots calls to impose strong economic and diplomatic sanctions against Germany. In a coordinated citywide protest against the Kristallnacht pogroms, thirty thousand New York storekeepers closed their shops for an hour. New York's Local 65 of the CIO's Retail and Wholesale Workers Union staged a two-day work stoppage.[54] Anti-Nazi activists picketed German consulates and German liners docked in New York. The grassroots protestors demanded that diplomatic and trade relations with Germany be severed and that immigration barriers be immediately lowered to permit the entry of Jewish refugees—appeals that went far beyond what the American and British governments even considered.

Despite the Kristallnacht, the British government resolved to maintain friendly relations with the Reich. Thus, it failed to take strong action against its government or to assist German and Austrian Jewish refugees. It had always considered Britain as at most a temporary stopover for Jewish refugees, who would quickly move on to destinations outside the United Kingdom. Ellen Wilkinson's exchange with Prime Minister Chamberlain's undersecretary for foreign affairs, R. B. Butler, in the House of Commons exposed the government's determination to continue its policy of appeasing Germany and its indifference to the Jewish plight in Germany and Austria. Wilkinson demanded to know why His Majesty's Government had invited Hitler government officials and German press representatives to a government-funded reception at London's Carlton Hotel. Undersecretary Butler responded that the reception "scarcely requires justification," emphasizing His Majesty's Government's policy of "extending hospitality to distinguished foreign visitors." The undersecretary noted that the Nazi government had similarly provided friendly receptions to English visitors to the Reich. MPs in attendance called out, "Hear, hear!" Wilkinson then asked sardonically whether such British hospitality should be continued in view of the recent savage pogroms in Germany. This elicited cries of "Oh!" from shocked cabinet ministers.[55]

SEALING EUROPEAN JEWRY'S DOOM

On April 27, 1938, the *Völkischer Beobachter* warned, "Jews, abandon all hope! Our net is so fine that there is not a hole through which you can slip!"[56] Emigration remained the only chance of survival for German and Austrian Jews, but no country was willing to provide a haven. Peter Gay recalled that after the Kristallnacht, "at the Dutch frontier, as frenzied German Jews pleaded for asylum literally on their knees, the [Dutch] government doubled its border patrol to keep out all the Nazis' victims."[57] In July 1938, a few months before the Kristallnacht, in an effort to deflect charges by journalists like Dorothy Thompson, a few members of Congress, and American Jews that the US government was indifferent to European Jewry's plight, the Roosevelt administration had invited thirty-two countries to send delegates to a conference at Evian, France, to talk about the situation.

But from the beginning, the Roosevelt administration conveyed that no country would be asked to accept any more refugees than its immigration legislation allowed. Only the Dominican Republic was willing to admit a sizeable number of Jewish refugees. The Roosevelt administration, fearing that their entry into the Caribbean would facilitate their passage into the United States, discouraged it from doing so. The United States was also determined to honor the British government's demand that the conference not discuss opening Palestine to more Jewish refugees.[58] At the Evian Conference, as Richard Evans noted, "one delegation after another... made it clear that it would not liberalize its policy towards refugees; if anything it would tighten things up." Peter Gay commented that at the "justly maligned" conference, "there was much humane talk and no humane action."[59]

The years of appeasing Nazi Germany culminated in a new Munich, this time involving Palestine: in May 1939, the British government issued a White Paper that overturned the Balfour Declaration in which it had promised to support a homeland for the Jews there. Jewish immigration to Palestine was to be terminated in five years and rigorously restricted to a mere seventy-five thousand until then. Palestine had represented the best prospect of refuge for the Jews. The White Paper of 1939 meant permanent Arab domination in Palestine and transformed the Jewish settlements into a ghetto. Using antisemitic tropes to defend the White Paper in the House of Commons, British colonial secretary Malcolm MacDonald explained that "the Arabs were afraid that if Jewish immigration continued indefinitely these energetic, clever, wealthy incoming people would dominate them." By contrast, in an editorial entitled "A Disastrous Policy," the *Manchester Guardian* vehemently denounced the White Paper, characterizing it as a "headlong repudiation of our pledges" to the Jews. The Chamberlain government had caved in to the Arabs' "long course of violence," inspired and intensified in recent years by Nazism's successes in Europe, and sealed their victory over the Jews.[60] Winston Churchill called the White Paper a "mortal blow" to the Jews.[61]

As always, Jews at the grassroots in the United States, backed by some non-Jews, mounted strong protests against this latest act of appeasement. When word circulated several months before the release of the White Paper that Britain was considering terminating Jewish immigration to Palestine, the Emergency Committee on Palestine, a coalition of major American Jewish groups, disclosed that Americans had sent more than sixty-four thousand telegrams to the White House and the State Department calling on the government to take action to maintain "an open door in Palestine for homeless Jews in Central and Eastern Europe." Twenty newspapers in the Hearst chain, which had a disproportionately working- and lower-middle-class readership, prominently featured an article "demanding that Britain should fulfill its pledges" in Palestine to the Jews. The distinguished American columnist Walter Lippman observed that it was not coincidental that the Munich accord, a clear sign of British weakness, had been followed by the increase in Arabs' violence and pressure on the British to accede to their demands to end Jewish immigration to Palestine.[62]

After the British government announced the White Paper, a capacity crowd jammed New York's Hippodrome for a protest meeting, at which Mayor Fiorello La Guardia, Senator Robert Wagner, and Rabbi Stephen S. Wise condemned the Chamberlain government for shutting the doors of Palestine to European Jews. At the New York World's Fair, a crowd of fifty thousand nearly swamped the stage at the dedication of the Jewish Palestine Pavilion, a celebration of the Jewish homeland. From the stage, Albert Einstein called for solidarity with the Jewish community in Palestine, "exposed to constant attack," where every Jew was "forced to fight for his very life."[63] In Washington, DC, heads of major Zionist organizations presented a joint statement at the British embassy, addressed to the ambassador, condemning Britain's capitulation to Arab terrorism and repudiation of the Balfour Declaration, when "thousands of Jewish refugees look to Palestine as . . . their main hope."[64] But it was all to no avail.

Similarly, the callousness of the Roosevelt administration toward Jewish refugees was dramatized when the Cuban government prevented the ocean liner *St. Louis*, carrying 907 Jews fleeing Nazi Germany, from landing at its destination, Havana, in early June 1939. The passengers had paid for "landing permits" signed by Cuba's minister of immigration, who had no intention of honoring them and who kept the money for himself. Cuba's president refused to allow the passengers to disembark, and the ship's decks became "a stage for human misery." Treated like a "plague ship," in the words of the *New York Times*, for seven days the *St. Louis* anchored about twelve miles off Havana. During that time two passengers attempted suicide. The Roosevelt administration refused to provide the passengers an obvious site such as the US Virgin Islands.[65]

With the Cuban government forbidding the liner to dock, it headed for Florida, hoping its passengers could find refuge there. Sailing along the Florida coast for three days, the *St. Louis* came close enough to shore for the passengers to see "the shimmering towers of Miami rising from the sea." Many American Jews telegraphed President Roosevelt imploring him to admit the refugees. But a US Coast Guard cutter and airplanes hovered close to the *St. Louis* to make sure it would not attempt to land and to prevent passengers from diving overboard and swimming ashore. The US government was aware when Cuba "slammed the door" that no other Western Hemisphere country would offer them asylum.[66] When Roosevelt had the coast guard prevent the *St. Louis* from landing in Florida, he "had no reason to believe [it] would be going anywhere except back to Nazi Germany."[67]

In 2013, when historians Richard Breitman and Allan Lichtman denied that US officials had "ordered the coast guard to prevent any passengers [of the *St. Louis*] from reaching American shores," four survivors of the "voyage of the damned" were outraged: "We saw the Coast Guard planes that flew around the ship to follow its movements. We saw the Coast Guard cutter that trailed us and made sure the *St. Louis* did not come close to the Florida coast. We heard the cutter blaring its warning to the *St. Louis* to stay away." The survivors emphasized that "it was President Franklin Roosevelt who decided our fate, who denied us and our families permission to land, forcing us to return to Europe, where many of the passengers were murdered by the Nazis."[68]

As the *St. Louis* turned back to return its passengers to the Third Reich, officials of Jewish organizations tried desperately to arrange their transfer to other European nations. They finally worked out an agreement for the passengers to be divided among England (287), France (224), Belgium (214), and the Netherlands (181). When the refugees arrived in Belgium, "they were strictly isolated from the beginning and were placed in wooden third-class coaches" on a railroad siding, separated by an iron barrier from the street. Belgian police drove away friends, relatives, and sympathizers hoping to speak with the refugees and warned reporters that they risked being charged with a misdemeanor and jailed if they even tried to interview them. A year after the agreement, Hitler's armies overran France, Belgium, and the Netherlands, and a sizeable percentage of the passengers were killed or would not survive. When England accepted 287 of the refugees, the British Home Office undersecretary made clear that this would not be considered "a precedent for the reception in [the] future of refugees."[69]

On June 21, 1939, not long after the *St. Louis* made its futile attempt to deposit its passengers in Cuba or the United States, Pulitzer Prize–winning journalist H. R. Knickerbocker reported that numerous other ships packed with Jewish refugees from Nazi Germany were "plying along the coast of Palestine, forbidden [by the British] to discharge their despairing burdens in the Promised Land." The Jews were jammed in the ships' holds like "Negro slaves on Levantine ships." The Royal Navy hunted them "like animals along the corridors of . . . No Man's Sea."

Knickerbocker emphasized, "There is not a country in the world in which [these Jews] have not sought a crevice within which to creep." A thousand had "lived more than three months aboard ship." He reported that "within the last sixty days alone eighteen ocean-going steamers carrying 5,627 Jewish refugee men, women, and children have set forth from Europe and been turned back from their destination." Unscrupulous ship captains had stripped many of the Jewish refugees of their belongings. They charged "first-class Atlantic fare for deck space on a freighter across the Mediterranean." On one ship, the captain forced the passengers to hand over their watches, rings, and any remaining money to get food and water.

Compared to the voyages of many ships carrying Jewish refugees, the *St. Louis*'s was "a pleasure cruise." Knickerbocker described the experience of the 552 Jewish men, women, and children from Germany, Czechoslovakia, and Danzig who sailed from Greece for Palestine on the *Agios Nicolaos* on March 1, 1939. As the *Agios Nicolaos* tried to land the Jews on the Palestine coast on March 31, a British naval patrol fired at them, killing one Jew and wounding two others, forcing the ship to turn back to Greece. The wounded died soon after. When the *Agios Nicolaos* arrived at the port of Kandia on April 4, the Greeks did not permit the Jews to disembark. For the next four weeks, the ship sailed "among the small islands of the Aegean," the passengers subsisting on a diet of tea and stale bread. A week before Knickerbocker's *Journal-American* article appeared, the *Agios Nicolaos* had tried to dock at the Romanian port of Balcic, but Romanian police had driven it back from the shore. The refugees had been at sea for more than one hundred days.[70]

Angered by the British attack on the *Agios Nicolaos*, Labour MP Josiah Wedgwood reminded Colonial Secretary MacDonald in the House of Commons that during the 1870s that body had passed a law requiring the Royal Navy, which was then attempting to suppress the Arab slave trade in the Red Sea, to provide refuge to any fugitive slave who reached its vessels. Wedgewood castigated Britain's Palestine administration for failing to show any sympathy for severely persecuted German Jewry. He demanded that the colonial secretary explain why the British government undermined its Fugitive Slave Law by assisting "the slave owners in Germany today" (the German government) in its "dirty work"—preventing Jewish slaves escaping from the Reich from gaining their freedom.[71]

Knickerbocker reported that another Greek vessel bound for Palestine, the *Astir*, with 641 Jews aboard, turned away by the British, had anchored off the Greek ports of Kea and Laurium during the two months before the publication of his article. These refugees "were near starvation." After leaving the Palestine coast, the *Astir*, sailing about the Mediterranean searching for somewhere to land, had encountered "a colony of 424 destitute Jewish refugees living like savages on the coast of Crete." Another Greek vessel, the *Marmora*, with five hundred Jewish refugees, that had sailed for Palestine from the Romanian Black Sea port of Mangalia in early June had "not been reported since."

The two hundred Jewish refugees on the *Orinocco*, which departed from Hamburg for Cuba on May 28, had suffered "the worst fate." Learning of the Cuban and American refusal to accept the *St. Louis* passengers, the *Orinocco* docked at Cherbourg for three days and then returned to Hamburg. Forced to disembark there, its Jewish passengers "now await concentration camp."

Knickerbocker made clear that his discussion of Jewish refugees' desperate efforts to escape Nazi Germany by sea was incomplete. He had described only the plight of the Jews "who wandered on the water" or who were trapped near it, huddling "in ragged groups on deserted islands . . . in the wine-dark Aegean" and "crouching on the docks of Black Sea ports, waiting vainly for a ship to carry them away." But these, Knickerbocker emphasized, were only "a few of the visible victims of the Modern Pharaoh during the last sixty days." On land were many more.[72]

* * *

Shortly after the passage of the Nuremberg laws, almost four years before the doomed voyage of the *St. Louis*, the London *Jewish Chronicle* had described German Jewry's plight as the torment "of a people in a cage."[73] From the cold pogrom at the very beginning of Hitler's rule through the *Anschluss* and beyond, the Western press repeatedly reported that Jews were being degraded in the most abhorrent ways. They were displayed in garbage wagons and pig sties, made to crawl on all fours and eat grass like cattle, and forced to their hands and knees and made to scrub streets and gutters. After the *Anschluss*, Jews in Austria were compelled to clean excrement from toilets with their bare hands before jeering crowds.

From the inception of their movement, the Nazis had cast the Jews not only as subhuman but as the major threat to non-Jews' lives, routinely equating them with lepers and microbes and characterizing them flatly as a cancer. Thus, the solution to the Germans' problem could only be the eradication of the Jews. Sir Horace Rumbold, the British ambassador to Germany when the Nazis came to power in 1933, reported to Foreign Secretary Sir John Simon that Hitler had told him the Jews constituted a disease that was infecting all of Germany.[74] Less than two months after the Nazis came to power, rabbis presiding at Purim services compared Hitler to Haman, who had tried to destroy the Jewish people. In late 1933, the highly respected journalist Pierre van Paassen warned that unless 150,000 German Jews were immediately brought to Palestine, none would be left to send there. In June 1934, after the Harvard administration had warmly welcomed Hitler's foreign press secretary Ernst Hanfstaengl to campus, Rabbi Joseph S. Shubow confronted him in Harvard Yard and demanded to know whether the German plan for the Jews was extermination.

Yet year after year went by without any significant action by the American or British government on behalf of the Jews. Neither seriously considered the implications for European Jewry of failing to check Germany's rapid military buildup and expansionist designs. AJCongress leader Joseph Tenenbaum would recall that President Roosevelt "was always patronizingly affable, but in practical matters quite ineffectual. . . . He failed us in time of stress." Tenenbaum characterized the Roosevelt administration as "honeycombed with men of a twisted bent to 'go easy on the Jewish question,' not to speak of the outright anti-Semitic staff of his State Department."[75] Even as a second world war loomed in 1939, Britain closed off Jewish immigration to Palestine, European Jewry's last means to escape annihilation, and the United States government broadcast its lack of concern by blocking entry to the last ship attempting to land Jewish refugees on its shore.

NOTES

1. Karl Dietrich Bracher, *The German Dictatorship* (New York: Praeger, 1970), 296–98; H. N. Brailsford, "Hounded—from Cradle to Grave," *Daily Herald*

(London) clipping, March 16, 1936, HNB 59, H. N. Brailsford Papers, People's History Museum, Manchester, UK.

2. *The Yellow Spot: The Extermination of the Jews in Germany* (London: Victor Gollancz, 1936); *New York Times*, March 16, 1936, 9; *Manchester Guardian*, March 17, 1936, 7. The American edition of *The Yellow Spot* was issued by Knight.

3. James MacGregor Burns, *Roosevelt: The Lion and the Fox* (New York: Harcourt, Brace, and World, 1956), 262.

4. Rafael Medoff, *FDR and the Holocaust: A Breach of Faith* (Washington, DC: David S. Wyman Institute for Holocaust Studies, 2013), 2. During the 1930s, Secretary of Labor Frances Perkins was the only member of Roosevelt's cabinet to call for a "liberalization of immigration procedures" to help Jewish refugees gain entry into the United States. Bat-Ami Zucker, "Frances Perkins and the German-Jewish Refugees, 1933–1940," *American Jewish History* 89 (March 2001): 38.

5. *New York Times*, March 8, 1936, 1, 31.

6. Harold Macmillan, *Winds of Change, 1914–1939* (New York: Harper and Row, 1966), 422–26; Harold Nicholson, *Diaries and Letters, 1930–1939*, ed. Nigel Nicholson (New York: Atheneum, 1966), 248–49.

7. Robert Dell to Sylvia, March 26, 1936, and Dell to Sylvia, April 2, 1936, Dell/1/13, Robert Dell Papers, London School of Economics and Political Science Library Archives, London, UK.

8. Norman Bentwich, *Wanderer between Two Worlds* (London: Kegan Paul, Trench, Taubner, 1941), 241.

9. *Chicago Tribune*, March 8, 1936, 6; *Washington Post*, March 8, 1936, 1.

10. Sir Eric Phipps to Mr. [Anthony] Eden, March 13, 1936, 1/16, Sir Eric Phipps Papers, Churchill College, University of Cambridge, Cambridge, UK.

11. *New York Times*, March 8, 1936, 1, 31.

12. Horace Rumbold to Geoffrey Dawson, June 13, 1936, MS-78, Pols. 1–18, Geoffrey Dawson Papers, Bodleian Library Special Collections, University of Oxford, Oxford, UK.

13. Gerhart Seger, "Remove the Olympic Games from Nazi Germany!," *New Leader* (US, December 14, 1935; *Boston Evening Transcript*, August 20, 1935; "Confidential Report Issued by the Jewish Telegraphic Agency, Inc.," no. 3, December 16, 1935, The Economic Position, box 174, Arthur Hays Sulzberger Papers, New York Public Library, New York, NY. Seger called for shifting the Games to Prague, the capital of "a free country," whose Sokol Stadium could seat 250,000.

14. B. C. Newton to Mr. [Anthony] Eden, August 20, 1936, C 5983/306/18, Foreign Office Records, National Archives, Kew Gardens, London, UK.

15. George S. Messersmith to Secretary of State, June 17, 1933, MS 109 0195-00, George S. Messersmith Papers, University of Delaware Library, Newark, DE; "Sport—More Discrimination against Jews," *Jewish Chronicle* (London), January 4, 1935, 13.

16. *Boston Evening Transcript*, August 20, 1935.

17. "Confidential Letter on Germany: The Visit of Under-secretary of State Phillips to Berlin," n.d., but late 1935 or 1936, ACC/3123/C11/12/21, Board of Deputies of British Jews Papers, London Metropolitan Archives, London, UK.

18. Morris D. Waldman to Dr. [Cyrus] Adler, September 24, 1935, box 11, Cyrus Adler Papers, American Jewish Committee Archives, New York, NY.

19. *Boston Herald*, August 8, 1935; *New York Times*, September 1, 1935, 12, October 4, 1935, 18, and January 31, 1936, 20; "Monster Petition in U.S.A.: A Million Signatures against Persecution," *Jewish Chronicle* (London), October 11, 1935, 15; Richard A. Hawkins, "'Hitler's Bitterest Foe': Samuel Untermyer and the Boycott of Nazi Germany, 1933–1938," *American Jewish History* 93 (March 2007): 47.

20. *Times* (London), March 7, 1936, 13.

21. Frank Rodgers, Organizing Secretary, British Non-Sectarian Anti-Nazi Council, to Mr. [G. E.] Harriman, December 10, 1935, box 111, Non-Sectarian Anti-Nazi League (hereafter, NSANL) Papers, Rare Book and Manuscript Library, Butler Library (hereafter, RBML), Columbia University (hereafter, CU), New York, NY.

22. Cyril Q. Henriques to G. E. Harriman, January 17, 1936, box 111, NSANL Papers, RBML, CU.

23. G. E. Harriman to Cyril Q. Henriques, January 11, 1936, and C. Q. Henriques to Dr. Boris E. Nelson, August 6, 1937, box 111, NSANL Papers, RBML, CU.

24. *Times* (London), March 24, 1936, 9.

25. "The Olympic Games: American Labour Urges Boycott," *Jewish Chronicle* (London), October 25, 1935, 19; *New York Times*, October 18, 1935, 1.

26. Peter Gay, *My German Question: Growing Up in Nazi Berlin* (New Haven, CT: Yale University Press, 1998), 83. Marty Glickman believed that Brundage and Cromwell "did not wish to . . . embarrass their Nazi friends by having two Jewish athletes stand on the winners' podium." Marty Glickman with Stan Isaacs, *The Fastest Kid on the Block: The Marty Glickman Story* (Syracuse, NY: Syracuse University Press, 1996), 28–29.

27. Newton to Eden, August 20, 1936.

28. Deborah Lipstadt, *Beyond Belief: The American Press and the Coming of the Holocaust, 1933–1945* (New York: Free Press, 1986), 84.

29. Richard D. Mandell, *The Nazi Olympics* (Urbana: University of Illinois Press, 1987 [1971]), 280.

30. Joseph Tenenbaum, "The Anti-Nazi Boycott Movement in the United States," *Yad Vashem Studies* 3 (1959): 148; *New York Times*, June 20, 1937, 12.

31. Tenenbaum, "Anti-Nazi Boycott," 145; *New York Times*, January 13, 1938, 4, and January 14, 1938, 3.

32. *New York Times,* January 14, 1938, 3.

33. Associated Press article appeared in *Washington Post,* March 14, 1938, X7; *Times* (London), March 15, 1938, 14.

34. William L. Shirer, *The Rise and Fall of the Third Reich* (New York: Simon and Schuster, 1960), 351.

35. *New York Times,* April 3, 1938, 1; G. E. R. Gedye, *Betrayal in Central Europe, Austria and Czechoslovakia: The Fallen Bastions* (New York: Harper and Brothers, 1939), 299.

36. Gedye, *Betrayal in Central Europe,* 293; *New York Times,* April 3, 1938, 1. As a result of Gedye's published reports of such horrors in Vienna, Nazi authorities there notified Gedye on March 25, 1938, of his expulsion from Austria and Germany, effective March 28.

37. *Times* (London), March 15, 1938, 13, and June 3, 1938, 13.

38. *Times* (London), March 21, 1938, 12.

39. *Times* (London), June 18, 1938, 15; Gedye, *Betrayal in Central Europe,* 346–47; "Desperate Austrian Refugees Pour into Czechoslovakia without Invitations," *Life,* August 8, 1938, 23. Six British Christians, in a letter to the editor of the London *Times,* stated, "We have before us a credible report that since Herr Hitler and his forces entered Vienna some 7,000 Jews have committed suicide in that city alone. The degree of suffering, terror, and hopelessness thus attested defies imagination. No comment is needed on Field-Marshal Göring's wireless statement at the end of March that the Jews had better do away with themselves if they wanted to, and that he could not put a policeman behind every Jew to prevent suicides." William Ebor Lytton, George Cicestr, Violet Bonham Carter, Victor Cazalet, Dorothy Gladstone, and Evelyn Jones, letter to the editor, *Times* (London), July 19, 1938.

40. Keith Eubank, "Munich," in *A History of the Czechoslovak Republic, 1918–1948,* ed. Victor S. Mamatey and Radomir Luža (Princeton, NJ: Princeton University Press, 1973), 239, 241–42, 251; John W. Wheeler-Bennett, *Munich: Prologue to Tragedy* (New York: Viking, 1964 [1948]), 194. Wheeler-Bennett noted that Czechoslovakia's fortifications, "yielded up without a fight" at Munich, were "formidable" and "might well have held up" any German assault "for a considerable period." These fortifications provided the Germans with "much valuable information for future reference in dealing with the French defenses." Wheeler-Bennett, *Munich,* 333.

41. Shirer, *Rise and Fall of the Third Reich,* 383.

42. *Manchester Guardian,* October 18, 1938, 6; *New York Times,* October 11, 1938, 16.

43. Burns, *Roosevelt,* 385–87. On the Kellogg Pact, see John D. Hicks, *Republican Ascendancy, 1921–1933* (New York: Harper and Row, 1960), 150–52.

44. Martin Weil, *A Pretty Good Club: The Founding Fathers of the U.S. Foreign Service* (New York: W. W. Norton, 1978), 42–45.

45. Ibid., 60–61.

46. Richard J. Evans, *The Third Reich in Power, 1933–1939* (New York: Penguin, 2005), 619; Shirer, *Rise and Fall of the Third Reich*, 456; *New York Times*, May 30, 1938, 4, October 10, 1938, 1, and March 20, 1939, 3. A 1920 treaty made Poland responsible for conducting Danzig's foreign relations and gave it the right to use the port facilities. It also placed Danzig within Poland's customs frontier. *Chicago Tribune*, May 5, 1939, 5.

47. *New York Times*, August 31, 1938, 3; "Troubles of Jews," *Time*, September 12, 1938, 30; *Manchester Guardian*, August 10, 1938, 5.

48. *Manchester Guardian*, September 5, 1938, 13.

49. *New York Times*, August 31, 1938, 3; "Troubles of Jews, 30."

50. *New York Journal-American*, November 27, 1938, *New York Journal-American* morgue, Dolph Briscoe Center for American History, University of Texas at Austin, Austin, TX (hereafter, Briscoe Center).

51. Gay, *My German Question*, 131, 136–38.

52. Martin Gilbert, *Kristallnacht: Prelude to Destruction* (New York: HarperCollins, 2006), 165–66.

53. Saul Friedländer, *Nazi Germany and the Jews*, vol. 1, *The Years of Persecution, 1933–1939* (New York: HarperCollins, 1997), 299.

54. Stephen H. Norwood, *The Third Reich in the Ivory Tower: Complicity and Conflict on American Campuses* (New York: Cambridge University Press, 2009), 233; Stephen H. Norwood, "The Expulsion of Robert Burke: Suppressing Campus Anti-Nazi Protest in the 1930s," *Journal for the Study of Antisemitism* 4:1 (2012): 112.

55. *Times* (London), November 22, 1938, 8.

56. Gedye, *Betrayal in Central Europe*, 347.

57. Gay, *My German Question*, 140.

58. David S. Wyman and Rafael Medoff, "America's Response to Nazism and the Holocaust," in *Encyclopedia of American Jewish History*, ed. Stephen H. Norwood and Eunice G. Pollack (Santa Barbara, CA: ABC-CLIO, 2008), 1:218; Medoff, *FDR and the Holocaust*, 46–47.

59. Evans, *Third Reich in Power*, 559–60; Gay, *My German Question*, 120.

60. Arthur Koestler, *Thieves in the Night* (New York: Macmillan, 1946), 162; Walter Laqueur, *A History of Zionism* (New York: Schocken, 1976), 509, 528; *Manchester Guardian*, May 18 and 23, 1939.

61. Martin Gilbert, *Churchill and the Jews: A Lifelong Friendship* (New York: Henry Holt, 2007), 161.

62. *Manchester Guardian*, October 17, 1938, 12.

63. *New York Times*, May 22, 1939, 1, and May 29, 1939, 7.

64. *Washington Post*, May 18, 1939, 3.

65. *Manchester Guardian*, June 3, 1939, 15; *New York Times*, June 8, 1939, 24, and March 31, 1999, A21; Medoff, *FDR and the Holocaust*, 52.

66. Medoff, *FDR and the Holocaust*, 8–9; *New York Times*, June 8, 1939, 24, and March 31, 1999, A21; *Washington Post*, June 11, 1939, B8. Santo Domingo turned the *St. Louis* away when it tried to land there. *Manchester Guardian*, June 14, 1939, 11. Mexico's immigration department denied the refugees entry permits after they tried to land in Cuba. Argentina and Paraguay also denied entry to Jewish refugees. *Washington Post*, June 3, 1939, 5. As the *St. Louis* "idle[d] off the Florida coast," Costa Rica "ordered the departure of a large number of Jewish refugees whose ninety-day permits to remain in the country ha[d] expired." *New York Times*, June 5, 1939, 4.

67. Rafael Medoff, *The Jews Should Keep Quiet: Franklin D. Roosevelt, Rabbi Stephen S. Wise, and the Holocaust* (Philadelphia: Jewish Publication Society, 2019), 87–88.

68. Statement by passengers on the refugee ship *St. Louis*, signed by Herbert Karliner, Professor Hans Fisher, Col. Phil Freund, and Fred Buff, "*St. Louis* Survivors Dispute New Book's Absolving of FDR and U.S. Coast Guard," March 21, 2013, https://www.algemeiner.com/2013/03/21/st-louis-survivors -dispute-new-book%E2%80%99s-absolving-of-fdr-and-u-s-coast-guard/; Richard Breitman and Allan J. Lichtman, *FDR and the Jews* (Cambridge, MA: Harvard University Press, 2013), 137.

69. *New York Times*, March 31, 1999, B4; *Manchester Guardian*, June 14, 1939, 11; Medoff, *FDR and the Holocaust*, 8–9.

70. H. R. Knickerbocker, "10,000 Exiled Denied 'Promised Land'—Treated Like Slaves, Hunted Like Animals," *New York Journal-American*, June 21, 1939, *New York Journal-American* morgue, Briscoe Center.

71. Knickerbocker, "10,000 Exiled; "Parliament: The Ships off Palestine," *Jewish Chronicle* (London), June 9, 1939, 24.

72. Knickerbocker, "10,000 Exiled." Knickerbocker noted, for example, that thirty-six hundred Jews of Polish origin residing in Germany had been deported by the Gestapo in a special train to the Polish frontier village of Zbonszyn eight months before and had been held captive there since then in abandoned stables, forbidden by Polish authorities from entering Poland. He reported that the fifteen thousand Jews deported from Germany to Poland were "entirely dependent on outside charity." The Polish Jewish Refugee Committee, with only $400 left in its treasury, had been forced to reduce its per capita food donation from $1.25 to 65 cents a month. H. R. Knickerbocker, "Jews' Plight Likened to Black Death of Middle Ages," *New York Journal-American*, June 22, 1939, *New York Journal-American* morgue, Briscoe Center.

73. "Tormenting People in a Cage: Denied the Right to Live," *Jewish Chronicle* (London), November 15, 1935, 14.

74. Sir Horace Rumbold to Sir John Simon, May 15, 1933, MS-40, Sir Horace Rumbold Papers, Bodleian Library Special Collections, University of Oxford, Oxford, UK.

75. Joseph Tenenbaum, "The Contribution of American Jewry towards Rescue in the Hitler Period" (paper read at the Annual Session of the American Jewish Historical Society), *Yad Vashem Bulletin*, April 1957, 2–3, RG 21.001.02*05, Joseph and Sheila Tenenbaum Collection, US Holocaust Memorial Museum Archives, Washington, DC.

BIBLIOGRAPHY

Manuscript Collections

American Jewish Committee Archives, New York, NY
- American Jewish Committee Papers
- Cyrus Adler Papers

American Jewish Historical Society, Center for Jewish History, New York, NY
- Jewish War Veterans of the United States of America Collection

Bodleian Library Special Collections, University of Oxford, Oxford, UK
- Geoffrey Dawson Papers
- Sir Horace Rumbold Papers
- Sir John Simon Papers

Churchill College Archives, University of Cambridge, Cambridge, UK
- Sir Eric Phipps Papers
- Lord Robert Vansittart Papers

Columbia University, Rare Book and Manuscript Library, Butler Library, New York, NY
- James G. McDonald Papers
- Michael Florinsky Papers
- Non-Sectarian Anti-Nazi League Papers

Dolph Briscoe Center for American History, University of Texas at Austin, Austin, TX
- *New York Journal-American* morgue
- Walter Winchell Papers

Franklin D. Roosevelt Presidential Library and Museum, Hyde Park, NY
- Documents Relating to the Holocaust and Refugees, 1933–1945
- Franklin D. Roosevelt, Papers as President: The President's Secretary's File
- Press Conference Transcripts

John Rylands Library, University of Manchester, Deansgate, Manchester, UK
- Manchester *Guardian* Archives

Leo Baeck Institute, Center for Jewish History, New York, NY
- Florence Mendheim Collection of Anti-Semitic Propaganda

Library of Congress, Washington, DC
- Wilbur J. Carr Papers
- Norman Davis Papers
- William E. Dodd Papers
- Cordell Hull Papers
- David Foote Sellers Papers

London Metropolitan Archives, London, UK
- Board of Deputies of British Jews Papers

London School of Economics and Political Science Library Archives,
   London, UK
- Walter Citrine Papers
- Robert Dell Papers

National Archives, Kew Gardens, London, UK
- Admiralty Records
- Cabinet Office Records
- Colonial Office Records
- Foreign Office Records

National Archives, College Park, MD
- Department of State General Records, Record Group 59
- General Records Seized from the German-American Bund, Department of
   Justice, Office of Alien Property, Record Group 131

National Archives, Washington, DC
- Office of Naval Intelligence Records, Record Group 38

New York Public Library, New York, NY
- Adolph Ochs Papers
- Arthur Hays Sulzberger Papers

People's History Museum, Manchester, UK
- H. N. Brailsford Papers
- William Gillies Papers
- Ellen Wilkinson Scrapbook

St. Antony's College Library Archives, University of Oxford, Oxford, UK
- John Wheeler-Bennett Papers

University of Delaware Library, Special Collections, Newark, DE
- George S. Messersmith Papers

University of Maryland, Archives and Manuscripts Department, Hornbake
   Library, College Park, MD
- Millard E. Tydings Papers

US Holocaust Memorial Museum Archives, Washington, DC
- Board of Deputies of British Jews Papers
- Jewish Labor Committee Papers
- Joseph and Sheila Tenenbaum Collection
- Ligue Internationale Contre l'Antisémitisme Papers
- Records of the Religious Society of Friends of Great Britain: Friends Committee for Refugees and Aliens
- World Jewish Congress Office Papers

Wiener Library for the Study of the Holocaust and Genocide, London, UK
- Anti-German Protest and Prayer Meeting Records
- Board of Deputies of British Jews Defence Committee Papers
- Central British Fund for World Jewish Relief Records
- Documents concerning Antisemitism and Ritual Murder
- Microfilm P.C.

Wisconsin Historical Society, Madison, WI
- Toni Sender Papers

Newspapers

American Israelite (Cincinnati), 1932, 1933, 1935
Atlanta Constitution, 1899
Austin American, 1935
Bakersfield Californian, 1935
Baltimore Sun, 1934, 1935, 1936
Boston Evening Globe, 1933, 1934
Boston Evening Transcript, 1934, 1935
Boston Globe, 1899, 1919, 1933, 1934, 1935
Boston Herald, 1933, 1934, 1935
Boston Post, 1933, 1934
Brooklyn Jewish Examiner, 1932, 1933
Charleston News and Courier, 1935
Chicago Tribune, 1899, 1919, 1930, 1931, 1932, 1933, 1934, 1935, 1936, 1939, 1949
Christian Science Monitor, 1933, 1935
Cleveland Plain Dealer, 1933
Columbia Spectator, 1933, 1934
Daily Californian, 1935
Daily Chronicle (Centralia, WA), 1934
Daily Herald (London), 1933, 1934, 1935
Daily Mail (London), 1933
Daily Mirror (New York), 1933, 1934
Daily Worker (US), 1933, 1934
The Day [*Der Tog*], 1934

Detroit Jewish Chronicle, 1934

Figaro, 1933

Harvard Crimson, 1934

Honolulu Advertiser, 1934, 1936

Houston Post, 1935

Jewish Advocate (Boston), 1931, 1933, 1934, 1935

Jewish Daily Bulletin, 1933, 1935

Jewish Examiner (Brooklyn), 1933

Jewish Exponent (Philadelphia), 1930, 1931, 1932, 1933, 1934, 1935

Jewish Telegraphic Agency, 1931, 1932, 1933, 1934, 1935, 1941

Le Droit de Vivre (Paris), 1933, 1935

Le Petit Parisien, 1935

Le Temps, 1933

Los Angeles Examiner, 1934, 1935

Los Angeles Times, 1919, 1930, 1933, 1934, 1935, 1936

Manchester Guardian, 1930, 1931, 1932, 1933, 1934, 1935, 1936, 1938, 1939, 1944, 1957

New Leader (UK), 1934, 1935

New Leader (US), 1933, 1935

New York Evening Post, 1933

New York Herald Tribune, 1930, 1931, 1933, 1935

New York Times, 1899, 1919, 1922, 1930, 1931, 1932, 1933, 1934, 1935, 1936, 1937, 1938,
   1939, 1949, 1999

New York World-Telegram, 1934

Oakland Tribune, 1935

Observer (London), 1928, 1935

The Oklahoman (Oklahoma City), 1936

Palestine Post, 1933, 1934, 1935

Philadelphia Inquirer, 1933

Pittsburgh Press, 1933

Public Ledger (Philadelphia), 1934

San Diego Union, 1934, 1936

San Francisco Chronicle, 1935

San Francisco Examiner, 1935

Seattle Post-Intelligencer, 1934

Stanford Daily, 1935

St. Louis Post-Dispatch, 1933, 1934

Tacoma Daily Ledger, 1934

The Tech (MIT), 1934

Times (London), 1930, 1931, 1932, 1933, 1934, 1935, 1936, 1938

Vancouver Sun, 1935

Wall Street Journal, 1934

Washington Post, 1899, 1919, 1931, 1932, 1933, 1934, 1935, 1936, 1938, 1939

Books and Pamphlets

Australian Dictionary of Biography. Melbourne: Melbourne University Press, 1996.

Bendersky, Joseph. *The "Jewish Threat": Anti-Semitic Politics of the U.S. Army.* New York: Basic Books, 2000.

Bentwich, Norman. *The Refugees from Germany: April 1933 to December 1935.* London: Allen and Unwin, 1936.

———. *Wanderer between Two Worlds.* London: Kegan Paul, Trench, Traubner, 1941.

Berkow, Ira. *Maxwell Street: Survival in a Bazaar.* Garden City, NY: Doubleday, 1977.

Bondy, Louis W. *Racketeers of Hatred: Julius Streicher and the Jew-Baiters' International.* London: Newman Wolsey, 1946.

Bonham-Carter, Lady Violet. *Child Victims of the New Germany: A Protest.* London: McCorquodale, 1934.

Bracher, Karl Dietrich. *The German Dictatorship.* New York: Praeger, 1970.

Brailsford, H. N. *The Nazi Terror: A Record.* London: Hereford Times, 1933.

Breitman, Richard, and Allan J. Lichtman. *FDR and the Jews.* Cambridge, MA: Harvard University Press, 2013.

Breitman, Richard, Barbara McDonald Stewart, and Severin Hochberg, eds. *Advocate for the Doomed: The Diaries and Papers of James G. McDonald, 1932–1935.* Bloomington: Indiana University Press, 2007.

The Brown Book of the Hitler Terror and the Burning of the Reichstag. New York: Alfred A. Knopf, 1933.

Bullock, Alan. *Hitler: A Study in Tyranny.* New York: Harper and Row, 1962.

Burns, James MacGregor. *Roosevelt: The Lion and the Fox.* New York: Harcourt, Brace, and World, 1956.

Churchill, Winston. *The Gathering Storm.* Boston: Houghton Mifflin, 1948.

Cohen, Israel. *The Jews in Germany.* London: John Murray, 1933.

Conradi, Peter. *Hitler's Piano Player: The Rise and Fall of Ernst Hanfstaengl, Confidant of Hitler, Ally of FDR.* New York: Carroll and Graf, 2004.

Dawidowicz, Lucy. *The War against the Jews, 1933–1945.* New York: Bantam Books, 1986 [1975].

Dell, Robert. *Germany Unmasked.* London: Martin Hopkinson, 1934.

Eksteins, Modris. *Rites of Spring: The Great War and the Birth of the Modern Age.* New York: Doubleday, 1989.

Evans, Richard. *The Coming of the Third Reich.* New York: Penguin, 2003.

———. *The Third Reich in Power, 1933–1939.* New York: Penguin, 2005.

Florinsky, Michael. *The Saar Struggle.* New York: Macmillan, 1934.

Foreign Relations of the United States: Diplomatic Papers. Vol. 2, 1933. Washington, DC: Government Printing Office, 1949.

Friedländer, Saul. *Nazi Germany and the Jews.* Vol. 1, *The Years of Persecution, 1933–1939.* New York: HarperCollins, 1997.

Friedman, Saul S. *The Oberammergau Passion Play*. Carbondale: Southern Illinois
    University Press, 1984.
Fritz, Regina, Grzegorz Rossoliński-Liebe, and Jana Starek, eds. *Alma
    Mater Antisemitica: Akademisches Milieu, Juden, und Antisemitismus an den
    Universitäten Europas zwischen 1918 und 1939*. Vienna: New Academic, 2016.
Fromm, Bela. *Blood and Banquets: A Berlin Social Diary*. New York: Harper and
    Brothers, 1942.
Gay, Peter. *My German Question: Growing Up in Nazi Berlin*. New Haven, CT: Yale
    University Press, 1998.
Gedye, G. E. R. *Betrayal in Central Europe, Austria and Czechoslovakia: The Fallen
    Bastions*. New York: Harper and Brothers, 1939.
Gilbert, Martin. *Britain and Germany between the Wars*. London: Longmans, 1964.
———. *Churchill and the Jews: A Lifelong Friendship*. New York: Henry Holt, 2007.
———. *The Holocaust*. New York: Henry Holt, 1985.
———. *In Search of Churchill: A Historian's Journey*. New York: John Wiley and
    Sons, 1994.
———. *Kristallnacht: Prelude to Destruction*. New York: HarperCollins, 2006.
———. *The Roots of Appeasement*. London: Weidenfeld and Nicholson, 1966.
———. *Sir Horace Rumbold*. London: Heinemann, 1973.
Gilbert, Martin, and Richard Gott. *The Appeasers*. Boston: Houghton Mifflin, 1963.
Glickman, Marty, with Stan Isaacs. *The Fastest Kid on the Block: The Marty
    Glickman Story*. Syracuse, NY: Syracuse University Press, 1996.
Goldhagen, Daniel Jonah. *Hitler's Willing Executioners: Ordinary Germans and the
    Holocaust*. New York: Alfred A. Knopf, 1996.
Granzow, Brigitte. *A Mirror of Nazism: British Opinion and the Emergence of Hitler,
    1929–1933*. London: Victor Gollancz, 1964.
Griffiths, Richard. *Fellow Travellers of the Right: British Enthusiasts for Nazi
    Germany, 1933–39*. London: Constable, 1980.
Hicks, John D. *Republican Ascendancy, 1921–1933*. New York: Harper and Row, 1960.
Higham, John. *Strangers in the Land: Patterns of American Nativism, 1860–1925*.
    New York: Atheneum, 1970.
Hoenicke Moore, Michaela. *Know Your Enemy: The American Debate on Nazism,
    1933–1945*. New York: Cambridge University Press, 2010.
Janowitz, Morris. *The Professional Soldier*. New York: Free Press, 1971 [1960].
Johnson, Gaynor, ed. *Our Man in Berlin: The Diary of Sir Eric Phipps, 1933–1937*.
    London: Palgrave Macmillan, 2008.
Koestler, Arthur. *Arrow in the Blue: An Autobiography*. New York: Macmillan, 1952.
———. *Thieves in the Night*. New York: Macmillan, 1946.
Kohler, Max J. *The United States and German Jewish Persecutions: Precedents for
    Popular and Governmental Action*. Cincinnati: B'nai B'rith Executive Committee,
    1934.

Kühl, Stefan. *The Nazi Connection: Eugenics, American Racism, and German National Socialism*. New York: Oxford University Press, 1994.

Langhoff, Wolfgang. *Rubber Truncheon: Being An Account of Thirteen Months Spent in a Concentration Camp*. New York: E. P. Dutton, 1935.

Laqueur, Walter. *A History of Zionism*. New York: Schocken, 1976.

Leff, Laurel. *Buried by the Times: The Holocaust and America's Most Important Newspaper*. New York: Cambridge University Press, 2005.

Lipstadt, Deborah E. *Beyond Belief: The American Press and the Coming of the Holocaust, 1933–1945*. New York: Free Press, 1986.

Macmillan, Harold. *Winds of Change, 1914–1939*. New York: Harper and Row, 1966.

Mamatey, Victor S., and Radomir Luža, eds. *A History of the Czechoslovak Republic, 1918–1948*. Princeton, NJ: Princeton University Press, 1973.

Mandell, Richard D. *The Nazi Olympics*. Urbana: University of Illinois Press, 1987 [1971].

Medoff, Rafael. *FDR and the Holocaust: A Breach of Faith*. Washington, DC: David S. Wyman Institute for Holocaust Studies, 2013.

———. *The Jews Should Keep Quiet: Franklin D. Roosevelt, Rabbi Stephen S. Wise, and the Holocaust*. Philadelphia: Jewish Publication Society, 2019.

Morse, Arthur D. *While Six Million Died: A Chronicle of American Apathy*. Woodstock, NY: Overlook Press, 1998 [1967].

Mowrer, Edgar Ansel. *Germany Puts the Clock Back*. New York: William Morrow, 1933.

———. *Triumph and Turmoil: A Personal History of Our Time*. New York: Weybright and Talley, 1968.

Nicholson, Harold. *Diaries and Letters, 1930–1939*. Edited by Nigel Nicholson. New York: Atheneum, 1966.

Norwood, Stephen H. *Antisemitism and the American Far Left*. New York: Cambridge University Press, 2013.

———. *The Third Reich in the Ivory Tower: Complicity and Conflict on American Campuses*. New York: Cambridge University Press, 2009.

Norwood, Stephen H., and Eunice G. Pollack, eds. *Encyclopedia of American Jewish History*. Santa Barbara, CA: ABC-CLIO, 2008.

O'Connell, Robert L. *Sacred Vessels: The Cult of the Battleship and the Rise of the U.S. Navy*. New York: Oxford University Press, 1991.

Pedersen, Susan. *Eleanor Rathbone and the Politics of Conscience*. New Haven: Yale University Press, 2004.

Penkower, Monty. *The Jews Were Expendable: Free World Diplomacy and the Holocaust*. Urbana: University of Illinois Press, 1981.

Perry, Marvin, and Frederick Schweitzer. *Antisemitism: Myth and Hate from Antiquity to the Present*. New York: Palgrave Macmillan, 2002.

Prinz, Joachim. *Joachim Prinz, Rebellious Rabbi: An Autobiography—the German and Early American Years.* Edited by Michael Meyer. Bloomington: Indiana University Press, 2008.

Rose, Jonathan, ed. *The Holocaust and the Book: Destruction and Preservation.* Amherst: University of Massachusetts Press, 2001.

Rosenbaum, Ron. *Explaining Hitler.* New York: HarperCollins, 1998.

Sender, Toni. *The Autobiography of a German Rebel.* New York: Vanguard, 1939.

Shapiro, James. *Oberammergau: The Troubling Story of the World's Most Famous Passion Play.* New York: Pantheon, 2000.

Shirer, William. *Berlin Diary: The Journal of a Foreign Correspondent.* New York: Alfred A. Knopf, 1941.

———. *The Rise and Fall of the Third Reich.* New York: Simon and Schuster, 1960.

Steinberg, Michael Stephen. *Sabers and Brownshirts: The German Students' Path to National Socialism, 1918–1935.* Chicago: University of Chicago Press, 1977.

Stern, Fritz. *Five Germanies I Have Known.* New York: Farrar, Straus and Giroux, 2006.

Taylor, A. J. P. *English History, 1914–1945.* New York: Oxford University Press, 1965.

Tenenbaum, Joseph. *Race and Reich.* New York: Twayne, 1956.

Toller, Ernst. *I Was a German.* New York: William Morrow, 1934.

Turner, Henry Ashby Jr. *German Big Business and the Rise of Hitler.* New York: Oxford University Press, 1985.

Vansittart, Lord Robert. *The Mist Procession.* London: Hutchinson, 1958.

Vernon, Betty D. *Ellen Wilkinson, 1891-1947.* London: Croom Helm, 1982.

Weil, Martin. *A Pretty Good Club: The Founding Fathers of the U.S. Foreign Service.* New York: W. W. Norton, 1978.

Wheeler-Bennett, John W. *Munich: Prologue to Tragedy.* New York: Viking, 1964 [1948].

White, Theodore H. *In Search of History: A Personal Adventure.* New York: Harper and Row, 1978.

Wilkinson, Ellen. *The Terror in Germany.* London: British Committee for the Relief of German Fascism, n.d.

Wise, James Waterman. *Swastika: The Nazi Terror.* New York: Harrison Smith and Robert Haas, 1933.

Wootton, Graham. *The Official History of the British Legion.* London: MacDonald and Evans, 1956.

Wyman, David S. *The Abandonment of the Jews: America and the Holocaust, 1941–1945.* New York: New Press, 2007 [1984].

———. *Paper Walls: America and the Refugee Crisis, 1938–1941.* Amherst: University of Massachusetts Press, 1968

The Yellow Spot: The Extermination of the Jews in Germany. London: Victor Gollancz, 1936.

Zucker, Bat-Ami. *In Search of Refuge: Jews and US Consuls in Nazi Germany, 1933–1941.* London: Vallentine Mitchell, 2001.

Articles in Journals and Anthologies

Bessel, Richard. "The Potempa Murder." *Central European History* 10 (September 1977): 241–54.

Cohen, Naomi. "The Transatlantic Connection: The American Jewish Committee and the Joint Foreign Committee in Defense of German Jews, 1933–1937." *American Jewish History* 90 (December 2002): 353–84.

Eubank, Keith. "Munich." In *A History of the Czechoslovak Republic, 1918–1945,* edited by Victor S. Mamatey and Radomir Luža, 239–52. Princeton, NJ: Princeton University Press, 1973.

Florinsky, Michael. "The Lesson of the Saar." *Hungarian Quarterly* 2 (Autumn 1936): 11–25.

Gottlieb, Moshe. "The Berlin Riots of 1935 and Their Repercussions in America." *American Jewish Historical Quarterly* 59 (March 1970): 302–28.

———. "The First of April Boycott and the Reaction of the American Jewish Community." *American Jewish Historical Quarterly* 57 (June 1968): 516–56.

Hawkins, Richard A. "'Hitler's Bitterest Foe': Samuel Untermyer and the Boycott of Nazi Germany, 1933–1938." *American Jewish History* 93 (March 2007): 21–50.

Hill, C. J. "Great Britain and the Saar Plebiscite of 13 January 1935." *Journal of Contemporary History* 9 (April 1974): 121–42.

Hill, Leonidas E. "The Nazi Attack on 'Un-German' Literature, 1933–1945." In *The Holocaust and the Book: Destruction and Preservation,* edited by Jonathan Rose, 9–46. Amherst: University of Massachusetts Press, 2001.

Kovács, Mária M. "The Numerus Clausus in Hungary, 1920–1945." In *Alma Mater Antisemitica: Akademisches Milieu, Juden und Antisemitismus an den Universitäten Europas zwischen 1918 und 1939,* edited by Regina Fritz, Grzegorz Rossoliński-Liebe, and Jana Starek, 85–111. Vienna: New Academic, 2016.

Lewy, Guenter. "The German Roman Catholic Hierarchy and the Saar Plebiscite of 1935." *Political Science Quarterly* 79 (June 1964): 184–208.

Norwood, Stephen H. "The Expulsion of Robert Burke: Suppressing Campus Anti-Nazi Protest in the 1930s." *Journal for the Study of Antisemitism* 4:1 (2012): 89–113.

Sheramy, Rona. "'There Are Times When Silence Is a Sin': The Women's Division of the American Jewish Congress and the Anti-Nazi Boycott Movement." *American Jewish History* 89 (March 2001): 105–21.

Spear, Sheldon. "The United States and the Persecution of Jews in Germany, 1933–1939." *Jewish Social Studies* 30 (October 1968): 215–42.

Tenenbaum, Joseph. "The Anti-Nazi Boycott Movement in the United States." *Yad Vashem Studies* 3 (1959):141–159.

Walter, John C. "Congressman Carl Vinson and Franklin D. Roosevelt: Naval
    Preparedness and the Coming of World War II." *Georgia Historical Quarterly* 64
    (Fall 1980): 294–305.
Zucker, Bat-Ami. "Frances Perkins and the German-Jewish Refugees, 1933–1940."
    American Jewish History 89 (March 2001): 35–59.

Magazine Articles (signed)

Aronsfeld, C. C. "A Refugee's Memories of London, 1933." *Jewish Frontier,* April
    1980.
Brown, James Oliver. "Annapolis—Stronghold of Mediocrity." *Forum and Century,*
    October 1936.
Cohen, Israel. "A Letter from Berlin: The Menacing Situation." *Jewish Chronicle*
    (London), June 24, 1932.
———. "The Situation in Germany." *Jewish Chronicle* (London), February 19, 1932.
Dell, Robert. "Hitler over Europe." *Nation,* May 3, 1933.
Delman, J. David. "Haman, 'Yemach Shemoh!'" *Jewish War Veteran,* April 1933.
E. G. L. "News from Germany: Ernst Heilmann Remembered." *AJR Information,*
    March 1982.
Fabricant, Noah. "Intolerance in Vienna." *Nation,* October 21, 1931.
Fisher, Barbara E. Scott. "Notes of a Cosmopolitan." *North American Review,*
    March 1934.
Hanfstaengl, Ernst F. S. "My Leader." *Collier's,* August 4, 1934.
Hertz, J. H. "In Ancient Egypt and Present-Day Germany." *Jewish Chronicle*
    (London), April 21, 1933.
Hodess, J. "Oberammergau: An 'Evil Play.'" *Jewish Chronicle* (London), August 22,
    1930.
Langdon-Davies, John. "Nazi Science and Ourselves." *Forum and Century,* May
    1934.
Laski, Neville, and Leonard G. Montefiore. "A Call to Self-Restraint." *Jewish
    Chronicle* (London), March 31, 1933.
Rubin, Ruth. "I Heckled Luther!" *Student Review,* January 1934.
Seger, Gerhart. "The Hitler Hells." *Labour,* April 1934.
Tenenbaum, Joseph. "The Contribution of American Jewry towards Rescue in the
    Hitler Period." *Yad Vashem Bulletin,* April 1957.
Vorse, Mary Heaton. "Getting the Jews out of Germany." *New Republic,* July 19,
    1933.

Magazine Articles (unsigned)

"The American Boycott." *Jewish Chronicle* (London), August 16, 1935.
"The Anglo-German Football Match." *Jewish Chronicle* (London), December 6,
    1935.

"Anti-Jewish Riots Sweep Berlin." *American Hebrew*, July 19, 1936.

"Anti-Nazi Demonstration in Hyde Park." *Jewish Chronicle* (London), November 1, 1935.

"Anti-Semitic Rioting at Universities." *Jewish Chronicle* (London), July 3, 1931.

"Anti-Semitism Crops Out among French University Students." *Jewish Chronicle* (London), December 4, 1930.

"Austria: The Nazi Boycott Campaign." *Jewish Chronicle* (London), December 23, 1932.

"Being a Jew Means Being Less than an Animal." *Jewish Chronicle* (London), March 24, 1933.

"The Black Forest Well Named/German Jewry's Ordeal/The Situation in the Provinces." *Jewish Chronicle* (London), January 23, 1931.

"Boycott German Goods!" *Jewish Chronicle* (London), March 31, 1933.

"The Boycott in America." *Jewish Chronicle* (London), July 12, 1935.

"The Boycott in France Goes On." *Jewish Chronicle* (London), May 19, 1933.

"The Boycott in Poland: Imports of German Goods Drop to 7%." *Jewish Chronicle* (London), April 7, 1933.

"Boycott Scenes." *Jewish Chronicle* (London), March 31, 1933.

"British Reactions: Protests in Parliament." *Jewish Chronicle* (London), March 31, 1933.

"The Concentration Camps." *Jewish Chronicle* (London), March 16, 1934.

"Concentration Camps: Jews Still Imprisoned." *Jewish Chronicle* (London), November 23, 1934.

"Count Helldorf Acquitted." *Jewish Chronicle* (London), February 19, 1932.

"The Debate in the House." *Jewish Chronicle* (London), April 21, 1933.

"Decorating the Kurfurstendamm." *Jewish Chronicle* (London), November 1, 1935.

"The Deputies." *Jewish Chronicle* (London), May 19, 1933.

"The Deputies." *Jewish Chronicle* (London), April 20, 1934.

"The Deputies: Special Meeting of Protest." *Jewish Chronicle* (London), October 4, 1935.

"Desperate Austrian Refugees Pour into Czechoslovakia without Invitations." *Life*, August 8, 1938.

"Emden at Ft. Stevens." *Army and Navy Journal*, February 1, 1936.

"The English Press—the Manchester *Guardian*'s Exposure." *Jewish Chronicle* (London), April 21, 1933.

"The Evasive Herr Rosenberg." *Jewish Chronicle* (London), May 19, 1933.

"Extremists in the Saddle: Jews Boycotted Everywhere." *Jewish Chronicle* (London), August 30, 1935.

"An Eyewitness Account." *Jewish Chronicle* (London), March 24, 1933.

"Foreign Reactions: Boycotting German Goods." *Jewish Chronicle* (London), March 24, 1933.

"French Public Feeling Aroused: Many Protest Meetings." *Jewish Chronicle* (London), April 7, 1933.
"Frustrated Jewish Hopes in Germany." *New Statesman*, April 20, 1935.
"The Fur Trade Boycott." *Jewish Chronicle* (London), May 12, 1933.
"German Anti-Semitic Theatre Riots." *Jewish Chronicle* (London), December 12, 1930.
"The German Barbarism: Branding the Children." *Jewish Chronicle* (London), March 16, 1933.
"The German Jewish Agony." *Jewish Chronicle* (London), May 5, 1933.
"German Vessel Visits Baltimore." *Army and Navy Journal*, April 25, 1936.
"Germany: The Berlin Riots." *Jewish Chronicle* (London), July 19, 1935.
"Germany: Bibliocaust." *Time*, May 22, 1933.
"Germany: Boycott of Jews in Berlin." *Jewish Chronicle* (London), July 19, 1935.
"Germany: Disgraceful Jew-Laws." *Jewish Chronicle* (London), September 20, 1935.
"Germany: The Jewish Agony." *Jewish Chronicle* (London), April 21, 1933.
"Germany/Nazis' Resolution for 1934." *Jewish Chronicle* (London), January 5, 1934.
"Germany/New Acts of Terrorism." *Jewish Chronicle* (London), March 16, 1934.
"Germany: The Saar." *Jewish Chronicle* (London), January 25, 1935.
"The Ghetto Walls Contract: Jews Barred from Trams, Cinemas, and Shops." *Jewish Chronicle* (London), August 30, 1935.
"Glass Dealers Boycott German Goods." *Jewish Chronicle* (London), April 21, 1933.
"Hitler and His Government 'Guilty!'" *Jewish Chronicle* (London), March 16, 1934.
"Hitler's Part in University Riots." *Jewish Chronicle* (London), July 10, 1931.
"The House of Lords." *Jewish Chronicle* (London), April 7, 1933.
"In Darkest Germany." *Jewish Chronicle* (London), December 2, 1932.
"Jewish Students in Germany." *Jewish Chronicle* (London), December 5, 1930.
"Jewry's New Courage." *Jewish Chronicle* (London), February 22, 1935.
"Jews Boycotting German Ships." *Jewish Chronicle* (London), May 12, 1933.
"Jews Expelled from Villages: A Countrywide Campaign; Towns Refuse Aid." *Jewish Chronicle* (London), August 30, 1935.
"Jews' Hopes Shattered." *Jewish Chronicle* (London), February 1, 1935.
"The Jews in Danzig: Persecution Intensified." *Jewish Chronicle* (London), February 1, 1935.
"Jews Not Wanted." *Jewish Chronicle* (London), August 2, 1935.
"A Letter from Berlin: Tear Bomb Outrages." *Jewish Chronicle* (London), December 23, 1932.
"Manchester." *Jewish Chronicle* (London), March 24, 1933.
"The Martyrdom of German Jewry: Brutal Process of Economic Extinction." *Jewish Chronicle* (London), April 7, 1933.
"Monster Jewish Protest Demonstration." *Jewish Chronicle* (London), July 21, 1933.
"Monster Petition in U.S.A.: A Million Signatures against Persecution." *Jewish Chronicle* (London), October 11, 1935.

"More Gruesome Activities Revealed." *Jewish Chronicle* (London), June 9, 1933.

"Nazi Justice in Speech and Action." *Jewish Chronicle* (London), August 30, 1935.

"Nazis Defy Hitler: More Anti-Jewish Terrorism." *Jewish Chronicle* (London), September 20, 1935.

"Nazis Flout Saar Pledges." *Jewish Chronicle* (London), September 13, 1935.

"Nazism Abroad: The Threat of the Saar." *Jewish Chronicle* (London), April 27, 1934.

"Nazis Proclaim a Ghetto." *Jewish Chronicle* (London), September 20, 1935.

"New York Hotels Bar German Assemblies." *Jewish Chronicle* (London), August 8, 1935.

"The Numerus Clausus." *Jewish Chronicle* (London), February 6, 1931.

"The Olympic Games: American Labour Urges Boycott." *Jewish Chronicle* (London), October 25, 1935.

"Our Protest Parade." *The Jewish Veteran*, April 1933.

"Paperhangers Refuse to Handle German Goods." *New Leader* (US), October 25, 1933.

"Parliamentary Notes." *Jewish Chronicle* (London), April 27, 1934.

"Parliament: The Ships off Palestine." *Jewish Chronicle* (London), June 9, 1939.

"Prayers and Atrocities." *Time*, April 3, 1933.

"Professor Haldane Hits Out." *Jewish Chronicle* (London), May 19, 1933.

"Professor Richard Gottheil: American Savant Reviews the Situation." *Jewish Chronicle* (London), June 30, 1933.

"Prussian Nazis Invade Danzig." *Jewish Chronicle* (London), August 9, 1935.

"Riots in Paris." *Jewish Chronicle* (London), May 1, 1931.

"Rosh Hashanah in Berlin: Anti-Jewish Rioting." *Jewish Chronicle* (London), September 18, 1931.

"Saar Terrorism Protest." *Jewish Chronicle* (London), September 17, 1935.

"The Shadow of the Swastika: A Letter from Berlin." *Jewish Chronicle* (London), May 6, 1932.

"Shamming Blind." *Jewish Chronicle* (London), May 19, 1933.

"The Silent Parade." *Jewish Chronicle* (London), July 28, 1933.

"Sport—More Discrimination against Jews." *Jewish Chronicle* (London), January 4, 1935.

"Streicher on Jesus." *Jewish Chronicle* (London), November 16, 1934.

"Teaching the Children to Hate." *Jewish Chronicle* (London), September 6, 1935.

"These Jews Are Dead." *Jewish Chronicle* (London), August 16, 1935.

"Tormenting People in a Cage: Denied the Right to Live." *Jewish Chronicle* (London), November 15, 1935.

"Torturing Jewish Children in Schools." *Jewish Chronicle* (London), June 16, 1933.

"The Tragedy of German Jewry—Vigorous Economic Persecution Continues—Starvation for 600,000 Jews." *Jewish Chronicle* (London), April 14, 1933.

"Troubles of Jews." *Time*, September 12, 1938.
"United States." *Jewish Chronicle* (London), September 7, 1934.
"U.S. Senate Speaks." *Jewish Chronicle* (London), June 16, 1933.
"Where Is That World-Conscience?" *Jewish Chronicle* (London), January 4, 1935.
"World Alliance for Combatting Anti-Semitism." *Jewish Chronicle* (London), March 31, 1933.

Class Report

Entry for Ernst Hanfstaengl, Harvard College, 25th Anniversary Report, Class of 1909. Harvard University Archives, Pusey Library, Harvard University, Cambridge, MA.

Oral History Transcript

"The Reminiscences of Gerhart Henry Seger." December 1950. Oral History Research Office, Butler Library, Columbia University, New York, NY.

Published Proceedings

The Labour Party. "Report of the 33rd Annual Conference Held in the White Rock Pavilion, Hastings, October 2nd to 6th, 1933."

INDEX

Page numbers in *italics* indicate photographs.

303–4, 310; Börgemoor, 41; Brandenburg, 41, 66, 71n49; Dachau, 64–65, 261, 280, 284n46, 300; Oranienburg, 40–41, 65–67, 158–59; Osnabrück, 65; Siegburg, 65; Sonnenburg, 41
Conservative Party (British), 96, 99, 180, 200, 293, 297
conscription, German reintroduction of, 252
Coralnik, Abraham, 113
Crosfield, George, Col., 258, 261
Crozier, William P., 51, 98, 118–19, 145n19
Cuba, 64; and St. Louis affair, 308–10, 316n66
Curley, James Michael, 89, 270
Czechoslovakia, 130, 132, 158, 213, 299, 309; alternative for boycotted German goods, 130, 132, 273–74; hostility to Jewish refugees, 301–3; German seizure of, 301–2; impact of Munich conference, 301; and refugees, 42, 159, 210, 301, 314n40

Daniels, Josephus, 80
Danzig, 219n80, 309, 315n46; and "bleeding borders campaign," 213–14; persecution of Jews in, 214–15, 303–4
Dawson, Geoffrey, 295, 300
deicide accusation, and Oberammergau Passion Play, 177; Nazi use of, 24, 62, 175
Dell, Robert, 8; on British appeasement, 293; on German militarism, 220–21, 253; on Nazi antisemitism, 118
Department of Labor, US, 116; and Saar plebiscite, 203
Department of the Navy, US, assists Nazi warships improve combat readiness, 242; friendly reception of Nazi warships, 238–39
Department of State, US, 29, 49, 73n76, 89, 158, 307; antisemitism in, 29–30, 108n65, 221, 302–3, 311; assists Nazi warships improve combat readiness, 231, 242; deluged with grassroots demands to condemn Nazi antisemitism, 6, 78, 88, 101; displeased with Massachusetts House of Representatives condemnation of Nazi antisemitism, 270–71; Hitler government appeals to suppress anti-Nazi protests and boycott in US, 104, 116, 167–68,

251, 268; indifference to German persecution of Jews, 64, 75n106, 86, 91, 93, 104, 186, 267–69 pleasure over German victory in Saar plebiscite, 207; opposition to boycott of German goods and services, 83; opposition to Tydings resolution, 164–65, 187; unwillingness to condemn Rhineland invasion, 294
Der Stürmer, 16, 33, 47, 62–63, 185, 250–51; and July 1935 Berlin pogrom, 265; special blood libel issue, 175–77
Deutsch, Bernard, 157; and boycott, 274; condemns Hans Luther, 141; and March 27, 1933, protest, 78, 85; and 1934 mock trial of Hitler, 166, 168
Deutsche Front, 198–200, 204–5, 207
Dewey, John, 157, 166
Dickmann, Bernard, 169–70
Dickstein, Samuel, 173, 203
Dodd, Martha, 58, 61
Dodd, William E., 57–58, 61, 132, 302; on German preparations for war, 253–55; on Jews' dire situation in Germany, 299
Dreyfus, Pierre, 97
Dreyfus Affair, 76, 82–83, 96–97, 102–3, 132, 138
Dubinsky, David, 182
Dunn, Bishop John, 86
Dunn, James Clement, 268

East End, London, 6, 279; and boycott, 94–96, 124, 135, 153; and July 20, 1933, demonstration, 129–30, 143, 154; and October 27, 1935 demonstration, 271–72
East Prussia, 25, 241, 250
Easterman, A. L., 276
Eden, Sir Anthony, 207, 251–52, 278, 280–81, 294–95, 298
Edinburgh, Scotland, 241
Effigies, 89, 209, 214, 234, 268
Egypt. See Alexandria; Cairo
Ehrhardt Brigade, 16
Einstein, Albert, 27, 33, 121, 159, 187; books burned, 58, 171; and Brown Book, 163; commencement in absentia, 119–20; and The Romance of a People, 126; and Yishuv, 307
Elliott, John, 53

STEPHEN H. NORWOOD is the author of six books, most recently *Antisemitism and the American Far Left* and *The Third Reich in the Ivory Tower: Complicity and Conflict on American Campuses*, which was a Finalist for the National Jewish Book Award in Holocaust Studies. He coedited the prize-winning two-volume *Encyclopedia of American Jewish History* (with Eunice G. Pollack). Norwood is Professor of History and Judaic Studies at the University of Oklahoma. He received his PhD from Columbia University.

Lightning Source UK Ltd.
Milton Keynes UK
UKHW010038230621
385978UK00002B/53